ADVANCE PRAISE FOR
A TASTE OF MADAGASCAR

"I have had the distinct joy of guiding Emmanuel through the vibrant landscapes of Madagascar. He dared to play the adventurer with us to get as close as possible to the various growers and producers.

"Guided by a passion for discovery and a respect for both the traditional and the innovative, Emmanuel's writing captures the essence of Madagascar's food world. He brings to life the flavors of our island with the discernment of a true connoisseur, but it is his genuine fascination and connection with our food culture and local people that truly enriches his narrative.

"His work not only celebrates but also deepens the appreciation for our diverse ingredients, destined to inspire the palates of chefs and food lovers globally."

—**NIRINA RAMANANDRAIBE**
Assistant direction, Chocolaterie Robert; chairman, Mikéa Lodge

"With *A Taste of Madagascar*, Emmanuel Laroche invites readers around the world to discover the Madagascar I know and love—not only its unique flavors and breathtaking landscapes, but also the stories of those who bring them to life. This book is a heartfelt tribute to the artisans, chefs, and farmers who shape our identity. From the richness of our seafood, chocolate, and caviar, to the warmth of our culture, Madagascar's gastronomy is an experience like no other. I am deeply touched by how this book brings Madagascar to the world with such sincerity and beauty. It is a bridge between cultures and a heartfelt ambassador for our country, inviting the world to experience a nation that is as generous as it is unique."

—**VIVIANE DEWA**
Minister of Tourism, Republic of Madagascar

"In the fall of 2022 I went on a wild adventure with another chef, a mixologist, Emmanuel, and others from his team at Symrise.

"We studied the vanilla orchid and met with farmers and specialists from every step of the process, including the selecting and curing and the unbelievable hand-pollinating of 80 percent of the world's vanilla.

"We traveled all over the island, we cooked, we went to markets, and we tasted many of the dishes of this unique place and were able to meet with many people who supply exotic and fragrant ingredients like clove, wild peppercorn, vetiver, wild ginger, ylang-ylang, and patchouli. We got a true taste of Madagascar!

"You'll find glimpses of our experience in *A Taste of Madagascar*, Emmanuel's upcoming book that captures the soul of this unforgettable island."

—**ELIZABETH FALKNER**
Chef and author; ChEF Productions

"While my time in stunning Madagascar with Emmanuel was initially a mission to study vanilla as a singular commodity, we came away with an elevated understanding of the island's incredible depth, both culinarily and culturally. From the aromatic markets to the endemic spices and the traditional Malagasy dishes, we uncovered flavors and stories that connect people to their land. Emmanuel's sense of curiosity, deep love for incredible food, and passion for the world at large turned this journey into something truly transformative. *A Taste of Madagascar* vividly showcases the intricate interplay between the island's biodiversity, resourceful communities, and culinary traditions. This book offers readers an inspiring glimpse into the complex tapestry of all that this inspiring place has to offer."

—**SHANNON TEBAY**
Specialist and consultant, Cocktail & Spirits

"I spent ten unforgettable days in Madagascar with Emmanuel. My first glimpse of the capital revealed a place marked by visible hardship. But as we traveled to the lush SAVA region—where eighty percent of the world's vanilla is grown—I discovered a vibrant culture full of life, color, and generosity.

"The markets overflowed with friendly faces and unbelievably ripe, delicious fruit. I cooked with spices pulled straight from the field—fresh, fragrant, unforgettable. We took river taxis to hidden mountain farms to witness how cocoa is grown and fermented. And the process of producing vanilla—hand-pollinated, harvested, cured, dried, and fermented over months—was a true labor of love.

"We met locals who had taught themselves to cultivate tropical plants for essential oils—used in perfumes—as a way to generate more income between vanilla harvests.

"Just as we were heading home—on a flight Emmanuel was sure I'd miss (long story)—he told us he wasn't leaving. He would return again and again to explore the island, even across difficult terrain, to tell the full story of this incredibly complex and beautiful place.

"Emmanuel's drive and dedication to deep, human-centered storytelling are incredible and praiseworthy."

—**MICHAEL GULOTTA**
Chef-owner, Mopho, Maypop, and Tana

"I have had a fascination with Madagascar long before I used my first vanilla bean from this island nation as a pastry chef at Spago. And now, with Emmanuel Laroche's stunning new book, *A Taste of Madagascar*, my intrigue has grown even more. And after learning about Mariette Andrianjaka, the 'Queen of Malagasy Gastronomy,' I know my dream of going to Madagascar will come true. Buy this wonderful book, and you will be on your way as well."

—**NANCY SILVERTON**
Chef; co-owner, Mozza Restaurant Group; founder, La Brea Bakery

"Emmanuel Laroche's book, *A Taste of Madagascar*, comes along as a rich and welcome surprise to me. I have been studying the transformation of cuisines from the Old World to the New and back for thirty years. Tucked behind vast Africa to the east, 'the Red Island' is deliciously rediscovered here. This is a new and exciting revelation to take in! He is an intrepid explorer with a vast curiosity. This is an adventure tale as one of culinary wonder!

"In reading it, one can discover the stories behind ingredients such as cocoa, vanilla, pink peppercorn, wild pepper, tiger prawns, colossal cashew nuts, zebu meat, and even caviar. Additionally, interviews with local farmers, food artisans, and companies that cultivate ingredients tell how the foods are used in traditional and modern dishes.

"Eighteenth-century Frenchman Jean Anthelme Brillat-Savarin famously stated, 'The discovery of a new dish confers more happiness of the human race than the discovery of a new star.' The 'star' in this case is Madagascar and the 'astronomer' is Emmanuel Laroche!"

—**NORMAN VAN AKEN**
Chef, author, and TV personality

"My first reaction as I read this book was fascination at the dazzling array of ingredients and dishes as described by a flavor professional. My second was envy for Emmanuel Laroche, who had these opportunities to explore a unique and, for most of the world, little-known island and habitat. A third response was admiration for the people Emmanuel introduces us to, who are not only chefs and gourmands but are also advocates for the threatened natural environment and the marvelous culinary cultures it has made possible."

—**PAUL FREEDMAN**
Author and professor of history, Yale University

"I've known Emmanuel Laroche for several years, and I've always admired his deep expertise and passion for the culinary industry. In *A Taste of Madagascar: Culinary Riches of the Red Island*, Emmanuel combines rich historical insight with a vibrant exploration of Madagascar's unique culinary landscape. The book not only showcases the island's diverse flavors but also tells a compelling story of its culture and history. Emmanuel's ability to weave together these elements makes this book an essential read for anyone interested in the history and evolution of food, as well as those who appreciate the intersection of culture and cuisine. I highly recommend this book to culinary enthusiasts, history enthusiasts, and travelers alike—it offers a truly immersive experience of Madagascar's gastronomic treasures."

—**NINA COMPTON**
Chef; owner, Compère Lapin and Bywater American Bistro

"*A Taste of Madagascar* is a remarkable journey through the cultural and culinary richness of Madagascar, capturing the nuances of the island's diverse landscapes, traditions, and flavors. At a pivotal moment in Madagascar's history—one that will determine the fate of its lemurs, unique biodiversity, and culinary heritage—Emmanuel Laroche has created a work that brings Madagascar's story to life.

"More than a celebration of cuisine, this book is a profound exploration of an island's identity, narrated through its flavors, customs, and environmental challenges. This is a story that needs to be told now more than ever, as Madagascar faces critical choices for its future.

"*A Taste of Madagascar* is an essential read for anyone passionate about culture, ecology, and conservation, offering a heartfelt window into Madagascar's soul at a time when its story must be heard."

—ABBY ROSS, PhD
Primatologist; founder, The Dr. Abigail Ross Foundation for Applied Conservation

"From bustling markets to remote villages, Emmanuel Laroche captures the essence of Madagascar—a place where food tells stories of resilience, community, and an unforgettable dance of flavor."

—DANIEL STONE
Bestselling author of *The Food Explorer* and *American Poison*

"*A Taste of Madagascar* is a real travel adventure to a place most of us know so little about. Through good storytelling, Emmanuel Laroche paints a compelling picture of the beauty of this magnificent landscape and the dire need for protecting it and the food culture that lives within."

—JASON EVANS
Dean, College of Food Innovation and Technology, Johnson & Wales University

"*A Taste of Madagascar* is deeply and thoughtfully researched, illuminating the many culinary treasures and stories to be found on Madagascar. Cooks, travelers, readers, and adventurers of all types will find much to love in these pages."

—LAURIE WOOLEVER
Author of *Care and Feeding: A Memoir* and *Bourdain: The Definitive Oral Biography*

"Madagascar, a very real place, is a mythical and magical place. Home to some of the world's most precious wildlife, ecosystems, and as Laroche shows us, some of humanity's most revered gastronomic indulgences. From chocolate to caviar, Laroche is your guide to discovering how special and unique the gastronomy of Madagascar is; it's second to none!"

—JEREMY UMANSKY
Chef; owner, Larder Delicatessen and Bakery; author of *Koji Alchemy*

"I wish I'd had Emmanuel Laroche's book when I was traveling Madagascar. He opens up a new dimension, often overlooked by visitors: flavor. In this intriguing culinary exploration, he brings to life a whole world of exotic fragrances, textures, and tastes. It takes a great enthusiast like him to do a job like this. Malagasies simply assume that the rest of the world enjoys what they enjoy. So, Emmanuel Laroche, thank for this delicious and delightful journey."

—JOHN GIMLETTE
Author of *The Gardens of Mars: Madagascar, an Island Story*

"Madagascar is an island of contrasts. It is full of riches in culture and biodiversity but has one of the poorest economies in the world. And with its culture firmly planted in the past, its young population is racing towards globalization. Many who set foot on Madagascar find it never quite leaves them. With *A Taste of Madagascar*, it's clear that author Emmanuel Laroche has joined those of us who can't help but return for repeat visits. Along with renowned local and international chefs, he explores the fascinating history and culture of Madagascar and Malagasy people through their spices, food, and traditions. The island's biodiversity and local conservation heroes play a starring role in a chapter about lemurs and their conservation, with a visit to a community-led reforestation project in the eastern rainforest. *A Taste of Madagascar* is fun to read, and a unique travelogue of this place I love."

—LYNNE VENART
Director, Lemur Conservation Network

"This is a must-read for anyone interested in flavors, food, and adventure. Emmanuel Laroche combines a career in flavor science with a journalist's eye for detail as he travels the hinterlands of Madagascar looking for interesting flavors, food—and the truth. The result is a captivating narrative. Informative. And fun."

—TIM MCCOLLUM
Founder and CEO, Beyond Good

A TASTE OF MADAGASCAR

CULINARY RICHES OF THE RED ISLAND

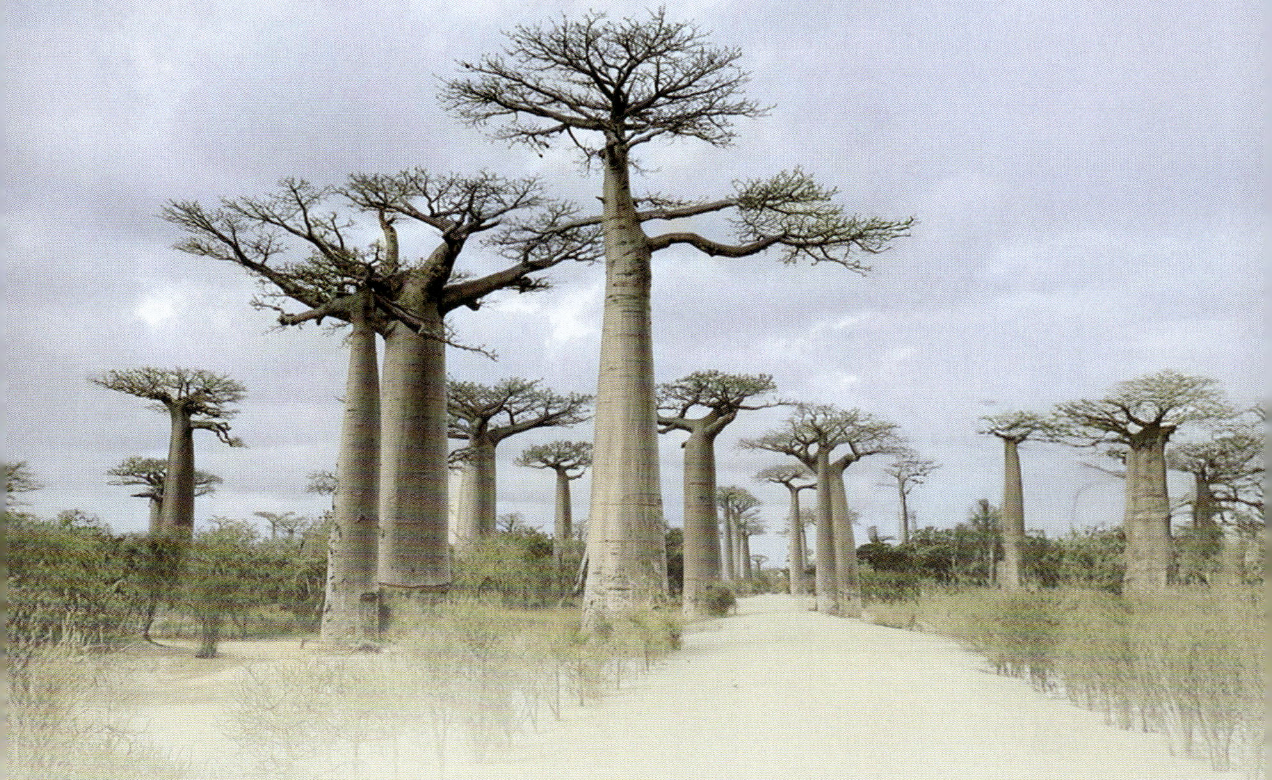

EMMANUEL LAROCHE

A POST HILL PRESS BOOK

A Taste of Madagascar:
Culinary Riches of the Red Island

ISBN: 979-8-89565-014-1
ISBN (eBook): 979-8-89565-015-8

Cover design by Jim Villaflores
Cover photo by Emmanuel Laroche
Art direction, interior design, and composition by Greg Johnson, Textbook Perfect

This book contains information relating to the health benefits of certain ingredients. It should be used to supplement rather than replace the advice of your doctor or another trained health professional. All efforts have been made to ensure the accuracy of the information in this book as of the date of publication.

This is a work of nonfiction. All people, locations, events, and situations are portrayed to the best of the author's memory.

Post Hill Press
New York • Nashville
posthillpress.com

Printed in Canada
Published in the United States of America

1 2 3 4 5 6 7 8 9 10

To my children—Frederic, Laura, and Alexandre...

"Twenty years from now you will be more disappointed
by the things that you didn't do than by the ones you did do.
So, throw off the bowlines. Sail away from the safe harbor.
Catch the trade winds in your sails.
Explore. Dream. Discover."

—H. JACKSON BROWN JR.

"Travel isn't always pretty. It isn't always comfortable.
Sometimes it hurts, it even breaks your heart. But that's okay.
The journey changes you; it should change you."

—ANTHONY BOURDAIN

"The real voyage of discovery consists not in seeking new
landscapes, but in having new eyes."

—MARCEL PROUST

"Preservation of one's own culture does not require
contempt or disrespect for other cultures."

—CESAR CHAVEZ

Contents

BARON
-Baie ds AssassinS M6-
22°13'30" Sud
43°14'16" Est
-Merci-
PAUL

Author's Note

As a child growing up in France, I dreamed of Madagascar—a faraway island that felt mythical in name alone. Decades later, that dream came true.

A Taste of Madagascar is a work of narrative nonfiction shaped by three immersions I made to the island between 2022 and 2025. Each visit pulled me deeper into the island's layers—culinary, cultural, relational, and personal.

Madagascar is often described in fragments—its unique biodiversity, its poverty rankings, its vanilla production. But behind those fragments are lives and landscapes that resist simplification.

The chapters combine reported conversations, field interviews, culinary experiences, and firsthand observations. While every effort has been made to ensure accuracy, some dialogue has been lightly edited for clarity. The content of these chapters was written from interviews, field notes, and recordings to preserve the spirit and truth of the experience. In a few cases, timelines have been condensed or reordered to preserve narrative cohesion without altering the substance of events.

The people featured in these pages—chefs, beekeepers, farmers, entrepreneurs—generously opened their lives and work to me. Their stories are presented as they were shared: personal, layered, and grounded in lived experience.

Traditional Malagasy proverbs appear throughout the book, not just for literary effect, and not only to honor cultural context, but to reflect the values at the heart of these stories: resourcefulness, humility, and perseverance.

This book is not a comprehensive guide to Malagasy cuisine, nor a technical study of agriculture or biodiversity. Rather, it is a portrait of a place told through food—through ingredients shaped by environment and memory, and through the people who grow, transform, and elevate them.

To enhance the sensory experience of reading, a QR code on the "My Malagasy Soundtrack" page at the end of the book links to a curated playlist of local music. You'll also find a section highlighting select companies featured in the book, for those interested in continuing the journey beyond the page.

One more way to extend the experience: during my first trip, I was joined by three American chefs whose perspectives and impressions added unexpected depth to our culinary exploration. I captured that shared adventure in a special episode of my podcast, *Flavors Unknown,* titled, "Exciting Culinary Adventures in Madagascar with Three American Chefs." This QR code will take you directly to that conversation.

Finally, while introductions are often skipped, I urge you not to overlook this one. It has been written and structured as a full chapter—offering essential context, framing key themes, and introducing places and people whose stories will unfold across the book. Reading it will deepen your understanding of what follows and provides a more connected experience from the outset.

—***Emmanuel Laroche***

Foreword

By Lantosoa Rakotomalala

Ambassador Extraordinary and Plenipotentiary
of Madagascar to the United States of America

In Madagascar, we have a saying: "*Ny teny toy ny atody: raha foy manan'elatra*," meaning, "Words are like eggs: when they are hatched, they have wings." This encapsulates the transformative power of storytelling—how ideas can take flight and travel far, connecting people across borders. Emmanuel Laroche's *A Taste of Madagascar* embodies this wisdom, offering readers a glimpse into the beauty, flavors, and ingenuity of our island.

Madagascar is known for its breathtaking biodiversity, from its vibrant landscapes to its rich flora and fauna. Yet, as we strive to share the treasures of our land with the world, our cuisine and the ingredients that shape it are emerging as symbols of cultural and economic significance. In this book, Emmanuel journeys through Madagascar to uncover the stories behind our vanilla, cocoa, rice, caviar, and spices—ingredients that are not only integral to the island's economy, but also a reflection of its potential and creativity.

Emmanuel's dedication to capturing the essence of Madagascar is evident in every page. He ventures beyond the familiar narratives of exoticism to explore the people, traditions, and innovations that define the island today. He engages with farmers, chefs, mixologists, and environmentalists, weaving together a narrative that highlights both the challenges and triumphs of a nation rich in heritage and ambition.

Like the resilience behind our national dish, Malagasy Romazava, life is a slow-simmered harmony: rich, earthy, unexpected, unforgettable, and best when shared.

During his travels, Emmanuel witnessed efforts to balance cultural evolution with respect for ancestral traditions. He encountered individuals and communities working tirelessly to preserve biodiversity, combat deforestation, and promote sustainable practices. Their stories reflect the resilience and resourcefulness of the Malagasy people, who are committed to shaping a brighter future while honoring their past.

Madagascar's culinary landscape is evolving, with a new generation of chefs and mixologists reimagining the possibilities of our local ingredients. Emmanuel captures this dynamic transformation, showcasing how Malagasy cuisine is embracing creativity while staying rooted in authenticity. From the bustling streets of Antananarivo to the tranquil shores of the Indian Ocean, he paints a vivid picture of an island brimming with opportunity and inspiration.

If you've never been to Madagascar, this book is an ideal companion to traditional travel guides, offering an immersive journey beyond the familiar paths and into the heart of the island's untold stories. By following in Emmanuel's footsteps, you won't simply tour Madagascar; you'll experience it as few ever have, uncovering its essence through its people, landscapes, and culinary treasures. Even if you've already visited, this journey provides fresh perspectives. With Emmanuel as your guide, you'll discover not only the visible beauty of Madagascar but also its hidden wonders—the secrets that make our island truly unique.

This book is more than a culinary exploration; it is an invitation to appreciate Madagascar's unique place in the world. By celebrating the stories of those who cultivate and transform its natural bounty, Emmanuel shines a light on the interconnectedness of culture, economy, and environment. His work reminds us that food is not only nourishment but also a powerful medium for understanding and connection.

It is my hope that *A Taste of Madagascar* will inspire readers to discover the richness of Malagasy ingredients and the stories they carry. May it encourage respect for the environmental and cultural heritage that sustains them, and may it deepen the appreciation of Madagascar's contributions to the global culinary landscape.

As the Ambassador of Madagascar to the United States, it is my honor to introduce this journey. Emmanuel Laroche has crafted a tribute to our island—one that I am confident will resonate with readers around the world, inviting them to savor the flavors of Madagascar and glimpse into the heart of its people.

—***Lantosoa Rakotomalala***

THE
LOWER
THIRD

INTRODUCTION

Where the Story Takes Root

Ny lalana no fetra, ny atao no hita.

The path sets the boundaries;
what is done is what becomes visible.

—TRADITIONAL MALAGASY SAYING

Ever wondered where your favorite ice cream flavor originated? The answer lies in the heart of Madagascar, a paradise known to some but a mystery to many. Many people in the US think of Madagascar as an animated film. Some people even think it is an imaginary world. But this island nation is real, pulsing with stories that connect the past to our plates. It's a huge island in the Indian Ocean, home to plants and animals that exist nowhere else in the world. Here, in this secluded part of the planet, exist many culinary flavors, tales, and traditions not yet fully discovered.

◂ *From left to right: Chef Elizabeth Falkner, me, Mixologist Shannon Tebay, and Chef Michael Gulotta.*

The first time I set foot on this island was the fall of 2022, the year of my fifty-ninth birthday. Like many French people, I grew up aware of the island and its history as part of France's colonial empire, but I never knew the details. I perceived it as an exotic place with the same beautiful fauna, flora, and landscapes illustrated in my childhood stamp collection. Each stamp was a miniature window into tropical paradises, rugged coastlines, and gorgeous atolls. Lemurs, baobabs, and heavenly beaches were visuals I often associated with this country. There was also a large Malagasy diaspora in France, so Malagasy culture had a certain visibility, and I had friends in elementary school whose families were originally from the island. I never paid much attention to it though.

Then, in the early '90s, when I started my professional career in the flavors industry, Madagascar resurfaced in my life—the first time since childhood. I discovered that the island accounted for 80 percent of the worldwide vanilla bean production, and suddenly, I could connect it to a familiar ingredient from my everyday cooking.

While vanilla, known as the "queen of spices," undeniably marks a prominent chapter in Madagascar's food narrative, it only scratches the surface of the country's current rich food landscape. Regrettably, Madagascar is infrequently highlighted in the news. When it does make headlines, it's often due to negative events like famine, the loss of endangered species, threats to its unique biodiversity, cyclones, political instability, and corruption. A report from the World Bank Group mentioned that due to the country's "location, topography, and socioeconomic conditions, Madagascar is highly exposed to extreme weather events, especially cyclones, flooding, and drought." But through this book, I wanted to present lesser-known facets of this nation. In my journey through the island, I uncovered a plethora of food ingredients and spices such as indigenous blossom honey, endemic wild pepper, pink peppercorn, blue ginger, and more. Each tells its own story, and each is deeply connected to courageous entrepreneurs, resilient people, and local terroirs.

Zsoil, is a land shaped by its isolation. Just a little larger than California, this world's fourth largest island rests 250 miles off the African coast in the

Indian Ocean, yet it feels a world apart. For me, the journey from New York to Antananarivo, the capital, was not just a physical one—it was a trip into the unknown, spanning nine thousand miles and nearly eighteen hours, including a layover in Paris, with each mile deepening my anticipation of what lay ahead.

This nickname, "Great Red Island," isn't just poetic—it stems from the island's laterite-rich soils, deeply tinted by iron and aluminum, formed under hot and wet tropical conditions. Once exposed to the air, the iron in the soil oxidizes, giving it a characteristic red color. The prominence of this reddish soil in many parts of the island, especially in the central highlands, makes the landscape appear red, hence the name.

Madagascar can be divided into five geographical regions: on the east, the coast stretches out, while the Tsaratanana Massif rises in the north, crowned with the island's highest peak. The backbone of Madagascar, the central highlands, run the length of the island and range from 2,600 to 5,800 feet (800 to 1,800 meters) in altitude. To the west, the coast plays host to dramatic limestone formations known as *tsingy*, sculpted patiently by years of relentless rains. And finally, the southwest area, primarily semi-arid, receives less rainfall than other parts of the island.

Yet, the tale of Madagascar isn't solely etched in its soil and stone. Madagascar's isolation, dating back to its split from the supercontinent Gondwana, shaped a land where time stood still. For millennia, its flora and fauna evolved in solitude, untouched by human hands. This pristine isolation remained until the eighth or ninth century, when the first settlers

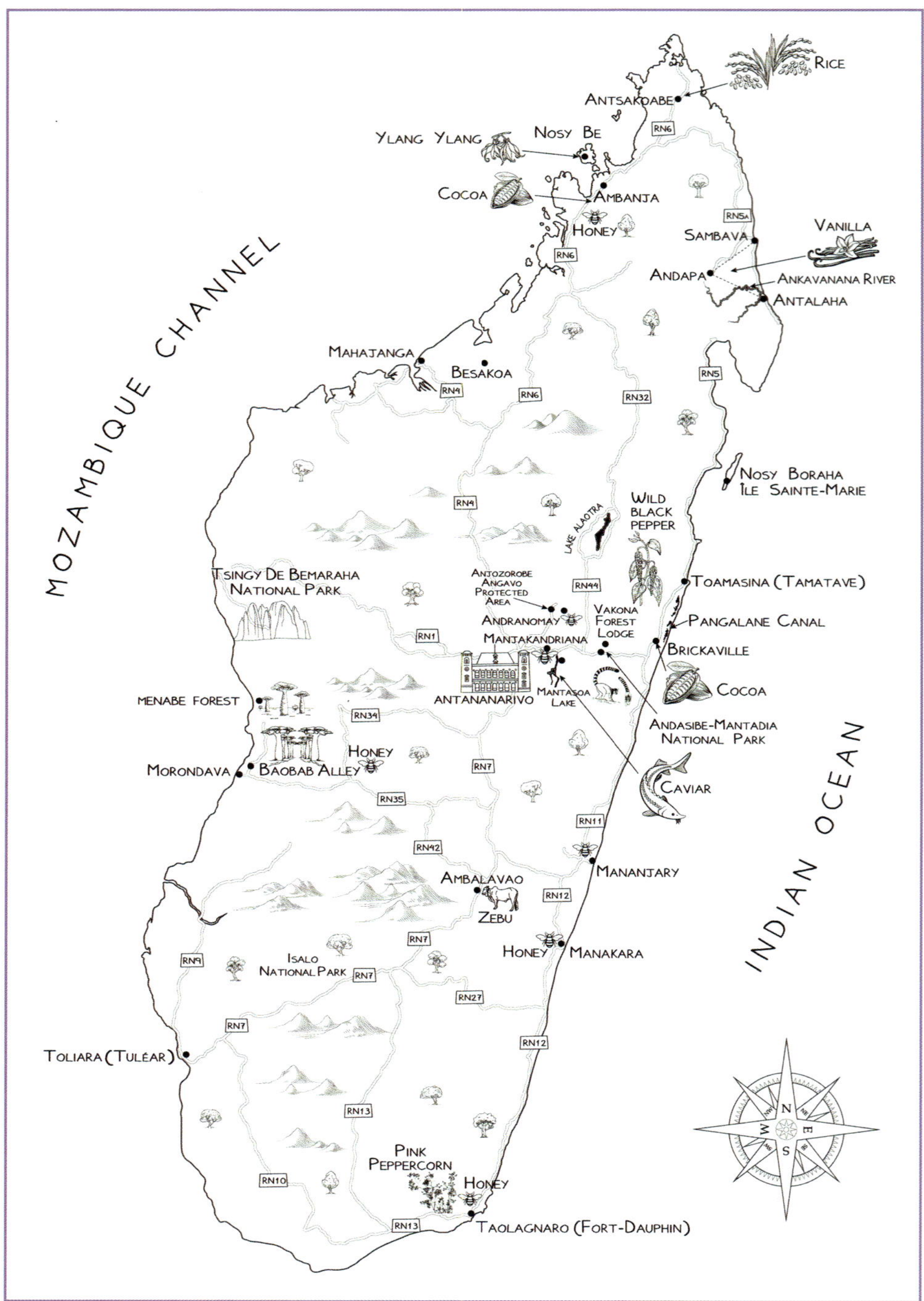

Madagascar—follow the flavor trail: Every dot a story, every stop a taste.

arrived. By the time of my visit, Madagascar was home to 29 million people, but its wild heart—a place where nature and culture coexist—still felt untouched, waiting to be discovered.

While delving into Madagascar's history, I discovered a land that began its narrative around two millennia ago, when seafarers—possibly of Indonesian and African descent—began to settle on this previously uninhabited land. Their legacy remains in the Malagasy language that evolved in isolation, branching into varied dialects. So profound is this diversity that the dialect spoken in the capital, Antananarivo, can sometimes sound foreign in regions like Tuléar (now Toliara) in the south, or Diego Suarez (now Antsiranana) in the north.

Madagascar's cuisine is a mosaic woven from its rich history of migration and cultural exchange. Each flavor reflects the island's journey, blending influences from across the globe into a uniquely Malagasy identity.

The Indonesian Connection

The earliest threads of Madagascar's culinary fabric can be traced to Indonesia, brought by Austronesian ancestors:

- **Rice as a Foundation:** Both Madagascar and Indonesia share a deep cultural and culinary reliance on rice, or *vary* in Malagasy. This staple mirrors the agricultural expertise of the Austronesian settlers.
- **Familiar Flavors:** Variations of Indonesian *satay* (grilled skewered meats) appear in Madagascar's own satay-like dishes.
- **Koba's Sweet Parallels:** The Malagasy snack *koba*—a steamed or baked mixture of rice, bananas, and peanuts wrapped in banana leaves—bears a striking resemblance to Indonesian sweet treats.
- ***Mofo Gasy:*** This Malagasy snack rice cake echoes the ingredients and preparation methods of Indonesian snacks, reinforcing a shared culinary heritage.

The African Influences

As Austronesian practices intermingled with African traditions, Malagasy cuisine evolved to include distinct elements from the African mainland:

- **Stews with Depth:** Many Malagasy stews feature ingredients like groundnuts (peanuts) and pulses, reflecting African culinary techniques.
- **Staples of Maize and Cassava:** Originally from the Americas, these crops arrived in Madagascar through Africa and became integral to local diets. Cassava is especially versatile, consumed both as a root and in leafy dishes.
- **Vegetables with Roots in Africa:** Greens like amaranth (*anamamy*) and okra have become cornerstones of Malagasy cooking, showcasing the island's connection to its African neighbors.

The Arab Influence

Arab traders arrived between AD 800 and 900, leaving an indelible mark on Madagascar's food culture:

- **Spices and Trade:** Through Arab trade routes, spices like cloves, cardamom, and black pepper became staples in Malagasy cuisine, enriching its flavor profiles.
- **Aromatic Rice Dishes:** While rice cultivation originated with Austronesian settlers, the Arab influence introduced spices like saffron to enhance traditional preparations.
- **Sweet Temptations:** Arab settlers brought pastries and desserts made with honey, dates, and deep-fried dough, inspiring Malagasy sweets with Middle Eastern flair.
- **Coffee's Arrival:** Though coffee's origins lie in Ethiopia, Arab traders spread its cultivation and consumption to Madagascar, embedding it in the island's cultural landscape.

The Portuguese Encounter

The unexpected arrival of Portuguese sailor Diogo Dias in 1500 marked a pivotal moment, albeit with subtler culinary contributions compared to earlier influences:

- **Chili Peppers:** Introduced by Portuguese explorers, chili peppers added heat and complexity to Malagasy dishes, including the now-popular chili oil.
- **Spice Trade Expansion:** Portuguese engagement in global spice routes further integrated Madagascar into this network, solidifying its role as a hub for aromatic ingredients.

From Indonesian-inspired satay skewers to African groundnut stews and Arab-spiced rice, Madagascar's cuisine narrates a story of migration and adaptation. Each bite serves as a reminder of the island's rich cultural exchanges, celebrating its position as a crossroads of culinary traditions.

The island soon became the envy of European powers. Their numerous attempts to colonize were met with formidable resistance from the native Malagasy warriors, proving the island was no easy conquest. In the shadow of these global powers, pirates found solace on the island's eastern coast in the 1600s. Their tales of hidden treasures and high-sea adventures added to Madagascar's mystique. As the pirate era weakened, Madagascar witnessed the emergence of its own kingdoms. The Sakalava monarchy in the west and their rivals, the Merina, rose to prominence. In 1810, the Merina Kingdom, under King Radama I's leadership, expanded its dominion across the island. Introducing Christianity, forming alliances with the British, and industrializing the region, his reign marked a renaissance. However, the wheel of time turned, and under Queen Ranavalona I, Madagascar witnessed a resurgence of its ancient rituals and a persecution of Christians. Her reign was both revered and reviled.

By 1896, after years of resistance, Madagascar became a French colony, with its lands being exploited for timber (especially rosewood and ebony), its shores for exotic spices, and its people for cheap labor. The Malagasy spirit, however, remained unbroken. It roared to life in the uprisings of 1918 and 1947, eventually attaining independence on June 26, 1960, with Philibert Tsiranana as its first president.

The post-independence journey was anything but smooth. Leaders like Didier Ratsiraka and Marc Ravalomanana, each with their distinctive leadership styles, shaped the nation's destiny. Ratsiraka's reign oscillated between dictatorship and political unrest. While Ravalomanana, once a humble yogurt seller, rose to become one of Madagascar's most influential leaders by focusing on economic and cultural revitalization.

As we reflect on Madagascar's journey, it's not just the milestones but the everyday life that adds color to its narrative. In 1960, as the island transitioned from a French colony into an independent state, the Malagasy people blended their traditional agricultural and fishing lifestyles with the new political changes.

Today, Madagascar reflects a complex history shaped by resilience. From Antananarivo's busy streets to the historical fortress of Ambohimanga, the country reveals a layered past marked by both challenges and progress. Influenced by Malayo-Indonesian, African, Arab, and European cultures, Madagascar continues to evolve as a society defined by adaptability and cultural diversity.

Madagascar's history reflects the intersection of indigenous and colonial influences. This is evident in the dual naming of some cities—for example, Antananarivo, the capital, is also known by its French colonial name, Tananarive. These parallel names highlight the administrative legacy of French rule and serve as reminders of the country's complex past.

In October 2022, I embarked on a journey to the island of Madagascar, accompanied by three American culinary maestros. This wasn't just a whimsical journey; it was a voyage to the very heart of vanilla production, organized by my employer, Symrise, a global flavor and natural ingredient company.

At the time, Symrise just launched a new vanilla extract for culinary professionals in the US market. As vice president of marketing, I developed a nationwide contest in partnership with StarChefs, a platform serving the restaurant industry. The challenge brought together leading chefs, pastry chefs, and mixologists to craft standout dishes, desserts, and cocktails using

our vanilla extract. From hundreds of entries, three winners were selected to travel to Madagascar and explore the origin of the ingredient firsthand.

Based in Los Angeles, Elizabeth Falkner is an award-winning chef recognized for her contributions to food, film, and culinary media. She has competed on shows such as Food Network's *Tournament of Champions*, *Iron Chef America*, *Food Network Challenge*, and *Top Chef Masters* and also served as a judge on episodes of *Top Chef*. Beyond her culinary achievements, Falkner is an advocate for LGBTQ+ visibility and gender equity in the industry, adding another dimension to her public presence.

Michael Gulotta hales from New Orleans—he is a chef and an entrepreneur. The mastermind behind Mopho, Maypop, and Tana restaurants has been a semifinalist two times for James Beard's "Best Chef: South" category. Gulotta's endeavors stretch beyond mere culinary passion, displaying an entrepreneurial flair.

Shannon Tebay's tale begins in Albuquerque and continues now in New York City. Her mixology expertise reverberates through famous establishments like Death & Co in New York and the American Bar at the Savoy Hotel in London. She also worked at The Lower Third in London's Soho, where she mixed more than just spirits. She's a fervent advocate for inclusivity, tirelessly pushing the envelope for underrepresented bartenders.

United by their insatiable curiosity, adaptability, and a shared ethos of collaboration, these three well-traveled American culinary experts were not just passengers but also pivotal players in my first trip to Madagascar.

I have been fortunate to share and promote Madagascar's esteemed vanilla extract at Symrise for two decades. Throughout this time, I felt a growing desire to visit the Red Island. I wanted to come closer to the source of this timeless flavor I worked with and wholeheartedly supported for years.

I commenced on this adventure with a mindset primed for professional growth. *It's about understanding the business better, meeting my Symrise colleagues on the island, engaging with farmers, and exploring vanilla plantations*, I told myself. But Madagascar had surprises in store.

This trip was a transformative experience. The beauty of Madagascar is not just in its scenery; it is in its soul. And beyond the stunning ingredients and rich biodiversity, it was the people who truly captured my heart.

In the lead-up to my 2022 expedition, a local colleague of mine introduced me to Herilalaina Ravelomanana, better known as Chef Lalaina, Madagascar's most renowned chef, a disciple of Auguste Escoffier and recipient of nine international awards. Chef Lalaina, who is self-taught, created from scratch an outstanding gourmet restaurant, Marais, in Antananarivo. Months before setting foot on Malagasy soil, a shared dream materialized. Together with the American chefs and Chef Lalaina, we envisioned a cocktail dinner at Marais—where cutting-edge dishes would be served together with exotic cocktails, each bursting with Madagascar's iconic spices, vanilla, and even caviar. Picture this: American culinary artists working alongside the most famous Malagasy chef and his brigade, promising a night like no other to several hundred local guests.

And speaking of cocktails, the presence of Shannon Tebay on this expedition ignited a spark. It fueled an ambition to forge a unique blend of Malagasy tradition with American cocktail flair. We worked on a cultural exchange of cocktail-making by incorporating the island's local ingredients to develop new cocktail recipes. We connected with Randrianarisoa Mahery Tiana, bartender and mixologist at Comptoir des Artistes, situated in the heart of Antananarivo's creative hub, La Teinturerie. He is known as K-Mëc, a title that embodies his unique approach to mixology. Each letter reflects a key element of his craft: "K" stands for knowledge, the dash symbolizes art, "M" is for mixology, while "ë" stands for experience, and, finally, "c" represents cocktail. La Teinturerie is a space where art comes to life in a myriad of forms, from exhibitions and concerts to debates and workshops. But above all, it's home to the Comptoir des Artistes—a bar where local ingredients are

mixed in a glass to celebrate the Malagasy culture.

With the news of American visitors, K-Mëc's excitement was palpable; so much so, he took it upon himself to launch the first ever craft cocktail competition, and the American chefs would be the judges. Yet, woven through these feelings of excitement were threads of uncertainty. Along with Chef Lalaina and K-Mëc, our American collaborators grappled with a mix of emotions: exhilaration from the prospect of uncharted flavors and some hesitancy in navigating unfamiliar terrains of tools and organization. However, it's worth noting that these seasoned professionals thrive in dynamic situations. They're no strangers to last-minute ingredient swaps, orchestrating dinners alongside fellow chefs, or the pressures of televised competitions. Their adaptability and expertise are precisely what cooled my concerns.

What I had anticipated as a business trip was rapidly transforming before my eyes. Madagascar wasn't just about understanding vanilla better; it was also about understanding myself. I found an unexpected connection, a bond so strong that just seven months after my initial trip, I was back on a plane. This time was for a personal vacation and to research a book I felt I should write—this book.

There's an uncanny contrast between my structured professional life at Symrise and the free, untouched beauty of Madagascar. This contrast, however, brought clarity. And when it comes to vanilla, it made me look beyond mere transactions and business dealings. It reminded me of the beauty of the human component and the importance of the craftsmanship in vanilla bean production. The art of extracting the beans wasn't solely about commercial exchange or chemical processes; it reflected the dedication of the people cultivating and curating it. These trips to the island taught me the harmony of science and tradition—how the science and technological precision I focused on for years was only one part of the story, complemented by the tradition and devotion of those who dedicate their lives to vanilla.

It's a rare privilege for a place to reshape one's narrative; to change not just the way one sees the world, but also oneself. For me, Madagascar was that touchstone. While initially a business exploration, it became a trip of self-discovery and introspection. As I look ahead to creating more memories on the Red Island, one truth stands out: the essence of my journey lay not in reaching a destination, but in the stories uncovered and the revelations shared.

On Chef Lalaina's recommendation, I set foot into Chocolaterie Robert with little expectation other than to taste local chocolate. I met with a man named Nirina Ramanandraibe. I learned that in Madagascar, names like Nirina don't conform to the gender expectations I was familiar with. As the doors of the chocolate factory swung open, a sense of destiny lingered in the air. Nirina's passion for his family business and legacy, combined with the history of the island, was contagious. After exchanging stories, sharing laughter, and despite our vastly different backgrounds, we developed a connection. Spending those hours with him deepened my connection to this place beyond just business. After my first trip, Nirina and I kept in touch. I told him about my plan to write a book. "It would highlight Madagascar's unique flavors loved worldwide, especially by French and American chefs," I told him. I also mentioned wanting to share genuine stories and spotlight companies helping local communities. His eyes sparkled. "Let me introduce you to this land's change-makers," he said, offering along the way to be my guide. He kept his word. I chose to collaborate with Nirina, who truly represents the spirit of Madagascar.

With a rich business education from Australia, Nirina returned to Madagascar to work for the family business. The first part of his career was mainly to look after the group's real estate assets. He also wanted to uplift his people and became involved in a number of social projects, from nurturing the youth through sports and Boy Scouts to launching reforestation initiatives and supporting agritourism. More recently, he created Mikéa Lodge on the southwestern side of the island and is currently developing culinary tourism tours. A testament to his devotion was the family farm at the edge of Antananarivo. Once a childhood haven, it transformed under Nirina's vision into an organic sanctuary, buzzing with life, from horses to the unexpected presence of crocodiles. Each corner of this farm hinted at his ethos: a harmonious balance between nature and nurture.

Nirina was the perfect collaborator for my book, connecting me to the heart and soul of Madagascar. Through his eyes, I didn't just see Madagascar; I felt it.

Among the many individuals with whom Nirina connected me was Chef Farah Rabekijana. A two-wheeler aficionado and prominent influencer, Farah helms the Facebook page "My Road Trip Culinaire." Here, she documents her gastronomic adventures across Madagascar, collaborating with the Madagascar Ministry of Tourism to spotlight the island's tourist, cultural, and culinary treasures. Actively engaging with local communities, she crafts dishes from indigenous ingredients. Moreover, Chef Farah oversees Nirina's family farm and accompanied us during my return visit in spring 2023.

Foreigners usually recognize only a handful of Malagasy dishes, primarily Romazava (a national dish of zebu, or humped cattle, meat stew combined with tomatoes, onions, ginger, and greens—a hearty and flavorful affair) and *ravitoto* (boiled cassava leaves with either pork or zebu, prepared over an open fire). As our tastebuds can attest, Madagascar offers an expansive and culinary repertoire based on a flavorful mélange. What I found, traveling with Chef Farah, was a cuisine deeply entrenched in Madagascar's storied history and influenced by its diverse set of settlers, including those from Indonesia, Africa, France, India, and China.

Traveling between Antananarivo in the Central Highlands and the SAVA region on the northeast coast (SAVA is short for Sambava, Antalaha, Vohemar, and Andapa), to the western coast, it was evident that Madagascar's size and varied climate played a significant role in regional specialties. But one thing remained constant: the importance of zebu, ginger, garlic, chili peppers, and soy sauce undoubtedly pays tribute to its Asian and Indian connections.

Rice is a staple. Few countries honor rice like Madagascar does. It's not just a side dish; it's a centerpiece. Consumed during all three meals, Malagasy's take on rice is unique. The preferred smokey crust that forms at the pot's bottom, after traditional cooking, is a delight. What's even more intriguing is the practice of deglazing the pot with water. The "burnt rice water" is not wasted; it's consumed as a calming after-dinner tea. This drink is called *ranovola*. It differs from Korean rice tea in its smoky flavor and preparation, as it is made from burnt rice and water without added tea leaves.

Some might find certain dishes slightly on the oilier side, but that's where the ubiquitous rice comes in, sopping up the juices and balancing out the dish. Plus, adding a light broth can always cut through the richness. The fusion of local ingredients and international influences makes Madagascar not just a must-visit for its scenic beauty, but also for its culinary culture.

In a world increasingly drawn to authenticity and untapped culinary frontiers, Madagascar stands as a beacon of opportunity. This book highlights the island's remarkable agricultural legacy, focusing on the passionate farmers and visionary entrepreneurs who cultivate its treasures while giving back to local communities. Although vanilla reigns as Madagascar's signature export, the island offers a wealth of underappreciated ingredients with extraordinary potential on the global stage.

Take the fruit of the baobab, a burgeoning superfood, or *voatsiperifery*, a wild pepper coveted by elite chefs yet largely unknown to broader audiences. Madagascar also produces exceptional cacao with distinctive red fruit and citrus notes, often overlooked in favor of larger commodity-grade cacao-exporting nations. Its vast coastline provides a bounty of seafood, with tiger prawns, one of the few products to make a notable mark internationally.

Though much of Madagascar's agricultural infrastructure is dedicated to vanilla, its unparalleled biodiversity holds untapped potential for the global market. As culinary explorers seek ever more distinctive flavors, the hope is that more of Madagascar's extraordinary produce will find its rightful place on tables worldwide.

On our journey from the east coast in (now Toamasina) to the west coast in Majunga (now Mahajanga), I conducted in-depth interviews with local farmers, artisans, and businesses. This book is a blend of travelogue and cultural exploration, offering a vivid narrative of Madagascar's unique agricultural and culinary landscape.

At the end of each chapter, you'll find a curated selection of recipes—not as the primary focus, but as a complement to the stories within. These recipes, both traditional and modern, showcase how local chefs are reinterpreting Madagascar's cuisine, alongside contemporary creations from American and French chefs celebrating the island's exceptional ingredients.

This book is not a collection of recipes; it's an immersive journey into the heart of Madagascar's culinary and agricultural world, enriched by captivating anecdotes and personal encounters that bring the island's remarkable food culture to life.

As you flip through this book, I hope you'll share my excitement for the untapped potential of overlooked Malagasy ingredients and see them through the lens of global culinary trends, all while understanding the profound impact of food tourism on our shared adventure.

Set against the lively backdrop of Antananarivo, our adventure commences at the restaurant Marais, a tribute to the country's rich culinary landscape. Whether accompanied by the three American chefs or alone on my subsequent visits, I explore the eclectic landscapes of Madagascar:

traversing the cocoa-rich soils of Ambanja and Brickaville, the aromatic vanilla from the triangle of the SAVA region, to the peaceful Lake Mantasoa, home to Africa's and the Indian Ocean's only caviar.

Our journey is as varied as the terrain itself. In the disparate regions of Ambanja and Brickaville, cocoa beans unveil stories of unique flavors, molded by the terroir and refined by the craftsmen at Chocolaterie Robert. Our journey unfolds narratives of dedication, and the transformative journey from soil to soul. Near Antalaha, at Domaine d'Ambohimanitra, we met Dina Rasanjison, an expert of vanilla history on the island. She revealed a realm of diverse vanilla strains and shared tales of its illustrious past, lesser known outside the island. Under Dina's guidance, we attempted the delicate art of hand-pollinating vanilla orchid blossoms. Venturing further east to Andapa, the vanilla heartland, we met the true heroes: the committed vanilla farmers. Their stories, struggles, and victories enriched our appreciation of this prized bean. At Lake Mantasoa, a short distance from Antananarivo, lies Acipenser, a sturgeon farm yielding the southern hemisphere's exclusive caviar. I met with three French visionaries who transported fertilized sturgeon eggs here years ago. Today, the lake shelters six sturgeon breeds, including the scarce Persicus and Nudiventris. Rova Caviar, an Indian Ocean jewel, is enhanced by Madagascar's unique environment.

From these focal points, our narrative sprawls out, unveiling the spicy charm of the endemic *voatsiperifery* pepper, the citrusy aroma of pink peppercorn during crop season near Fort-Dauphin (now Taolagnaro), and the cultural significance of zebu (hunchback cattle). We delve into the sweet allure of honey with the Beekeeper, igniting a revolution one droplet at a time. Experience the new buzz around town with the fragrant rice of Madame Rose from the Antsiranana region, and get lost in the fragrant embrace of Nosy Be's ylang-ylang flower, a quintessential component in perfumes like Chanel No. 5.

As we explore Madagascar's culinary treasures, the looming threat of deforestation casts a shadow over the island's future. Driven by slash-and-burn farming, overgrazing, and charcoal production—practices with roots stretching back to the French colonial period—deforestation remains a persistent challenge. From honey-producing blossoms to the island's endemic wild peppers, the delicate balance between biodiversity and human activity grows increasingly fragile. Madagascar's distinctive ecosystem, once thriving beneath its forest canopy, is steadily diminishing, eroding not only its natural heritage but also the ingredients that shape its culinary identity. Despite these challenges, there is hope. Initiatives like Ecovision Village in Andasibe are championing forest conservation and restoration, safeguarding both the environment and the island's culinary future. Through community engagement and partnerships with scientists, they extend their efforts beyond ecological preservation to provide tangible support for local communities. New projects, such as sustainable cocoa farming, are also showing promise, demonstrating that reforestation and agricultural innovation can go hand in hand.

Our voyage culminates by showcasing the contemporary culinary faces of Madagascar—with chefs Lalaina, Henintsoa Moretti, Kakulé, and Farah Rabekijana rekindling our appreciation for the island's large, diverse, and continually evolving gastronomic landscape.

Beyond the narrative of ingredients, this book also traces the lives and efforts of the Malagasy people: the farmers, food artisans, and small enterprises that sustain the global palate.

Madagascar generates 80 percent of the world's vanilla beans. It's imperative that we lend our support to the local population to ensure that the enduring impact of this cherished flavor continues for generations to come.

Vanilla, an aroma and flavor familiar to countless societies worldwide, has etched a distinct place on our collective memory. This singular ingredient has transcended its culinary origins to become a symbol of intangible emotions and memories of our past. The story of vanilla encapsulates the threads of generational recollections, evoking nostalgia and serving as a bridge between generations of human experience. With its soft, sweet, warm aroma, vanilla has been infused into countless societal events and personal milestones. From birthdays celebrated with vanilla cakes and ice cream, to the scent of vanilla candles illuminating family gatherings, these moments become deeply embedded in our personal and collective memories.

One importer explained Madagascar vanilla this way: "Vanilla is the most complex spice flavor on earth, which is what makes this high-quality bean so special—floral, sweet, and earthy undertones of dried dark fruits, oak, and leather all at the same time."

The flavor and aroma act as a thread, weaving together tales of our past and present. Imagine a grandparent sharing a cookie recipe that they once baked with their own grandparents. As they bake with their grandchildren, the kitchen is filled with that familiar, comforting scent. It is not just a cookie being shared, but memories, stories, and a sense of belonging. The act transforms into a rite of passage, and vanilla extract becomes the medium through which generational stories, values, and love are transmitted.

As the world primary cultivator of the vanilla orchid, the local communities of Madagascar are the backbone of the vanilla industry. Given the vast sociocultural importance and nostalgic value of vanilla worldwide, supporting these communities becomes an essential ethical and economic prerogative. Madagascar, as the heartland of vanilla production, plays a monumental role in ensuring the flavor's continuity in our lives. Beyond the economic and ecological reasons, there is an intrinsic cultural and ethical need to champion these local communities. The global love affair with this flavor, replete with its nostalgic resonances and generational memories, owes a debt of gratitude to the tireless efforts of Madagascar's vanilla cultivators. Supporting them ensures that these legacy flourishes, bridging past traditions with future aspirations.

For the avid gastronomes, culinary travelers, food writers, and chefs among you, this book serves as both a cookbook and a passport. It's an invitation to explore the intricate relationship between Madagascar's environment, culture, and cuisine, and to immerse oneself in its vibrant traditions, stories, and people. Whether you're savoring the recipes, crafted by both local experts and renowned American and French chefs, or picturing the vivid landscapes and gastronomic scenes, each page offers a slice of Madagascar, ready to be savored. And as we go on this journey, one must reflect: In the context of global culinary heritage and sustainability, what might we lose if we don't preserve Madagascar's culinary bounty, and how might we support the local communities, farmers, and food artisans responsible for the flavors ending up on our tables and in chefs' menus around the world?

As we delve into these pages, we explore not just the traditional and modern recipes inspired by the Red Island but the soul of a culture—woven with passion, resilience, and a touch of Malagasy enchantment.

As we taste the wonders of Madagascar's rich culinary tableau, let us remember that every flavor tells a story, and every tradition holds a legacy. Yet these stories and tastes remain fragile, threatened by the tides of time and change. Beyond savoring the delights, consider how we might play a part in the preservation of this legacy. Whether by supporting sustainable practices, promoting Malagasy cuisine, or simply sharing these stories with others, together we can ensure that Madagascar's culinary heritage thrives for generations to come.

Embark on this journey with both your palate and your heart.

CHAPTER 1

Landing in Madagascar

A Taste of Antananarivo's Diversity

Izay rehetra velona ambanin'ny lanitra dia mitambatra toy ny tsihy iray lehibe.

All who live under the sky are woven together like one big mat.

—TRADITIONAL MALAGASY SAYING

The scent arrived before the chef did: earthy truffle caramel on a black olive crisp, a citrus-and-chili bite of marinated red tuna, a frothy cappuccino of wild *Salicornia* (a genus of succulent that grows wild in salty marshes and mangroves) with *tsiperifery* pepper (a wild pepper that only grows on the island), and cauliflower paired with a sweet-tart passionfruit gel and local caviar. It was unexpected, precise, and unmistakably Malagasy.

◀ *Perched above the heart of Antananarivo, the Rova of Madagascar.*

Not served on a traditional plate, but in a sleek, minimalist bento box, the four elegant appetizers stood like edible vignettes—playful in form, complex in flavor. At that moment, inside the modern ambiance of Marais restaurant, everything else—our week of travel, the long roads north, the bustle of Antananarivo—fell away.

Just beyond the walls, Antananarivo buzzed with its evening ritual: streetlights flickering over busy intersections, taxis honking in tangled traffic, the scent of grilled meat curling through narrow alleys. But here, the city's rhythm gave way to something else—a curated quiet, soft lighting, minimalist lines, and the gentle clink of glassware.

We spent a week on the island, traveling from the capital in the Central Highlands, to the lush northeast, guided by our insatiable appetite for discovery and a deepening appreciation for the island's unique ingredients. Each day unfolded like a revelation: farmers, artisans, and locals welcomed us into their world, sharing their passion, stories, and expertise. It was as if we were unearthing culinary secrets hidden within the very heart and soul of Madagascar. Our time in the famed "vanilla golden triangle" only deepened our appetite for discovery and left us hungry for more. Now, we enthusiastically anticipated the pinnacle of our journey: a meal that would marry the island's flavors with the expertise of its most celebrated chef, Lalaina Ravelomanana.

One bite was all it took to understand why Madagascar's ingredients captured the hearts and palates of chefs who accompanied me on the trip. This wasn't just the beginning of a meal; it was the beginning of a deeper story, one I had come here to taste, and now felt compelled to tell.

While the symphony of flavors played out before us, my thoughts drifted back to the nonstop flight a few days ago that set this incredible journey in motion. Our group of culinary adventurers had come together on a plane from Paris to Antananarivo, each of us hailing from wildly different worlds, with a common excitement and anticipation for what this country had in store. I had the pleasure of knowing two of the three culinary leaders before the trip, Chef Elizabeth Falkner, the Los Angeles–based culinary dynamo, and Chef Michael Gulotta, the master chef behind New Orleans' culinary gems Mopho and Maypop. Both esteemed chefs graced my podcast, *Flavors Unknown*, with their presence, sharing their culinary journeys and unique approaches to cuisine. Chef Elizabeth Falkner, renowned for her innovative spirit and determination to challenge the status quo, captivated listeners with her inspiring story. She even penned the foreword for my first book, *Conversations Behind the Kitchen Door*. On the other hand, Chef Gulotta, known for his creative fusion of Asian-inspired cuisine with Louisiana pantry staples, enriched the podcast with his passion for melding diverse flavors and techniques. Tagging along for this wild ride was Shannon Tebay, a London mixologist who has become known for her beautifully crafted cocktails. We crossed paths before, back when she was shaking things up as the beverage director at Death & Co in the heart of East Village in Manhattan.

The trio were the fortunate winners of a competition orchestrated by my employer, Symrise, a multinational purveyor of flavors and natural ingredients, and StarChefs. The contest was part of the marketing plan for the introduction of the company's vanilla extract to the American market, catering to both consumers and industry professionals. The grand prize: an expedition to Madagascar, to intimately experience the world biggest region of vanilla cultivation. Alongside traveled a Symrise vanilla product manager, a flavorist expert in vanilla, and a marketing manager from my team, eager to partake in this remarkable journey.

During the ten-hour flight, as the aircraft's hum steadily carried us nearer to the adventure that awaited, we shared stories and expressed our aspirations for this trip. At one point during this lengthy voyage, I invited Elizabeth, Shannon, and Michael to accompany me to the plane galley, intrigued to discover their most cherished moments of exploring unfamiliar destinations.

"When I arrive in a new place," said Elizabeth, "it's the smells that really capture my attention. It's like getting a sneak peek into the local culture, the people, and their lives. Then it's about the food and the ingredients." Elizabeth explained that she was anxious to explore the local scene, wanting to learn about the kind of food people eat and wondering about their topics of conversation. Shannon agreed, emphasizing her love for creating lasting memories through flavors. Michael, on the other hand, shared his fascination with cultural diversity and the historical depth of the places he'd visited. "Experiencing other cultures is like unlocking a treasure trove of knowledge. Working in other countries has really opened my eyes to the diversity of the world. Living in the United States, we can sometimes forget how much history other countries have."

As we continued discussing our expectations, I couldn't help but ask, "What do you all think we'll find in Madagascar? Is it going to be anything like what you've experienced before?"

"I'm really curious to see the parallels between New Orleans and Madagascar," said Michael, "both being French colonies. It's fascinating to see how the influence of a colonizing power manifests differently in various places." I pointed out the distinct timelines of their independence, noting that Madagascar gained its independence in 1960, whereas Louisiana's dated back to Napoleon's reign. This prompted a lively conversation about the island's unique history and how our individual perspectives would shape our experiences there.

I confided in them my own enthusiasm for the opportunity to witness firsthand the comprehensive process of producing vanilla beans, spanning from the delicate hand-pollination of orchid flowers to the artisanal task of curing the green vanilla beans. I was particularly keen on meeting the vanilla farmers themselves. Familiar with Symrise's narrative on the island and having relayed it to numerous clients, I anticipated enriching my presentations with personal anecdotes and experiences. I obviously had no idea, at that moment, that this trip would have a tremendous impact on me, and I would establish great connections that would bring me back to Madagascar.

Shannon chimed in. "Honestly, I'm trying to keep my expectations broad. I have no idea what to expect! We might be exploring the jungle with machetes, wading through rice paddies in rubber boots, or staying at fancy hotels. I'm just keeping an open mind and looking forward to experiencing the beauty of Madagascar and meeting interesting people."

"I've never been anywhere near Africa before," added Elizabeth. "I've never been to a vanilla-growing region before either. I've been in many cacao regions around the world. I'm eager to explore the vanilla-growing region and compare it to my experiences in cacao-producing areas. I've been to Dominica and Venezuela in the equatorial belt, but Madagascar is in the southern part of it. So that's very different. I want to understand the unique vegetation, agriculture, and climate of this island." Elizabeth's focus seemed to be on embracing Madagascar's culinary offerings and expanding her knowledge by working with local chefs and bartenders. She expressed her excitement to experiment with the spices and other ingredients she would find at the local markets. For her, the opportunity to cook and make cocktails alongside local chefs and mixologists was a thrilling prospect. Beyond studying vanilla, she was excited to discover other ingredients and learn more about the local vegetation in the area.

Michael shared that while he understood the culinary excitement, the real thrill for him was experiencing a completely foreign place, which felt almost like being on another planet. He indicated that one of the most significant aspects of the trip was the human factor. "Meeting new people and forming lifelong connections along the way is truly special. People that you may end up being friends with for years that you end up doing other things with later on down the line. That's always one of the big ones that people don't think about."

We all agreed on our shared enthusiasm not only for the journey itself but also for the company we were keeping along the way—undoubtedly one of the more exhilarating aspects of the experience. We returned to our seats, and as the flight progressed, I noticed Michael slumbering peacefully. I considered him fortunate, as I have never been able to sleep on planes, regardless of the flight duration. I examined the flight itinerary displayed on the in-flight TV screen, always fascinated by the altered perspectives international travel provides. As the world map materialized, my mind grappled with the unfamiliar arrangement before me. I was so accustomed to seeing the Americas to the left and Europe to the right; however, this time, my usual landmarks eluded me. It took some moments of contemplation to comprehend that I was, in fact, observing the globe from above the African continent. Paris airport, now on the left, and our ultimate

destination, Madagascar, on the right—we soared over Tanzania. This disorientation, a subtle foreshadowing, hinted at the frequent instances of losing my bearings that would later unfold throughout our adventure on the island.

The anticipation and excitement radiated from Falkner as she discovered that the menu offered on the plane was curated by the esteemed chef Anne-Sophie Pic of La Maison Pic in Valence, France. Anne-Sophie Pic, the most accoladed female chef across the globe, boasting ten Michelin stars—including three in her native France—graced us with her culinary expertise. Her exquisite dishes, celebrating local ingredients, captivate the palate with their harmonious flavors, robust tastes, and refined delicacy.

A shrimp tartare was served as the appetizer, accompanied by a pea cream infused with lemon and ginger. For the main dish, I opted for the *conchiglie* pasta, adorned with Swiss chard and a zesty lemon coulis, while Michael savored the beef cheek and coffee pot-au-feu, complemented by a sweet onion consommé. The enticing dish was completed by a creamy, lightly smoked, ash-coated goat's cheese and a sprinkle of toasted pumpkin seeds. Though my distance from Elizabeth and Shannon prevented me from discerning their choices, they selected the succulent poultry and poulette sauce with tonka bean, accompanied by a creamy polenta brimming with mushrooms, or perhaps the pollock with seaweed, enrobed in a lovage sauce and a spinach and fennel compote. My taste buds rejoiced as I indulged in an assortment of fine French cheeses: the distinctive Crottin de Chavignol, the rich Fourme d'Ambert, and the flavorful Cantal.

Several hours later, the pilot announced the commencement of our descent into Antananarivo, or "Tana," as the locals called it. As we touched down, I couldn't help but feel a sense of awe. Madagascar's vibrant history as a pirate stronghold and a unique blend of cultural influences from Indonesia and Africa casts an air of mystique and intrigue. As I stepped off the plane, I felt a mix of excitement and apprehension, as I yearned to discover the island's wonders while remaining cognizant of its challenges.

The journey from the airport to Antananarivo left us drained after the long haul from Paris. In the hotel shuttle, no one spoke. All of us had our eyes open wide, captivated by this unfamiliar landscape. The novelty of everything overwhelmed us. Our driver led us down a narrow road from the airport to the capital. The sunlight was delicate, crisp, and sharp. The sky was vast and seemingly endless. It reminded me of my impression of the sky during my first visit to Kenya, almost forty years ago. Kenya remains a distant yet vivid recollection, where the boundless sky was adorned with colossal white clouds, a sight forever etched into my mind. Here, in the moment, the azure streams flowed down on either side of the road, trickling onto the still surface of the flooded rice fields.

I took my first picture, wanting to capture the striking contrast of the light green color of the rice fields against the blood-red tint of the soil, with the hills visible in the backdrop. The city of Antananarivo was nestled atop one of the twelve sacred hills. I read before my trip that, in the late eighteenth century, King Andrianampoinimerina unified several tribes and established a kingdom ruled from twelve sacred hills. Before they were conquered, each of them was the center of a little kingdom rivaling the hill of Analamanga (the blue forest), now called Antananarivo.

Each country, each region of the world has its own unique colors, and those of the highlands of Madagascar at three thousand feet above sea level are an astonishing mix of orange and the rich red of laterite lands (a red soil rich in iron). I would discover in the following days that, as night falls, these colors blend into a hypnotic array of purple and violet, transforming the hills of Tana into a painting that reminded me of the ones from Georgia O'Keeffe. I remember at that moment the words from Michael on the plane; it is indeed a city that seems to have been transplanted from another planet and another era.

As our chauffeur weaved his way toward the capital, I found myself unexpectedly captivated by the sight of the rice fields. For some reason, I was not expecting to see rice fields in Madagascar. Even though the Red Island was located 150 miles from the east coast of Africa, there was a strong Southeast Asian influence. We would soon experience the evident Southeast Asian cultural influence in Malagasy cuisine, in which rice was consumed at every meal.

These lush, verdant paddies stretched out on either side of the road were strong proof of the integral role rice plays in the lives of the Malagasy people. This scenery added a sense of tranquility to the otherwise chaotic traffic, vans spitting out black smoke and dust clouds. As we approached the city, the hill loomed large, topped by the Rova of Antananarivo, also known as the Queen's Palace. This striking fortress of red stone and age-old wooden design stood as a living, breathing symbol of the colorful heritage that Madagascar has to offer and the echoes of its storied past. I later learned the palace was built on top of a hill in 1834 by Queen Ranavalona, so that it could be seen from anywhere in the city. She was a powerful and controversial figure in the history of the island, who sought to preserve the island's political and cultural autonomy in the face of increasing European influence.

As we came closer to the city, winding around other hills, the neighborhoods grew more animated, and navigating the traffic became increasingly challenging. Tana could be an enigmatic maze for newcomers like us.

The traffic ground to a halt. Street vendors pressed so close to our minibus I could have reached out and touched the strings of sausages and slabs of meat dangling from their hooks. Pedestrians moved like water between the cars and buses, slipping through gaps with practiced ease.

"Close your window," our driver said quietly but firmly. "Someone could reach in and take your backpack."

The street narrowed. The crowd thickened. We inched forward, hemmed in by a tide of bodies. Children peered into the windows, palms outstretched. Men and women passed in worn shirts and dusty sandals.

I sat back, my bag clutched tightly, flooded by a feeling I hadn't expected: guilt, helplessness, discomfort at watching so much need from behind a pane of glass. It felt intrusive, like witnessing something I had no right to observe without offering more than a glance.

In that moment, Madagascar's famed natural riches faded into the background. What confronted us instead was a harsher truth: the beauty of the landscape cannot hide the deep economic inequality faced by so many who call this island home.

The city of Tana was structured across three distinct tiers: the "*ville basse*" (lower level), the "*ville intermédiaire*" (mid-level), and the "*haute ville*" (high level). The evolution of these levels unfolded throughout history, testifying of the indelible impact of the French colonization. Tana's "altitudinal" partitioning remained emblematic of a wealth-based hierarchy. The most affluent neighborhoods and opulent residences occupied the highest points of the capital, while, in contrast, the poorest neighborhoods predominantly lay within the plains of the lower town.

Our journey took us along the Avenue de l'Indépendance, a creation of the French who opted to drain some fifty acres of marshes and rice fields to forge a new district, Analakely—the "little forest"—at the foot of the upper town. As we ascended, we marveled at the resplendent jacaranda trees in full bloom—symbols of Antananarivo's innate beauty. Their vibrant lilac blossoms provided a striking counterpoint to the urban scenery. Advancing to the mid-level, the streets intersected with several grand stone staircases linking the mid-level to the lower level. The "*ville intermédiaire*" was the domain of the professional classes: doctors, pharmacists, bankers, and jewelers. Then, the "*haute ville*," an urban site of great heritage quality, both in terms of architectural buildings and its exceptional landscape situation. It was the place of kings and queens before the French colonization.

The climb of the hill was almost over. The hotel shuttle maneuvered onto a narrow lane, flanked by towering walls, and came to a halt before a subdued gray metallic gate. A single honk prompted the gate to reveal a cobblestone courtyard, where the hotel's modest facade greeted us in shades of ochre, beige, and white. Two flags fluttered proudly: one of Madagascar, the other of an unknown origin. The driver parked opposite to an unusual display of vintage cars, aged French street signs, and gas station memorabilia. La Varangue, at first glance, felt more like a charming, rustic, and cozy guest house, exuding the charm of a former era, nestled in a lush, verdant surrounding.

The peculiar decor continued inside, as the white walls of the foyer were adorned with old photographs and numerous antique lantern oil lamps, suspended beneath a wooden staircase. To the right, a quaint bar beckoned, its walls festooned with a symphony of musical instruments. It was as if an entire wind section of the local orchestra left their instruments behind before partaking in a drink. Yet, the room lay empty, save for the bartender who welcomed our group with fruity mocktails.

Our hostess distributed room keys and led us onward. The foyer's opposite door opened to reveal a spacious dining area, its eccentricity surpassing that of the entrance. A dozen tables were impeccably dressed in white linens, fine china, and gleaming silverware. Glass cabinets showcased an array of incongruous collections: ancient clocks, gramophones, old manual telephones, and more vintage oil lamps.

"All these objects are local and were collected by the hotel's owners," our hostess explained.

French doors led from the dining room to a covered deck, where breakfast would be served. Descending a few steps, we found ourselves on a wide terrace, surrounded by lush vegetation and a breathtaking view of houses clinging to the opposite hill. To our right, the Queen's Palace stood in plain sight, nestled on top of the hill behind a line of banana trees and swaying bamboo.

Ascending the stairs to my upper-floor bedroom, the unmistakable hum of mosquitoes filled my ears. The corridor's lighting was subdued, casting a shadowy veil over my dark bedroom door at the far end. I could not be sure if mosquitoes were drawn to the darkness and the shade, but a swarm of them greeted me as I fumbled to unlock my door. Though Antananarivo is free of malaria cases, I couldn't help but feel relieved that I'd taken my preventive medication a day prior to embarking on this journey.

Upon entering, I found the room to be airy and well-lit, featuring a lovely balcony overlooking the terrace. The sight of the mosquito net draping the bed transported me back to my readings of Somerset Maugham's novels. Though the settings and times were distinct—Maugham's tales unfolding in the 1920s south seas, while I stood in present-day Madagascar—the atmosphere in the room evoked a similar sense of exoticism and adventure. Maugham's vivid descriptions in his novels often conveyed a sense of mystique within the sultry, tropical landscapes of Southeast Asia. My introductory experience on the island echoed that sentiment, and the mosquito net serving as a delicate barrier, both functional and symbolic, added a touch of the exotic to my stay in this mysterious land.

In the morning, we gathered under the covered deck for breakfast, a charming outdoor terrace bathed in morning sunlight. A grand wooden pergola entwined with vibrant, flourishing greenery created a captivating canopy overhead. This picturesque cover produced a serene atmosphere, diffusing the sun's rays as they filtered through, casting a soft, dappled light on the tables below. We indulged in a delicious breakfast buffet as we basked in the warmth of the morning sun. The setting captured the essence of a relaxed morning, embracing the vibrant garden and the natural beauty of the city. The terrace, graced by a traveler's tree, overlooked the picturesque cityscape. Its hills were dotted with traditional Malagasy houses and buildings. The vivid colors of the architecture contrasted with the abundant foliage of the surrounding panorama, forming a captivating visual harmony. Each element contributed to the sensation of experiencing an unfamiliar setting for the first time. It was on that morning that I first savored the local *corossol* (or soursop) juice, which soon became my daily indulgence. Examining the buffet before me, I decided upon a generous scoop of mango fruit salad,

several small bananas, a croissant, and a steaming café au lait. Instantly, I was smitten with the small bananas. Their pronounced flavors and fruity taste left an indelible mark on my palate.

These were no ordinary bananas. The hotel employees explained that they were unique cultivars grown in Madagascar, though they weren't entirely sure of the exact variety. They might have been Iva, a local favorite known for its honeyed sweetness and subtle tang—a perfect blend of tropical fruit and candy. Or perhaps they were *Bonbon* Bananas, a cultivar cherished for its floral aroma and candy-like intensity. Whatever their origin, these tiny bananas, with their delicate flavors and sun-drenched sweetness, became one of the simplest yet most unforgettable pleasures of my journey.

The croissant, though flaky, possessed a denser texture compared to its French counterparts. The arabica coffee, sourced from the Itasy region merely two hours west of Tana, proved to be a delectable surprise, its bouquet of floral notes intermingling with delicate hints of coconut and citrus.

As the remainder of our group departed from the table to prepare for the day's adventures, I lingered, savoring the tranquility of the moment and the beauty of the view before me. Mere hours had passed since my arrival in Madagascar's capital city, yet I was already struck by the fascinating juxtaposition of affluence and poverty, a reflection of the island nation's intricate social and economic tapestry. Tana, home to nearly three million people, presented a striking contrast between the opulence of certain neighborhoods and the humble living conditions of others. This juxtaposition can be traced back to Madagascar's complex history, from being a pirate stronghold and slave trading center in the seventeenth to nineteenth centuries, to being a colony of France, and eventually regaining independence in 1960.

In the affluent districts, luxurious villas, gated communities, and well-maintained public spaces abounded. On the other end, the city's less privileged areas presented a starkly different scene. Here, homes constructed from wood, corrugated metal, or other materials cluttered the narrow streets, and access to fundamental necessities such as clean water, electricity, and sanitation remained scarce. Staying at a hotel in the upper part of the city, I felt a sense of uneasiness, realizing the harsh contrast between these lavish surroundings and the struggling communities just a few streets below. Despite these disparities, Tana pulsed with life, energy, and cultural richness. The indomitable spirit of the Malagasy people, rooted in diverse tribal heritages and customs, with ancestor respect and traditional festivals at its heart, was evident through the city's bustling markets, animated music scene, and effervescent street life. This melding of wealth and poverty created a singular urban scenery, a testament to the resilience, ingenuity, and determination of the local populace.

Located in the southwestern Indian Ocean and separated from the African coast by the Mozambique Channel, Madagascar has a rich history of migrations and colonization. The myriad faces encountered en route from the airport to Hotel La Varangue revealed a surprising tapestry of ethnic diversity—faces evocative of Indonesia and Africa, smiles from India and China, and features echoing Arabian heritage. These faces reflected the island's intricate past, woven together through migration, commerce, and colonization. The Malagasy people, who form the predominant ethnic group on the island, were believed to possess roots in both Southeast Asia and East Africa, creating a blend of physical attributes that tells a story of connection across oceans and centuries. Their presence was a vivid reminder of the Malagasy saying: *All who live under the sky are woven together like one big mat.* This saying resonated throughout my journey, as if the island itself whispered its truth—a mosaic of humanity, each thread contributing to the fabric of a shared history.

At Chef Lalaina's table, this tapestry of diversity was reimagined on the plate, where French techniques entwined with local ingredients and Asian inspirations to create something both familiar and entirely unique. One dish in particular—a tasteful combination of foie gras, oyster mushrooms, vanilla, and cocoa—embodied this harmony. This delightful medley featured foie gras *ravioles* (smaller, more delicate versions of ravioli) and grilled oyster mushrooms, their flavors elevated by a silken vanilla cream, the dish serving as a testament to Madagascar's rich culinary diversity. The smoked cocoa nibs added an evocative touch, evoking the ever-present scent of woodsmoke that accompanied us across the island. It was a significant reminder of the challenges posed by charcoal production and deforestation in this country. This interplay of flavors carried echoes of the landscapes we explored, from the charcoal-hewn paths of the highlands to the lush, fragrant fields of the SAVA region. With that, the memory of our travels dissolved, and we returned to the present—seated in the warm glow of Marais, the taste of Madagascar still alive on our tongues, and the story of its iconic vanilla ready to be told.

CHAPTER 2

The Heart of Global Vanilla Production

Ny vanim-potoana no manamasina ny lavanila.

It is time that gives vanilla its true flavor.

—TRADITIONAL MALAGASY SAYING

Vanilla, with its warm, sweet aroma, is more than just a flavor—it's a bridge between generations, a fragrant thread that weaves memory, ritual, and love into the foods we hold dear. In Western cultures, vanilla is inseparable from celebration. It's the soul of birthday cakes and holiday pies, the secret in a grandmother's custard, the scent that fills a kitchen and lingers in memory long after the oven cools. Through these rituals, vanilla becomes more than an ingredient—it becomes a vessel for tenderness, for time shared, for stories passed down across tables and time.

◀ *Vanilla beans drying process in the sun.*

Each vanilla-laced dessert—pudding, crème brûlée, custard, cookies, or a simple slice of cake—carries echoes of family gatherings and the unspoken comfort of home. In many cultures, the act of baking with vanilla is both a pleasure and a preservation, where culinary heritage is safeguarded through repetition, guidance, and shared hands. Making these dishes together becomes a way not only of honoring the past, but of creating new memories with each batch, each bite.

Vanilla's story doesn't end at the kitchen door. In Japan, a culture that reveres craftsmanship and quality, Madagascar's high-grade vanilla has become a prized treasure. There, it elevates confections into refined expressions of art and emotion. It isn't just used—it is honored.

Vanilla has found a home in Japan, a country renowned for its dedication to quality and craftsmanship, vanilla has also found a home. The Japanese market, with its emphasis on premium ingredients, has embraced vanilla, particularly the high-grade varieties imported from Madagascar. There, vanilla is not just an ingredient; it resonates with the soul of Japanese culinary art, transforming sweets into experiences that are both refined and comforting.

Beyond the plate, vanilla's calming presence has long shaped the emotional architecture of space. In feng shui, its scent fosters harmony and peace, supporting the Earth element's grounding energy. In homes around the world, the warm smell of vanilla—whether wafting from a cake tin or a diffuser—offers a quiet promise of safety, nurturing, and balance.

Vanilla's power lies not in novelty but in its familiarity. It connects us to where we've been and reminds us of who we've shared it with. In many cultures, vanilla carries a sense of belonging and a connection to family, but its true power lies in its ability to evoke memories. Vanilla is a potent symbol of nostalgia that makes us feel at home, no matter where we are in the world.

In 2019, Symrise, my employer, tested a new series of vanilla extracts in the US market. The marketing team organized a competition with StarChefs, a community and resource for the restaurant industry, receiving nearly one hundred recipe submissions from American chefs, pastry chefs, and mixologists. This competition was what first brought me to the island, along with Chefs Elizabeth Falkner and Michael Gulotta, and Mixologist Shannon

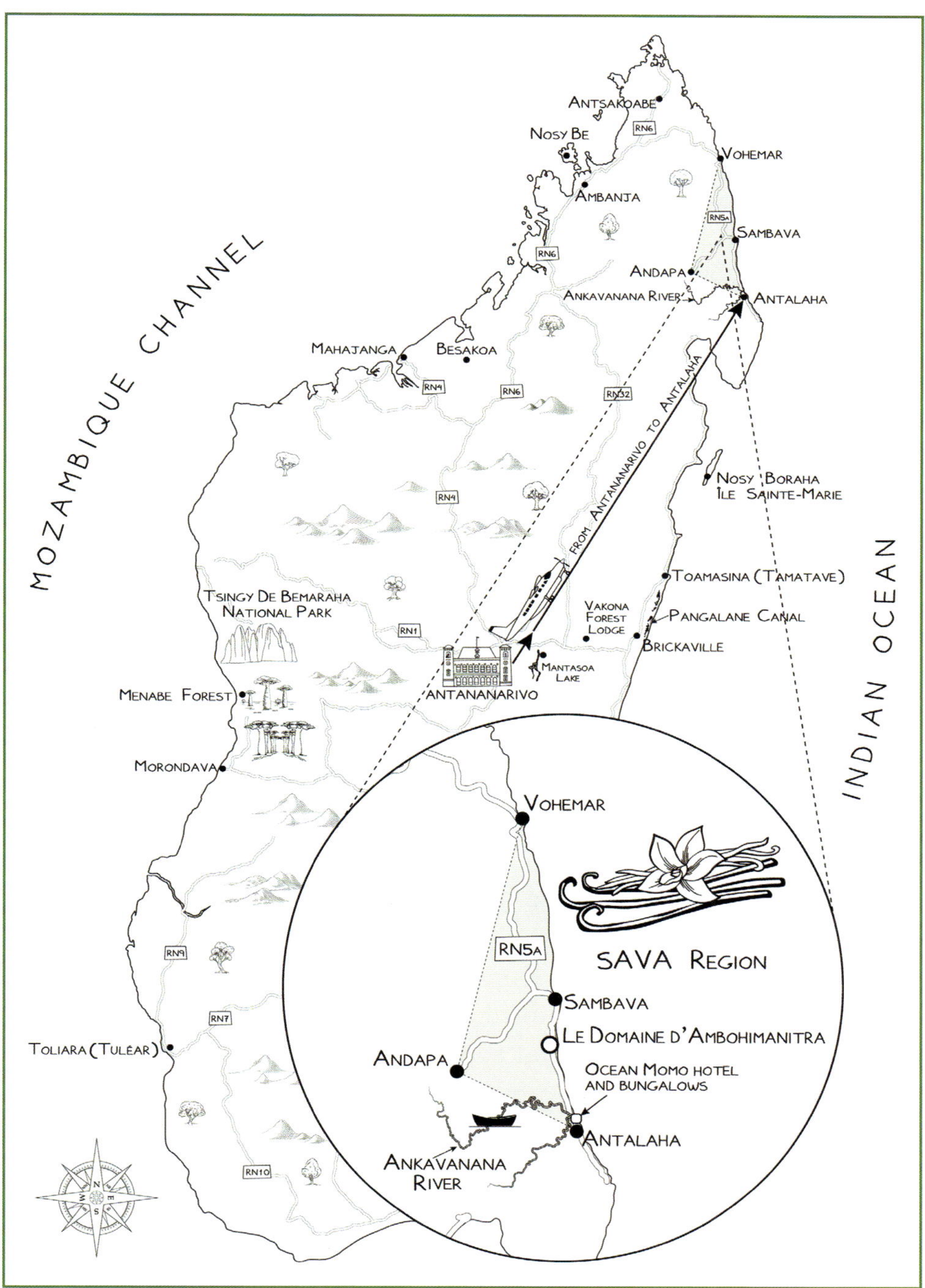

Madagascar's Vanilla Triangle: The SAVA region.

Tebay. Each of them weaved the essence of vanilla into their creations with creativity to win a spot on the trip.

Chef Michael Gulotta, whose culinary roots run deep in the rich soils of Louisiana, proposed a dish called Gnocchetti with Crawfish Tom Yum. It celebrates the vibrant flavors of Madagascar while honoring both Southeast Asian and New Orleans cuisines.

During crawfish season in New Orleans, at Mopho restaurant, Michael and his chefs would toss their boiled crawfish in a spicy lime butter. This simple yet flavorful preparation reminded him of a delicious tom yum soup he savored during a trip to Bangkok. Inspired by this experience, he decided to marry the two culinary worlds by combining the bright, aromatic flavors of tom yum with the hearty richness of a traditional New Orleans crawfish étouffée. The dish, served over gnocchetti pasta, captured the essence of both regions. He felt the vanilla extract orange blend from Symrise added a tropical, floral umami that elevated the sauce to new heights. His final touch? A pickled *mirliton* (*chayote* in Spanish or *christophine* in French) that added a bright crunch, tying the dish together while honoring an ingredient cherished in both cultures.

Mixologist Shannon Tebay submitted a cocktail named Star Fox—a bold reimagining of the Ramos Gin Fizz, a classic cocktail that originated in New Orleans in 1888. The frothy and creamy texture was what made the original drink so popular.

Shannon explained that the Star Fox cocktail was crafted in the style of a classic Ramos Gin Fizz. However, instead of the traditional light and airy texture, she chose to juxtapose it against the smoky spice of mezcal and pepper. The result was a drink that danced on the palate, with the Symrise vanilla extract orange blend adding depth and complexity. Shannon mentioned she chose this style because, while a Ramos Fizz typically uses orange flower water, the vanilla orange extract played beautifully in that role, showcasing vanilla's versatility as a culinary ingredient.

Chef Elizabeth Falkner presented A Veil of Vanilla, which used the Symrise pure vanilla extract as an addition to a chiffon cake made with cooled cooked oats and oat milk. The result was a dessert where vanilla sang in different tones, from the caramel sauce to the crumb, with minimal sugar, allowing the natural sweetness to take center stage. A touch of Meyer lemon zest added brightness, rounding out a dessert that was as elegant as it was flavorful.

Together, these three creations demonstrated not only the boundless creativity of these culinary artists but also the rich possibilities that vanilla extracts unlock. Whether in a savory dish, a cocktail, or a dessert, vanilla proves to be a bridge between cultures, a note that elevates every ingredient it is combined with.

As our small aircraft took off from Antananarivo, the city's outskirts quickly gave way to a patchwork of rice paddies stretching across the plains. We reached Antalaha, a key town in the vanilla golden triangle of the SAVA region, renowned for its rich vanilla production. The panorama on the ground below changed to a dense vegetation of forest interspersed with clearings and winding rivers. Clouds were drifting lazily above the earth.

As we made a wide turn over the Indian Ocean, my breath caught at the sight—my first ever glimpse of its vast, shimmering expanse. Moments later, we touched down on the short landing strip from the Antsirabato airfield of Antalaha, the memory of that beautiful view still vivid in my mind.

Two vans carried us to Symrise's vanilla curing facility in town for an early dinner. As we traveled along the rural dirt roads, the reddish-brown earth provided a striking contrast to the dense vegetation that bordered the path. The vehicles seemed to glide through small groups of houses, where glimpses of daily life flashed by. Upon reaching the town of Antalaha, we stopped in front of a gated property. After the guards opened the gates, we drove onto a wide, flat area that was covered with row after row of vanilla beans, carefully laid out to dry under the

bright sun. The air was thick with the rich, intense aroma of vanilla. Wooden racks, meticulously arranged, cradled the vanilla beans across a paved surface, creating an orderly display. It was here that we learned a few days later how this crucial stage—curing—transformed the green vanilla pods into the flavorful beans. The design of the racks allowed for optimal air circulation, ensuring the beans dried evenly and remained free from mold. In the background, workers dressed in blue uniforms were beginning to transport the racks back into large warehouses as evening approached.

For the moment, we followed our hosts and made our way to a grand white house nestled within a garden filled with abundant plants, flowers, and exotic trees, including ylang-ylang, lychee, yellow and pink plumerias, hibiscus, and the striking bright red heliconia, also known as the false bird of paradise.

Meet the Weatherman

The weatherman sits perched on his worn stool, eyes fixed on the sky, reading signs that are invisible to most. His role, as ancient as the vanilla trade itself, is to ensure that the beans drying in the sun are protected from the whims of nature. He listens to the whispers of the wind, deciphers the shifting language of the clouds, and feels the pulse of the air—his instincts honed over years, guiding the fate of the harvest.

In the curing process, timing is everything. The vanilla beans must ripen under the sun, absorbing just enough heat without ever getting wet. This is where the weatherman becomes indispensable. At his signal, a ripple moves through the entire curing facility. Workers rush to action, lifting wooden frames filled with dark, fragrant beans, carrying them swiftly back inside, away from the approaching rain. Moments later, the skies open, torrents of water flooding the courtyard where the beans once lay. Without the weatherman's keen eye, the entire crop could be lost.

He knows the rhythm of the seasons better than anyone. The wind, shifting from the northeast to the south, tells him that a change is near. He has learned to trust these subtle shifts, recognizing how the weather turns when the full moon begins to set. The cycle repeats itself year after year, but no two days are ever the same. And in this delicate balance between sun and rain, the weatherman's vigilance ensures that the vanilla beans are always one step ahead of the storm.

A dinner lovingly prepared by the local community was waiting. We were welcomed with a traditional beverage known as *ranovola*, a refreshing drink made from rice water. Our meal began with a comforting bowl of rice pudding, accompanied by *brèdes*, a leafy green commonly used in Malagasy cuisine, and succulent local pork sausages. One of the highlights was the vibrant *achard*, a pickled vegetable and fruit salad made from fresh, seasonal produce sourced directly from the garden. Ours featured a delightful mix of mango, papaya, carrot, and zucchini, all infused with ginger, turmeric, and *combava*—local Makrut lime. Alongside these dishes were delicate pastry rolls filled with savory meat and a rich, flaky quiche. The table was set with an array of condiments and jams, including the fiery homemade *sakay* sauce—a blend of chili, garlic, and ginger—as well as sweet papaya and *corossol* (soursop) preserves. To quench our thirst, we were served fresh *corossol* juice, and for dessert, we indulged in creamy homemade coconut and vanilla ice creams.

After dinner, our hosts brought the group to Ocean Momo, our base hotel for the next few days. The full moon cast its silver glow upon the shore. I distinguished isolated dark and silver silhouettes with flashlights, armed with long sticks in hand. Our hosts explained that with the skill and finesse of seasoned marksmen, the fishermen aimed their sticks at the elusive creatures of the sea—squid, calamari, sea urchins, and octopus. It was as if they were pulling diamonds from the waves or the sand, each one shining in the moonlight like a precious gem. The beach and the sea at night were their playground. They enjoyed the excitement of the hunt, and we could hear their laughter from the shore as they collected their catch in the baskets.

At 5:00 a.m. the next day, I woke up to the hum of the electric fan, with the bright sunlight filtering through the Bermuda shutters of my bungalow and dappling the room. The mosquito net swayed with the back-and-forth movement of the fan, creating a peaceful dance. The dark brown wooden furniture of the room stood in stark contrast against the bright white walls, and the blue light from the insect electric plugs striped the room like neon streaks. The temperature was perfect, not hot or sticky, very different from what I had imagined before my trip to the island. The Ocean Momo bungalows were located next to the beach, with white sand and the sound of waves crashing onto the shore as a constant background melody. It was the first time I experienced the sound of the Indian Ocean.

The landscape surrounding the bungalows transported me back to my trip to Kenya many years ago. As I gazed upon the shore on my way to breakfast, I recognized that distinct shade of green—the grass and short palm trees dotting the landscape—that was unlike any other. The warm, golden light that bathed the scene, unique to this part of the world, infused the grass with a magical glow. It was as if the sun had cast a spell upon the land, imbuing it with its own vibrant life and energy. Once you've experienced this feeling, it becomes a part of you, staying with you for the rest of your life.

The restaurant was quiet. The black-and-white tiles beneath my feet were a testament to elegance from another era. Wooden chairs, each cushioned with vibrant colors of blue, red, and yellow, invited guests to sink in and enjoy their breakfast. The tables, modestly arranged, were embellished with fresh tropical flowers from the garden that brought color into the room. Some tables were draped in crisp white linens, hinting at a more formal ambiance, while others were left bare, revealing the rich grain of the wood—a contrast that echoed the harmonious blend of comfort and rustic charm at Ocean Momo. The air was filled with the inviting aroma of freshly brewed coffee, mingling with the sweet, tropical scents, creating a warm and welcoming atmosphere. I chose a table outside on the porch, eager to take in the view. The shaded outdoor area provided both a pause from the sun and a cool breeze off the Indian Ocean. As I settled in, the staff brought me an espresso crafted from local coffee beans, a glass of fresh *corossol* juice, sweet little bananas, and a simple omelet. It was then that my traveling companions arrived.

Our local hosts kept the day's final destination a mystery, but we were advised to prepare for a long journey by boat, as we would be venturing up the winding course of the local river.

The mouth of the Ankavanana River lays just outside of Antalaha, originating seventy-eight miles north, just south of Andapa, in the heart of the vanilla golden triangle. The river, renowned for its scenic beauty, meandered gently into the Indian Ocean. We parked the cars along the riverbank, near where the river met the sea. Several simple, long metallic boats were docked, likely used for ferrying people and goods across the river or to nearby locations. The sky was partly cloudy, casting a soft glow over the tranquil scene. Nearby, a light brown zebu calf, with its soft fur and a small, developing hump typical of the breed, stood on the sandy ground close to the cars. Each of us took turns gently scratching the top of the calf's head, and it seemed to relish the attention, choosing to follow us as we made our way toward the boats.

We split into two groups and boarded the boats, ready to embark on the journey ahead. I sat on a simple, tiny wood bench next to Elizabeth; Michael and Shannon were behind us. The boat ride to our destination took about two hours, offering us ample time to soak in the sun.

As we started along the river, the gentle hum of the boat's engine mingled with the sounds of nature. The dense vegetation was punctuated by the presence of breadfruit trees. Now and then, the bright orange blooms of tulip trees added a splash of color to the scene. I spotted massive kapok trees—known as cotton-fiber trees—that loomed large, their trunks thick and their branches crowned with soft, cotton-like fibers that moved with the wind.

By the riverbank, narrow walkways descended to sandy edges where life in scattered dwellings unfolded in a rhythm as old as the river itself. Cattle meandered down to the water's edge, lazily drinking in the coolness. Nearby, people bathed or knelt by the river, washing clothes in the steady flow. Men, women, and children stood knee-deep in the shallow waters, casting their nets with practiced hands, hoping for a bountiful catch. Every so often, clusters of wooden sticks jutted out of the water, marking the spots where fish lay hidden in holes beneath the surface—a signal to the knowledgeable fishermen.

We occasionally crossed paths with other boats, their passengers journeying from one point to another along the river. These were the "taxi boats," ferrying people and goods—banana bunches or sacks of produce, just the simple necessities of daily life.

Our own boat ride was not without its moments of exhilaration. At times, we found ourselves racing alongside our group's other boat, the two vessels skimming across the water's surface, sending up sprays that sparkled in the sunlight. The sound of our boat's engines echoed off the riverbanks, mingling with the distant chirping of rare birds hidden in the trees.

The sun hung heavy in the sky, its heat pressing down on us as we drew closer to our destination, the plantation of "Mama Alexia," where we would soon be initiated into the delicate art of hand-pollinating the vanilla orchid flower.

As we approached the riverbank to park the boats, ours decided it needed a little more adventure and got itself stuck on a sandbank. Without hesitation, Michael jumped into the water, waded to the front, and heaved against the hull until it floated free, saving the day. Unfortunately, the river had other plans. The sand at the bottom was more "sift" than solid, and before he knew it, one of Michael's flip-flops made a break for freedom, sinking into the depths of the Ankavanana River. That flip-flop is probably still down there, a lone witness to Michael's brief, yet memorable, struggle with the nature of the red island.

Ascending from the river's edge, we were greeted by hills blanketed with fields of black pepper vines. Our group moved along narrow paths that wound through the wild pepper fields, the air heavy with the earthy scent of the vines. Mama Alexia, our guide and the soul of this plantation—renowned for its grapefruit, wild pepper, lemongrass, cinnamon, and pink peppercorn—pointed through the bushes lining the pathway. "There," she gestured with a knowing smile, directing our gaze to a cluster of green vines with large, thick leaves clinging to thin leafy trees.

Nestled among the foliage were our first vanilla vines, their delicate flowers and buds at various stages of development. Two flowers had already opened, their pale petals soft against the vibrant green of the surrounding leaves, while others seemed poised to unfurl. Alongside these open blossoms were numerous elongated, firm green buds, waiting for their moment to bloom. The sight was both humbling and mesmerizing, as these fragile flowers held the potential for the rich, fragrant vanilla beans we so love.

One of the workers, a man who had clearly spent years perfecting his craft, stepped forward to demonstrate the delicate art of hand-pollination. With a practiced hand, he carefully approached one of the open flowers and explained the process as he went. "This is where the magic happens," he said, his voice tinged with both reverence and practicality.

Hand-pollination of the vanilla orchid is a race against time, he explained. The flowers bloom only once a year, and their window of opportunity lasts just a few short hours. It was now or never. The process began with a gentle yet precise movement. He used a small tool, a thorn plucked from a nearby bush, to carefully open the flower further. Inside, he located the rostellum, a thin barrier of tissue that separates the orchid's male and female reproductive parts. With a deft motion, he lifted the flap and pressed the pollen from the male anther onto the female stigma, ensuring fertilization.

Then, with a nod and a smile, it was my turn. The seemingly simple act now felt daunting. The flower, so delicate in my hand, required a steady touch and sharp eyes. As I followed his instructions, lifting the rostellum and pressing the pollen into place, I realized how much care and skill this work demanded. Each flower that was successfully pollinated will develop into a vanilla green bean. Each American chef then took their turn, experiencing the delicate process of pollinating a vanilla orchid flower for the first time. This wasn't merely a task—it was a deep connection to the island, its traditions, and the essence of vanilla itself. In that moment, I realized we were embracing a craft painstakingly passed down through generations. It became clear that in the world of vanilla, the craft—rooted in tradition and carried forward by skilled hands—was the backbone of the entire process, from flower to extract, far more than science or technology could ever be.

The river guided us back to Antalaha, where we gathered in the kitchen of Ocean Momo's restaurant for what promised to be an unforgettable culinary experience. Our hosts welcomed us with a bounty of local ingredients, an abundant array that showcased the island's rich offerings and provided endless inspiration for the chefs. Shannon, Elizabeth, and Michael joined forces to craft a meal that was as much a reflection of the island's vibrant flavors as it was of their own diverse backgrounds.

Shannon kicked off the evening with an *aperitivo* featuring Malagasy rum as the base. Its earthy sweetness was elevated by the bitterness of Campari and the floral notes of Martini Rosato. The unexpected addition of peach tea introduced a subtle fruitiness that lingered on the palate, perfectly setting the stage for what was to come. We were deeply appreciative of Shannon's creativity and resourcefulness, especially given the limited ingredients available at the hotel bar.

Elizabeth followed with the first dish, her fish laab—a refreshing tribute to the vibrant street food of Southeast Asia. She seasoned the dish with fish sauce, *combava* juice, and the deep umami of *padaek*, a traditional Lao fermented fish sauce made from freshwater fish and salt, placing it atop a bed of crisp lettuces, mustard leaves, and cress, with the spicy kick of African basil or clove basil (*Ocimum gratissimum*) cutting through the flavors. A generous sprinkle of toasted peanuts added a satisfying crunch to complete the dish.

Michael's initial preparation was both decadent and delicate: lobster roasted to perfection, bathed in a sauce that seamlessly blended the warmth of vanilla with the subtle bite of pink peppercorns, all tied together with the richness of cocoa butter. The dish was a testament to Michael's ability to elevate familiar ingredients, transforming them into something extraordinary.

For his second dish, Michael presented a shrimp curry. The Makrut lime leaf infused a fragrant citrus note, while the coconut oil and freshly made coconut milk provided a silky smoothness that enveloped the tender shrimp. Both lobster and shrimp were harvested fresh from the morning sea, adding an extra layer of authenticity to the experience.

The second day in the SAVA region took us to the Domaine d'Ambohimanitra, a vanilla plantation of 150 acres, located north of Antalaha on the road to Sambava. The plantation is owned by the Ramanandraibe family. Perched on a hill with a breathtaking view of the Indian Ocean, the estate's name, meaning "hill of perfume," was a fitting tribute to its fragrant surroundings. In addition to vanilla, the plantation cultivates other spices and botanicals such as ylang-ylang, cloves, cinnamon, and pink peppercorns.

We were welcomed by Dina Rasanjison, in charge of the Ramanandraibe agency in the Antalaha region, the plantation, and its touristic activities.

We commented that we were utterly stunned by how little emphasis the locals placed on vanilla and that it is not part of their culinary culture. Coming from a place where terroir is deeply intertwined with the culinary culture, we expected SAVA, a region renowned for vanilla, to be immersed in it. But instead, we found it strange and unexpected that vanilla, despite being so closely associated with the region, wasn't as prominently featured or celebrated as we had imagined.

The region breathes vanilla, yet almost 99 percent of the island's production is exported. Very little vanilla is consumed locally by the Malagasy people. And traditionally, the cured vanilla pods were placed in sugar and then left in there for months, even years sometimes. Dina commented that adding vanilla in dishes in some refined restaurants of the capital was a totally new cuisine style, not even a decade old. For locals, vanilla was more than a "food" plant. It was the plant that supported the family. She explained that farmers (who own their vanilla plantations), producers, and processors—everyone whose livelihood depended on vanilla—shared a deep connection with it. Yet they did not view it as merely a consumer product. "Vanilla is a currency. Vanilla is the 'friend' that enabled Malagasy people to make a decent living," she said.

There is an invisible bond between the farmers and the vanilla vines. When new vines are planted, raffia or vetiver ties are often used to secure them to stakes, as the orchid's natural tendrils have not yet gripped the support. Dina explained that it was the farmer who must tie the vine. And she often teased them by saying, "The vine grows stronger because, from the moment you plant it, you're completely bound to it." She meant that the vine held farmers with unseen connections, requiring constant care and attention. "Farmers must carefully loop the vine, protect it from sunburn, guard against fungi and insects, pollinate the flowers, thin them out, and prepare them for harvesting." This ritual repeats every year, making it impossible for farmers to detach themselves from the vanilla, unlike with other plants.

We learned that historically, vanilla was not native to the island. Its origins trace back to the Totonac people of what is now Veracruz, Mexico, who were recognized as the first to cultivate the vanilla orchid. However,

the earliest known use of vanilla predates even the Totonac cultivation, appearing in the rituals of the pre-Columbian Maya. They incorporated vanilla into a spiced cacao beverage, a practice later adopted by the Aztecs after they conquered the Totonac empire. For the Aztecs, vanilla became a prized addition to *chocolatl*, a drink reserved for nobility. In the early sixteenth century, Spanish conquistadors led by Hernán Cortés introduced vanilla to Europe following their conquest of the Aztec Empire. From there, vanilla began its journey around the globe, eventually reaching the fertile soils of Madagascar.

Vanilla was cultivated in botanical gardens in France and England, but never offered up its glorious seeds. Growers could not understand why until centuries later, when a Belgian horticulturist reported that vanilla's natural pollinator was the Melipona, a bee that did not survive outside of Mexico.

In the early 1800s, Europeans brought vanilla to La Réunion, a thirty-nine-mile-long volcanic island in the Indian Ocean, forever altering its history. Dina shared the remarkable story of Edmond Albius, which took place around 1840. Edmond was a young teenage slave on the island, working for a master with a passion for botany. One day, during a heated moment while being scolded, Edmond, overwhelmed by anger and frustration, threw his farming tools in a fit of clumsiness.

Months later, something unusual happened: vanilla pods began to form on the vines—an occurrence that hadn't happened before, as vanilla flowers typically require manual pollination in the absence of their natural pollinators. Reflecting on the incident, Edmond realized that his actions unknowingly caused the flowers to be manipulated. Intrigued, he began experimenting with the flowers intentionally, eventually discovering how to manually pollinate the vanilla flower. His accidental discovery revolutionized vanilla cultivation, enabling the industry to flourish on La Réunion.

Dina explained that the discovery of vanilla pollination was often attributed to Edmond Albius, not only for its historical significance but also because the story carried a certain allure—a compelling narrative of luck, ingenuity, and resilience, even within the harsh conditions of slavery. In actuality, a Belgian researcher by the name of Charles Morren discovered the fertilization if vanilla in 1833, three years earlier. But he had discovered it in a laboratory and could not reproduce it in the wild by planters. If Charles Morren was more likely to be credited with the actual discovery, it was readily attributed to Edmond Albius, who, following his discovery, was baptized by his master before setting him free. Hence the name Albius, which in Creole language meant "light yellow," the color of the vanilla flower. And Dina emphasized that the "matchmakers" (name given to the women hand-pollinating the orchid flowers) always use the same manual gesture that Emond pioneered. She added that Edmond spent the rest of his life working on the plantation and lived in poverty. He died in 1880, at the age of fifty-one, with little recognition for his contribution to the vanilla industry. However, his legacy lived on, as the method he discovered is still used today, and the vanilla industry is one of the most important agricultural sectors in Madagascar.

Vanilla's arrival in Madagascar was a story of careful cultivation and discovery. The first settlers on Réunion Island brought vanilla to Madagascar around 1880, beginning its journey on the island of Nosy Be before spreading to Ambanja on the mainland. Over time, vanilla cultivation expanded further, reaching the east coast and the SAVA region. Those who established the plantations soon recognized that the SAVA region offered the ideal conditions for growing vanilla. Its unique balance of rainfall and temperature created an environment perfectly suited for the plant's growth, cementing the region's reputation as a global hub for vanilla production.

It is ironic that vanilla was first introduced on the west side of the island, only to discover that it thrived on the east side, while cocoa, initially planted on the east side, was later found to be better suited to the Sambirano region on the west side.

The Vanilla Vine Looping Technique

Looping is a cultivation method used to promote vertical growth and enhance the productivity of vanilla vines. As a climbing orchid, the vanilla plant naturally ascends by wrapping itself around a support structure, such as a tree or wooden stake, and can grow several meters in length if left unmanaged.

The looping technique involves gently guiding the vine back down to the soil and passing it through the growing medium to encourage new root development. This process boosts the vine's vigor, making it more productive and more resistant to disease.

Looping also helps maintain the vine at a manageable height, facilitating key agricultural tasks like hand-pollination and harvesting. The technique is typically performed when the vine reaches a length of about two meters. At that point, the grower carefully detaches the vine from its support—before it grows out of reach—and lays it back down toward the ground.

In addition to improving resilience and yield, looping encourages the growth of lateral branches, which can lead to the production of more flowers and, ultimately, more vanilla beans.

Wherever vanilla was cultivated, efforts were made to introduce the Melipona bee from Mexico. However, since the introduction methods of the time were not advanced enough and relied solely on open-environment releases, the bee could not adapt and ultimately disappeared. The timely discovery of manual pollination was crucial, as it became clear that the Melipona bees were no longer present, either on Réunion Island or in Madagascar. Manual pollination quickly became the standard practice, which is why vanilla exports surged so rapidly. By 1900, Madagascar was exporting one thousand tons of vanilla.

Dina invited us to discover a part of the domain where she demonstrated the "looping technique" of the vanilla vine. Elizabeth, Shannon, and Michael were able to practice in the field.

A year later, during my second trip to the island, with memories of that first visit still fresh in my mind, I found myself retracing my steps—this time with Nirina Ramanandraibe to lead me back to his family's vanilla plantation. I was eager to speak with Dina again and to delve further into the history of vanilla. This time, I had the opportunity to stay in one of the three tourist villas on the estate, which we had only briefly glimpsed during our tour with the American chefs.

Each villa at the lodge was designed to blend seamlessly with the vibrant tropical environment. Two stories tall, it boasted an open design that invited ample natural light and promoted air circulation. The exterior, a harmonious mix of wood and brick, was anchored by a grand central walkway leading to the entrance. A staircase ascended to the upper level, where an open deck exuded a warm, inviting ambiance, enhanced by the rich tones of polished wood and soft lighting. The floor, ceiling, and railings—all crafted from wood—created a cohesive, natural aesthetic. In the background, partially concealed behind a delicate white mosquito net, was access to a spacious, fully opened master bedroom. An ideal setting for unwinding at the end of the day. At the rear of the first floor, the space opened onto a wide deck with a large table and benches.

The table was elegantly set, with a tray of large green coconuts complete with straws, inviting Chef Farah, Nirina, and me to quench our thirst. As night fell, the soft lighting created a dimly lit, tranquil atmosphere. Our drivers, who brought their guitars, began to play, filling the air with live music that perfectly complemented the relaxed ambiance. The meal was an enjoyable, laid-back affair, starting with smoked white fish spread on toast, followed by a delicate vol-au-vent (a small round case of puff pastry filled with a savory mixture, typically of meat or fish in a rich sauce) infused with vanilla, and culminating in a generous platter of roasted langoustes (lobsters). This intimate gathering, with its harmonious blend of simple yet exquisite local food, live music, and serene surroundings, made for a truly memorable and pleasant experience.

As I settled into the rhythm of the estate, each day revealed new details.

The next day began early, 5:45 a.m., as a sharp bird whistle jolted me awake. The sun was already peeking over the horizon. I sat up in bed beneath the mosquito net, looking out at a sky still cloaked in the dark clouds of the receding night. From my vantage point above the treetops of the domain, the ocean was visible. The sky held a silver-gray hue, the remnants of a passing storm, with the horizon offering the only touch of color, streaked with pink and white brushstrokes, hinting at the promise of another beautiful day on the island.

During breakfast, I asked Dina to revisit the history of vanilla on the island, beginning with the French colonization. She explained that the French were instrumental in developing the infrastructure necessary for large-scale vanilla cultivation. Dina stressed the importance of understanding the events that shaped and affected the industry over the years.

"Everything related to vanilla beans operates in cycles," Dina explained. She added that as a natural product, vanilla beans experience fluctuations in price that are inevitable. She described how these cycles involve years of high production followed by periods of lower yields as the vines recover. The cycle might see a slight increase before another substantial harvest, but this pattern is natural. Dina also stressed that climatic events, such as cyclones, could either intensify or mitigate these cycles. "Typically, these vanilla price cycles span around ten years," she said.

Dina continued. "It's clear that people have a short memory. Those who have been around for a long time have this knowledge and history, but unfortunately, the ones who love vanilla aren't always the ones who talk the loudest in the industry."

She added that one of the biggest gaps today is in the transmission of the history of vanilla. She said that those who know it are becoming fewer and fewer, and decisions continue to be made without taking the time to learn more about the product.

From her own experience in the flavor industry, she acknowledged that technical knowledge is crucial when making strategic decisions about a product. Unfortunately, this effort is no longer systematically made. This gap sometimes leads to decisions that are misguided, decisions that might have been well-considered at one point, but with the market changing so rapidly, adaptability becomes essential. "Decisions are often made at the wrong time, or too late," she commented.

Vanilla History, from Colonial Times to Today

By the mid-twentieth century, Madagascar solidified its position as the leading producer of vanilla. By this time, the SAVA region became the center of vanilla production, producing most of the world's supply.

In the late 1940s, the Malagasy Uprising against French colonial rule caused some disruption in production, but the vanilla industry continued to thrive after Madagascar gained independence in 1960. However, the French saw the potential of the SAVA region, where the climate was perfect for vanilla orchids. They expanded its cultivation, with investments in processing and curing, intertwining the destiny of vanilla with Madagascar's history.

In the 1960s and 1970s, post-independence, Madagascar's vanilla industry continued to grow, with the government supporting agricultural exports. However, fluctuations in global prices and political instability affected the industry's stability.

In the 1980s and 1990s, the global vanilla market faced challenges due to synthetic vanillin, which reduced the demand for natural vanilla. Despite this, Madagascar remained the top producer of high-quality vanilla beans.

In 1994, Cyclone Geralda severely damaged vanilla crops in Madagascar, leading to a spike in global vanilla prices. This event highlighted the vulnerability of vanilla production to environmental factors.

By the late 1990s, efforts to modernize the industry began, including improving quality control and establishing better market conditions for farmers.

From the early 2000s to present time, Madagascar continues to dominate the global vanilla market, producing around 80 percent of the world's vanilla beans. The industry is now characterized by a focus on sustainability, fair trade practices, and efforts to combat the volatility of vanilla prices.

In 2004, Cyclone Gafilo hit Madagascar. It was one of the stronger cyclones of the decade and caused considerable damage to the vanilla-producing regions, particularly in the SAVA region.

Then, in 2008, Cyclone Ivan struck Madagascar, causing extensive damage to the island, particularly in the SAVA region, which is the heart of vanilla production. The cyclone destroyed a significant portion of the vanilla crops, leading to a shortage of vanilla beans in the global market.

In 2017, another major cyclone, Enawo, hit Madagascar, again causing significant damage to vanilla crops. This led to a dramatic increase in prices and brought attention to the need for more resilient agricultural practices.

Today, the vanilla industry in Madagascar is focused on improving the livelihoods of farmers through environmental and social programs to mitigate the impacts of natural disasters.

Dina admitted that motivations are not always the same. "If the initial decisions by the government to set prices were made to protect farmers, that was completely reasonable and understandable. However, when it becomes clear that the market isn't keeping pace, it's crucial to be able to respond swiftly."

She warned that if prices are kept too low, there is a risk that farmers might decide to replace their vanilla plants with other crops like pepper, cinnamon, or cloves. Companies have now established many sustainable programs to address this risk. Many farmers, as members of cooperatives or associations that offer a range of benefits, have seen their partners make significant efforts to provide alternative income-generating opportunities. Ultimately, the work done by international producers and exporters has been focused on mitigating this risk. Companies like Symrise and Ramanandraibe, among others, have been working on this for more than ten years. After the 2004 crisis, these companies organized themselves to ensure that vanilla knowledge was passed down from generation to generation, allowing growers and producers to continue producing vanilla.

The aim was to support farmers in a way that would inspire their children to continue the tradition. Of course, "modern" farmers would approach their crops differently than their parents and grandparents, given their different education, but the key question was how producers and exporters could collaborate to ensure that vanilla production provided a decent living for everyone.

Dina reflected that passing down knowledge is deeply ingrained in Malagasy culture. "A Malagasy child will be cooking rice before they're even tall enough to see into the pot," she said. "They'll stand on a stool to check if the rice is cooked. This tradition of transmission is very natural. It's simply because children support their parents in the farming activities that are accessible to them when they're out of school."

Her words echoed a deeply rooted tradition—but they also prompted a reflection on the fine line between cultural transmission and labor in a country where poverty shapes daily life.

Child labor remains a concern in Madagascar, where high poverty rates continue to affect vulnerable households. In some communities, children risk being pulled out of school to work as daily laborers in rice cultivation or other off-farm activities. Recognizing the risks and the often-blurred lines between child labor and acceptable child involvement in family farming, the Malagasy government, together with vanilla exporters, took action. In December 2015, they signed the Vanilla Code of Conduct (CoC)—a key step in Madagascar's commitment to combating child labor within the vanilla supply chain. As part of this initiative, companies have pledged to raise awareness and implement programs that support children's education and promote ethical labor practices.

Dina went on to explain that it was not just about passing down knowledge; it was also about sharing family time. On the island, children did not always have extracurricular activities, so spending time with their parents became a shared experience. "By accompanying them," she added, "it becomes a moment of connection and transmission." She emphasized that pollinating the vanilla flower was not something parents wait until their children are eighteen or twenty-one to teach. "It's a natural curiosity," she said. "Children watch their parents do it and quickly learn. A child isn't going to pollinate eight hundred or a thousand flowers a day like an experienced worker. In any case, I don't think any Malagasy parents would entrust their child with fertilizing so many flowers if they didn't yet have the skill to do it."

Dina pointed out that this transmission is natural, just as it is with preparing vanilla. Historically, she noted, the harvest took place in June, July, and August, right in the middle of the vacation season. As parents worked, their children, being on vacation, naturally spent time with them. She did not believe they could be accused of subjecting their children to dangerous work. "A bundle of vanilla weighs, at most, ten pounds. It's not eighty pounds, which is the limit for the proper development of a child's bones, and so on. To me, it was a debate that never should have existed. We were unfairly criticized and pressured to make commitments. Yes, we made those commitments, but only because we were threatened with an embargo on Madagascan vanilla. Everyone complied, even though we were quite clear about our stance."

From Green Pods to Vanilla Beans

From late May until August begins the harvest of green vanilla pods. Once the pods have reached full maturity—about nine months after pollination—they are carefully hand-picked. These pods, though rich in potential, are yet to develop the complex flavors and aromas that make vanilla. The journey from green pod to vanilla bean is a delicate transformation.

The first step in this transformation is known as the "killing" stage, where the life of the green pod is halted to kickstart the curing process. In Madagascar, this is often achieved by immersing the pods in hot water, a method that not only stops the maturation process but also initiates the crucial enzymatic reactions needed to develop vanilla's signature flavor.

Next comes the sweating stage. The pods, now blanched and pliable, are wrapped in thick blankets and stored in insulated containers. Here, in the warm, humid environment, the pods sweat for days, their complex compounds breaking down into the rich, aromatic molecules that define high-quality vanilla. This is the stage where enzymatic reactions are most intense. The enzymes within the vanilla pod break down precursor compounds like glucovanillin into vanillin, the key aromatic molecule in vanilla. This is a form of biochemical transformation rather than microbial fermentation.

After sweating, the pods enter the drying stage, where their moisture content is carefully reduced to preserve the newly developed aromas. Initially, the pods are laid out in the sun, where they are turned regularly to ensure even drying. This is followed by a more prolonged drying period in shaded areas, where the pods are allowed to slowly lose the remaining moisture, concentrating their flavor. This stage can last several weeks and is critical in defining the final quality of the vanilla. The drying process halts enzymatic activity and promotes oxidation. As moisture is removed, the chemical reactions continue at a slower pace, concentrating and stabilizing the aromatic compounds developed earlier. This stage ensures that the pods retain their desired aroma without microbial degradation.

She added that if those who pressured them to make this commitment had taken the time to understand how the industry actually works, they would have realized there was no need for such measures.

In response to these concerns, the Malagasy government, in collaboration with the International Labour Organization and industry stakeholders, took measures to combat child labor. Notably, in December 2015, a code of conduct for combating child labor in the vanilla sector was signed, aiming to address and reduce child labor practices.

Dina observed that vanilla remains a favorite flavor for many consumers because it evokes such strong emotions. "It takes people back to their childhood, to those carefree years and cherished memories. Vanilla truly has the power to transport us through time, simply by triggering its scent."

She added that she would like people to recognize beyond those beautiful memories, there is also a tremendous amount of hard work that ensures these exquisite vanilla pods reach them. "These are truly 'love' pods," she said, "crafted not by a single person, but by a team of individuals who have devoted great care to them." Dina highlighted the effort involved, from planting the vine, to the care given during the three years before it produces, and the meticulous attention required during the nine months of preparation. "It's said," she continued, "that, on average, a pod is touched at least forty times during its preparation: massaged throughout the six months of processing and stabilization, it is checked, watched, listened to, and handled by multiple people. It truly receives special attention." Dina elaborated that very few ingredients require as much attention before reaching the final consumer. It takes a great deal of passion to produce vanilla. If someone was not passionate about the product, they would likely turn away from it due to the immense effort involved and move on to something simpler. "I think that's what gives this spice its nobility," she said.

Producing a vanilla pod is not just about hard work; it's the culmination of experience passed down from grower to grower and processor to processor. In the end, it's the accumulation of a rich history—a true fruit of passion handed down from one person to another.

The planifolia variety Madagascar exports is the one that is approved by the food industry and the perfume industry. This is essentially because planifolia is the variety with the widest olfactory and gustatory range, hence the different qualities of vanilla. There are different notes depending on the respective moisture content.

Dina explained that there are different qualities of vanilla beans. Cut vanilla beans are typically lower-grade beans that had been cut to remove

Meet Estelle: The Heart of the Curing Process

At just twenty-seven years old, Estelle has already spent nearly a decade perfecting the art of vanilla curing. Married with three children, she began working at Symrise when she was only eighteen. Her day starts at seven in the morning, and if the weather is favorable, she and her team spread the vanilla out to dry under the sun. Later, they bring the beans back to the warehouse to begin the meticulous process of sorting and grading.

"Before we start the killing process, we sort the vanilla beans and put them in boxes based on their length and maturity," Estelle explains. "This helps us tailor the killing process to each bean's needs. After killing, we let them sweat for two days in special boxes, then let them dry for a whole month before we sort them again."

The vanilla undergoes a drying process in the sun, often wrapped in blankets or laid out on rocks for up to a month and a half. Every batch is carefully monitored, and the sorting is done daily. During sorting, any beans that are not fully dried are returned to the racks, while the dried ones are moved to the crates, where the final classification by grade occurs.

But before the beans are packed for shipment, Estelle and her colleagues rely on the seasoned noses of more experienced women. "We make sure there's no bad smell (mold) before sending them off," she says.

blemishes or damaged parts. These beans are often shorter and might have splits or cracks. Gourmet or Grade A vanilla beans are high-quality beans that are plump, moist, and have a strong aroma. They are typically longer in size and more flexible. "Cuts have less moisture content," said Dina, "at around fourteen percent, and they do not offer the same flavor impact as a Gourmet, at thirty-five to thirty-eight percent of humidity. Water molecules really do support olfactory and gustatory molecules!"

Dina elaborated that although vanillin is the primary component of natural vanilla beans, there are more than three hundred additional molecules that contribute to its complex aromatic bouquet. When people smell vanilla, they experience a symphony of these varied notes, which distinguishes natural vanilla from synthetic vanillin, where only a single, dominant vanillin note is present. She emphasized that this complexity is crucial during anti-fraud testing, as most tests focus on detecting these unique natural molecules.

But the journey of Malagasy vanilla has not always been sweet. With the advent of artificial vanilla flavoring, the market faced stiff competition. The cheaply produced flavor, although lacking the genuine taste and aroma, posed a threat. And nature, too, hasn't always been kind. The scars of climate change and the wrath of cyclones often challenge the robustness of the crops. Added to this is the shadow of thievery, driven by the bean's high value, leading to premature harvesting and a dip in quality.

Despite these challenges, the vanilla trade has continued to pulse through the heart of Madagascar. When I returned to Tana on my first trip, I met with Laurence Briand, Symrise general manager in Madagascar, at the Grand Urban Hotel. I knew that Symrise Madagascar's commitment stretched beyond just the vanilla pods, but I wanted to hear from Laurence how her team delved into the day-to-day lives of the vanilla farmers.

She explained that Symrise provided measures like health insurance and promoting diversification in agriculture. They not only wanted to ensure a consistent quality of vanilla but also a holistic well-being of the local communities.

According to Laurence, Madagascar stood at a critical juncture, where the intertwining challenges of environmental conservation, farmer welfare, and sustainable agriculture converged. As one of the leading figures in this landscape, the focus for our company remained steadfast on reinforcing the initiatives that not only support the environment but also ensure a living income for the farmers who are the backbone of this vibrant ecosystem.

The years ahead promised to be challenging, marked by high inflation and economic pressures. However, Symrise's commitment to these farmers—spread across more than one hundred remote communities—is unwavering. The challenge lies not just in the actions taken but also in effectively conveying these efforts to consumers, clients, and colleagues, especially in a country where digitization and data collection are fraught with difficulties.

At the heart of Symrise's mission is a multifaceted approach to environmental support. On the farms, the emphasis is on supporting the ecosystem by encouraging tree planting and protecting endemic species, essential for maintaining the delicate vanilla agroforestry system. Yet, the environmental efforts extend beyond vanilla. The destructive slash-and-burn practices used to cultivate rice on steep slopes led to severe soil erosion, rendering the land barren within a few years. To combat this, there has been a concerted effort to promote regenerative agricultural techniques, diversified income sources with other botanicals like patchouli, and sustainable alternatives that protect the soil and ensure its fertility for future generations.

Community involvement for Symrise is crucial to these efforts. In collaboration with local leaders and villagers, risks were identified, and solutions, such as reforesting key areas to protect vital water sources, have been implemented. This approach was not merely about preserving the environment; it was about connecting these actions to the everyday lives of the people, making the link between their behaviors and the health of their environment clear and actionable. Laurence stated that the passion with which these communities engaged, sometimes walking hours to reforest their land, was a testament to their commitment to a sustainable future.

"Yet, the challenges faced by vanilla farmers in Madagascar went beyond environmental concerns," said Laurence. "The lack of social security nets meant that any misfortune—a sick child, a destroyed home—could push a family into a financial crisis." She continued to explain that cash-flow management became a daily struggle, exacerbated by the inability to secure loans from banks due to the lack of collateral. In desperation, many farmers previously turned to local moneylenders, pre-selling their vanilla crops at unfavorable rates just to make ends meet. This cycle not only affected their financial stability but also impacted the quality of the vanilla, as there was less incentive to produce a high-quality product when the crop had already been sold at a low price.

Recognizing this, Symrise introduced a groundbreaking health insurance system for these farmers. For the first time, they could cover medical expenses for their families without plunging into debt, breaking the cycle of financial vulnerability. This initiative was coupled with a push for food security through regenerative agriculture and income diversification, encouraging farmers to grow ginger, vetiver, and other crops alongside vanilla to ensure a steady income throughout the year.

This holistic approach—analyzing the household as a whole and addressing not just agricultural productivity but also factors like health, education, and food security—created a sustainable ecosystem that supports both the present and future generations. Laurence stated Symrise's goal was twofold: to provide high-quality vanilla today while ensuring that the farmers' families were secure and thriving, and that the next generation would be prepared to continue this vital work.

On a personal level, Laurence shared how her work in Madagascar was not just a professional endeavor but a deeply rewarding journey. Leading a passionate and dedicated team, contributing to the country's development, and witnessing the tangible impact on local communities has provided her with profound fulfillment. Her connection to Madagascar ran deep, whether she was engaging with farmers she had known for more than a decade or exploring the countryside with just a backpack. The island's diverse landscapes and rich biodiversity, both above and below the water, offered her endless opportunities for discovery and reflection.

When I asked her to share some of her most memorable moments, she spoke not of grand achievements but of the simplest pleasures. She recalled a day on the beach, enjoying freshly grilled fish prepared by local fishermen, enhanced by nothing more than a squeeze of lemon. In that simplicity, she found the essence of Madagascar—a place where purity and connection flowed effortlessly between the land and its people.

While Laurence found fulfillment in her connection to the land and its people, I was equally intrigued by how others might be transformed by their time in Madagascar. As our first trip drew to a close, I sat with the three American chefs on the deck of the Grand Hotel Urban in Tana, eager to discover how their experiences would inspire new interpretations of their award-winning vanilla recipes.

Chef Michael Gulotta reflected on his Gnocchetti with Crawfish Tom Yum: "I've fallen in love with Madagascar's pink peppercorns," Michael shared enthusiastically. "The floral, fruity notes they add, along with their subtle spice, are just incredible." This newfound appreciation for an ingredient he once overlooked spoke volumes about the transformative power of travel and exposure to new culinary landscapes. "In classical cooking, pepper often serves as a baseline flavor," he continued, "but pink peppercorns can really make a dish pop." He added that the local cocoa nibs would complement the existing flavors beautifully, adding a rich, earthy dimension that he had not considered before.

For Mixologist Shannon Tebay, the vibrant flavors of Madagascar sparked new ideas for her Star Fox cocktail. Originally a smoky, peppery twist on the classic Ramos Gin Fizz, Shannon now envisioned incorporating the tropical fruits and spices she encountered on the island.

"If I were to redo the recipe, I'd definitely bring in more of the local ingredients—fresh mango, pink peppercorns, cacao, and coffee," she explained. "These elements make perfect sense together. Generally speaking, if it grows together, it goes together, and the flavors of Madagascar blend beautifully with the vanilla extract." Shannon's reflection underscored the importance of location in crafting a drink that was not only delicious but also deeply connected to its origins.

Chef Elizabeth Falkner, always attentive to texture and flavor balance, shared her thoughts on revising A Veil of Vanilla, which was originally a delicate balance of oats, vanilla, and minimal sweetness. However, her experiences in Madagascar inspired her to push the boundaries further. "I would toast, or even slightly burn, the oats, similar to how rice is treated here, in the beverage called *ranovola*." She also considered incorporating cashews instead of streusel, drawing on the nut's natural pairing with vanilla. For Elizabeth, these adjustments would not only enrich the dish's mouthfeel but also integrate the authentic flavors she experienced during her travels.

Through these reflections, Michael, Shannon, and Elizabeth demonstrated how their culinary journeys were ever evolving, shaped by the places they visited and the ingredients they encountered. The influence of Madagascar, with its bounty of flavors and aromas, not only deepened their appreciation for vanilla but also sparked new ideas and possibilities for their craft. Through their willingness to adapt and experiment, they demonstrated the dynamic nature of culinary arts—always curious, always evolving, always inspired by new experiences.

In my first book, *Conversations Behind the Kitchen Door*, and in each episode of my podcast, *Flavor Unknown*, I explored the deep-rooted connection between chefs and their home regions—a culinary anchor that grounds their creativity and shapes their identity. But where was the true home of vanilla, this beloved and ubiquitous flavor? Was it nestled in the sun-drenched hillsides of Madagascar, where the precious pods are cultivated, cured, and selected with care? Or was it in the elegant patisseries of Paris or New York City, where pastry chefs transformed it into decadent desserts? Perhaps, more than anywhere else, vanilla's true home was in "mom's kitchen"—a place where the aroma of vanilla-infused treats brought warmth and comfort to homes around the world.

Indeed, it was in those home kitchens, where recipes were passed down like treasured heirlooms, that vanilla truly belonged. It was where the alchemy of family time took place, where the simple act of baking became a connection to parents, grandparents, and the cherished memories of childhood. Vanilla was far more than just an ingredient; it was a symbol of love, continuity, and the heritage of our most treasured moments.

But this heritage, this connection to our past, shouldn't be taken for granted. Vanilla is not just "plain old vanilla." It is a thread that ties generations together, the generation of vanilla farmers from Madagascar as well as the generations of consumers around the world. Vanilla is a flavor that holds the power to evoke memories and create new ones. If we wish to protect the heritage of our childhood memories for the next generation, we also must protect the source of this cherished flavor—the farmers, the matchmakers, the weathermen, the women in the vanilla curing facilities in the SAVA region of Madagascar, who work tirelessly to make vanilla that enriches our lives and theirs. By supporting these people from the Red Island, we ensure that the magic of vanilla, and the memories it helps create, continue to flourish in kitchens around the world. It's a small but significant way to honor the alchemy of family time and safeguard the connections that make us feel at home, wherever we may be.

Star Fox

Recipe by Mixologist Shannon Tebay

Yields 1 cocktail

INGREDIENTS

Orange Vanilla Syrup

5 cups white sugar
4¼ cups water
1½ teaspoons vanilla extract
½ teaspoon orange extract

Cocktail

1½ oz. Del Maguey Chichicapa Mezcal
½ oz. Aperol
½ oz. lemon juice
½ oz. lime juice
3 drops black pepper tincture
1 egg white
1 oz. orange vanilla syrup
1 oz. heavy cream
2 oz. soda water, plus more to top
Misted vanilla extract

PREPARATION

For the Orange Vanilla Syrup

Combine sugar with water and whisk until dissolved. Add extract and stir to combine.

TO ASSEMBLE AND SERVE

1. Combine mezcal, Aperol, lemon, lime, black pepper tincture, egg white, and orange vanilla syrup. Dry shake to incorporate.
2. Add approximately 50 grams of ice and shake until ice is almost melted. Before the ice is completely gone, add cream and shake again to incorporate.
3. Pour cocktail into a Collins glass bottomed with soda water. Allow the cocktail to set up and stiffen for 20 to 30 seconds, then gently top with more soda.
4. Garnish with extract mist and black pepper.

Gnocchetti with Crawfish Tom Yum

Recipe by Chef Michael Gulotta (Chef-owner at Mopho, Maypop, and Tana, New Orleans, Louisiana)

Serves 3 to 4 people

INGREDIENTS

Vanilla Tom Yum

½ oz. virgin coconut oil
2 shallots, minced
1 red bell pepper, small diced
1 Thai chili
3 cloves garlic, sliced
1 fingerroot ginger, minced
1 stalk lemongrass, sliced thinly into rings
1 lime leaf
1 tsp. crab paste
1 cup shellfish stock
3 oz. coconut milk
4 oz. butter
1 oz. rendered bacon fat
2 tsp. vanilla extract
½ bunch cilantro, thinly sliced
Juice and zest of 2 limes
Fish sauce to taste

Citrus Herb Crust

½ cup neutral oil
1 clove garlic
½ bunch cilantro
Juice and zest of 1 orange
¼ cup grated Grana Padano
1 cup panko breadcrumbs, lightly toasted

Vanilla Pickled Mirliton

1 tbsp. seasoned rice wine vinegar
1 tbsp. sugar
2 tsp. vanilla extract
½ tsp. *yuzu kosho*
1 *mirliton*, peeled, seeded, diced small

TO ASSEMBLE AND SERVE

8 oz. gnocchetti pasta, cooked until al dente, with some pasta water reserved
8 oz. picked crawfish tails
⅓ cup grated Grana Padano
1 tbsp. sliced chive

Recipe continues →

PREPARATION

For the Vanilla Tom Yum Butter

1. In a nonreactive pan, warm the coconut oil over medium-high heat.
2. Add in the shallot, red peppers, Thai chili, garlic, ginger, and lemongrass and sweat for 3 minutes; do not caramelize.
3. Add in the lime leaf and crab paste and sweat for an additional 2 minutes.
4. Pour in the shellfish stock and coconut milk and bring to a simmer.
5. Whisk in the butter and bacon fat to emulsify.
6. Finish with the vanilla extract, cilantro, lime juice and zest, and fish sauce; cut the heat and let steep.
7. Check seasoning and adjust as needed.

For the Citrus Herb Crust:

1. In a blender, purée together the oil, garlic, cilantro, orange juice and zest, and Grana Padano to a fine paste.
2. In a medium bowl, fold together the herb purée and toasted panko then lay out on a baking sheet to dry.

For the Vanilla Pickled Mirliton

1. In a nonreactive pot, bring the vinegar and sugar to a simmer.
2. Allow the vinegar mixture to cool then whisk in the vanilla extract and yuzu kosho.
3. Pour the pickling liquid over the mirliton, cover, and let sit overnight in the cooler.

TO ASSEMBLE AND SERVE

1. Simmer the cooked gnocchetti in 16 ounces Vanilla Tom Yum Butter for 2 minutes.
2. Gently fold in the crawfish tails and heat just to warm through.
3. Separate the pasta into four bowls and top each with a healthy sprinkle of Vanilla Pickled *Mirliton* then Citrus Herb Crust, chives, and Grana Padano.

A Vail of Vanilla

Recipe by Chef Elizabeth Falkner (ChEF Productions, Los Angeles, California)

INGREDIENTS

Chiffon Cake

1½ oz. canola or sunflower oil
1½ oz. egg yolks
2½ oz. oat milk
1 tsp. vanilla extract
4 oz. all-purpose flour
½ tsp. baking powder
3¼ oz. sugar
2½ oz. egg whites
¼ tsp. Diamond Crystal kosher salt

Caramel

3 oz. sugar
1 tbsp. glucose or corn syrup
1 tbsp. butter
2 oz. heavy cream
½ tsp. vanilla extract
1 pinch of salt

Vanilla Biscuit Crumb

1 oz. white sugar
3 oz. white flour
2 tbsp. cornstarch
½ tsp. Diamond Crystal kosher salt
1½ oz. butter
1 tsp. vanilla extract

Vanilla Oat Milk

4 oz. oat milk
1 tsp. vanilla extract

TO ASSEMBLE AND SERVE

4 oz. cooked steel-cut oats, cooled
2 oz. crème fraîche
2 oz. low-fat Greek yogurt
Meyer lemon or tangerine zest

Recipe continues →

PREPARATION

For the Vanilla Chiffon Cake

1. Preheat the oven to 375°F and prepare a greased, parchment-lined quarter baking sheet.
2. Combine the oil, yolks, oat milk, vanilla extract, flour, baking powder, and 1.25 ounces sugar and whisk until smooth. In a separate bowl, make a French meringue by whipping the egg whites with salt and gradually adding the remaining sugar to form stiff peaks.
3. Fold French meringue into the other mixture then spread onto a baking sheet. Bake for 10 to 15 minutes or until the cake springs back slightly to the touch. Cool.

For the Vanilla Caramel

1. In a saucepan over high flame, combine sugar and glucose or corn syrup to caramelize.
2. Remove from heat then add butter and cream. Bring back to a rolling simmer.
3. Remove from heat then add vanilla extract and a pinch of salt. Let cool.

For the Vanilla Biscuit Crumb

1. In a bowl, mix sugar, flour, cornstarch, and salt with butter, then add vanilla extract to form the crumb.
2. Bake on a parchment-lined sheet pan at 350°F for about 20 minutes, raking halfway through baking.

For the Vanilla Oat Milk

Combine oat milk and extract. Keep cold.

PLATING

1. Spoon cooled, cooked oats into the center of bowls and make a small well or indentation.
2. Spoon small amount of Vanilla Caramel in the center of the oats. Cut Vanilla Chiffon Cake into 2-inch squares.
3. Set a square of cake on top of each of the Vanilla Caramel–filled oats.
4. In a small bowl, combine crème fraîche and Greek yogurt, then make a small quenelle of the mixture on top of each piece of Vanilla Chiffon Cake.
5. Grate Meyer lemon or tangerine on top of crème fraîche.
6. Top with a little of the Vanilla Biscuit Crumb. Pour Vanilla Oat Milk over the Vanilla Chiffon Cake square and oats at the bottom of the bowl, then serve.

CHAPTER 3

From Brickaville to Ambanja

A Journey Through Madagascar Cocoa Terroirs

Ny voankazo avy amin'ny hazo sarobidy no manana tsirony tsara.

The fruits from a precious tree have a good taste.

—TRADITIONAL MALAGASY SAYING

The drive along Route Nationale 2 (RN2) was a true test of endurance and focus. The narrow road, crowded with lumbering container trucks and weathered 4x4s, moved at a sluggish pace, each mile challenging our patience. Deep potholes turned the journey into a relentless obstacle course. At one bend, we passed an overturned truck. "It happens all the time here," Nirina remarked casually, as if it were just another part of the journey.

◀ *Cocoa pods with rows of seeds inside—cocoa beans in the sticky, sweet white pulp.*

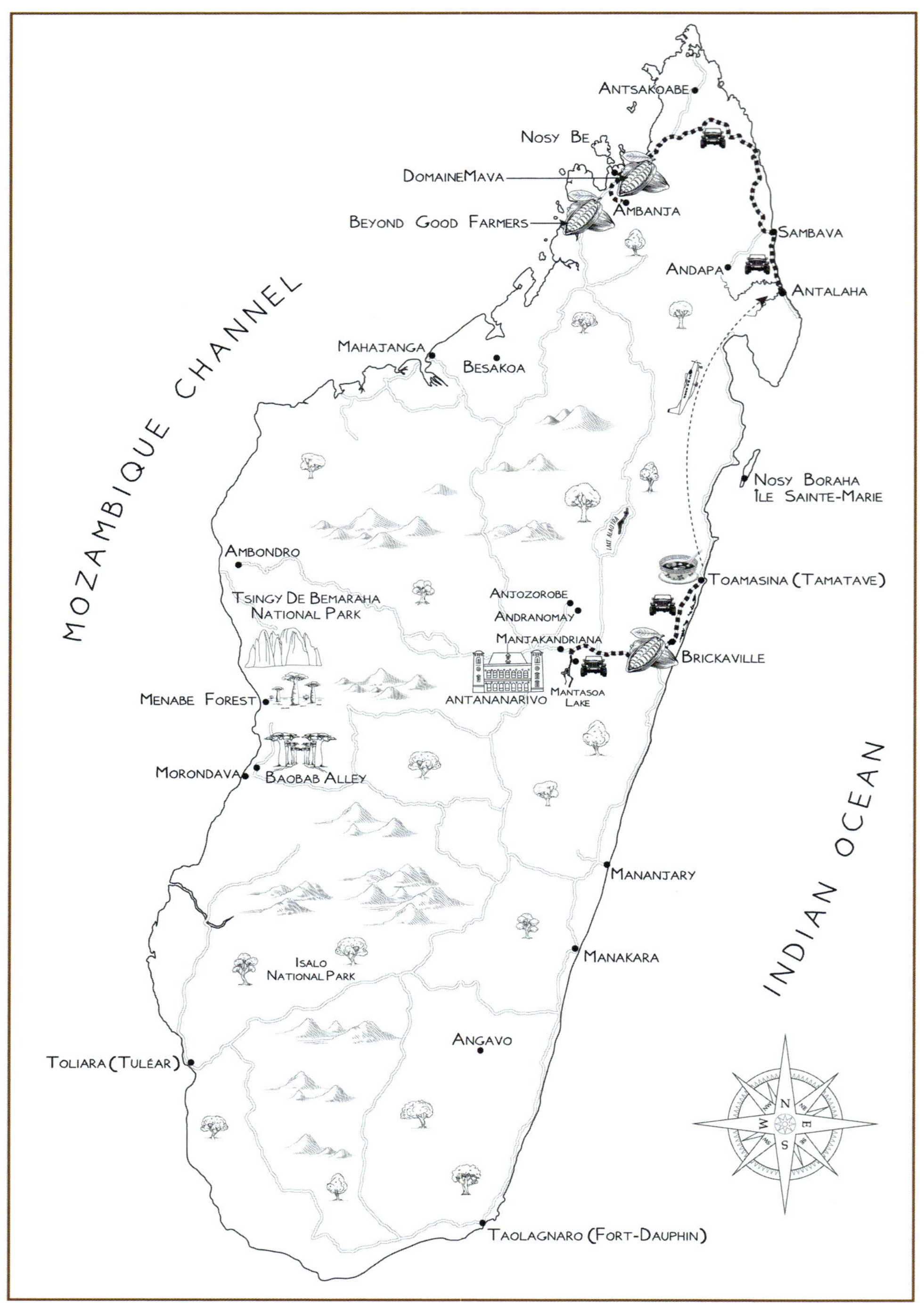
Antsakoabe
Nosy Be
DomaineMava
Ambanja
Beyond Good Farmers
Sambava
Andapa
Antalaha
Mozambique Channel
Mahajanga
Besakoa
Nosy Boraha
Île Sainte-Marie
Ambondro
Toamasina (Tamatave)
Tsingy De Bemaraha
National Park
Anjozorobe
Andranomay
Mantakandriana
Brickaville
Menabe Forest
Antananarivo
Mantasoa
Lake
Morondava
Baobab Alley
Indian Ocean
Mananjary
Manakara
Isalo
National Park
Angavo
Toliara (Tuléar)
N
E
S
W
Taolagnaro (Fort-Dauphin)

The road wound its way through small villages, where locals sold fresh produce and handmade goods. The proximity of pedestrians and vendors to the road's edge required careful navigation. At one curve, we stopped to admire vibrant bunches of small bananas, artfully arranged under a traditional thatched roof. The price was three thousand ariary per kilogram—just sixty-four cents. Nirina purchased a large bunch and placed it in the space between the front seats so we could snack as we continued our drive.

As we approached Brickaville (known today as Vohibinany), we stopped at the busy produce market in Antsampanana. While Nirina stepped aside to handle a series of business calls, Chef Farah invited me to explore the vibrant stalls with her. The market was brimming with exotic produce that offered a glimpse into Madagascar's rich and diverse bounty of fruit.

Our tasting began with *mokotra*, the so-called "monkey orange." Its tough, intriguing shell required as much effort to crack as a coconut, but the reward inside was worth it: tangy, caramel-like pulp with a flavor as bold and surprising as the fruit's appearance. The pulp's sharp acidity contrasted with the consistency of a custard. It was unlike anything I had ever tasted before.

Next, we sampled *bananes séchées* (dried bananas), whose chewy texture and concentrated sweetness offered a satisfying contrast to the tang of the *mokotra*. Nearby, rambutan, with its spiky red skin and juicy, lychee-like flesh, provided a refreshing burst of tropical flavor.

The stall also displayed *voamadilo* (tamarind pods), *pomme cannelle* (custard apple) known for its soft, creamy flesh, and *corossol* (soursop). That spontaneous stop to explore Madagascar's flavors was an unforgettable experience for a food enthusiast like me.

As we left the market and continued our journey toward Brickaville, I took a moment to thank Nirina. Despite his busy schedule and the constant buzz of calls and messages on his phone, he had taken the time to guide me through his country with unwavering enthusiasm. It was clear that this balance—between entrepreneur and ambassador—was second nature to him.

During one of the quieter moments on the road, I inquired about his life, his heritage, and the path that brought him back to Madagascar after studying abroad. As we talked, his personality began to unfold—pragmatic and deeply rooted in his family and the traditions of his country, yet undeniably shaped by his experiences beyond its borders. Raised in a family of leaders, he spoke of his childhood dreams with a hint of humor.

"When I was fourteen," he chuckled, "I wanted to be either a fighter pilot or a stock trader. I was pretty good with numbers, but my father had a different vision for me. He wanted me to return to Madagascar, to carry on the family's work."

Even as Nirina pursued his education abroad, first in Paris and later in Australia, the call to return home was ever-present. "I always knew I'd come back," he said. "That clarity gave me a sense of calm during my studies. I wasn't chasing external pressures—I knew I'd eventually return as an entrepreneur."

Upon returning to Madagascar, Nirina immersed himself in the family business, starting with construction and property management. While these roles weren't initially his passion, they laid the foundation for his leadership within the group's diverse operations, which include export, real estate, plantations, and even microfinance. Over time, he began to focus on what truly excited him: agriculture and tourism. "I told my family," he said, "that after twenty years of managing routine tasks, I wanted to dedicate myself to what I love. It wasn't an easy conversation, but it was the right decision."

Nirina's vision, however, extends far beyond personal fulfillment. He spoke passionately about improving the livelihoods of Madagascar's local communities by creating more value within the country. "Too often," he explained, "we export products in bulk at a fraction of their final market value. It's essential that more of that value stays here, benefiting the people who work so hard to produce it. For me, it's about building a sustainable, equitable system."

As we continued our conversation, the topic shifted to the world of cocoa. Nirina confirmed what I read before my trip: Madagascar produces only about 0.1 percent of the world's cocoa. To put that into perspective, the world produces approximately 5.76 million tons of cocoa annually, with Africa dominating, at almost 70 percent. Major players like the Ivory Coast (2.23 million tons) and Ghana (683,000 tons) lead the charge. In contrast, Madagascar's 15,000 tons occupy a niche position, though the country is celebrated for its fine cocoa.

The World of Cocoa

The global cocoa production is approximately 5.76 million tons, with Africa contributing 68.4 percent, the Americas 17.3 percent, Asia 13.5 percent, and Oceania 0.8 percent.

Ivory Coast: 2,230,000 Tons
Ghana: 683,000 Tons
Indonesia: 667,000 Tons
Ecuador: 337,000 Tons
Cameroon: 295,000 Tons
Nigeria: 280,000 Tons
Brazil: 270,000 Tons
Peru:170,000 Tons
Dominican Republic: 75,000 Tons
Papua New Guinea: 42,000 Tons
Uganda: 35,000 Tons
Mexico: 28,000 Tons
India: 28,000 Tons
Madagascar: 15,000 Tons

Source: Food and Agriculture Organization of the United Nations (2023)

Malagasy cocoa has gained global acclaim, thanks to the efforts of local and international chocolatiers such as Chocolaterie Robert and Valrhona. By leveraging new marketing strategies that emphasize its unique terroir and exclusivity, Madagascar successfully positioned itself as a niche player in the luxury cocoa market.

Nirina traced cocoa's journey to Madagascar, a tale of global migration and adaptation. First introduced by French colonizers in the late nineteenth and early twentieth centuries, the cocoa tree's roots stretched back to Latin America. From there, it traveled through Asia, arriving in Java, Mauritius in 1755, and Réunion Island in 1777, before finding fertile ground on Madagascar's eastern shores. Early efforts focused on Criollo beans in Brickaville, where plantations initially thrived—until sugarcane replaced them as the dominant crop.

Nirina hypothesized that the decline of cocoa cultivation in this region was primarily due to the plant's poor adaptation to the humid tropical climate of Madagascar's east coast. The high rainfall created an environment where cocoa trees struggled to thrive, resulting in low yields per tree and increased susceptibility to mold and disease. In contrast, sugarcane was far more resilient and economically viable. At the same time, the growing demand for rum from Réunion Island made sugarcane an even more attractive crop for farmers. This combination of environmental and economic factors

likely led to the conversion of cocoa plantations into sugarcane fields, shifting cocoa cultivation to more suitable areas of the island.

"The real story of cocoa in Madagascar, however, took place in the northwest, in the Sambirano Valley near Ambanja," Nirina explained. He emphasized that the valley's fertile soil, enriched by the alluvial deposits of the Sambirano River, along with its unique microclimate, created ideal conditions for cocoa cultivation. It was in this region, starting in the mid-twentieth century, that Madagascar's fine cocoa production found its true home.

Nirina explained that the global cocoa market categorizes beans into three main varieties: Forastero, Trinitario, and Criollo. Forastero dominates as the commodity cocoa of the world, prized for its disease resistance but often lacking complexity in flavor. Trinitario, a hybrid of Forastero and Criollo, combines the former's hardiness with the latter's nuanced taste. Madagascar stands out as one of the few places in the world that exclusively produces fine cocoa, largely Criollo or Criollo-dominant Trinitario varieties. The result is cocoa celebrated for its bright citrus, red fruit, and floral notes. This distinctiveness has cemented Madagascar's reputation as one of the world's premier sources of fine cocoa.

Although Ambanja is Madagascar's prime cocoa region, Nirina included Brickaville in our itinerary to explore efforts to revive cocoa cultivation in its original Malagasy home. From there, our journey would lead to Tamatave, a bustling port city shaped by Chinese influence. He added, "I also have someone to meet, someone I'd like to introduce to you—he's been instrumental in the efforts to reintroduce cocoa trees to the Brickaville region."

We turned off RN2 onto a dirt road marked by deep ruts, patches of mud, and puddles. Nirina stopped the car along a rustic bamboo gate. Outside the nursery entrance, potted plants were displayed, likely available for purchase. A handwritten sign prominently displayed the name "*Pépinière* Les Amadi," a plant nursery in Madagascar specializing in agroforestry plant production. Near the entrance, a Malagasy flag fluttered atop the roof of traditional thatched structures. As we stepped out of the car, a tall, thin man welcomed us with a warm smile, inviting us to come inside.

We wandered among neat rows of young potted plants—lychee trees, bamboo, tender cocoa saplings, vanilla vines, and noni trees—all thriving under the nursery's care. Our host pointed toward a modest shed, its corrugated roof providing shelter for a collection of garden tools and clay pots.

Nirina gave the context of the project. With limited land in Ambanja, efforts began to revive cocoa in Brickaville, where it was first cultivated in Madagascar. His team propagated high-quality varieties from the Sambirano Valley and partnered with local nurserymen to plant one hundred thousand cocoa trees across 128 hectares. This initiative not only expanded cocoa production but also empowered farmers in the region. Today, we were here with one of them.

They brought the cocoa pods here from Ambanja, where the nurseryman germinated them and oversaw the entire process. Nirina had a personal arrangement with him, providing access to the market for selling the cocoa trees. "Today, he continues his work as a nurseryman," commented Nirina. "Of the one hundred thousand plants, eighty thousand are under contract with me. These will be released in five or six years because I signed a fifteen-year contract—five years for growth and ten years for amortization."

As we lingered at the nursery, news of Nirina's visit quickly spread. A local farmer soon approached him, eager to talk. Their exchange was brief but animated, with the farmer gesturing toward the rows of cocoa plants. Afterward, Nirina turned to me, his voice thoughtful.

"This farmer wanted to know if I could help him with cocoa plants," Nirina explained. "I told him, 'I don't do that anymore, but you don't need to sign a contract with me. Just focus on quality—buy your plants from here because they're the best, and you'll have no issues.' My goal isn't to tie farmers to contracts. Who knows? Tomorrow, he might connect with a chocolatier searching for a specific origin, opening new opportunities for him."

Nirina's commitment to improving cocoa quality was as personal as it was professional. "It's simple," he said, "when farmers realize that quality brings rewards, they embrace the process." His words carried the weight of experience, underscored by countless conversations with the very farmers who had transformed their livelihoods through this approach. "More farmers are now delivering their cocoa directly to us instead of relying on middlemen who offer lower prices."

He shared a vivid example of the impact this approach has had. "There was a farmer who used to ask for small advances just to make ends meet," he recounted. "I told him, 'You have no idea how much you're going to earn today.' When he received his payment, it was far beyond what he expected. That moment created a ripple effect in his village—he bought a motorbike and became an example of what's possible when value is returned to the producer."

For Nirina, the cocoa project in Brickaville represents more than just an agricultural initiative; it's a cornerstone of his mission to foster development through fairness, quality, and respect for the farmers. "When the prices are right, and the quality is there, everyone benefits. That's how we move forward together," he said firmly.

This approach has yielded significant benefits. Brickaville now contributes to Chocolaterie Robert's second single-provenance dark chocolate bar, the 70 percent cacao "Terroir Brickaville." At the same time, it provides a sustainable and substantial income for local farmers, who are capitalizing on the global demand for fine cocoa from Madagascar. This demand is driven by the island's unique distinction as one of the few places in the world that exclusively produces fine cocoa. Such recognition stems from the careful cultivation and postharvest practices championed by local organizations and chocolatiers.

Nirina acknowledged the challenges faced during transition periods, such as the two-year wait for cocoa trees to mature. "Farmers need to survive in the meantime," he said, gesturing toward the surrounding fields. "That's why intercropping with bananas, lychees, and patchouli is essential. These crops provide temporary income while also improving soil health and biodiversity through agroforestry practices." Once mature, the cocoa trees offer farmers a stable, long-term income, with some trees producing yields for up to fifty years.

He detailed efforts to enhance farmer resilience through technical training and financial incentives. "We've introduced standardized quality control measures, like fermentation and drying protocols, to ensure premium beans fetch significantly higher payments—sometimes more than double the average rate. This motivates farmers to maintain high standards and fosters a culture of excellence within the local cocoa industry."

Additionally, local fermentation centers in Brickaville have reduced dependency on intermediaries, enabling farmers to sell directly and earn fairer prices. These centers play a crucial role in maintaining the distinct quality of Malagasy cocoa by ensuring optimal fermentation and drying conditions. "Farmers who once depended on collective trading now find themselves more empowered," Nirina observed. "Direct sales and consistent quality bonuses have given them a level of financial security they never had before."

As we stepped out of the nursery, bidding farewell to our gracious host, I turned to Nirina, reflecting on Madagascar's well-established reputation as a producer of fine cocoa. "It seems to me," I said, "that the real challenge now is gaining greater recognition for the quality of this cocoa—earning the respect it truly deserves on the global stage."

Nirina nodded. "By encouraging adherence to proper fermentation processes," he said, "we can elevate Madagascar's cocoa to a level that rivals the finest plantation-grown cocoa in the world."

Nirina reflected on the future of Malagasy cocoa with a mix of ambition and realism. "We need to keep moving forward—planting for those who can plant—because this can be something enduring," he said. Although South American chocolates and cacaos could be considered as the best, largely due to their high Criollo content, he remains proud of Madagascar's unique place in the world of cocoa, a direct result of its exceptional aroma and flavor.

"Madagascar has its own identity," he emphasized. "Even if it's not universally considered the very best, it's undoubtedly among the best. More importantly, we have something no one else can replicate—our distinct identity. That's what we need to focus on: embracing and promoting the fact that we are the cocoa of Madagascar, with a character and quality that stand out in every chocolate shop where origins are highlighted."

After leaving the nursery, Nirina shared the thoughtful strategy behind the Brickaville plantation's location near a river. He explained his preference for alluvial soils, which are enriched by nutrient-rich sediments deposited during periodic flooding. This choice reduces the need for artificial fertilizers and underscores how cocoa cultivation can align with sustainable agricultural practices, enhancing both crop health and the surrounding ecosystem.

Nirina elaborated on the intricate agroforestry systems used in cocoa farming. Young cocoa trees, for example, are often intercropped with banana plants, which provide essential shade for the delicate saplings. This practice not only shields the young trees from overexposure to sunlight—particularly critical during their early stages when they require 70 to 80 percent shade—but also creates a favorable microclimate that supports healthy growth. The intercropping of bananas and other tall tree varieties, as practiced in Brickaville, enhances soil health, boosts biodiversity, and contributes to a unique environmental dynamic.

"Cocoa cultivation," Nirina added, "is often linked to reforestation rather than deforestation." Cocoa trees thrive in shaded environments, making them well-suited for agroforestry systems that restore tree cover and create habitats for local wildlife. In regions like Brickaville and the east coast of Madagascar, farmers are now being encouraged to preserve existing trees rather than clear land entirely for cocoa planting. Instead, they selectively remove species that are incompatible with cocoa or deplete soil quality. These practices enhance ecological stability, demonstrating how sustainable cocoa farming can benefit both the land and the farmers who depend on it.

Although we couldn't visit the cocoa plantation in Brickaville due to its remote and challenging location, Nirina assured us that we would not miss the opportunity to explore the expansive plantation owned by La Chocolaterie Robert in the Ambanja region. There, we would witness firsthand the large-scale efforts that have made Ambanja a cornerstone of Madagascar's cocoa legacy.

On our way to Toamasina, Nirina described Chocolaterie Robert's robust quality control system, designed to ensure optimal fermentation and bean consistency. Incoming cocoa beans are rigorously tested for key metrics, such as fermentation quality, humidity levels, and the proportion of purple beans, with cross-sectional sampling used to evaluate their interior characteristics. This meticulous process helps maintain high standards and identifies beans that meet premium quality benchmarks.

In regions like Brickaville, producers are encouraged to follow detailed protocols, with significant financial rewards for delivering exceptional quality—sometimes earning up to 90 percent above the market rate. This system has motivated many farmers to commit to quality improvement. However, challenges persist with beans sourced from smallholders, where inconsistent fermentation practices often lead to variable quality. By contrast, plantation-grown beans, managed under strict fermentation protocols, consistently achieve superior results.

Nirina also highlighted ongoing efforts to improve cocoa genetics through selective breeding, focusing on pods with higher Criollo content. Though strong genetics provide the foundation, he stressed that fermentation and postharvest practices remain critical for achieving the exceptional quality that Madagascar's cocoa is known for.

Madagascar Cocoa Beans

In Madagascar, the terms "plantation beans" and "collected beans" distinguish two postharvest processing methods for cocoa, which directly affect the final quality of the beans.

PLANTATION BEANS

On-site fermentation: Plantations manage the fermentation of beans themselves, ensuring strict control over the process.

Uniform quality: This control allows for consistent quality, which is essential for chocolatiers seeking specific flavor profiles.

COLLECTED BEANS

Fermentation by farmers: Smallholder farmers ferment the beans individually before selling them to collectors or cooperatives.

Quality variability: Fermentation methods may vary, resulting in differences in quality and flavor.

Plantations have complete control over the process, while collected beans depend on the individual practices of farmers.

Plantation beans offer predictable quality and traceability, which are crucial for premium markets.

Collected beans allow many small farmers to participate in the cocoa supply chain but require concerted efforts to standardize practices and improve overall quality.

When we arrived in Toamasina, Nirina was eager for me to experience the city's vibrant Chinese culinary influence. As Madagascar's principal port city, Toamasina has long been shaped by its significant Chinese community, whose roots trace back to the late nineteenth century. Chinese laborers were originally brought to Madagascar to work on major infrastructure projects, most notably the railway linking Antananarivo and Toamasina. Over time, the community flourished, contributing to commerce, culture, and, most notably, the city's food scene. Today, Chinese restaurants are a defining feature of Toamasina's culinary identity, reflecting the seamless integration of Chinese traditions into the local fabric.

Nirina was particularly excited to take me to his favorite spot: Fortuna Restaurant, located at 11 Rue de la Batterie. A well-established eatery serving patrons for more than thirty years, Fortuna is a must-visit for Nirina every time he came to Toamasina. The restaurant is renowned for its Chinese dishes, especially its soups and fish specialties. Nirina had been raving about their famous soup since we left the nursery in Brickaville, building my anticipation.

We started with "Pork Nems," a popular appetizer. Although they were flavorful, they didn't offer anything new to me. The main event, however, was the "Rice Soup with Demi-Lune Dumplings," and it fully lived up to Nirina's enthusiastic praise. The soup was simple yet deeply comforting, with rice grains simmered in a delicate broth that created a porridge-like texture. The highlight was the crescent-shaped dumplings, generously stuffed with shrimp and vegetables, their subtle flavor perfectly complementing the soup's light seasoning. Nirina watched me with a wide smile, clearly delighted that I was enjoying a dish he held so dearly.

Next, we tried "Mine Sao," a stir-fried noodle that was equally memorable. The pork was minced and marinated in a fragrant blend of soy sauce, oyster sauce, sesame oil, garlic, ginger, and a touch of sugar, creating a perfect balance of savory and sweet. The noodles were expertly prepared, capturing the essence of Toamasina's Chinese culinary heritage. Sharing this meal with Nirina, I could see how these dishes reflected not only the blending of cultures but also the pride and warmth of the community that made them their own.

Later that night, we ventured to the vibrant beachfront area, lined with small restaurants and food stalls where locals, expats, and tourists alike gathered. We tasted local shellfish from the scallop family and zebu skewers, known locally as *masikita*. A staple of Madagascar's street food scene, these skewers featured tender cuts of zebu meat marinated in a blend of local spices and grilled over open flames.

After several days of travel—from the vibrant streets of Toamasina to the greenish landscapes of the SAVA region and onward across Madagascar's interior—we found ourselves heading northwest. The journey, with its winding roads and shifting scenery, was a reminder of the island's vastness and diversity. With each mile, I felt a growing sense of anticipation to witness firsthand the large cocoa farm that had drawn us to this part of the island.

In 2015, the Ramanandraibe family, Nirina's family, collaborated with the TAF Products Madagascar to acquire the MAVA Plantation. TAF is a Malagasy company specializing in the production of food products sourced from local ingredients.

The MAVA Plantation encompasses approximately 635 hectares of single-estate cacao farms spread across the upper and lower Sambirano Valley in northwest Madagascar, near Ambanja.

As we approached the plantation, a large concrete sign came into view, proclaiming its identity: "Mava—Madagascar Pure Origin." The straight dirt road stretched ahead, flanked by towering trees whose canopy filtered the sunlight. Beneath them lay rows of cocoa trees, their branches heavy with reddish pods, painting a scene of abundance and meticulous cultivation. The sheer vastness was breathtaking, with the road disappearing into the horizon.

Nirina explained that the plantation spans two thousand acres and produces more than two hundred metric tons of cocoa annually. It was a vast operation; unlike anything I had seen before. The scale was particularly striking, as I recalled visiting a much smaller plantation the year prior with the American chefs. Nestled along the Ankavanana River in the SAVA region, that plantation covered just forty acres—a world apart from the magnitude of what now lay before me.

Despite the difference in scale, the tasks on both plantations were similar. Teams collected pods from the cocoa tree trunks using sharp tools, while others were responsible for the sucker pruning of the cocoa trees. Nirina explained that pod collection took place daily, from 6:00 a.m. to 11:00 a.m., with each worker gathering about four hundred pods.

The process with cacao pods otherwise was similar. Groups of women worked together to process the freshly harvested pods. Vibrant cacao pods, varying in colors of red, yellow, and green, were piled beneath the shade of trees or under a simple open-air shed. With practiced precision, a swing of a machete split each pod open, revealing its hidden treasure.

Inside, rows of seeds—cocoa beans—were encased in a sticky, sweet white pulp. Drawn by curiosity, I plucked a seed or two and tasted them, the pulp still clinging to the surface. To my surprise, the flavors were delightful: slightly acidic yet fragrant, with a tangy, fruity brightness.

The seeds themselves were oval, about the size of almonds, and arranged in tight clusters. Nirina explained their remarkable composition: rich in fat, known as cocoa butter, and brimming with the raw precursors of the chocolate flavors that would later emerge during fermentation and roasting.

Cocoa Bean Fermentation Process in Madagascar

COLLECTION AND PREPARATION

After harvesting, the ripe cocoa pods are opened to extract the beans, which are still coated in their sweet white mucilaginous pulp. These beans are transported to the fermentation site.

PLACEMENT IN WOODEN BOXES

The beans are placed in the first of a series of wooden fermentation boxes, typically constructed to allow airflow and drainage of excess liquid (cocoa "sweatings").

The boxes are lined and covered with banana leaves, which help retain heat and maintain humidity. They provide an optimal microclimate and encourage the growth of natural yeasts and bacteria, crucial for effective fermentation.

THE SIX-DAY FERMENTATION PROCESS

Day 1–2: Yeast Fermentation (Anaerobic Phase): The sugars in the pulp are broken down by yeasts into alcohol and carbon dioxide. This produces heat, raising the temperature inside the box to about 40–45°C (104–113°F). The banana leaves trap heat and moisture, accelerating this phase.

Day 3–4: Lactic Acid Bacteria and Acetic Acid Bacteria (Aerobic Phase): The beans are transferred to the second and third boxes. Here, oxygen exposure activates lactic and acetic acid bacteria. Alcohol is converted to acetic acid, further raising the temperature to about 50°C (122°F). This is when the flavor precursors for chocolate start to develop, as the acids penetrate the beans, killing the embryo and halting germination.

Day 5–6: Oxidation and Drying Readiness: The beans are turned multiple times (using wooden paddles) for even fermentation and aeration. By the sixth day, the fermentation process is complete, and the beans are ready for drying.

Nirina explained that this fermentation process for cocoa varies significantly across regions, influenced by cultural practices, environmental conditions, and postharvest techniques.

"In Madagascar," he noted, "fermentation lasts six days and involves regular turning to ensure even aeration. In Central America, the process can take place in slatted wooden boxes, pits, or even directly on the ground, depending on the scale of production. The duration typically ranges from five to seven days, though some regions extend it to nine days for fine-flavor cocoa. In Indonesia, for contrast, the process is often shortened to just two or three days."

We drove to one of the main fermentation farms on the MAVA property, arriving at a spacious compound with an open concrete courtyard surrounded by structures likely used for processing and storage. The courtyard spanned a significant area, suggesting the facility was equipped for large-scale cacao production.

The fermentation area featured several large, sturdy wooden boxes arranged in tiers. The structure itself was open and airy, with a corrugated metal roof designed to promote airflow during the fermentation process. The wooden boxes, each fitted with lids that could be opened and closed, were labeled with letters and numbers to systematically track fermentation batches.

Outside, drying platforms sat on rails, allowing them to be rolled out into the sun during the day and retracted under shelter to protect the beans from rain.

A woman wearing a straw hat and a vibrant orange and red *lamba*—traditional Malagasy clothing made of lightweight fabric with intricate patterns—was using a wooden rake to evenly spread cacao beans across a large concrete drying platform. Her colorful clothing stood out against the rich brown tones of the cacao beans and the bright concrete surface. The scene captured the meticulous manual labor involved in cacao processing, blending traditional practices with the natural elements of the craft.

Nirina explained that after completing the six-day fermentation process, the cocoa beans are removed from the fermentation boxes and briefly placed on cement drying platforms for no more than half a day. In high-quality cocoa plantations like MAVA's, this short resting period—typically no longer than six hours—prevents excessive acidity from developing in the beans. Immediately afterward, the beans are transferred to sliding tray dryers, where they remain for five to ten days, depending on the weather. During this drying phase, their moisture content is reduced from around 55–60 percent to 6–7 percent, ensuring proper storage and optimal flavor development. The beans are turned or raked regularly, typically every couple of hours, to ensure even drying and to prevent mold growth. The sunny, tropical climate of Madagascar provides ideal conditions for this stage, contributing to the beans' bright and fruity flavor profile.

While tasting the mucilage coating the cocoa seeds, I noticed variations in its color within the opened pods. Most had a white mucilage, while others exhibited subtle pink or purplish tones.

"Is the color linked to the species, Criollo or Trinitario?" I asked.

"Yes," Nirina replied. "It's correct to say that the color of the white mucilage coating the cocoa seeds is somewhat correlated with the species or variety of cocoa. However, it's not solely dependent on the species. Genetic variation, terroir, and environmental conditions also play a role in influencing the color and appearance." He added that the shape and color of the cocoa pods themselves are often more reliable indicators of the specific variety of cocoa, providing valuable clues about the genetic lineage of the trees.

He went on to explain that the white mucilage is more commonly associated with Criollo cocoa beans. Criollo beans themselves often have a pale white to light pink or ivory inside the seed. Trinitario, being a hybrid of Criollo and Forastero, exhibits traits from both parent species. The mucilage in Trinitario beans can range from white to slightly pink or purplish, depending on the genetic dominance of Criollo or Forastero traits. He added that the purplish color seen in some cocoa beans, especially Forastero-dominant ones, is caused by anthocyanin pigments.

Nirina further explained that the Criollo and Trinitario varieties are the most widely cultivated in Madagascar. These varieties are central to the island's reputation for producing some of the world's finest cocoa beans, celebrated for their distinctive and complex flavor profiles.

This legacy of excellence, however, stands in stark contrast to the global cocoa butter industry, where the emphasis has historically been on quantity over quality.

For many years, the standard practice in cocoa butter production was to deodorize the butter, stripping it of its natural aroma and flavor. This approach arose mainly because the raw materials—purple beans or flat beans—were often of lower quality and cheaper to purchase. These beans, characterized by a stronger bitterness, were commonly used in cocoa butter production, making deodorization necessary to make the butter palatable and suitable for various applications. As a result, most chocolatiers disliked white chocolate, as the process eliminated much of its inherent aroma and flavor.

At one point, Chocolaterie Robert in Madagascar invested in a large cocoa press, far exceeding the scale of their regular chocolate production needs. This led to an overproduction of cocoa butter, prompting the company to explore selling the surplus. Unlike many industrial producers, however, they chose not to deodorize their cocoa butter. This decision was a commitment to preserving the natural quality and beneficial properties of the butter, maintaining its distinct aroma and flavor.

Years later, this decision proved to be a pivotal differentiator. When renowned chocolatier Pierre Marcolini visited Madagascar and tasted Chocolaterie Robert's cocoa butter, he was astonished by its distinct, rich flavor—a characteristic absent in most deodorized cocoa butters. This unaltered cocoa butter retained the authentic chocolate aroma and taste, setting it apart in a market where white chocolate is often criticized for its lack of chocolate flavor. The addition of milk and other ingredients typically masks any residual chocolate essence, but Chocolaterie Robert's cocoa butter offered a unique sensory experience.

The decision to preserve the natural flavor of their cocoa butter became a defining feature for Chocolaterie Robert. At industry events like Sirha Lyon, even seasoned professionals were captivated by its unique profile. One anecdote recounts how a chocolatier, after tasting a sample, immediately called over colleagues to experience it themselves. The unadulterated cocoa butter became a key ingredient in Chocolaterie Robert's award-winning white chocolate, celebrated for its exceptional flavor and distinctiveness.

Today, Chocolaterie Robert fully embraced this approach, reversing the trend of deodorization. Their cocoa butter is now pressed from high-quality beans—the same premium beans used in their chocolate production. By focusing on quality ingredients and preserving the butter's natural aroma, they carved out a niche in the global market, showcasing the rich flavors of Madagascar's cocoa and redefining standards in chocolate craftsmanship.

Reflecting on my journey, I recall my first encounter with Madagascar's cacao—a 70 percent Ambanja bar from Dandelion Chocolate in San Francisco during a StarChefs event. It was a sensory awakening to the island's unique flavors. Later, I came across Beyond Good chocolate bars at Whole Foods, produced in Madagascar through a direct-trade approach that supports local farmers. At trade shows, I also tasted Valrhona's renowned Manjari chocolate, a hallmark of Madagascar's beans. These experiences cemented my understanding of why Madagascar's cocoa is globally sought after by artisanal chocolatiers and revered brands like Valrhona. Their use of Madagascar's beans exemplifies the island's legacy as a cornerstone of premium chocolate production.

While my time with Nirina in Madagascar revealed the deeply personal and labor-intensive process of cacao farming, I sought a different perspective—one that connected these remarkable beans to the American consumers. I wanted to understand how brands like Beyond Good balance storytelling about Madagascar's heritage with the expectations of a discerning market. This curiosity led me to connect with Tim McCollum, Beyond Good's co-founder, to explore how their work not only uplifts local farmers but also brings the essence of Madagascar to shelves across America.

Like Nirina, Tim emphasized how Madagascar distinguishes itself on the global stage as a producer of exclusively fine cocoa, a distinction that underscores its unmatched quality and flavor. Cocoa from the island is celebrated for its distinctive profile, marked by vibrant, fruity notes with hints of red berries, citrus, and tropical nuances—a flavor range that enchants both experienced chocolatiers and discerning chocolate lovers.

This unique flavor profile is central to Beyond Good's value proposition and messaging, which always prioritizes flavor and product quality. However, it wasn't always this way. When I spoke with Tim, he reflected on the company's early days. "The first thing we always used to tell people," he admitted, "was that this is made in Africa, and that's why they should like it." He paused thoughtfully before adding, "The mistake early on was—well, that's what was important to me, but it wasn't important to people who just wanted a good chocolate bar."

Over the years, Beyond Good came to recognize the uniqueness of Madagascar's cocoa. Its genetic variety and amazing flavor profile set it apart from any other chocolate on the market. Tim explained how the company initially emphasized its African roots to appeal to conscious consumers but soon realized the importance to lead with quality. "Flavor wins over everyone," he said. "When consumers taste Madagascar cocoa, their eyes light up—they notice the difference instantly. Quality and education go hand in hand, and once people understand the story behind the bean, they're hooked."

Curious about his perspective, I asked Tim how he would describe the cocoa from Madagascar and what makes it different from other chocolate on the market.

To get his point across, Tim explained that 90 to 95 percent of the world's cocoa is considered commodity cocoa. "It's been hybridized over the years," Tim added, "to be more disease and drought tolerant. In that process, it's been dumbed down from a flavor profile point of view. There are three main genetic varieties of cocoa."

For Tim, Forastero is the commodity cocoa. It dominates the global chocolate and the grocery industry. "It's the same cocoa that goes into a Lindt chocolate bar, a Hershey Kiss, a Kit Kat, Nesquik, or Oreo cookies.

It's a very ubiquitous flavor, primarily derived from one variety of cocoa," he explained.

Tim stressed that this wasn't the Earth's original cocoa. In pockets around the world, there are strains of cocoa that remain much closer to the varieties that originally grew in the wild. "What you have in Madagascar is the Earth's original genetic variety, in some cases perfectly intact with no hybridization—which is extremely rare—and it's a different variety altogether," he said. "There's even a strain called Pure Ancient Criollo documented in Madagascar and has never been proven to exist anywhere else in the world."

Tim recounted an experiment conducted over a decade ago in partnership with the USDA. He explained that the test came at a pivotal moment for the craft chocolate movement in the United States. "This was around the time the Fine Chocolate Industry Association was just starting out, and the craft chocolate community really began to grow here," he noted. Back then, there was no established link between cocoa varieties and their flavor profiles—something we often take for granted today. "What we did know," he continued, "was that certain regions produced beans with extraordinary flavors. For example, Madagascar beans always had this incredible flavor profile. And you could find similarly fascinating beans in parts of Ecuador, Peru, and Venezuela. The chocolate made from those beans offered a much richer, more unique experience."

"But here's the thing," he emphasized, "At the time, no one had ever connected those amazing flavors to the genetic variety of the cocoa beans themselves. That link just hadn't been established yet."

While the complex aroma of Criollo and Trinitario beans and the careful craftsmanship of Malagasy farmers were celebrated here, I wondered how these qualities translated to an audience thousands of miles away. In my conversation with Tim, I was eager to explore this connection. How do they convey the unique story of Madagascar's cocoa to American consumers who might not be familiar with its origins? And, perhaps more importantly, how does this origin story resonate in a market that often prioritizes convenience over provenance? These questions lingered as I thought about the role of storytelling in bridging the gap between Madagascar's farms and America's shelves.

"The American consumer is still in the very early stages of understanding single-origin chocolate," he began, drawing a parallel to the coffee industry. "It's probably twenty years behind where coffee is today. Most people now recognize that origin matters, that roasts matter, and that processing methods make a difference when it comes to coffee. But with chocolate, we're just at the beginning of that journey."

He leaned forward, his tone shifting to one of optimism. "The great thing is, when people taste really good chocolate—whether it's ours or from another craft maker—it's a game changer. All it takes is a side-by-side taste test. The moment they try it, their eyes light up, and you can see the realization hit them. They're enlightened, educated, almost instantly. It's incredible to watch."

The transformation he described isn't just about flavor; it's about unlocking a new understanding of what chocolate can be. "And here's the thing," he added, "the price difference isn't huge. It's not like we're talking about doubling the cost. You're going from spending three dollars on bad chocolate to maybe four or five dollars for something truly exceptional. Once people make that leap, there's no going back."

Tim truly believes that consumers will soon embrace chocolate as more than just a sweet treat—as a product with depth, complexity, and a story worth savoring.

Tim McCollum's first encounter with Madagascar traces back to his decision to join the Peace Corps after graduating. Dissatisfied with traditional career paths and inspired by transformative experiences abroad in Mexico and Scotland, Tim remembered a high school exchange program where he wrote letters to students in Togo, facilitated by a Peace Corps volunteer. This planted a seed for his interest in cultural immersion and meaningful work.

Tim was drawn to the idea of living within a community and building deep connections, making the Peace Corps a natural fit. Assigned to Madagascar, he arrived with little knowledge of the island but embraced the experience with curiosity. Immersed in communities facing poverty, he gained a profound perspective on humanity, opportunity, and inequality—an outlook that stayed with him long after his two years of service.

One moment stood out in shaping his understanding of poverty. Tim suggested to neighbors that feeding rice to their chickens could yield larger, healthier birds. But they couldn't spare even a handful—every grain was essential for their own survival. This simple exchange revealed a harsh truth: extreme poverty leaves no room for future planning when daily survival takes precedence. The experience transformed Tim's view, showing how poverty not only deprives resources but also stifles hope and the ability to invest in anything beyond the present.

Over time, Tim's role in the community evolved. Initially seen as an outsider, or *vazaha*, he eventually earned the respect and affection of locals, who began calling him *gasy*—a term meaning Malagasy. This shift underscored the power of connection and mutual respect, leaving him with a lasting sense of shared humanity.

Tim's time in Madagascar ultimately inspired him to view business as a means for meaningful change. This realization led to the co-founding of Beyond Good, a company focused on empowering communities through commerce. His transition from nonprofit work to entrepreneurship reflected his belief that sustainable impact is best achieved through private enterprise.

He and his partner's vision was bold: to create finished products in Madagascar, starting with chocolate bars—a concept virtually unheard of across Africa, where 70 percent of the world's cocoa is produced, yet almost none of its chocolate is manufactured. Determined to challenge the colonial-era norm of exporting raw materials, they sought to prove that high-quality, finished products could be made in the country of origin. It was a steep learning curve, with little initial understanding of the food industry, chocolate manufacturing, or cocoa sourcing, but a strong belief in their mission carried them forward.

Fifteen years later, Beyond Good continues to grow, crafting chocolate in Madagascar and expanding its reach, all while staying true to its founding principles of empowering local communities and redefining what's possible in the global cocoa industry.

Tim and his team set out to manufacture entirely in Madagascar, believing that creating value locally was the best way to support the country's development. By sourcing packaging, manufacturing, and keeping operations on the island, they aimed to foster a more sustainable future for one of the world's poorest nations. Their motivation was straightforward—Madagascar needed more value-added activities to progress.

As the business expanded, an unexpected benefit emerged. Operating directly in Madagascar allowed them to bypass traditional supply chains and source cacao straight from smallholder farmers—an option unavailable to most chocolate companies reliant on global logistics. The conventional model, built around large shipments, excludes small-scale farmers and limits direct connections with manufacturers.

By eliminating intermediaries, Tim's team disrupted this system, paying farmers more and ensuring pricing transparency. This direct-sourcing model became central to their mission, demonstrating that staying close to the source not only improves efficiency but drives real impact for farmers and the cacao industry.

I was eager to learn how Beyond Good affected the life of a farmer. Tim shared a powerful story that underscored the transformative impact of his company on the lives in Madagascar. During a visit to a village near Ambanja, a farmer proudly showed Tim his pen of ducks, calling them "the biggest in the village." This unexpected moment symbolized a shift. The farmer's pride and success with his ducks represented a growing sense of urgency and possibility that hadn't existed before.

Later that same day, a cooperative leader expressed an ambitious vision to grow their partnership into a model for all cocoa farmers in Madagascar. For Tim, who worked in Madagascar for two decades, this level of forward-thinking optimism was unprecedented, especially in such remote areas. Farmers now believed they could achieve something extraordinary, breaking the cycle of static poverty and imagining a brighter future.

These moments reaffirmed Tim's belief that the most meaningful change often lies in fostering optimism and aspiration—qualities rarely found in communities grappling with generational poverty. Whether it was a farmer's fattened ducks or a cocoa cooperative's bold vision, these stories demonstrated his company was making a real impact, not just economically but in shifting mindsets toward what's possible.

What Tim shared echoed Nirina's words about reforestation, offering a hopeful perspective on cocoa farming in Madagascar. While Nirina spoke about the potential for cocoa to restore the landscape, Tim described how Beyond Good's program was helping farmers actively reforest their land. The unique variety of cocoa grown in Madagascar requires a shade canopy to thrive, unlike commodity cocoa, which depends on herbicides and pesticides. This essential need for shade creates a harmonious agroforestry system, with farmers cultivating a three-tiered canopy of trees that not only supports cocoa growth but also resembles a natural rainforest from above.

During a visit to a cocoa farm, Tim realized the cocoa forest resembled a rainforest, prompting research that revealed five lemur species thriving and reproducing there alongside humans. This unexpected discovery added an environmental focus to Beyond Good's mission, leading to regular wildlife assessments and reinforcing cocoa farming as a driver of regeneration and biodiversity in Madagascar.

When I shared with Tim how my trip to Madagascar had been a deeply personal journey—so transformative that it inspired me to write a book—he immediately understood. He recognized the desire to capture the experience in a way that went beyond scrolling through photos on a phone. Madagascar, with its raw beauty and deeply rooted traditions, isn't just a place you visit—it's a place that changes you. Curious about how he might introduce someone else to the island's wonders, I asked him two questions that revealed not only his personal connection to Madagascar but also the values that make the island so extraordinary.

I first asked Tim, "If you could take an American food enthusiast to Madagascar for just one day, where would you take them, and what would you want them to experience?"

Without hesitation, he replied he'd take them to the most remote village on the coast he could find. "I'd head up to Ambanja," he explained, "and then drive along a dirt road until we were maybe fifty kilometers from the nearest town." The journey itself, he implied, was part of the experience—a gradual departure from the modern world. "I'd want them to eat local food, prepared the way people in the countryside have made it for generations. And this might sound strange to a trained chef or someone from the culinary world, but when you go into rural Madagascar, it's like stepping back in time. Serious time travel—five hundred years back, at least. There's no refrigeration and very little has changed in terms of how people cook."

For Tim, the magic lies in the simplicity and purity of the food. "When I eat with farmers," he said, "the amount of flavor that comes from food that's fresh and unprocessed is always stunning. Imagine eating chicken that was running around just an hour earlier, or fish that was caught from the ocean two hours before it's on your plate. It's a meal that's one hundred percent sourced from within a kilometer. One farmer I visit grows his own

rice—everything he serves comes directly from his land. And honestly, the best meals I've ever had in my life were on very remote farms in Madagascar."

The way he described it, these meals weren't just about the food but about an entire way of life. One that connects people to the land, tradition, and a slower, more deliberate rhythm of living.

Then I asked him a second question, one that lingered in the air before he could answer: "If you had one story from Madagascar that every chocolate lover in the world should hear, what would it be?"

Tim paused, clearly wrestling with the weight of the question. "It's hard to pick just one," he admitted. "The journey from the tree, to the farm, to the factory—it's such a rich, layered story. But honestly, more than any single story, I wish every chocolate lover could go there themselves and spend time in Madagascar. You can't understand the country in a week; you'd need to visit at least three or four regions just to grasp how vast and diverse it is."

Then his tone shifted, becoming more reflective. "I wish every chocolate lover could have the chance to harvest a cocoa pod right off the tree, cut it open with a machete, and taste the pulp. That's where the story of chocolate begins—with that pulp, which is sweet and tangy, nothing like the finished product we know. I've always thought of chocolate as the most commonly consumed food in the world that people know nothing about. They don't know the backstory, the supply chain, or what goes into making great chocolate truly great."

Tim's voice grew more passionate as he continued. "To follow the journey of the bean—from the farmer to the factory, all within the same country—would show people how dynamic and complex it all is. It's not just a product; it's the story of the people who grow it, the land it comes from, and the centuries of tradition behind it."

His words lingered, a reminder that the essence of Madagascar's cocoa lies not only in its remarkable flavors but also in the stories of the people who nurture it. For Tim, Madagascar wasn't just a place to visit—it was a place that reveale essential truths about connection, resilience, and the beauty of living in harmony with the land. And for anyone willing to look closer, the island offers a journey far deeper than the taste of chocolate—a journey into the heart of what it means to truly know where your food comes from.

Crispy Chocolate with Citrus and Basil Mousseline

Recipe by Chef Lalaina Ravelomanana (Marais Restaurant in Antananarivo, Madagascar)

Serves 8 people

INGREDIENTS FOR 8 PEOPLE

Chocolate Discs

14 oz. (400 g) dark couverture chocolate (preferably 64–70%)
1½ tsp. (6 g) cocoa butter (optional, for shine and snap)

Citrus Mousseline Cream with Basil

¾ cup + 2 tbsp. (200 g) fresh-squeezed orange juice
Zest of 1 orange
2 tsp. finger lime pearls or lime zest (substitute for *citron caviar*)
¼ cup (50 g) instant pastry cream powder, *poudre à crème.*
(Substitute: 1½ tbsp. cornstarch + 2 tsp. flour + 1 tsp. vanilla pudding mix)
4 large egg yolks (80 g)
½ cup (100 g) granulated sugar
¾ cup (180 g) unsalted butter, cubed and chilled
Fresh basil leaves, chiffonade (to taste)
Crushed roasted cacao nibs, optional for garnish

PREPARATION

For the Chocolate Discs

1. Place 7 ounces of the chopped dark couverture chocolate in a heatproof bowl over a barely simmering water bath (*double boiler*).
2. Stir gently with a rubber spatula until fully melted—smooth and glossy.
3. Remove bowl from the heat.
4. Add the remaining 7 ounces of chopped chocolate and 1½ teaspoon cocoa butter to the melted chocolate.
5. Stir continuously until everything melts completely.

Recipe continues →

TIP: This is a shortcut tempering method using seeding to bring down the temperature and encourage stable crystals.

6. Place a sheet of acetate (guitar sheet) or parchment paper on a flat tray.
7. Pour the tempered chocolate on top and spread it thin and even using an offset spatula. Aim for 1–2 millimeter thickness.
8. Allow the chocolate to crystallize at room temperature (65–70°F / 18–21°C is ideal).

TIP: Don't refrigerate yet—we want partial setting first.

9. As soon as the surface starts to lose its shine but is still soft, use a round cookie cutter (~2¾ inches or 7 centimeters) to gently score circles into the chocolate.

TIP: Press gently, but don't lift the discs yet.

10. Place the tray in the refrigerator for 10–15 minutes until fully hardened.
11. Once firm, carefully peel off the chocolate discs from the sheet.

For the Mousseline

1. Wash the oranges and finger limes (or citron caviar) thoroughly.
2. Zest the orange(s) and squeeze about ¾ cup + 2 tablespoon fresh orange juice into a metal mixing bowl (bain-marie safe).
3. In a separate bowl, whisk together 4 large egg yolks and ½ cup granulated sugar.
4. Whisk until the mixture is pale, thick, and smooth (this is called *blanching*).
5. Add the instant pastry cream powder and whisk the mixture.
6. Place the bowl with the orange juice and zest over a gentle bain-marie (simmering water bath).
7. Pour in the egg yolk mixture, whisking constantly.
8. Cook slowly and gently, whisking until the mixture thickens to a curd-like consistency (approximately 170–175°F if using a thermometer).
9. Remove from heat.
10. While still warm, stir in ¾ cup (1½ sticks) unsalted butter, a few pieces at a time, until fully melted and emulsified.
11. Transfer to a clean bowl and cover the surface directly with plastic wrap (*film à contact*) to prevent a skin from forming.
12. Let cool to room temperature, then refrigerate until cold and slightly firm (at least 2 hours).

13. Once chilled, stir in the finger lime pearls or zest and pulp of 1–2 limes, a handful of finely chopped fresh basil leaves, and a sprinkle of roasted cacao nibs, crushed if desired.
14. Transfer the finished cream into a piping bag fitted with a plain or star tip.
15. Keep chilled until ready to pipe onto your chocolate discs.

PLATING

1. Base Layer: On a flat dessert plate, place one chocolate disc as the base.
2. First Cream Layer: Pipe a large dollop (or rosette) of the chilled citrus mousseline in the center of the disc using a pastry bag.
3. Second Disc: Gently place a second chocolate disc over the cream, pressing lightly to settle it.
4. Second Cream Layer: Pipe another smaller swirl or quenelle of the mousseline on top.
5. Top with Final Disc: Cap with a third chocolate disc, aligned or slightly offset for a modern presentation.
6. Garnish and Serve: Decorate with a few micro basil leaves or young basil sprouts. Add a few pearls or flecks of finger lime pulp (*citron caviar*) for brightness and texture.

CHAPTER 4

Luxury with a Cause

The Ripple Effect of Caviar Farming

Izay mahakoloko manana ny soa.

Those who care for something, even if it's difficult, are the ones who will be rewarded.

—TRADITIONAL MALAGASY SAYING

The first bite was unexpected—Madagascar caviar, nutty and creamy, nestled against a spoonful of crème fraîche, peas, and a whisper of vanilla. It was both daring and delicate, an association of flavors that surprised my palate. We came to the celebrated Marais restaurant that evening for a cocktail dinner celebrating local Malagasy ingredients revisited by two American chefs and Chef Lalaina—it was a convergence of stories, identities, and a new kind of Malagasy luxury.

◀ *Like ink dropped on water, the net pens at Mantasoa Lake float in quiet formation—cultivating caviar in the heart of Madagascar.*

The evening was hosted by Delphyne, Christophe, and Alexander, the visionaries behind Rova Caviar, the Indian Ocean's first caviar house. The two American chefs, Elizabeth Falkner and Michael Gulotta, were invited by Chef Lalaina to reimagine this prized delicacy through their own lenses. Elizabeth's dish was a study in restraint and refinement, her caviar mingling with soft notes of crème fraîche, peas, and vanilla. Michael offered a wilder vision: local oysters sharpened by passion fruit, finished with a briny burst of caviar. Their creations were not merely culinary feats; they were moments of connection, bridging global expertise with Madagascar's distinctive ingredients.

The dinner, held in the heart of Tana, came after a week of discovery: the sun-splashed vanilla fields of SAVA, a visit to Chocolaterie Robert with Nirina, and now, this unexpected meeting of tradition and innovation. But it was here, with a glass in hand and a spoonful of sturgeon pearls on my tongue, that a new question began to take root: What did I really know about caviar?

When Delphyne, Christophe, and Alexander later extended an invitation to visit their sturgeon farm at Lake Mantasoa, it felt like a call I couldn't ignore. Until then, caviar had been a delicacy I admired—but hadn't truly understood. That night at Marais planted a seed of curiosity—one that would pull me back the following year across the ocean, not just to witness the journey from hatchery to lake to table, but to understand the land, the labor, and the legacy behind Madagascar's most luxurious export.

In the dark chill before dawn, Lake Mantasoa was quiet, its surface murmuring stories only early risers like me could hear. The cold enveloped and prickled my skin—a kind of cold that that heightened my awareness. The world was painted in deep blues and muted grays. The moon hung high, casting a faint light over distant houses scattered around the lake. I stood still and embraced the near silence, interrupted only by the gentle lapping of water against the shore.

I waited for my host, Delphyne Dabezies, who soon emerged from the house with a camera crew in tow. That June morning, they were there to film the lake's raw beauty for a promotional project. I joined them on a boat, and we ventured into the lake's dark wilderness. As dawn approached, the

sky and water transformed, shifting from soft blues to pale purples and traces of gold. The first rays of sunlight spread across the water, gradually unveiling the world around us.

In the dim light of early morning, the precise nature of the trees fringing Lake Mantasoa remained a mystery. Their silhouettes, especially those on the hills, appeared as ghostly figures. Slowly, the shoreline revealed its familiar terracotta tone, characteristic of Madagascar's soil. The scent of burning wood was in the air—a sharp reminder of the land's ongoing battle against deforestation. Overhead, three white ibises glided gracefully across the quiet sky, their presence punctuating the stillness.

The lake itself was glassy and serene. In the distance, local fishermen—dark shapes etched against the brightening horizon—casted their nets with practiced precision only years could teach. We slowed the boat, letting them work undisturbed. The rhythmic sound of nets hitting the water echoed the timeless bond between these fishermen and the lake.

As morning unfolded, the colors in the sky and the lake's reflection brightened, heralding the freshness of a new day. Each moment felt like stepping out of a dream. Through the lingering morning mist, massive structures began to take shape in the distance. Emerging from the haze were fifty-three immense net pens, each spanning more than 150 feet across, anchored in a wide arm of the lake. Their scale was breathtaking and stirred questions in my mind: Who designed these? Why were they placed here? And what did their existence mean for those who call Lake Mantasoa home?

The first time I learned about Delphyne's journey, I was struck by the contrast between her past and present. From navigating the bustling streets of Paris to finding her footing along the tranquil shores of Madagascar, manufacturing clothing for the global luxury and haute couture markets. Her story was one of bold reinvention. The sparkle in her eyes hinted at a life shaped by ambition and a willingness to embrace the unknown.

Now, as we glided across the lake under the morning sun, I reflected on the remarkable shift that had brought her and her companions here.

"Did you ever imagine you'd trade textile threads for sturgeon, Delphyne?" I asked.

She chuckled softly. "Not in a million years. But isn't life the most unpredictable of tales?"

Their journey to this lake was a testament to their vision and audacity. It was a story of risk and reward, of carving out something extraordinary in an unexpected place.

In Paris, during their engineering university days, Delphyne met Christophe and Alexandre. Their bond grew stronger through shared dreams, late-night study sessions, and weekend escapades. It was the unforgiving Parisian winters, however, that pushed them to seek warmer horizons and eventually set them on a path to Africa.

"Christophe introduced me to the magic of Africa," Delphyne mused, reminiscing about her days in Guinea Conakry. They had planned to travel the world, never settling for too long. Yet, Madagascar's enigma captivated them so much that it altered the plans. Delphyne dreamed of living no more than two years in each country, moving from one adventure to the next.

However, her deep affection for Madagascar kept her here for thirty years, much to her surprise.

She leaned back, a distant smile curving her lips. "Madagascar wasn't the plan. But it became the heart."

Delphyne and Christophe became husband and wife, and soon, joined by Alexandre, they first ventured into textiles. From a modest beginning to a flourishing business supplying fabrics for luxury children's-wear lines, their company, Akanjo, became synonymous with quality. Delphyne recalled with fondness that Alex brought a fresh energy, and the three working together led Akanjo to greater heights.

Despite success, they craved a new challenge—and a television program about Aquitaine caviar, in France, ignited their curiosity. "We knew nothing about caviar production," Delphyne admitted. "But that is what made it so exciting. We were novices, but sometimes, that's what the story needs."

The textile industry taught them the importance of quality and the art of crafting a compelling narrative around a product. With their deep understanding of the luxury market, they set out to apply those principles to caviar, aiming to create something equally refined and distinctive.

The transition was not without its challenges. She remembered Alexandre traveling endlessly, searching for the perfect spot. She laughed and said, "He'd call, desolate one day, euphoric the next." But finally, near the river flowing from Lake Mantasoa, they discovered their goldmine. The untapped lake, with its pristine waters and a bottom rich in ferruginous laterite, would be the setting for their next story.

Their conversation naturally turned to the ambitious caviar venture, and I found myself curious about what drove them to such an undertaking. Why caviar in Madagascar? And why such a strong emphasis on corporate responsibility?

Delphyne's answer reflected a conviction rooted in her guiding principle: "quality over quantity." It was a mantra carried from their textile days into this new chapter of their lives. Their mission, however, extended far beyond the product itself. For them, corporate responsibility wasn't a buzzword but a fundamental part of their purpose. They viewed their caviar venture as a chance to make a meaningful impact—elevating Madagascar on the global stage while honoring the environment and its people.

Delphyne and her team understood their position as guests in this land, embracing a philosophy of respect and reciprocity. Madagascar had given them so much, and they felt a duty to give back. For them, sustainability was not just a strategy but a moral imperative. The caviar venture was more than a business; it was a love letter to the island, a way of showcasing its potential and challenging preconceived narratives about it.

Profit, of course, was essential—Delphyne readily acknowledged that—but it wasn't the sole focus. To her, a true legacy was built on respect. Their vision was to position Madagascar as a source of exceptional products while preserving the land and its people for future generations.

It wasn't an easy journey. Launching a business while juggling the demands of raising a newborn tested their resilience. Delphyne recalled late nights filled with doubts and the looming shadow of failure. Yet, it was Alexandre's unwavering optimism that kept them grounded. More than a business partner, Alexandre became family—the godfather to their child and a steady source of hope during the most challenging moments.

Despite the hiccups, their passion saw them through. Today, Acipenser (the name of the sturgeon farm) stands as a testament to their tenacity, producing the brand Rova Caviar.

The founding of a successful pisciculture (fish farming) company, Acipenser, mirrored their textile ethos: unwavering quality, service, and a commitment to social responsibility.

As our conversation neared its end, Delphyne pointed out from textiles to caviar, their journey has been unexpected. "But then, isn't that the beauty of it?" she concluded. "To chart unknown territories and find your own narrative?"

Acipenser has become the second sturgeon farm in the southern hemisphere (the first one was created in Uruguay). From crafting dreams in textiles to producing eleven tons of caviar each year, their journey embodies true entrepreneurial spirit.

"You seem deeply connected to this land," I remarked, eager to uncover the roots of her relationship with Madagascar.

Delphyne paused, her gaze distant as if sifting through memories. "You know, our initial plan was to keep moving—one country, then the next. But this place...." She smiled, her voice softening, "It wrapped itself around my heart. It's a blend of African and Asian cultures, a mosaic that's both intriguing and endearing."

Her words carried a deep affection for the island, but I couldn't ignore its challenges. "But Madagascar also has its struggles," I said carefully, mindful of its reputation.

She nodded, her expression thoughtful. "Yes, and it breaks my heart. But where some see poverty and despair, I see potential. There's so much this country has to offer, so much untapped promise." Her voice carried the weight of both determination and hope.

For Delphyne, her vision extended beyond her immediate work. She spoke passionately about transforming Lake Mantasoa into "the lungs of Madagascar," a symbol of renewal and sustainability. As we parted after that first conversation, her parting words lingered with me, resonating with her sense of purpose: "*Faire rêver* Madagascar!" or, "Dream Madagascar!"

The day before, I left Tana, the capital, trading its chaotic energy for the serene embrace of Lake Mantasoa. The road unfurled like a ribbon, leading me eastward through landscapes that shifted dramatically with every mile. RN2, a vital artery in Madagascar, connects the capital with the port city of Toamasina, and its path seemed to mirror the island's diversity.

As we ventured further, the highlands gradually softened into rolling hills, their slopes blanketed with dense patches of forest. The road began to twist and wind, tracing the contours of the land's evolving topography. The descent toward Lake Mantasoa spanned more than seven thousand feet, a long and winding journey through towering mountains that offered breathtaking views at every turn.

Pockets of red soil stood out vividly against the verdant rice fields, a striking contrast that drew my eye again and again. Despite the road's rough patches and the occasional jarring pothole, the drive held its own rugged charm, a reminder of Madagascar's untamed beauty.

Lake Mantasoa, with a span of five thousand acres, stood as a testament to time. The dam and the artificial lake dated back to the mid-1800s.

It was created by Jean Laborde (a French adventurer and early industrialist in Madagascar who worked for Queen Ranavalona I) to build an industrial complex, long gone today. The lake was more than a vast body of water. It was a maze of arms stretching amidst forests and hills. This pristine environment remained untouched by factories or farms. It was a rare Eden, unspoiled in today's world.

Within this true green setting lies the Acipenser farm, occupying three hundred acres between two sites: The "Lake Site," with a mesh of fifty-three mighty structures for adult sturgeons, a testament to man's venture into aquaculture in an almost sacred spot; and the "Earth Site," with the ten pools for the young sturgeons. This corner of the world, untouched by the grinding gears of industry, offers a pristine backdrop for this adventure. And it's the lake's laterite bed that sets it apart. This iron-rich Madagascar soil, a sentinel against the unwanted growth of algae or geosmin (a naturally occurring compound that has an earthy and musty taste and odor), ensures the lake's treasures—its fish and caviar—remain unsullied by any earthy taint. Here, thanks to Madagascar's soil, there are no bad off notes in the taste of the fish, or the caviar.

Delphyne and I stood at the edge of the pool, watching young Belugas rise to the surface as they were fed. She spoke of the sturgeons with reverence, describing their unique life cycles. Some species, she explained, take as long as twenty years to produce caviar—a striking testament to nature's patience. These extraordinary fish, she added, can live for fifty to one hundred years, grow up to ten feet long, and weigh more than one metric ton.

As we walked around the pools, Delphyne shared how sturgeons have existed for 250 million years, surviving epochs that wiped out countless other species. Yet, their survival in modern times has been fraught with challenges. Industrialization and the construction of hydroelectric dams decimated their wild populations. "Wild sturgeons," she said, "can now only be found in Eastern Europe—in the Black Sea, the Caspian Sea, and a handful of other places."

Caviar and Sturgeons

Sturgeons are ancient fish, with fossils dating back approximately 174 to 201 million years, indicating their resilience through significant geological events.

These remarkable creatures can live up to sixty years, with some species like the lake sturgeon reaching lengths of more than six feet and weights exceeding two hundred pounds.

Historically, sturgeons inhabited various regions, including the Black Sea, Caspian Sea, and parts of North America. However, due to overfishing and habitat loss, their populations have significantly declined, leading to their current status as critically endangered.

Notably, sturgeons have a delayed sexual maturity, with some species taking up to twenty years to produce roe, reflecting their slow reproductive cycles.

The decline in wild sturgeon populations has led to a rise in aquaculture. China has become a leading producer, exporting over 3,700 tons of caviar and related products, valued at approximately $127.86 million.

In the United States, the Atlantic sturgeon is found along the east coast, from southern Canada to northern Florida. They spend most of their adult life in the ocean, migrating into coastal estuaries and rivers to spawn in spring and fall.

Traditionally, caviar production was dominated by the Caspian and Black Seas, with countries like Russia and Iran harvesting roe from species such as Beluga, Ossetra, and Sevruga sturgeons. At its peak, these regions provided substantial quantities of wild caviar annually. However, due to overfishing and habitat degradation, there has been a significant decline in wild sturgeon populations, leading to increased aquaculture efforts worldwide.

In recent years, the global caviar market has seen significant growth, with the market size valued at approximately $0.73 billion in 2023 and expected to reach $1.66 billion by 2032.

This growth is driven by increasing consumer interest in gourmet foods and the expansion of aquaculture production to meet global demand.

Her tone shifted as she spoke of Acipenser's bold endeavor to bring Madagascar into the world of caviar production. "We weren't just battling the stereotype of Madagascar," she said, her voice firm with pride. "We were stepping into one of the most competitive industries globally." The company's efforts felt monumental, yet Delphyne spoke with the confidence of someone who understood the stakes—and the potential.

"How do you distinguish yourself and carve a niche in a market teeming with relentless competition?" I asked.

"It starts with our unique environment," she explained. "We've already discussed how the laterite soil creates clean, pure flavors in our caviar. But beyond that, our climate is extraordinary. In winter, the water stays at a steady warmth of fifteen degrees Celsius (fifty-nine Fahrenheit), and in summer, it doesn't rise above twenty-five degrees (seventy-seven Fahrenheit). This consistency ensures optimal growth for our sturgeons."

She commented on how the mild climate of Madagascar provides a significant advantage over the extreme winters and hot summers of the northern hemisphere, where sturgeons either hibernate or experience stunted growth. "Here, their growth is uninterrupted, and over an eight-year cycle, we've reduced the time needed to raise sturgeons by almost two years. That was an incredible discovery for us."

Even more remarkable was their practice of multiple maturations. "Unlike traditional methods," Delphyne continued, "we allow the sturgeon to produce caviar two, three, even four times before harvesting. That characteristic is what's earning Madagascar's caviar its reputation for excellence."

This commitment to quality extends to their global competition. "Of the more than seven hundred sturgeon farms worldwide, only two are in the southern hemisphere—ours in Madagascar and one in Uruguay. Interestingly, we share a similar climate, which is crucial for high-quality production." Both farms produce around nine metric tons of caviar annually, though Delphyne's team has ambitious plans to reach eleven tons. Despite this growth, they remain dedicated to excellence. "We don't harvest all our sturgeons at once. Instead, we prioritize sustainable practices to ensure every batch meets the highest standards."

Curious about how they started with Baeri and Ossetra species, I probed further. "Why the Siberian sturgeon?"

Delphyne said, "It was a practical choice—these sturgeons are easier to raise and well-suited to aquaculture. The idea came from a television report on Aquitaine caviar that Christophe saw. It detailed how Siberian sturgeons were reintroduced in France, blending tradition with modern aquaculture. That vision inspired us to embark on this journey, combining respect for heritage with innovation to create something truly unique."

Their journey into caviar production began, fittingly, with fertilized eggs—the foundation of any sturgeon farm. I recalled my visit to the farm in October, where Delphyne explained the origins of their stock. They started with eggs sourced from France, later expanding to include shipments from Siberia. These careful beginnings laid the groundwork for what would become a remarkable endeavor.

A pivotal moment came four years into their farming efforts. Seeking to establish credibility, they invited major caviar brands to visit their setup in Madagascar. Among them, only one accepted: a century-old caviar house with roots in France and a strong presence in the US.

"They said, 'Yes, we'll come to visit your farm,'" Delphyne recalled, her pride evident. The representatives from this caviar house made the journey, their visit marking the start of a collaboration that would shape the future of Madagascar's caviar industry. Their insights weren't just technical—they were transformative. The savvy professional emphasized the importance of genetics, a key factor in determining the quality of caviar.

Acting on their advice, Delphyne connected with a leading expert, Dr. Mikhail Chebanov, from Krasnodar. Renowned for his work in sturgeon preservation, Chebanov's mission is to protect these ancient fish from extinction, focusing on reproduction rather than commercial meat or caviar production. His expertise and access to top-quality genetic stock played a vital role in strengthening the foundation of Madagascar's sturgeon population.

The conversation shifted to the challenges of producing caviar in today's world. Delphyne spoke about the 1998 restriction on wild sturgeon harvesting, enforced by the Convention on International Trade in Endangered

Species (CITES). These regulations protecting endangered species even extended to the circulation of fertilized eggs and required special certification similar to that for crocodiles, snakes, or elephants. The layers of complexity in this industry became evident as I listened.

One detail stood out. "Krasnodar—that's the name of one of your caviar brands, isn't it?" I asked, intrigued.

Delphyne smiled. "Not quite—it's Kasnodar, with an 'S.' We dropped the 'R.' It is a tribute to Dr. Chebanov's hometown, who supplied us with exceptional fertilized eggs. It's our way of honoring his role in our journey."

She went on to explain the farm's three distribution channels. The largest is white-label production, with much of it destined for the United States, which has embraced Madagascar's caviar. "Currently, sixty percent of our volume is exported there," she noted. The second channel is their Kasnodar brand, introduced to private clients and high-end restaurants and establishments. The brand is also present at trendy events such as Taste of Paris, La Folie Douce, and certain Nikki Beach events, where food lovers and chefs explore new culinary treasures. Finally, there is Rova Caviar, the pinnacle of their production. Representing just 2–3 percent of the farm's output, Rova Caviar is reserved for starred chefs, palaces, and discerning private clientele. "The difference lies in the maturation," Delphyne explained. "Rova Caviar comes from fish that undergo longer cycles, producing larger, firmer eggs, and from rare species like Persicus and Nudiventris—both incredibly unique."

Delphyne reminisced about a journey filled with challenges and success as she recounted their pursuit of the elusive Persicus sturgeon. Years ago, a century-old caviar house, their mentor on the market, presented them with a tantalizing challenge: integrate this rare species into their farm, and they'd buy the entire production. What followed was a worldwide hunt—reaching out to Iran, Russia, Italy, and beyond—met with repeated denials. Yet their determination paid off as the quest led them back to Dr. Chebanov.

Each year, the team ordered fertilized eggs from Russia, carefully orchestrating their journey through Moscow and Paris to Madagascar. But the process was fraught with setbacks. Delphyne laughed as she described one

incident at Roissy Airport, where a spilled bottle of Evian led authorities to discard an entire shipment. "We joked about our eggs getting a taste of luxury," she said, though the loss was no laughing matter.

The eggs required constant movement, mimicking the gentle rocking of water, to prevent suffocation—a detail they learned through painful trial and error.

Amid these challenges, Dr. Chebanov, who had been moved by their dedication, surprised them with a small pouch, discreetly marked with a black cross. Inside were fertilized Persicus eggs—an offering born of their shared passion for sturgeons. When the hatchlings emerged, the team celebrated, knowing they had something extraordinary. It was a promise of future prosperity. But their joy was tempered when they realized a critical oversight: the CITES certificate accompanying the shipment listed the wrong species.

Quickly, they photographed the sturgeons and sent the images to CITES Geneva. The response was both alarming and thrilling: "It's like discovering a herd of baby dinosaurs," the officials said. The Persicus, once thought extinct, was now reclassified as endangered, thanks to their stock.

Delphyne reflected on the mysterious origins of those eggs. "Perhaps Dr. Chebanov, as a scientist repopulating the wild seas, had rare permission to extract them. We'll never know for sure.

"The following year," she continued, "Dr. Chebanov, seeing our deep passion for sturgeons, sent us a list of about twenty names of sturgeons in Latin, names unreadable and incomprehensible to us."

They forwarded the list to their mentor, who guided them to the Nudiventris species—a sturgeon tied to the Shipova caviar of his childhood. This connection carried profound weight. For Delphyne and Alex, the stakes extended far beyond the caviar itself; it was about the future of Acipenser. If their Madagascar-grown caviar failed to meet their mentor's exacting memories, it could force a dramatic shift in their business plans.

In 2022, traveling to Paris with their carefully prepared sample, they presented it in the elegant tasting room of one of the most emblematic caviar houses.

"We held our breath as the founder tasted it," Delphyne recalled. Time seemed to stretch as he savored the glossy pearls. Finally, he declared, "It's exceptional. This is the Shipova of my childhood." Their joy was palpable.

Delphyne and Alex planned to allow three to four more maturation cycles—three to four more years—for their Nudiventris sturgeons to produce even larger eggs of superior quality. But that December, an urgent request came: Their client wanted the caviar in time for Christmas. The team worked tirelessly, scanning their stock and producing a modest three kilograms of the prized roe. The caviar debuted under the Rova Caviar banner, a testament to Delphyne and Alex's relentless pursuit of excellence.

"Each grain tells a story," Delphyne said as I prepared to leave. "It's not just about the taste—it's about the terroir and the journey behind it."

The day ended at the farm, where I experienced the intricate journey of caviar production. By the water ponds, I stood with Delphyne, watching as the elusive Beluga sturgeons glided beneath the surface, their tails occasionally breaking the water in elegant arcs. A photographer struggled to capture their movement, spending hours in search of the perfect shot.

Delphyne pointed to the lush greenery behind the ponds. "These plants aren't just decorative," she explained. They are part of a natural filtration system, absorbing ammonia and nitrates from the water. This sustainable practice ensures that the water returned to the river is clean—a testament to the farm's environmental responsibility and their dedication to quality.

As we approached the lab, a truck rumbled past, carrying six-year-old sturgeons destined for caviar production. Divers gently transferred the fish into chilled pools beneath the facility. I looked into the opening where the sturgeons were introduced and saw a lineup of several narrow and lengthy pools. Delphyne explained that the frigid waters calmed them in preparation for the next steps.

Inside the lab, we adhered to strict sterilization protocols before entering the cold, sterile environment. We gowned up, meaning that we wore sterile white uniforms, had to sanitize our hands, slipped gloves over them, wore sterile white boots. Only then were we permitted inside. We first approached the cold pools, home to the sturgeons being conditioned. One unfortunate creature had already been chosen and dispatched before our arrival.

A worker carefully sliced open a sturgeon, revealing a gleaming trove of silver-grey eggs. At 2.2 kilograms, this treasure would soon become caviar. The eggs were washed, salted, and refined, then packed into pristine one-kilogram containers.

In the final stage of the day, Georges, the production manager and caviar taster, guided me through my first tasting. Freshly prepared caviar shimmered on the spoon, its flavor bursting with complex notes—hazelnut, potato, and other descriptors that told a story of taste and texture. The burst of flavor, the silkiness—it was a culmination of my first day at the farm.

As I walked past the water ponds, now quiet after the photographers left, my path led me to Christophe's office for a panel discussion with some of Acipenser's employees. The building stood ahead, its sleek black facade perched on sturdy stilts, rising like a sentinel overlooking the pond and the surrounding landscape. The late afternoon sun cast long shadows, highlighting the clean lines of its container-like structure. Light played across the wide windows, reflecting fragments of the outside world while concealing the mysteries within.

Just before entering, something unexpected caught my eye—a vintage airplane wing, seemingly from the early twentieth century, affixed to the building's side. Its French registration, marked by the letter "F," hinted at its origins. The wing felt like a bold artistic statement, a testament to Christophe's creative spirit and his reverence for history.

Inside, the office revealed itself slowly, as though unveiling layers of Christophe's personality. "You'll find a bit of everything here," Delphyne said, gesturing around the room. The dark wood floors and walls were a backdrop for eclectic art and artifacts, each carrying its own story. Floor-to-ceiling windows flooded the space with natural light, creating a seamless connection with the outdoors.

The room was a curated selection of Christophe's passions: framed artwork arranged in a gallery-like display, white shelves holding an eclectic mix—from geological samples to tribal masks—hinting at his curiosity for both the natural world and cultural heritage. Vintage items like an old camera and classic typewriter sat comfortably alongside practical elements, such as a water cooler and storage crates. It was a space that balanced historical nostalgia with modern functionality.

Though my interactions with Christophe during my trips to Madagascar had been brief, standing in his office gave me a deeper sense of who he was. This room reflected a mind attuned to art, history, and culture, yet grounded in the practicalities of life and a pragmatic sense of organization. It was a place of quiet complexity, where the beauty of the past met the demands of the present.

As I stepped into the room, I was met by four individuals: William, Say, Manda, and Georges. Their stories, I would soon discover, mirrored the quiet revolution happening here at Acipenser—where sturgeon farming had taken root against all odds.

I turned first to William, whose soft demeanor belied his deep connection to the sea. "I'm from Tuléar," he began. For the Vezo people, one of the first ethnic groups of Madagascar, the ocean was not just a way of life; it was in their blood. These people of the sea make up a community of traditional, semi-nomadic fishermen and are great connoisseurs of the region's marine ecosystem. They live in villages scattered along the Mozambique Channel, on both sides of the Tropic of Capricorn, between the cities of Morondava and Tuléar.

Originally, William came to Acipenser to visit his brother, a diver on the farm, and stayed when a vacancy opened for a security guard. But his dream was waiting in the water.

"I always wanted to dive," William shared, his voice lifting with quiet pride. "When the opportunity came to join as a diver, I applied immediately. Being Vezo, we're attuned to the sea, and here, I'm finally doing what I've always wanted."

William's first dive among the sturgeons had been daunting—three hundred fish, some weighing more than two hundred pounds, gliding like prehistoric shadows through the water. “At first, I was a bit scared,” he admitted with a chuckle. “But now, I know them. I care for them.”

Say, sitting nearby, picked up the thread of conversation. She also was from Tuléar. Where William arrived through family ties, her journey began with a scholarly visit to Acipenser during her aquaculture studies. “The place called to me,” she said simply. She applied for a job, and what began as an assistant role quickly grew into something more. Today, Say is the deputy director of the site, overseeing the fish from hatchery to grow-out stage.

“Finding work here that matched my studies was rare,” she explained. “But beyond that, producing caviar in Madagascar—caviar made in Africa—that fills me with pride. It’s something no one expected to see here.”

Manda’s story had its own serendipity. A native of Antananarivo, he stumbled upon Acipenser during soccer matches with the former mayor’s team. “I noticed fishponds where there used to be rice fields,” he said, his curiosity piqued. As a student specializing in animal husbandry (the science of breeding and caring for farm animals), he arranged an internship to study feed production—work that would eventually become his expertise, and he is spearheading the process today.

“In the beginning, there was no feed manufacturing plant. I was part of testing and developing feeds locally, instead of importing them,” Manda shared. His ascent through the company mirrored Acipenser’s growth: meticulous, determined, and focused on creating the ideal environment for the fish. “My parents are proud,” he said quietly. “In their eyes, I hold a position of great responsibility, perhaps the most significant in our family, with a key position in a large company.”

At this point, Georges, the production manager, joined in. He explained he was born and brought up in Anjiro, a small farming, rural community in eastern Madagascar, located ten miles from Acipenser. He started at the sturgeon farm five years earlier as a general worker. “Back then, I didn’t even know what caviar was,” he said. “The first time I saw it, I thought of tilapia eggs!”

Through training, Georges had become one of the farm’s official caviar tasters, developing his palate to recognize the subtle, nutty, and creamy notes that define great caviar. “The funny part was learning to identify hazelnut flavors," he recalled. "We don't have hazelnuts here, so someone brought cookies with hazelnut cream from the gas station. That was my reference!"

Georges took pride in representing Madagascar's growing place in the world of caviar. "This is more than just a job. It's something I never imagined doing—something that shows what's possible."

As the conversation deepened, Say reflected on the changes Acipenser brought to the surrounding community. "Eight years ago, there were no permanent jobs here. Now I see families with stability and new opportunities. Ambatolaona, the nearby village, has a gas station now—a sign of growth."

Her words carried the weight of hope, a theme that seemed to bind all their stories together. Manda nodded in agreement. "This project is audacious. You won't find another sturgeon farm like this anywhere in Africa or the Indian Ocean. That's what makes it special."

As I listened, I couldn't help but feel the pull of their collective pride—a pride born not just from producing world-class caviar, but from redefining what was possible for Madagascar. In William's dives, in Say's leadership, in Manda's innovation, and in Georges' quiet expertise, I saw the beating heart of Acipenser: a story of ambition, perseverance, and a deep respect for the work they do.

The room felt warm and humid, and I absentmindedly wiped away a bead of sweat trickling down my forehead. Across from me, the others smiled knowingly—it was fall for them, and the air was already turning cooler. Say, with a playful grin, reminisced about William's first experience of autumn and winter at the farm.

"It was cold for William," she said, laughing. "Coming from Tuléar, where it's always hot, he'd often say, 'It's like winter in Tuléar here!'"

Over the years, Say had accumulated countless memories at Acipenser, but one in particular stood out—one that revealed both her dedication and the emotional connection she had forged with her work.

"It was in 2021," she recalled softly, "when I was tasked with sexing the Belugas from the 2016 batch. Handling fish that size—it's a massive responsibility." Working with her team, they carefully completed the process, ensuring everything was done properly.

“But then came the hard part,” she continued, her expression shifting. “I had to eliminate the males.” She shook her head slightly, as if reliving the moment. “It was painful for me. I’d watched them hatch; I called them ‘my babies.’ Letting them go was tougher than I expected.”

Before I left them, Georges shared a final thought that seemed to sum it all up. “When chefs visit, they ask to taste the feed we produce for the sturgeons,” he said, laughing. “It’s natural, so they’re curious. I always ask them, ‘Would you like it if you were a sturgeon?’”

It was a fitting note to end on—a mix of humor, pride, and the ingenuity that has made Acipenser’s caviar a story worth telling.

As the conversation ended, I left Christophe’s office with the stories of these four people in mind. William, the diver from Tuléar, a tale of simple aspirations, and brotherhood. The tale of Manda seeing in Acipenser a haven where nature, nurture, and human endeavors coalesced into a narrative of hope, growth, and sustainable future. I admired Georges, the humble man, whose journey was a testament to what one can achieve with determination and a love for what they do. Say's fervor for her work was infectious, leaving me with a profound sense of admiration for the young woman who embraced the essence of Mantasoa and made it her own.

Walking through the peaceful grounds of Acipenser, past the sturgeon ponds, the signs of the company's essence materialized—not as a mere fish farm, but as a living hub of community, sustainability, and cultural exchange.

Tucked into the quiet landscape near Lake Mantasoa, Acipenser stood as a model of thoughtful enterprise. For employees like William, Say, and Manda, work transcended the confines of labor—it was a life integrated with opportunities, camaraderie, and pride. Here, the company provided not just jobs, but homes, fostering a close-knit community, bound by common aspirations and a shared love for aquaculture. The accommodations, complete with recreational spaces like ping-pong tables, *pétanque terrains*, and communal areas, embodied a vision of work-life balance uncommon in such rural settings. Laughter and friendly competition filled the air as we walked toward the company restaurant, a place where employees gathered over shared meals, blurring the boundaries of hierarchy and tradition. That afternoon, Achille, the administrative director, proudly introduced a dish of local fried fish accompanied by *achard de légumes*—pickled vegetables—prepared using his own recipe, taught to the chef earlier that day. This simple act symbolized Acipenser's spirit: a leadership rooted in approachability, collaboration, and cultural exchange.

Yet, the impact of Acipenser ripples far beyond its gates. Georges, a long-standing member of the team, described the transformation of the surrounding villages—once marked by economic stagnation and limited opportunities. Acipenser's environmental initiatives, including waste management programs, have brought both awareness and action to the community. With new waste bins in place and education efforts under way, residents learned to sort their trash properly and developed a deeper respect for their land. The company's influence sparked economic activity, with local farmers selling vegetables, fruits, and livestock to meet growing demand. A once-quiet village had come alive with life and trade, providing a steady income for many households. What was once a hard-to-find steady job became a reality for many, bringing happiness to countless lives.

These testimonials provided insight into the professional opportunities and community impact generated by Acipenser in Madagascar, in addition to showing how local individuals can grow professionally and personally in a specialized field like aquaculture and caviar production.

Such change did not come without vision. The founders—Delphyne, Christophe, and Alex—saw their enterprise not only as purveyors of one of the world's most luxurious delicacies but as champions of social responsibility. They were acutely aware of Madagascar's paradox: the decadence of caviar set against the harsh reality of poverty. This awareness pushed them to act. Collaborating with Père Pedro, a revered humanitarian who built entire villages from Antananarivo's landfills, Acipenser began supplying fresh fish to children at the Akamasoa schools and orphanages.

Père Pedro transformed Antananarivo's vast landfills into thriving villages, offering shelter, education, and dignity to thousands living in extreme poverty. Over decades, his tireless work with the Akamasoa association brought homes, schools, and opportunity to tens of thousands of Malagasy families. Inspired by his mission, Delphyne, Christophe, and Alex joined forces with Père Pedro in 2016, focusing on improving sanitation at the Andralanitra landfill and supporting job creation in Akamasoa. Their collaboration culminated in the creation of the Vita Malagasy training school, where women from the most vulnerable backgrounds could learn valuable textile skills to build a better future.

Delphyne described her first visit to Père Pedro's community—children bright-eyed but malnourished, lacking critical nutrients like protein. Initially designed for caviar production, the sturgeon farm found a deeper purpose: fulfilling urgent nutritional needs. Every week, Acipenser distributed hundreds of kilograms of fish, offering essential sustenance to more than eleven thousand children. "The portions may seem small, just a medallion of fish," Delphyne reflected, "but each bite matters. It's a step toward healthier lives."

This commitment extended to ensuring access to affordable protein for Madagascar's poorest communities. Fish flesh from the sturgeon—often overlooked in favor of caviar—became a beacon of hope. "We want it to be the cheapest animal protein on the market," Delphyne explained, "cheaper than pork, chicken, or zebu, so that even the most vulnerable families can afford to eat well."

The introduction of sturgeon to Madagascar was not without challenges. Locals initially viewed the strange fish with suspicion, but over time, the fear gave way to pride. Today, Malagasy caviar is a symbol of national identity. It is celebrated by the nation's president, mentioned in his addresses, and embraced by the communities surrounding Acipenser as their own.

Most striking, however, was the human impact. Once an area devoid of industry, the company now employs more than three hundred people, directly supporting hundreds of families. A ripple effect of growth followed—small businesses, grocers, and farmers have emerged to serve this new economy. "It has truly developed an entire local ecosystem," Delphyne shared. "You see it in the stalls of fresh vegetables, the chickens, the fruits. Acipenser is more than a farm; it is a lifeline."

In this balance of luxury and necessity, Acipenser demonstrates how food, at its core, can transcend its purpose—nourishing not just the body but the community and culture from which it springs. It is a story of how one farm, dedicated to caviar, found itself feeding souls and sparking hope in one of the world's most overlooked corners.

Returning to the Marais restaurant in Antananarivo, I felt a sense of anticipation. Nestled on Rue Ravoninahitriniarivo—a street named after a historical figure from the court of Madagascar's last two queens—Marais is as intriguing as its location. Though I had visited before, this time I sought to explore deeper layers of its culinary world.

Ascending to the fifth floor of the Atrium building, I was greeted by the restaurant's modern, airy space. In its open kitchen, visible behind sleek glass walls, Lalaina's brigade was moving swiftly. Behind a secret bookshelf door leading to the bar, I found Chef Lalaina engaged in conversation with two bartenders. A warm smile spread across his face as he turned to greet me.

"Welcome to the bar of Marais," he said, pride gleaming in his voice. "I'm glad I can share this special place with you."

Lalaina is more than a chef; he is a storyteller through food, weaving Madagascar's natural bounty into dishes that celebrate its unique flavors.

As the executive chef of Marais, he also serves as the ambassador for Rova Caviar. His creations elevate this delicacy, using ingredients like vodka jelly, maize cream, and smoked cocoa to craft a repertoire of more than three hundred recipes.

Yet his approach to caviar is anything but overwhelming. "Caviar demands simplicity," he explained during our conversation. "Its luxury lies in its natural qualities, which need to shine, not be overshadowed." This philosophy drives his creations, from sweet potato *cromesquis* (a crispy sweet potato ball with a tender center, breaded and fried) paired with coconut *espuma* to mango and pineapple in a caviar crust. For Lalaina, caviar should not be hidden under too much complexity. "A beautiful quenelle of caviar, just placed next to the prepared product, will enhance your dish," he concluded.

Flipping through the menu, I paused at the Grilled Octopus with Rova Caviar. Lalaina shared the inspiration behind this dish: "It's a tribute to Madagascar's exotic fragrances, combining the iodine of the sea with the smoky aftertaste of octopus, which reminds me of the sturgeons at the Acipenser farm, where the caviar is sourced."

As we discussed his many creations, Lalaina highlighted two standout recipes. The first, *Œuf dans l'Œuf*, or "Egg within an Egg," layers an egg emulsion with Baeri caviar, apple, and delicate condiments. The second is a nest of glass eels cradling a heart of Rova Caviar, complemented by a light vanilla bisque. Each dish underscores his commitment to balancing flavors while respecting the integrity of his ingredients.

"Caviar's texture is unique," he said, describing the thought process behind his recipes. "It's about finding complements that enhance, not overpower. Starchy vegetables, cream, or fish are ideal—they support, rather than dominate, the caviar's profile." He also noted the importance of avoiding acidic products or cooking caviar, which could compromise its delicate nature.

Lalaina's deep involvement with Rova Caviar extends beyond the kitchen. "I've participated in tastings with almost every major caviar brand," he shared. "Rova Caviar stands out for its subtlety. It's less salty, delicate, and tells a story of sustainability and care."

One particularly unexpected pairing caught my attention: roasted bone marrow with caviar. Lalaina described how the buttery, neutral flavor of the marrow complements the caviar's saltiness, creating a perfect balance. He also mentioned experimenting with caviar in desserts, combining it with chocolate or exotic fruit chips for surprising results.

As our conversation drew to a close, Lalaina reflected on his mission to introduce caviar to new audiences. "A gentle introduction can make all the difference," he said. "Brioche pan-fried in sweet butter with a hint of caviar, or an asparagus carpaccio with citrus oil and creamy caviar sauce—these simple dishes allow the quality of the caviar to speak for itself."

I left Marais that afternoon with more than just an appreciation for caviar. Lalaina's passion for his craft, his reverence for ingredients, and his desire to honor Madagascar's culinary heritage transformed my understanding of what it means to truly elevate flavors.

Madagascar—better known for its rainforests, vanilla, and spices—seemed an unlikely setting for one of the world's most coveted delicacies. Yet, here I saw firsthand how a careful balance of nature, science, and human effort was redefining the industry.

What struck me most was not just the quality of the caviar but the people behind it. Nearly 80 percent of the workforce comes from the nearby villages, many of whom have never imagined a livelihood tied to luxury food production.

As chefs and consumers increasingly demand transparency in sourcing, Madagascar's caviar presents an alternative that goes beyond taste. It's a reminder that food is never just about what is on the plate—it's about the regions it comes from, the communities it sustains, and the choices we make when we decide what to serve.

Candied Potatoes, Light Bergamot Mousse, Smoked Crème Fraîche and Caviar

Recipe by Chef Christophe Chiavola (Relais & Châteaux le Prieuré Baumanière, France)

Serves 4 people

INGREDIENTS

Confit Potatoes

8 small potatoes (Ratte or fingerling potatoes)
7 oz (14 tbsp.) clarified butter (200 g) (or mild olive oil as an alternative)
2 garlic cloves, crushed
1 sprig fresh thyme

Bergamot Potato Mousse

3 large starchy potatoes (such as Yukon Gold)
¾ cup (6.8 fl. oz.) heavy cream (200 ml.)
1 gelatin sheet
A few drops of bergamot extract or essential oil (highly concentrated, use sparingly)
Salt, white pepper, to taste

Smoked Crème Fraîche

5.3 oz. (⅔ cup) crème fraîche (150 g)
Smoker or smoking dome (with wood chips, such as beech or applewood)

TO ASSEMBLE AND SERVE

1.4 oz. (40 g) Madagascar Rova Caviar (Ossetra, Beluga, or another variety of choice)
Edible flowers (optional)
Vegetable charcoal powder (optional, for visual effect)

PREPARATION

For the Confit Potatoes

1. Wash the potatoes thoroughly, leaving the skins on.
2. In a saucepan, gently heat the clarified butter over low heat with the crushed garlic cloves and thyme.
3. Submerge the potatoes fully in the butter and cook over very low heat for 40 to 50 minutes, until tender.
4. Carefully drain the potatoes and keep warm.

For the Bergamot Potato Mousse

1. Peel and cut the potatoes into pieces. Boil them in salted water until they are very tender.
2. Drain and mash into a fine purée.
3. Heat the heavy cream, then add the gelatin (previously softened in cold water) and mix well.
4. Incorporate the warm cream into the mashed potatoes and blend until smooth.
5. Add salt and pepper, and a few drops of bergamot extract (taste and adjust as needed).
6. Transfer to a siphon, charge with a gas cartridge, and keep warm in a bain-marie at 149°F (65°C).

For the Smoked Crème Fraîche

1. Place the crème fraîche in a shallow dish.
2. Use a smoker or a smoking dome to smoke the crème fraîche for 5 minutes.
3. Refrigerate, then lightly whip for a soft, airy texture.

PLATING

1. Place two confit potatoes on each plate.
2. Add a quenelle or small dollop of smoked crème fraîche beside them.
3. Top the quenelle with a generous portion of caviar.
4. Pipe a delicate rosette or light, airy mound of bergamot potato mousse using the siphon.
5. Garnish with edible flowers and optionally a light dusting of vegetable charcoal powder for a striking visual contrast.
6. Serve immediately to enjoy the contrasting textures and flavors. This dish is ideal as a starter or light course, accompanied by a glass of brut champagne.

Grilled Octopus with Reduced Cooking Juice and Rova Caviar

Recipe by Chef Lalaina Ravelomanana (Marais Restaurant in Antananarivo, Madagascar)

Serves 4 people

INGREDIENTS

11 oz. (¾ lb.) octopus (320 g)
2 large onions
2 carrots
1 leek stalk
8½ cups (68 fl. oz. or 2 L) of water
1 small glass (4 fl. oz. or ½ cup) white wine
Salt, pepper, mixed peppercorns, to taste
1 bouquet garni (assortment of herbs)
2.8 oz. (5½ tbsp.) butter (80 g)
Juice of ½ lemon
1 tbsp. olive oil
1 tbsp. honey
1 tbsp. soy sauce
1.75 oz. (1.8 oz. tin) Madagascar Rova Caviar (50 g)
Edible marigold flowers for decoration

PREPARATION

1. Thoroughly wash the octopus in cold water.
2. Peel the onions and carrots, and clean the leek, and cut into large pieces.
3. In a pot with the 2 liters of water, pour the white wine and add the peppercorns, vegetables, and bouquet garni. Bring to a boil, then add the octopus and cook for about 1 hour.
4. Test the tenderness with the tip of a knife, which should easily penetrate. Drain and cut into large pieces. Reserve the cooking broth.
5. Reduce the cooking broth by three-quarters. Whisk in butter. Season to taste with salt and pepper. Add a drizzle of lemon juice.
6. Mix the olive oil, honey, and soy sauce. Brush this mixture over the octopus pieces and grill. Set aside.
7. On a flat plate, pour a few drizzles of the reduced octopus juice. Then place the grilled octopus on top. Arrange two quenelles of caviar on the side. Decorate with marigold petals and the mixed peppercorns.

Broiled Oysters with Passionfruit, Pink Peppercorn, and Rova Caviar

Recipe from Chef Michael Gulotta (Chef-Owner at Mopho, Maypop, and Tana, New Orleans, Louisiana)

INGREDIENTS

16 oz. (2 cups) unsalted butter, room temperature (450 g)
½ oz. (1 tbsp.) garlic, minced (15 g)
½ oz. (1 tbsp.) ginger, grated (15 g)
4.2 oz. (½ cup) fresh passionfruit pulp (120 g)
¼ tsp. pink peppercorn, crushed (1 g)
1.4 oz. (2 tbsp.) sea salt (40 g)
7.7 oz. (2½ cups) panko breadcrumbs (220 g)
40 chives, thinly sliced
2 dozen oysters
4 oz. (110 g) Rova Caviar

PREPARATION

1. Whip the butter in a stand mixer with the whisk attachment for 3 minutes.
2. Add in the garlic, ginger, passionfruit, pink peppercorn, and salt, and blend for another minute.
3. Using a spatula, fold in the breadcrumbs and chives, and let sit for at least an hour.
4. Shuck the oysters, keeping as much liquor inside as possible.
5. Top each oyster with a large spoonful of the butter and breadcrumb mixture and spread it out to cover the oyster.
6. Place the oysters, a few at a time, in the broiler, and roast until the breadcrumbs are golden brown on top.
7. While the oysters are still bubbling, top them with a dollop of Rova Caviar and serve immediately.

ROVA CAVIAR
MALOSSOL CAVIAR MADAGASCAR

CHAPTER 5

Echoes from the Canopy

Voatsiperifery Pepper and Other Spices

Ny hanitra no mahatonga ny olona hifampiantso.

The aroma is what brings people together.

—TRADITIONAL MALAGASY SAYING

In the afternoon, the gentle hum of Delphyne's boat set the tone for my journey from their lakeside house back to the sturgeon farm. I looked forward to meeting my guides, Nirina and Chef Farah, for the rest of my journey across the island.

That day was driven with purpose: deepening my exploration of Madagascar's vibrant culinary culture and meeting with Olivier Ramaherison, an expert on voatsiperifery, the wild pepper unique to the island. How could a single spice encapsulate the essence of an entire culture? I was about to find out.

◄ *Madagascar's eastern forest offers its spice—the voatsiperifery pepper.*

I first met Olivier at a gala with the American chefs at the Marais restaurant more than a year ago, when the President of Symrise Madagascar introduced us. Olivier's passion for Madagascar's wild pepper immediately captured my attention. We stayed in touch, and he later gave me a rendezvous point tucked away somewhere along the serpentine RN2. The exact location was an enigma, though, and as I pondered over the coordinates, Nirina called him to confirm the rendezvous point. We eventually stopped our vehicle on a curve in the middle of nowhere, amid the buzzing tableau of road life—trucks rumbling by, children playing, and chickens scattering in their wake.

Olivier waived at us across the road.

While crossing the RN2, our senses razor-sharp, I saw the most amazing and terrifying scene. A group of young children daringly navigating downhill in soapbox cars amidst the traffic. A blend of amazement and concern gripped me.

On the other side of the road, a cluster of modest wooden structures marked the entrance to a path that led to a wooden bridge suspended over a large river—the gateway to our adventure. Dangling precariously over the river, the wooden bridge's planks weathered and creaked under my feet with each step. I could not stop thinking that it was put together by the same hands that had once built the children's soapbox cars for racing down hills of the RN2!

Walking uphill, surrounded by towering butterfly ginger bushes, our trail intersected with an old railroad track, a relic of times past when trains connected the city of Toamasina, on the Indian Ocean, to the capital. Now these old tracks were our guide westward. With each step on the stony track, we delved deeper into the heart of the land, and we soon forgot about the traffic noise coming from the RN2.

Olivier led us into this hidden world. Suddenly, he paused and pointed toward a hill that rose majestically to our right. A carefully crafted trail wound its way upward, its edges lined with neatly arranged wooden branches. Slender sticks were strategically embedded into the soil, securing the foundation and providing stable footing among the trees. At the entrance to this path stood a sign that read "*PROPRIÉTÉ PRIVÉE—TSY AZO IDIRANA*,"

(PRIVATE PROPERTY—NOT ACCESSIBLE). This was our destination for the day, a place steeped in mystery. Nestled within boundaries of private land, it was an uncharted territory where the wild *voatsiperifery* pepper thrived—a secret kept from the eyes of outsiders, but one that would now be unveiled to us.

Beyond the sign marking the threshold of this private domain—land Olivier inherited from his father—we stepped into a forest alive with signs of sustainable care. Evidence of selective logging, clearing underbrush, and the planting of young coffee plants revealed a thoughtful balance between use and preservation. Our trek was accompanied by the soft whispers of leaves swaying in the gentle breeze that coursed through the hill's vegetation. Olivier explained that he had started planting a unique coffee variety called "café Bourbon *Pointu*," renowned for its excellent flavor profile, often described as smoother and fruitier than other coffee types. Originating on the island of Réunion, which was formerly called Bourbon Island, hence its name. Bourbon Pointu coffee is a variety of the Arabica species, obtained from a mutation of the Arabica cultivar, known for its superior quality compared to most other types of coffee.

He pointed at the leaves of a vine and said, "Here's the *tsiperifery* pepper. As you can see, it's a treasure hidden in plain sight, growing wild on these hills."

I wiped the sweat from my forehead, panting, and welcomed the pause in our climb up the hill, grateful for the chance to catch my breath. "A hidden treasure that's making me work for it!" I remarked with a wry smile.

Nirina laughed. "Don't worry, we won't let the wild pepper outpace you!"

Chef Farah joined in, grinning. "At least we know you won't run off with all the pepper, huh?" The group chuckled. We all took a moment to rest, looking at the wild pepper vines.

"In the heart of Madagascar's rainforests and in this heat, these vines thrive, clinging to the tall trees," said Olivier. "It's here that *voatsiperifery* grows far from the reach of casual gatherers."

My gaze was immediately drawn to the youthful exuberance of a *voatsiperifery* with a few catkin-like structures present—the early stages of the plant's fruit development. I reached out and curled my fingers around a branch, feeling the subtle, burgeoning weight of green berries clustered together like small pearls.

Olivier shared how the *tsiperifery* epitomizes Madagascar's rich biodiversity, a spice deeply woven into local cuisine and tradition. He explained that its name came from the Malagasy word "*voa*," which means "fruit," and "*tsiperifery*."

"For centuries, the Malagasy people have been familiar with this pepper. Its use, however, was largely confined to traditional cuisine and medicine," said Olivier.

Olivier called our attention to a series of young fruit on the vine, future grains of wild pepper. He emphasized its interesting path, from being virtually unknown to recently recognized globally. "It was only a decade ago when western chefs started to catch on to its unique flavors."

Voatsiperifery's ascent to culinary fame owes much to its distinct taste profile—a harmonious blend of woody, floral, and citrus notes, much softer yet more aromatic than the common black pepper. French Chef Anne-Sophie Pic mentioned that "*voatsiperifery* pepper is one of the strong markers" of her cooking. On her Facebook page, she specified that she likes "to associate the Malagasy wild pepper with pigeon, scallops, but also with fruit tarts such as rhubarb or grapefruit. It is also very interesting to enhance the taste of chocolate or combine it with tonka beans (seeds from the *cumaru* tree) in infused butter."

As we climbed higher, the foliage began to open, and we were granted glimpses of the world below. The canopy broke away in places to reveal a patchwork of hills rolling into the distance, covered in the mist that concealed the horizon. There was a sense of isolation, of being in a world apart, where time held a different meaning.

Olivier explained that harvesting *voatsiperifery* was an art, traditionally carried out by local dwellers of Madagascar's remote rainforests. The vines grew along tall trees and spread their leaves on the top of the canopy. The berries, growing on vines as high as sixty-five feet, demanded a laborious and skillful collection process. He elaborated that the way they were harvested was a double-edged sword, as foragers often cut both the vines and the trees to reach the peppers and were, therefore, damaging the ecosystem.

Listening to Olivier describe the delicate balance of traditional foraging, I found myself pondering on the broader implications. *How do we honor tradition while protecting the future?* I wondered, realizing the weight of responsibility that comes with culinary heritage.

"It's a delicate balance, isn't it?" added Nirina. "Preserving nature while benefiting from its gifts."

The hike continued, with occasional banter and laughter.

Olivier mentioned that the journey of *voatsiperifery* from these remote forests to the global market is complex and multifaceted. It involves a series of transactions, beginning with the forest dwellers who pick the berries. These pickers sell their harvest to local intermediaries or "*collecteurs*," who play a pivotal role in bridging the fruits from the remote forests to global markets. These intermediaries navigate through a network of relationships, transportation issues, and market dynamics to bring this rare spice to the global stage. However, this journey is not without its challenges. The supply chain of *voatsiperifery* has been scrutinized for its lack of traceability and uneven benefit distribution. Intermediaries often face accusations of speculative practices and quality degradation. Despite these problems, they are essential in maintaining the flow of this spice from the depths of Madagascar to international cuisines.

Finally, as we reached the summit, we paused—our breath stolen not only by the climb but also by the awe-inspiring panorama that unfolded before us. "Look at this view! Worth every step and every drop of sweat, right Emmanuel?" said Farah with a smile.

The land stretched out before us, a verdant sea that met the sky in a distant, hazy line. We stood there, amidst the towering silhouette of the trees, and for a moment, the world below seemed inconsequential. I could not help but think that in places like this, we were just fleeting visitors. It was a humbling thought; the vastness of Madagascar's highlands was a reminder of the transient yet profound impact of our journey.

As we made our way down into the confined valley, the path zigzagged ahead, making its way to the bottom. On the opposite hill, we saw a section with terraced gardens carved out like giant steps. There, nestled on the valley floor, was a cozy little house. Right beside it was something quite unexpected—a rustic outdoor distillation setup with an old, weathered alembic distillation apparatus. It felt like stumbling upon a hidden treasure of traditional craftsmanship. The alembic, worn yet still standing, seemed to carry the stories of countless extractions, standing as a testament to traditional methods of distilling plant, blossom, or spice extracts. The open-air structure rested on a solid stone foundation with a concrete platform, its weathered appearance and signs of extensive use suggesting it had been an integral part of the landscape for generations.

Nearby, a wooden picnic table with peeling blue paint offered a quaint spot for gathering. It was here, in this tranquil setting, that we later sat down to enjoy a meal. A perfect spot to chat with Olivier and get a feel for the place. It was these kinds of simple, cool discoveries that made exploring new places so awesome. This setting was not just a workplace but also a slice of life in this remote little valley, where traditional distillation practice was likely intertwined with the daily lives of the people here, connecting them to the land and their heritage.

A rustic shed stood adjacent to the alembic structure. Its simple construction, evident in the tin roof and walls that had been discolored by smoke and time, was a hint at its frequent use for cooking or processing. A thick plume of smoke drifted from the shed, suggesting a fire burning within. To the left of the doorway, a meticulously stacked pile of firewood was evidence of the traditional methods that are still revered here, relying on natural resources to cook and process food.

Olivier held a colander filled with *voatsiperifery* peppercorns. Their colors ranged from green to brownish red, indicating different stages of ripeness. Each peppercorn had the characteristic little tail. The remaining drops of water on top of the fruits indicated that the peppercorns had been recently washed. He spoke with a mix of pride and concern. He described how these berries were more than mere spices—they embodied the legacy of the land. Their journey beyond Madagascar began in 2004, when a spice trader first introduced them to the world. Since then, they have become prized in the realm of fine dining, celebrated for their unique flavor. Yet, this success came at a cost. The rising global demand was putting increasing pressure on local supplies, a strain that threatened the very sustainability of the berries. It was a bittersweet story.

Earlier that morning, he had walked toward his plants of wild pepper with the anticipation of harvest. With care, he selected only the ripest fruit, delicately plucking the stems heavy with the fragrant, spicy orbs. The *voatsiperifery* would infuse its exotic flavor into the dishes we would soon cook together—Poulet et Steak au Poivre *voatsiperifery* (Chicken and Steak with Wild Pepper Sauce). This was a classic French recipe, Steak au Poivre Vert, but with a twist, showcasing the unique wild pepper from Madagascar.

Chef Farah and I entered the shed, volunteering to start working on the roasted potatoes. Inside, we found three traditional open-fire cooking setups, each made of stone. The design featured three holes on the bottom to arrange the firewood, allowing for good airflow, and three holes at the top to hold trays, pots, and pans over the flames.

With a playful nudge, she passed me a basket of potatoes. "These are yours," she said with a wink. "I'll brave the onions. After all, a chef's tears are the secret ingredient to culinary magic."

We placed a large metallic tray over the fireplace, where the flames eagerly licked its underside and the onions started sizzling in butter. When the onions became translucent and their edges caramelized to a golden brown, we added the potatoes. Despite our recent acquaintance, a comfortable rapport was beginning to form between Chef Farah and me, fostered by the shared task and the cozy warmth of the shed.

Nirina was leaning casually against the shed's wooden door. I turned to him, a smile playing on his lips. "You're not joining the cooking?"

Nirina shrugged with a grin. "My talents lie elsewhere. I'll stick to appreciating the results."

We left Farah to the potatoes and joined Olivier, who already started pouring some local rum in assorted glasses. While tasting the rum, I checked my recording equipment, and Olivier started preparing the Poulet et Steak au Poivre, using the wild pepper freshly harvested from his land. I couldn't wait for the moment I would finally taste green *voatsiperifery* for the first time.

Over the amber glow of the charcoal, Olivier masterfully sizzled the peppercorns in butter, giving the sauce a smoky depth. The high heat made

the butter bubble vigorously, coaxing the peppercorns to release their fragrant oils—an essential step to infuse the sauce with their distinctive flavor. With a deft hand, he flambéed the peppercorns in rum, the flames dancing in the pan, eliciting a chorus of impressed murmurs from the audience. This technique not only added a subtle, caramelized rum flavor but also burned off the alcohol, leaving only its essence to meld with the butter and pepper. Once the flames subsided, he poured in the cream, transforming the contents into a rich, velvety sauce speckled with the green and orange hues of the roasted and flambéed peppercorns.

As I watched Olivier masterfully sizzle the peppercorns, my thoughts drifted to the rich history of Steak au Poivre Vert. This quintessential French recipe, a culinary legacy of Auguste Escoffier, had been popularized by renowned chefs and introduced to American tables in the '60s by Julia Child. Yet here I was, in a secluded valley in Madagascar, witnessing a dish with such storied origins being prepared over an open flame with the simplest of tools. It was a profound testament to the far-reaching influence of French cuisine—a gastronomic bridge that connects continents and cultures. This moment was more than a culinary experience; it was a vivid reminder of how recipes transcend borders, evolve, and adapt. The Steak au Poivre Vert, rooted in French gastronomy, had found a new expression here, in the heart of Madagascar, reminding me that food is a universal language, endlessly adaptable and unifying.

Finally, the moment of truth arrived. Farah joined with the golden potatoes, their edges crisped to perfection. "Emmanuel, look at these beauties," she said with a grin. "Golden and crispy—just like you promised they'd be!"

We gathered around the picnic table, surrounded by the lush greenery of the secluded valley. The table was laden with our creations: the Chicken and Steak with Wild Pepper Sauce, generously coated in Olivier's exquisite sauce, accompanied by the golden, crispy roasted potatoes and tender green beans wrapped in a thin layer of crispy ham. The main dish was both spicy and smooth, with complex layers of flavors that celebrate the unique exotic flavor from the *voatsiperifery* pepper.

As we took our first bites, a collective roar of approval filled the space. The sauce was a revelation, spicy and smooth, with layers of flavor that celebrated the *voatsiperifery's* unique character. Olivier explained how, in culinary traditions, the fresh berries were often blended with fiery chilies to add a piquant twist to local dishes.

In a more somber tone, he spoke of the challenges facing the *voatsiperifery* due to its growing popularity. "With its export to markets across Europe, the United States, and Japan, we're facing a real dilemma," he explained.

Farah, with a thoughtful expression, asked, "But that's a good thing, right? Bringing attention to a local product?"

Olivier sighed. "In theory, yes. The pressure to harvest is immense, and it's affecting the sustainability of the species. With the development of these export markets, stocks are declining, and exporters face challenges obtaining sufficient quality and quantity. Our rural communities have become dependent on *voatsiperifery* as a vital income source, especially during lean periods. The situation risks worsening without adequate safeguards."

As Olivier turned his gaze toward the terraced gardens on his land, he spoke of the challenges and the ongoing efforts to secure the future of *voatsiperifery*. Ensuring the pepper's sustainability, he explained, requires a comprehensive approach. Research is being conducted to better understand its cultivation, strategic plans are being developed, and the involvement of the local community is central to every effort. These initiatives, though still in their early stages, are beginning to bear fruit. Steps are being taken to protect the delicate plants while ensuring that those who nurture them reap tangible benefits. It is a delicate balancing act, but one driven by a shared vision: to preserve the pepper not just as a resource, but as a symbol of the community's resilience and unity.

Voatsiperifery Pepper

Plant Characteristics: Voatsiperifery is a climbing vine from the Piperaceae family. It grows wild in the tropical rainforests of Madagascar, straight up the trunk of trees, to heights of up to sixty-five feet.

Environment: This pepper thrives in humid, shaded conditions at altitudes ranging from one hundred feet to 6,600 feet. The soil must be rich in organic matter, with Madagascar's climate providing the ideal combination of rainfall and temperature.

Fruits: The berries are small and oval with distinctive "tails," and their flavor profile is intensely aromatic, combining woody, citrus, and floral notes.

Challenging Harvest: The voatsiperifery pepper is wild-harvested by hand, and its location in the rainforest canopy makes it extremely labor intensive. Harvesters must often climb trees to reach the pepper vines, which is dangerous and requires great skill.

Seasonality: There are two seasons for voatsiperifery: May to July for the short season, and October to February for the long season. The berries are picked when ripe, showing shades of red, orange, or black, depending on the stage of maturity.

Sorting: Once collected, the fresh berries are sorted to remove unripe or damaged fruits. This ensures the highest quality for further processing.

Processing for Fresh Use: There is no fresh export for these rare berries. For those seeking to experience the unique flavor of fresh peppercorns, the berries are sometimes preserved in brine to maintain their texture. However, it is worth noting that this method can alter the peppercorns' delicate natural aroma.

Drying for Dried Peppercorns: Voatsiperifery pepper is also known as "Red Pepper." The berries are dried in the shade to retain as many red berries as possible—this is known as the dry method. In the past, some exporters scalded the berries before drying them, which caused many of the aromas to be lost in the water and resulted in uniformly black berries. Today, most producers use the dry method, as it preserves more of the pepper's natural aromas and highlights the distinctive red berries.

Final Cleaning: Once dried, the peppercorns are cleaned again to remove any impurities.

Rising with an air of purpose, Olivier's smile was a blend of pride and hope. "Come with me," he said. "I'll give you a peek into our world here and our efforts to safeguard the future of Madagascar's wild pepper."

Olivier led us to the terraced gardens, and to my dismay, we faced yet another ascent. This time, the incline was notably steeper, challenging me with each step. As we climbed, Olivier shared his vision with us. He spoke passionately about revitalizing the forest, aiming to conserve the remnants of the primary forest. He emphasized that *tsiperifery*, a symbol of Malagasy culture, held untapped potential as a product yet to be fully recognized by the world.

Determined to cultivate *tsiperifery*, he embarked on a journey of discovery. He delved into research, scouring the internet and consulting experts, only to find that no one had attempted to farm *tsiperifery* before. Undeterred, they studied existing *piper nigrum* plantations around the world, gleaning insights to guide their project. After about a year of rigorous trials and experiments, they achieved what many deemed impossible. They successfully propagated *tsiperifery*, a plant once thought to be unyielding to cultivation, proving the skeptics wrong and marking a significant milestone in their quest to preserve and promote this unique aspect of their heritage.

"What can you tell us specifically about this hybrid you've developed?" I inquired, eager to learn more.

Olivier quickly corrected me. "Actually, it's not a hybrid. It's a specific part of the *tsiperifery* vine that we propagate." His clarification sparked my interest, stirring memories of my college days filled with biology classes and evenings spent watching TV shows about the fascinating world of plants. My interest deepened as he delved into the vine's anatomy. "The part of the vine that naturally clings to trees is known as 'orthotropic,'" he explained, his voice reflecting a mix of expertise and enthusiasm. "In contrast, the horizontal branches that bear fruit are called 'plagiotropic.'" He continued, his eyes lighting up with passion, "It's from these plagiotropic branches that we take cuttings. Remarkably, these cuttings allow us to harvest seeds in just six months." His explanation, detailed yet accessible, opened a window into the intricate world of *tiperifery* cultivation, revealing the meticulous care and scientific understanding driving their innovative agricultural practices.

They discovered that the prostrate stems of the *tsiperifery* vine sprawled across the ground, rooting themselves and sprouting new plants—much like the way strawberry plants propagate. Over time, these stems were destined to blanket the entire surface of the terraces. "Our plan is to let them naturally expand and cover the area," Olivier shared, his eyes reflecting a vision of the future. "We envision the hills of terraces, one day, being completely enveloped in *tsiperifery*."

I closed my eyes for a moment, letting myself be transported into this future. In my mind's eye, I descended the hills, visualizing them draped in a lush tapestry of green, interwoven with earthy shades of brownish red.

Olivier brought me back to the present. "It'll take at least another three years before the plants we've set down begin to produce substantial yields. And to diversify, we've also entered the *tsiperifery* essential oil market, offering a novel ingredient to the world of perfumery." His words painted a picture of innovation and adaptability in the face of growing market pressures.

Olivier's journey to preserve and cultivate *tsiperifery* had reached a remarkable milestone: proving that the pepper could be successfully propagated. It was a breakthrough that underscored the possibility of sustaining this precious spice. Yet, Olivier acknowledged that the next challenge loomed large, scaling up cultivation while maintaining consistently high yields. Looking ahead, Olivier was resolute in his plans. Over the next three years, he intended to expand the terraces and planting areas on his land. This growth was vital, not only to preserve the legacy of the pepper but also to meet the rising demand from perfumers, whose interest in *tsiperifery* was steadily growing. The task was ambitious, but Olivier's determination and clear vision offered a hopeful outlook for the pepper's continued prominence and sustainability cultivation.

Wondering about the culinary world's reception of *tsiperifery*, I posed another question: "Do you know if any other chefs, particularly those from France, have taken an interest in *tsiperifery*?"

He nodded confidently. "I believe the majority of French chefs are now familiar with and appreciate *tsiperifery*. It's gradually becoming a luxury spice on French household tables."

"The next step is to introduce it to the American market," I added, "and expose Americans to the outstanding flavor of the *tsiperifery* pepper!"

His enthusiasm for spreading the recognition of *tsiperifery* was infectious, painting a future where this unique spice held a prominent place in kitchens around the world.

As we retraced our steps to the car, left waiting at the edge of the RN2, my mind lingered on the spice's potential impact. Once seated, I quickly scribbled in my notebook: *today's conversation with Olivier had left me pondering deeply on the future of Tsiperifery in global cuisine. Could its journey from Madagascar to the finest tables in Paris be just the beginning?*

After that day spent with Olivier, my appetite for exploring Madagascar's spice heritage had only grown. A handful of days later, our journey took us back to Antalaha to explore another facet of Madagascar's rich spice landscape.

Returning to the Ocean Momo Hotel along the Indian Ocean coast felt like stepping back into a familiar world. Overlooking the ocean, the hotel and its bungalows offered a peaceful setting, complemented by the soothing sound of the sea breeze. Yet, something was different from my previous visit. The wreckage of the old cargo ship was nearly gone—dismantled, with its rusted sheets of metal likely repurposed by the locals.

Nirina, Farah, and I decided to have lunch at the *kiosque* a traditional, thatched, hut-like structure. It provided a shaded spot where we could enjoy our meal, accompanied by the gentle ocean breeze around us. The *kiosque*, supported by wooden pillars, allowed us to feel connected to the surrounding landscape and the rhythmic sounds of the ocean. The area around was neatly maintained, with a variety of plants bordering a low stone wall that separated the garden from the beach. A simple concrete bench offered a place to sit and enjoy the view. Beyond the low wall, the beach stretched out, inviting a walk or a moment of reflection by the water's edge. Along the wall, colorful red, pink, and white poinsettias added touches of color to the serene atmosphere. This tranquil tableau embodied the essence of a coastal retreat along the Indian Ocean, where the natural beauty and peaceful environment provided a perfect backdrop for a relaxing lunch.

For lunch, we opted for grilled fish seasoned with local spices, served with white rice and a side of green papaya and carrot *achard*—pickled, shredded vegetables. The dish showcased the fresh seafood and produce of the area. The fish was caught that morning by a local fisherman and brought to the restaurant with other seafood. The food was simple but elegantly plated.

After the meal, I strolled on the beach, letting the rhythm of the waves align with my thoughts. Upon returning, I found Nirina lounging on the low wall; his posture spoke of calm relaxation.

The afternoon's calm was interrupted by the hum of a motorcycle. Gabriel Styvio, a young Malagasy man dressed casually in a t-shirt and shorts, arrived with an air of surprise. Our meeting had been hastily arranged by Nirina through local connections, a spontaneous opportunity sparked by my growing curiosity about Madagascar's spice cultivation—nutmeg, cloves, pink peppercorn, and more. Nirina and I settled comfortably with Gabriel at a sturdy table on the sheltered deck of the restaurant. He introduced himself in gentle tones that carried the warmth of his homeland. "My name is Gabriel Steev," he began. "I am native to Antalaha." At first, Gabriel seemed shy and reserved, but he carried a quiet confidence that suggested he had much more to share.

Gabriel said he was involved in the local production of cloves, vanilla, and coffee. His family had been in this business for generations, making it a family enterprise deeply rooted in the local culture and economy.

I asked Gabriel and Nirina to delve into the history of cloves on the Red Island. Cloves are primarily grown in tropical regions. The leading countries in clove production include Indonesia, Madagascar, Tanzania, and a few others. Indonesia has been the largest producer for many years, contributing a significant portion of the world's supply. Madagascar, while smaller in production volume compared to Indonesia, is notable for its quality and distinct flavor profile of cloves. Both highlighted Madagascar's unique "terroir"—the combination of factors including soil, climate, and sunlight—that give a distinctive profile on top of the eugenol—the major constituent (70 to 90 percent) in the aromatic oil extracted from cloves.

Cloves are not endemic to the Red Island. In the 1820s, clove trees were brought from Maluku Island in Indonesia to Sainte Marie Island, located off Madagascar's east coast, by Pierre Poivre, a noted seafarer, botanist, and administrator of La Réunion. From there, plantations began to spread north of Tamatave, where Malagasy farmers quickly mastered clove cultivation, producing both the clove spice and essential oil. By the 1920s and 1930s, Madagascar emerged as a major producer and exporter. The cultivation mainly occurred along the east coast, in regions like Analanjirofo, known for its dense clove forests. This area encompasses a significant portion of the Toamasina province, including places like Tamatave, Sainte-Marie Island, Mananara, Fenoarivo Atsinanana (Fénérive), and Soanierana Ivongo. About 90 percent of Madagascar's clove production is concentrated in these regions.

In terms of economic impact, cloves provided an important source of income for Malagasy farmers, especially during periods of shortfall in staple crops like rice and vanilla. In 2021, Madagascar exported $117 million worth of cloves, making it the world's top exporter of this spice.

I knew cloves in Madagascar had a rich history and significant economic impact, and I was curious to hear Gabriel's perspective of a small family business. Gabriel's family business, modest yet significant, contributed fifty-eight metric tons (produced and collected from many small local farmers) to Madagascar's noteworthy rank as the world's second-largest clove producer—after Indonesia—with twenty-five thousand metric tons.

"The harvest season peaks in November and December," Gabriel said, detailing the meticulous process, "with ten metric tons per week, over six weeks."

Our conversation steered back to the cultivation methods. Gabriel stressed the meticulous selection of terrain and the tender care in shaded nurseries—a crucial foundation before the young trees could face the sun. Gabriel explained it takes five to six years for a tree to fully produce, and each tree will produce twenty-two to thirty-three pounds of fresh cloves, which leads to eleven pounds of dry cloves. He took out his phone and showed pictures of nurseries where young plants sat individually potted neatly arranged in rows on the ground. They were aligned under a simple, makeshift shelter constructed with bamboo poles and covered with dried palm fronds. This shelter provided the necessary shade for the saplings, protecting them from direct sunlight.

Curious, I inquired about the flowers' hues. Gabriel presented another image—blossoms in shades of pink and yellow, nature's artwork pollinated by bees that buzzed around their farm's hives.

Gabriel's face lit up as he shared a childhood memory related to clove harvesting. "During the clove harvest, there are a lot of small beehives in the tree branches," he recalled, describing how getting stung by bees was a common, yet memorable, part of the experience. "It was a game when we were kids. There were three to five people harvesting each tree. When we got stung, we didn't say anything. We stepped aside and someone else immediately got stung too."

I shared my own recollections of clove trees in the Domaine d'Ambohimanitra during my previous trip to the island. I remembered noticing the younger leaves displaying a striking pinkish-red hue that gradually transitions to a deep green as they mature. Gabriel mentioned that it was common in many plant species as a signal to deter herbivores and attract pollinators. "The leaves were elongated and ovate with smooth edges," I said. "They seemed to emerge in clusters from the branches."

Finally, I showed a photograph of my hand holding a sprig from a clove tree with young clove fruits. "These are immature clove fruits," said Gabriel. "They are small, rounded, and puffed, transitioning in color from a pale yellow at the base to a soft pink at the tips, a common coloration for young cloves before they mature and darken."

When discussing quality and market dynamics, Gabriel said that in some regions, collectors mixed different qualities. Some unscrupulous local collectors would sometimes combine exhausted, low-quality cloves with higher-quality ones to sell locally, boosting profits due to low margins. However, he assured us that this was uncommon in the SAVA region, where we were, emphasizing their commitment to maintaining the purity and quality of their cloves for export.

Cloves

Plant Characteristics: Clove trees are evergreen trees that can grow up to ten to fifteen meters (thirty to fifty feet) tall. They belong to the Myrtaceae family and are native to the Maluku Islands, but have flourished in Madagascar's climate for centuries.

Environment: Cloves thrive in humid, tropical climates with well-drained soil, abundant rainfall, and consistent warmth. Madagascar's eastern coastal regions offer ideal growing conditions.

Flowers and Buds: The spice comes from the aromatic flower buds of the tree. These buds are harvested before blooming, when they transition from green to a vibrant pinkish-red hue.

Seasonality: Clove harvesting in Madagascar typically occurs between October and March, aligning with the region's rainy season. The timing is crucial, as the buds must be collected just before they bloom to retain their aromatic oils.

Labor-Intensive Work: The buds are hand-harvested, which is a meticulous process. Workers climb ladders or trees to reach the higher branches, carefully snipping off clusters of buds without damaging the tree.

Sustainability: Clove trees begin producing buds around their fifth year and can remain productive for decades if managed properly, making them a sustainable crop when cared for.

Sorting: After collection, the buds are sorted by hand to remove leaves, stems, or damaged buds. Only the best buds are processed further.

Sun-Drying Method: Cloves are laid out on mats or clean surfaces in the sun to dry. This process can take up to a week, during which the buds darken from reddish-pink to a deep brown color.

Turning and Monitoring: The buds are regularly turned to ensure even drying and to prevent mold or spoilage. Clove stems are sometimes collected and dried separately, as they also have industrial uses (e.g., in essential oil production).

Essential Oil Production: A significant portion of Madagascar's cloves are processed for their essential oil, rich in eugenol, which is used in perfumes, pharmaceuticals, aromatherapy, and even in the tobacco industry. The buds, stems, and leaves are distilled in steam to extract the oil, prized for its purity and potency.

Nirina commented that cloves carry with them a dual purpose. While their intense flavor enhances curries, fruitcakes, and mulled wines across continents, the clove's primary destiny lies in the smoke of Indonesia's *kretek* cigarettes. The common belief that associates cloves with gastronomy or their soothing touch in dental relief only scratches the surface of their story. In reality, it is in those aromatic cigarettes that cloves find their most extensive use, a fact that shapes their global demand and market value. Madagascar, with its bountiful clove harvests, finds a significant chunk of its exports bound for these tobacco products, revealing a surprising twist in the clove's narrative that is often overlooked in favor of its more traditional roles.

As our conversation neared its end, I saw Gabriel more engaged and reflecting on his family's history with a sense of responsibility. "It's about family," he said. "My parents started this, but now we are in charge."

Curious, I asked if taking over was always his plan. Gabriel's response was practical. "Someone had to do it. I grew up with this, and I want to see it grow even more."

As we wrapped up, it was clear that for Gabriel, this was more than just a transition of duties. It was about honoring the past while steering toward the future, ensuring the survival and growth of both his family's legacy and the agricultural heritage of Madagascar.

After Gabriel left, I found myself reflecting on the weight of legacy and tradition that rested on his shoulders. His story was one of continuity, a vital link in the chain of his family's history. It reminded me of another man I had met the previous year in the SAVA region.

During my first trip with the American chefs, we met Christiano Grosset, who had a family farm and essential oil distillery located just fifteen minutes north of Antalaha.

Like Gabriel, Christiano shared the experience of taking over from his father, carrying the weight of expectation and navigating the challenges of both initial struggles and eventual successes. Beyond managing the family business, Christiano was also the quality and security manager at Symrise Antalaha. During our spice evaluation session, he extended an invitation to tour his plantation, where twelve acres were devoted to pink peppercorn trees.

Since our first meals in the capital and the fresh spice evaluations at the Symrise facilities in Antalaha, Chef Michael Gulotta discovered a newfound appreciation for the island's pink peppercorns. Their unique and vibrant flavor had captivated his culinary imagination. We were all excited to hear more about pink peppercorn. We all jumped into a minivan, and on the way there, Michael reflected on how this journey on the Red Island had completely transformed his perception of this once-overlooked ingredient.

"Before this trip, pink peppercorns were merely a footnote in my recipes, an afterthought," said Michael. "But here, they've revealed their true potential. The floral, fruity notes, coupled with a hint of spice—they're not just an additive; they're a revelation!"

The Madagascar scene changed his viewpoint on this specific ingredient. He had fallen in love with pink peppercorns since the beginning of our journey.

Michael explained to Christiano that in classical cooking, pepper is often a background note—an ingredient so ubiquitous it's taken for granted and rarely noticed. However, in Southeast Asian cuisines—in places Michael traveled to—green or Sichuan peppercorns were more prominently featured in dishes, though they were still not usually the star ingredient. He went on to say that the pink peppercorns he had discovered here were surprisingly versatile.

"Here, in Madagascar, pink peppercorns are not just a spice; they're an experience, a burst of flavor that elevates a dish or a drink to something extraordinary. It's amazing; from now on, I easily think of pink peppercorns in my creative process."

The chef further commented that the pink peppercorns had an ability to transform a dish and make the other flavors pop. He wondered whether the pink peppercorns back in the US could achieve the same potent effect as those harvested here in Madagascar. He expressed his hope of finding pink peppercorns stateside that packed the same flavor punch as the locally sourced ones that had left him so impressed.

Although Christiano's farm was just a few miles from Symrise, the unpredictable nature of Madagascar's roads always held surprises. We reached the Ankavanana River—the same one on which we took a boat to visit the vanilla farms. The bridge was so slender that Christiano was compelled to stop, allowing clusters of tuk-tuks and various vehicles to clear the path before we could cross to the other side. We found ourselves trailing behind two tuk-tuks that dominated the road, their presence creating a challenging obstacle for Christiano to maneuver around.

As we patiently waited behind the tuk-tuks, Christiano seized the moment to share some enlightening facts about pink peppercorns. "Contrary to what many think, pink peppercorns aren't true peppercorns. They're actually berries harvested from trees," he explained.

He continued, his voice mixing with the hum of the idling engine. "There are two primary varieties: *Schinus terebinthifolius* and *Schinus molle*. Simply put, the first one is the type that flourishes in Brazil and Madagascar, while *Schinus molle*, commonly known as the Peruvian pepper tree, is found in Peru, various South American countries, the United States, South Africa, and Australia."

Amidst our amusement over the quirky sight of two tuk-tuks commandeering the road, we commented on the rising global prominence of pink peppercorns, not just in culinary circles but also in various non-culinary domains, like fine fragrance and cosmetics. This diversification in use added another layer to the cultural and economic importance of pink peppercorns.

Christiano, who finally was able to navigate around the tuk-tuks, further added that the distinction in flavor profiles between Madagascar's and Brazil's pink peppercorns made each region's produce unique. Madagascar pink peppercorns hold a special place in the culinary world. Their cultivation and use had been increasing due to their distinctive flavor and aroma.

Madagascar, though not a top producer, was recognized for the quality of its pink peppercorns in countries like Italy, France, and Japan.

When parking our minivan in front of a Christiano's family house, he told us that in Madagascar, pink peppercorns were cultivated in several regions, each contributing to the unique qualities and reputation of the spice on the island. The main region contributing to the overall production of pink peppercorns was Anosy, in the southeast, near Fort-Dauphin.

We started walking up a small hill on a large trail. On both sides, there were bushes of *longoza*—also known as the Phoenix Flower—a rare flower native to Madagascar with many uses, including in perfumery, skincare, and traditional remedies.

I utilized the duration of our hike to gain a deeper understanding of our guest.

Pink Peppercorn

Plant Characteristics: Pink peppercorns, though called "pepper," are not true pepper (Piper species) but the dried berries of the Schinus terebinthifolius, commonly known as the Brazilian pepper tree. These trees are introduced species that thrive in Madagascar's tropical climate.

Environment: The trees flourish in warm, sunny areas with well-drained soil. They are particularly well suited to Madagascar's eastern and southern regions, where they grow naturally or semi-cultivated, often found along roadsides, farms, and forests.

Berries: The vibrant pink to red berries grow in clusters and are known for their delicate, sweet, and slightly peppery flavor profile, with hints of citrus and floral undertones.

Seasonality: Pink peppercorns are typically harvested during the dry season, between May and October, when the berries are fully ripe and at their peak color and flavor.

Hand-Harvesting: Workers cut the branches from the trees and load them into large sacks, which women carry on their heads to a central collection area. There, the sacks are emptied onto wide tarps, and the branches are vigorously whipped to detach the peppercorns.

Sorting: After harvesting, the berries are sorted by hand to remove any unripe, damaged, or discolored fruits. Leaves, stems, and debris are

Christiano, originally from Antalaha, pursued a finance career in Tana after high school. He spent a decade there before returning to his hometown in 2013 to join Symrise, which is where I met him. His father, an experienced distiller of essential oils, was a supplier of Symrise. Christiano's early memories included helping his father plant twelve acres of pink peppercorn trees for a company contract when he was in middle school. Those days were simpler, with long journeys on dirt roads by bicycle to reach the planting sites.

Tragically, Christiano's father passed away a few years ago. By then, Christiano had begun working with him, but his father's sudden death left him in the dark on many aspects of the business. Despite this, Christiano chose to take up the mantle, dedicating himself to support his mother and continue the family's essential oil cultivation—a path that stood in contrast to his siblings, who preferred the city life.

separated to ensure a clean final product. Once harvested, the berries go through a detailed sorting process that determines their export potential.

- Grade 1 (Premium): Round, bright pink, and nearly blemish-free. Used by Michelin-starred chefs and high-end perfumers.
- Grade 2 (Select): Slightly irregular berries, minor blemishes, often used in spice blends and mid-range retail products.
- Extraction Quality: Less visually appealing but valued by the fragrance industry for their high essential oil content.

Sun-Drying: The berries are spread in thin layers on tarps for a pre-drying phase under the sun. This traditional method helps allows the pink peppercorns to be safely stored for several weeks before final processing.

Careful Monitoring: The drying process must be closely monitored to prevent over-drying or discoloration. Proper drying results in berries that are slightly wrinkled but maintain their characteristic pink color.

Packaging and Export: After harvest, the pink peppercorns are brought to the processing facility, where they undergo final drying in industrial dryers to ensure optimal humidity control. Once properly dried, they are packaged to preserve their flavor and prevent moisture absorption. Madagascar is the second producer of pink peppercorns after Brazil.

As we stood on the trail, Christiano gestured toward the expansive forest of trees stretching on the hill in front of us. "There," he said, his eyes gleaming with a mix of pride and reverence, "is the heart of our peppercorn cultivation." Nestled on the far side of a gently sloping hill, the trees were partly obscured by the crest of the terrain, yet what was visible spoke of a thriving, vibrant orchard. The trees, mature and robust, formed a verdant ocean that seemed to undulate gently over the rolling landscape.

We continued our hike, and as we approached a crossroads where multiple trails intersected, my attention was drawn to a white monument nestled within a small, gated area. The sight piqued my curiosity, compelling me to inquire about its significance. Christiano, with a somber yet thoughtful tone, revealed that it was his father's grave.

Seizing this unexpected yet poignant moment, I gently steered the conversation toward a deeper cultural aspect. "Christiano, seeing your father's grave here in such a serene setting reminds me of Madagascar's unique traditions. I've read about *Famadihana*, the 'turning of the bones.' Could you share your thoughts or experiences with this tradition?"

This respectful inquiry led to Christiano divulging more about his personal and cultural connections to this distinctive Malagasy ritual.

"You see," he started, "*Famadihana* is a practice that's very special to some tribes in Madagascar. It involves exhuming the remains of the deceased loved ones, wrapping them in fresh cloth, and then...people dance with them to live music. It sounds unusual, I know, but it's their way of celebrating life and death, of maintaining a connection with those who have passed on."

He paused, glancing back at the trail we had just traversed. "Every five to seven years, families come together for this ritual. It's not just a somber remembrance; it's a festivity, a reunion of sorts. In their beliefs, the ancestors hold power—they intervene in people's lives, guide them. *Famadihana* keeps that bond alive. But times are changing. The ritual isn't as common as it once was. Costs, the influence of other religions, and public health all play a role in this change. And my father, even though he was from this region, specifically requested not to have *Famadihana* after his passing. A personal choice, you see."

Christiano turned to me, a pensive expression on his face. "The *Famadihana* is mostly practiced by the Merina tribe in the central highlands. But even within our communities, beliefs and practices evolve. My father's decision was his way of embracing change."

Christiano changed the topic and explained that learning in this new role was largely self-directed. While there were local people to advise him, he quickly realized the necessity of making independent decisions, especially given Madagascar's unpredictable weather and the challenges of working in remote areas. He understood that practical experience, coupled with local wisdom, was essential for success in this environment.

"As you know," said Christiano, "in the SAVA region, people talk about nothing else but vanilla. That's all the people there know, vanilla!" He affirmed that asking to diversify agriculture was a challenge for the entire region in convincing people to grow things other than vanilla. People have difficulty switching to varied crops that could provide more regular income.

"Even as a distiller, I try to work on many different species. I can't just focus on pink peppercorns. If the market collapses tomorrow I need to have other options. On our plot of about 250 usable acres, we grow pink peppercorns, lemongrass, palmarosa (a grass cultivated for its essential oil), and allspice. We also have papaya, vanilla, patchouli, and more. That way, if one crop fails we can rely on the others. It's an important lesson."

Christiano stopped in front of a cultivated area filled with papaya trees. These trees stood tall with slender trunks and had a cluster of large, lobed leaves at the top. Hanging from the branches near the crown of each tree were several ripe papaya fruits. The landscape was somewhat hilly, and the papaya trees were planted in rows, ascending the slope of the terrain. The ground appeared to be recently cleared or tilled, and two workers from the farm were still working there. Christiano grabbed their attention and asked one of them to get a few papayas for us.

We saw a few vanilla vines on our way back to Christiano's family house. We were greeted by his mother, who had prepared fresh fruit juice for us, some freshly cut papaya, and carrot *achard*.

Our conversation turned to the future of his farm. Christiano talked about the importance of preserving and enhancing his father's legacy. He openly admitted regretting not becoming involved earlier, when his father was still around to mentor him. He reflected on how he had once been captivated by urban life and modern technology, overlooking the true value of the remote bush, forests, and the land his family owned. Now, however, his perspective has shifted dramatically. He finds greater contentment and a sense of belonging in nature more than he ever did in the city. Looking ahead, his goal is to fully realize his father's vision by not only maintaining the farm but also expanding its agricultural scopes. This commitment to continuing and broadening the cultivation of their land stands as a tribute to his father's legacy.

Christian expressed his deep fondness for his country. He recalled his time in France and how he once longed for opportunities abroad. However, as his perspective shifted, he has come to truly appreciate Madagascar's immense natural beauty and cultural richness. He stressed the importance of experiencing Madagascar firsthand to move beyond common stereotypes, highlighting the breathtaking beauty found in its landscapes and waters.

Yet, while Christiano spoke passionately about Madagascar's beauty, he didn't shy away from its challenges. I acknowledged the stark realities of poverty and limited educational access that affect so many Malagasy. Christiano noted that these challenges often shape foreigners' first impressions, especially when they encounter them upon arriving in the capital, where visible poverty can overshadow the country's many virtues. Still, he emphasized the resilience of Madagascar's people and that Madagascar's true wealth lies in its biodiversity and the rich tapestry of cultures found among its diverse ethnic groups. "Madagascar is rich in many things," he said, "but you have to get out of the capital to properly experience it."

I asked Christiano how he would describe Madagascar to a first-time visitor, hoping his words would ignite readers' imaginations. He smiled and said, "Though I haven't seen paradise itself, I certainly am not far from it! To truly know Madagascar, you must see it, breathe it, and let it change you."

In Madagascar's far south, where pink peppercorns flourish and opportunity is scarce, one man set out to redefine rural development—not through charity, but through a spice.

During my third trip to Madagascar in May 2025, I traveled to Fort-Dauphin, a city perched on the southeastern tip between the Indian Ocean and the island's mountain backbone. This region accounts for 80 percent of Madagascar's pink peppercorn production. Alongside Nirina, I met with Riaz Badouraly, founder of Eva Fruit, at one of the orchards during peak harvest season.

Just beyond the outskirts of Fort-Dauphin, we turned off the main road onto a narrow sand track lined with wooden dwellings. The path eventually opened into a clearing, where a simple, open-sided structure stood. Its floor was covered in large tarps, each blanketed with millions of bright reddish-pink berries.

We parked near a row of women, seated on small, colorful tarps, rhythmically whipping branches to dislodge the peppercorns. Nearby, others moved steadily through the orchard, harvesting by hand. Some balanced sacks of freshly cut branches on their heads as they returned to the clearing, where more women sat in circles, beating the branches against the tarps to free the tiny grains. A faint floral-citrus scent hung in the air, grounding the entire scene in both beauty and labor.

This was the heart of the harvest season.

Beneath the shade of the shed, we met Riaz, a man whose vision for rural development has redefined the spice trade in the region. "We didn't choose pink pepper," he told me with a knowing smile. "It chose us."

Born in Fianarantsoa and raised in Fort-Dauphin, Riaz had spent time in Europe before returning home with a mission: to build an agricultural model that worked for the people who lived off the land. His philosophy was simple—start with the end in mind. "Too many development projects fail because they never think past the planting stage," he explained. "If you can't create a market, what's the point?"

His answer came in the form of a small, glossy berry with global potential.

"We sourced the plants from Tamatave, where a horticultural center had already established collections," he explained. "From there, we took cuttings and replanted them in an orchard in Andakana." After testing multiple species, pink peppercorn stood out—early-fruiting, hardy, and highly sought after by both perfumers and chefs.

By 2005, Riaz had planted a mother orchard in Andakana. From those first trees, he began distributing cuttings to local farmers, partnering with international NGOs to introduce pink peppercorn cultivation across the Anosy region. "The first three hundred farmers didn't know what it was," he recalled. "They were skeptical. But we covered the planting costs, we promised to buy the berries, and we kept our word."

Two decades later, that initial group of growers has grown into more than 3,600 trained, certified producers, many of them now organized in cooperatives.

"I never opposed others getting involved," Riaz said of the project's growing popularity. "Even though I financed the start, I welcomed anyone, as long as they followed a shared vision. We're not just dealing with crops. We're working with people."

At the core of Eva Fruit's philosophy are four pillars: dignity, transparency, sustainability, and long-term vision. "These communities have been largely overlooked for decades. Let's be honest—they've been neglected. And without education, real development just isn't possible."

"It's not just about buying and selling," he added, reciting the pillars with quiet conviction, like someone who's repeated them to every farmer and official he's ever worked with. "It's about dignity, transparency, sustainability, and a long-term vision.

"Sustainability is essential. We have to take special care—not just with the product, but with the buyer. That's what allows us to think long term. Real development doesn't happen overnight—it's only after fifteen years that you begin to see the true impact. It took us fifteen years to reach international recognition."

We walked between rows of trees as he explained the phenological study they use to determine the precise start of harvest. "If you pick too early, you ruin the quality. Too late, and you risk spoilage. So we watch, we test, and then we decide—together." Once harvest is approved, each cooperative negotiates a fixed minimum price, based on inflation and global demand. "This isn't charity," Riaz said. "It's equity."

The harvested peppercorns undergo a meticulous process: manual destemming, sun-drying, and sorting into three grades. "Grade 1 is what Michelin-starred chefs and perfumers want," he explained, showing me a handful of perfect, vibrant berries.

A large portion of Madagascar's pink peppercorn exports now comes from this region, second only to Brazil in global volume, but first in quality, especially for essential oil extraction. "Our berries have a higher molecular yield for perfumery," Riaz said. "It's the terroir—our soil, our sun, and our way of working."

As we spoke, he paused to greet the women sorting berries under a tree. He examined the pile and nodded. "That's Grade 2—often used in spice blends and mid-range retail."

Behind the region's economic success lies a deeper human story—one of migration, resilience, and ownership. Riaz emphasized that the plants now belong to the farmers. "We don't bind them with contracts. If someone else offers a better price, they're free to go. That's freedom. That's dignity."

Eva Fruit has since expanded into lychees and macadamia nuts, now producing 320 metric tons of pink peppercorn annually. But this crop remains the heart of the story. "It was the first one that made people believe," Riaz said. "It showed them they could build something lasting."

Back in the clearing, the air was thick with the scent of drying peppercorn. I asked Riaz what he thought about the future of the island.

"The country is in a bad way. That's not a judgment—it's just a fact. I'm not assigning blame. But despite all the aid we've received, we're growing poorer and less educated. That's a dangerous combination. It means we're heading toward a society driven by hunger, but without the intellectual clarity to make better choices. If nothing changes over the next decade, we won't just see hardship—we might enter a different reality. One that could be marked by violence, by people who might no longer feel grounded, or good in their own skin."

He wasn't being dramatic—just honest. And I understood his frustration. Traveling across Madagascar, I had seen the realities he spoke of: broken roads, deep poverty, and a generation at risk. But I had also encountered something else, stories of purpose, of people investing in their land, in education, in future generations. This book is filled with those stories. Perhaps development is never as fast or as linear as we want it to be. But if Riaz's orchard proves anything, it's that small seeds—planted with vision and trust—can take root and grow. A berry may not fix a country. But it can help.

Later that day, back in the car, the smell of drying peppercorns lingered on my hands. I kept thinking about what Riaz said—that pink peppercorn chose them. But after witnessing the structure, the training, the care poured into this ecosystem, I saw it differently. It wasn't the berry that chose them. They chose to make the berry matter. And in doing so, they built a future around it.

Foie Gras Ravioli and Cream Infused with Wild Madagascar Black Pepper

Recipes by Chef Lalaina Ravelomanana (Marais Restaurant in Antananarivo, Madagascar)

Serves 8 people

INGREDIENTS

Ravioli Dough

2¾ cups all-purpose flour (400 g)
4 whole eggs
1 tbsp. water
1 pinch of salt
1 tbsp. olive oil

Voatsiperifery Pepper–Infused Cream

2 cups heavy cream (½ L)
1 tsp. crushed wild black pepper
⅓ cup salted butter (80 g)
Lime zest, to taste
Salt and pepper, to taste

Foie Gras Ravioli Filling

1.1 lbs. fresh foie gras (500 g)
⅓ cup raw cashews (40 g), lightly toasted and chopped, divided
1 pinch of ground voatsiperifery pepper
Lime zest, to taste
Salt and pepper, to taste

PREPARATION

For the Ravioli Dough

1. Place the flour on a clean work surface and form a well in the center. Add the eggs, beaten with the water, salt, and olive oil, into the well. Mix everything together by hand until a smooth, elastic dough forms that doesn't stick to your hands. Wrap the dough in plastic wrap and refrigerate for at least 1 hour to rest.
2. After resting, roll the dough several times through a pasta machine until it reaches the thinnest possible setting. Cut out medallions approximately 3 inches (8 centimeters) in diameter. Store them in the refrigerator with a slightly damp kitchen towel on top to prevent the dough from drying out.

Recipe continues →

For the Voatsiperifery Pepper–Infused Cream

1. In a saucepan, heat the heavy cream over medium heat, making sure it doesn't come to a boil. Add the coarsely crushed wild black pepper (*voatsiperifery*). Remove from heat, cover, and let the cream infuse for about 1 hour.
2. Strain through a fine mesh sieve to remove the pepper bits. Bring the infused cream to a boil, then whisk in the butter until fully incorporated. Add a touch of lime zest and salt and pepper, to taste. Keep warm until ready to serve.

Foie Gras Ravioli Filling

1. Cut the foie gras into thick slices, about 1 ounce (30 grams) each. Season with salt and pepper, then lightly dust with flour. Refrigerate the slices for about 30 minutes.
2. Heat a skillet over medium-high heat. Quickly sear the foie gras slices on both sides using a spatula to flip. Remove from heat and let cool.
3. In the same skillet, sauté the cashew nuts in the rendered foie gras fat. Add a pinch of wild pepper powder (*voatsiperifery*, if available). Set aside and refrigerate.

ASSEMBLY AND COOKING

1. Place one seared slice of foie gras in the center of each pasta medallion. Add a few toasted cashews on top. Finish with a touch of lime zest for brightness.
2. Cover with a second pasta medallion and press the edges gently with your fingers, lightly moistening the edges to seal.
3. Bring a large pot of water to a gentle boil. Simmer the ravioli for about 4 minutes until just cooked. Carefully remove with a slotted spoon and gently warm in salted butter before serving.

PLATING

1. In a soup plate, arrange 3 pieces of ravioli with a little cooking butter.
2. Pour over the infused cream.
3. Finish with a few pieces of pan-fried, grated cashew nuts, and serve piping hot.

Confit of Zebu Chuck and Crispy Cannelloni with Pink Peppercorn

Serves 8 people

INGREDIENTS

Smoked Eggplant Caviar

2 medium eggplants (about 7 oz. or 200 g each), diced
3 garlic cloves, minced
1 large yellow onion, diced
Zest of *combava* (Makrut lime), to taste
Juice of ½ lime
2 tbsp. olive oil
Salt, black pepper, and pink peppercorn powder, to taste
8 cannelloni pasta tubes

Confit of Zebu Chuck

½ cup sunflower oil
3.3 lbs. boneless zebu chuck roast (or beef chuck roast)
4 large yellow onions, sliced
2 heads of garlic, peeled and crushed
1 tbsp. pink peppercorns (crushed slightly)
3 bay leaves
Salt, black pepper, and pink peppercorn powder, to taste
8½ cups (16 fl. oz.) beef stock or broth
⅓ cup unsalted butter (about 6 tbsp.)

PREPARATION

For the Smoked Eggplant Caviar

1. Preheat the oven to 248°F. Wash the eggplants. Burn the skin completely over a high heat, using a grill. Remove when all the skin is well burnt (black). Gently scoop out the flesh with a spoon. On a plate, mash the flesh and add the pressed garlic cloves, chopped onion, combava zest, lime juice, and olive oil. Season with salt, pepper, and a little pink peppercorn powder.
2. Fry the cannelloni in sunflower oil. Stuff the cannelloni with the eggplant caviar. Place in the oven for about 1 hour.

Recipe continues →

For the Confit Chuck with Pink Berries

1. Preheat the oven to 320°F.
2. Over a high heat, pour in the oil in a frying pan and brown the chuck block on all sides.
3. Add the chopped onions and halved garlic. Sauté until caramelized. Add the pink peppercorn, bay leaves, and salt and pepper to taste.
4. Then add the golden chuck in an oven roasting pan, adding the meat stock at the end.
5. Cover the oven roasting pan with aluminum foil. Place in the oven for approximately 4 hours.
6. Baste the chuck with the cooking juices every hour, until the meat is very soft.
7. Reduce by half until the juices can coat a spoon. Beat with butter. Adjust seasoning by adding a little pink peppercorn powder.

PLATING

1. Cut up the chuck. Glaze with the reduced jus.
2. Sprinkle with a few pink peppercorns and arrange the chuck on a warmed flat plate. Place the cannelloni next to it. Decorate with sprouts and edible flowers. You can garnish this dish with a wedge of lightly roasted onion and a spoonful of mustard cream (mustard lightened with a little mascarpone).

CHAPTER 6

Zebu Nation

The Living Link Across Madagascar

Ny omby tsy miverina tsy mahita ny lalan-kaleha.

The zebu that does not retrace its steps
does not find its way.

—TRADITIONAL MALAGASY SAYING

I first met the baobab in the pages of *The Little Prince* by Antoine de Saint-Exupéry—a fantastical tree with roots of menace and mystery. Later, in my French schoolbooks, it returned as a symbol of Africa: grand and exotic. But those were ink on paper. I had yet to stand beneath one.

So, when the chefs and my business colleagues returned home at the end of our first trip, I stayed behind. I couldn't leave Madagascar without seeing the Avenue of the Baobabs with my own eyes.

◀ *Zebu: The animal that binds a people.*

My driver met me at Morondava Airport, on the island's west coast. Before heading north, I asked to stop at a bank. Each one we visited had a long queue of people waiting to withdraw cash. My driver grew uneasy, shifting from foot to foot. I brushed it off as impatience to hit the road. But the delay had its gift.

A few miles north along Route *Nationale* (RN8), the baobabs began to appear on the horizon—first as silhouettes, then shapes, then giants. Rising from the earth they looked like ancient sentinels, with their thick, bottle-shaped trunks and sparse, root-like branches reaching toward the sky. Against the vast blue horizon, dotted with drifting clouds, they seemed like almost unreal monuments of time itself.

The driver dropped me off at the entrance to the Avenue of the Baobabs. I knew this was one of the most photographed places in the world, and I dreaded sharing this long-awaited moment with crowds of tourists. But, thanks to the delay at the banks, most visitors had already come and gone. A few locals herded zebus across the road, and otherwise, it was just me and the trees.

I walked along a golden ribbon of sand, winding through the silent corridor of giants. Some stretched more than one hundred feet high, their massive trunks standing like fortress walls. Up close, their sheer scale was overwhelming. Here, along the legendary Avenue of the Baobabs, time seemed to slow, the world ancient and hushed. Pressing my palm to one

The Baobab Tree

The baobab tree, often referred to as the "Tree of Life," is integral to Madagascar's culture and ecology. Every part of the baobab is utilized.

Fruit Pulp: Rich in vitamin C, potassium, and fiber, the pulp is consumed fresh or processed into beverages and foods, like ice cream.

Leaves: Eaten as a vegetable, they are also used medicinally to treat various ailments.

Seeds: These can be ground into flour or pressed for oil, serving as a cooking ingredient.

Bark: Its fibers are crafted into ropes, mats, baskets, and cloth.

Baobabs play a crucial role in their ecosystems, providing food, water, and shelter for various species. Their flowers are primarily pollinated by fruit bats, which feed on the nectar, facilitating cross-pollination.

In Madagascar, six endemic species of baobab exist, with Adansonia grandidieri being the most renowned. This species, reaching heights of up to one hundred feet, is prominent in the famed Avenue of the Baobabs.

The baobab's significance extends beyond its nutritional value; it supports local economies and traditions, underscoring its status as a vital resource in Madagascar.

colossal trunk, then my ear, I imagined it whispering stories carried by the wind for centuries.

As I spotted my driver waiting in the distance, my attention was drawn to two round, earth-toned shapes resting in the sand near a towering baobab. Stepping closer, I recognized them—baobab fruits, also known as "monkey bread fruit." They resembled small coconuts, their hard, woody shells rough and faintly fuzzy beneath my fingers.

Curious, I grabbed a nearby rock and brought it down hard on one of the fruits. The shell resisted at first, then split open with a sharp crack. Expecting something moist inside, I was surprised to find a chalky, bone-dry interior. It crumbled into uneven, cream-colored chunks—fragile, powdery, almost like pieces of sun-bleached chalk. I picked up a piece and let it dissolve on my tongue. The flavor was tangy and slightly sweet—a mix of citrus, pear, and vanilla.

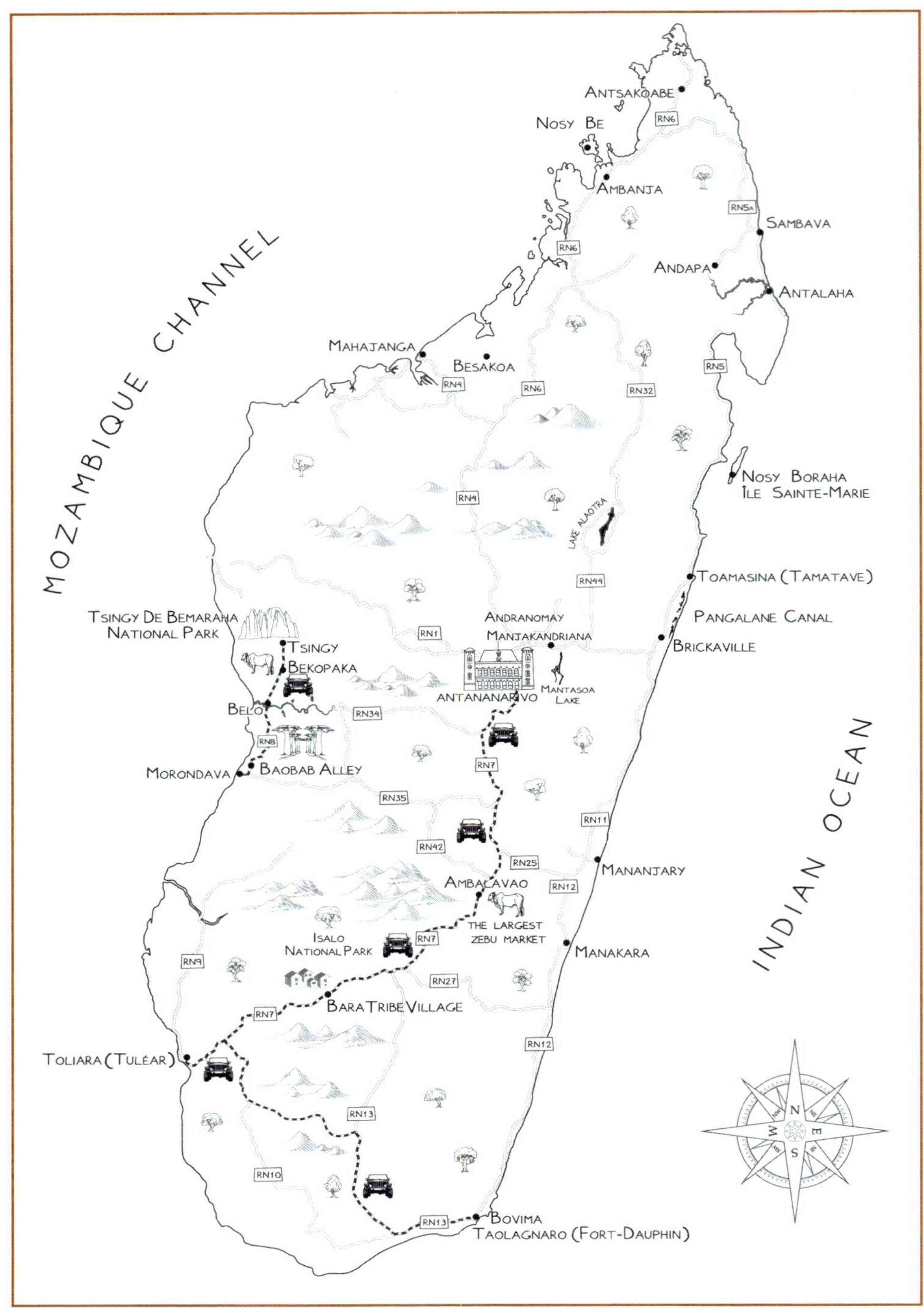
Mozambique Channel
Indian Ocean
Antsakoabe
Nosy Be
Ambanja
Sambava
Andapa
Antalaha
Mahajanga
Besakoa
Nosy Boraha
Île Sainte-Marie
Lake Alaotra
Toamasina (Tamatave)
Pangalane Canal
Brickaville
Tsingy De Bemaraha
National Park
Tsingy
Bekopaka
Andranomay
Manjakandriana
Antananarivo
Mantasoa
Lake
Belo
Morondava
Baobab Alley
Mananjary
Ambalavao
The largest
zebu market
Isalo
National Park
Manakara
Bara Tribe Village
Toliara (Tuléar)
Bovima
Taolagnaro (Fort-Dauphin)
RN6
RN5A
RN5
RN4
RN32
RN44
RN1
RN34
RN8
RN7
RN35
RN11
RN42
RN25
RN12
RN9
RN27
RN13
RN10
N
E
S
W

Back in the car, the road stretched endlessly ahead—an ochre ribbon winding through an untamed landscape. The engine hummed steadily, and the tires crunched over the sand, sending up clouds of dust that clung to the windshield and seeped through the cracks of the car doors.

For three hours, the scenery barely changed. At times, the road narrowed into a tunnel of bare branches, then opened again into a vast expanse, where a few baobabs receded into the horizon.

Time seemed to slow inside the vehicle. The rhythm of the bumps and sways became a song of discomfort, a constant reminder of how far we were from anything familiar.

Something about my driver's demeanor unsettled me. His hands gripped the wheel too tightly, his knuckles whitening with tension. As we neared Port Bac Tsimafana, where a ferry would take us across the Tsiribihina River, I heard him sigh—a sharp, weary exhale that didn't go unnoticed. Sensing his unease, I finally asked if something was wrong. He hesitated for a moment before offering a clipped response: "Everything is fine." But his tone—tight and unconvincing—suggested otherwise.

The river stretched wide and sluggish before us, a vast expanse of reddish-brown water. The air was thick with the scent of damp earth and sunbaked mud.

At the water's edge, four narrow metallic ramps lay half-buried in the mud. At first, I assumed they had been long abandoned—until, a few minutes later, I watched them put to use in a way I hadn't expected.

I heard the ferry before I saw it—the guttural roar of its twin engines cut through the thick, humid air. I had pictured a sturdy ferry. What emerged instead was a skeletal raft. The entire structure was a series of loosely laid wooden planks, teetering atop two long metal floats—each scarred by years of wear and haphazard repair. At the rear, two small, motorized canopies jutted out, shielding the engines—if they could be trusted to work at all. There were no guardrails, no safety ropes, and no clear indication of how this vessel was supposed to transport vehicles, let alone four of them. Just faith and balance.

I lingered on the riverbank, watching as my driver prepared to board. Three other cars were waiting their turn, and I couldn't help but wonder how

they would all fit. The two ferry operators, moving with practiced efficiency, aligned the narrow, mud-caked ramps. My driver inched forward, his concentration razor-sharp, maneuvering the four-wheel drive onto the platform with near-surgical precision. The ramps were barely wider than the tires.

After a careful series of back-and-forth adjustments, all four vehicles were finally positioned on the precarious wooden surface.

I carefully crossed the metallic ramps and settled at the front of one of the metallic floats. Turning to my driver, curiosity edged into concern, "Has a car ever fallen into the river?"

He barely hesitated. "Last week, a small truck went off the platform and into the water." He said it as if it were an unremarkable event, just another risk of daily life here.

An hour later, we reached the other side, arriving in the town of Belo. It was well past lunchtime when my driver pulled up in front of a small but well-known restaurant: The Mad Zebu. I invited him to join me for the meal, but he politely declined, explaining that all drivers had a designated area beside the restaurant, where they were served a fixed menu of rice and meat stew. It was a system in place at many stops like this—a structured, affordable routine for those constantly on the road.

Stepping inside, I was taken aback. The menu was unexpectedly refined—a gourmet surprise in the middle of the bush. After the rough, chaotic journey, it felt like a well-earned reward.

I started with a grouper fillet, served with leeks, spinach cream, and a *vierge* sauce—a lively blend of diced tomatoes, olive oil, fresh herbs, and lemon, its brightness lifted even further by a touch of candied lemon. Next came the pièce de résistance: a cut of zebu braised in red wine until fork-tender, accompanied by a delicate potato *millefeuille*—its golden layers crisp yet meltingly soft. A medley of vegetables completed the plate, their colors vibrant against the rich, dark sauce.

It was the second dish I had featuring zebu meat. The first was a zebu carpaccio at the restaurant of La Varangue Hotel in Tana.

After lunch, we continued on toward Bekopaka, the base for the Tsingy de Bemaraha. The journey would take the rest of the day, navigating dusty roads riddled with deep potholes. Fortunately, we were in the dry season—during the rains, the route would have been impassable.

I was impressed by my driver's skill—his smooth, effortless way of maneuvering through mud puddles and obstacles. But I also noticed something else. Whenever the road allowed, he would accelerate, pushing the car forward with an urgency I hadn't sensed before.

I asked him why. He hesitated before answering. He was trying to catch up to a convoy that had left Morondava earlier that morning. If we could reach them, we would be able to cross the second river—the Manambolo—before nightfall. "They should be waiting at the next village," he said.

But when we finally arrived at the heart of the village—a scattering of houses and a towering baobab standing in the center—there was no sign of the convoy.

I glanced at my driver. His grip on the wheel tightened, his fingers flexing and releasing as if resisting the urge to drum against the dashboard. He scanned the empty village, exhaled sharply, and without a word, turned the car back onto the road.

"What's going on?" I pressed.

He hesitated again. Then, finally, he spoke. He hadn't told me before because he didn't want me to worry. But now, there was no point in hiding it.

We had entered a stretch of road where the Dahalo were known to operate. For security reasons, convoys usually traveled in groups of twenty-five

Zebu: The Heartbeat of Madagascar

The zebu, a type of humped cattle originally from India, holds a place of profound importance in Madagascar, weaving into the very fabric of its cultural, economic, and spiritual life.

HISTORICAL ROOTS

Zebu were introduced to Madagascar around the ninth to twelfth centuries through maritime trade and migrations involving Austronesian and Bantu-speaking peoples. Originally domesticated in South Asia, these humped cattle (Bos indicus) adapted to Madagascar's environment and became integral to its society, influencing agricultural practices and cultural traditions.

CULTURAL SIGNIFICANCE

In Malagasy culture, zebu are more than livestock; they are symbols of wealth, status, and ancestral connection. They play a central role in various ceremonies.

Famadihana (Turning of the Bones): This funerary tradition involves exhuming ancestors' remains, rewrapping them in fresh shrouds, and celebrating their memory. The sacrifice of zebu during this ceremony honors the departed and reinforces bonds between the living and their ancestors.

Savika: Among the Betsileo people, young men participate in this traditional cattle-wrestling sport as a rite of passage, showcasing bravery and skill.

ECONOMIC IMPORTANCE

Zebus are vital to Madagascar's agrarian economy.

Agriculture: They are used for plowing fields and facilitating rice and crop cultivation.

Livestock Products: Zebus provide milk, meat, and hides, contributing to both subsistence and local markets.

Wealth Indicator: Ownership of zebus signifies wealth and social standing; larger herds often correlate with higher status within communities.

SPIRITUAL AND SYMBOLIC ROLE

Zebus serve as a bridge between the living and the spiritual realm.

Ancestral Connection: They are considered intermediaries to the ancestral world, especially during sacrificial ceremonies, reinforcing the Malagasy belief in the enduring presence and influence of ancestors.

In essence, the zebu is not merely an animal in Madagascar but a cornerstone of its identity, embodying the island's traditions, economy, and spiritual beliefs.

4WDs, with armed military personnel spread among three of the vehicles. But we were alone.

I had first heard about the Dahalo back in Tana. Once respected as warriors and herdsmen, some had turned to cattle rustling as a means of survival—or profit. They were no longer just thieves; they were outlaws, and their presence on this road meant danger.

Cattle raiding was historically a rite of passage for young men proving their bravery within ethnic groups like the Bara and Sakalava. Traditionally, stealing a zebu was a symbolic act that marked the transition to adulthood, often tied to securing a dowry for marriage. By the twentieth and twenty-first centuries, what had once been a cultural tradition evolved into organized banditry, fueled by poverty, political instability, and weak law enforcement. No longer just symbolic acts of manhood, Dahalo raids became violent economic threats, devastating communities dependent on zebu cattle for their livelihood. In response, the Malagasy government, along with local groups, launched military interventions, community defense initiatives, and social programs to address the escalating issue.

Though security operations persist, local actors are crafting grassroots solutions. I recall a meeting on RN2 with Heriniaina Ramboatiana, the CEO of Phael Flor Group—a family business sourcing essential oils, plant extracts, and organic spices across Madagascar. He had witnessed the Dahalo's impact on rural communities firsthand. His company works closely with small-scale farmers, especially in remote areas, promoting sustainable livelihoods through distillation and agricultural training.

He recalled a group of one hundred families near Andilamena, on the island's northeast side, whose lives were upended when the Dahalo torched their homes, fields, and tools. "Overnight, they had nothing," he said. The families fled to Behataza but faced new tensions there. "Locals saw them as outsiders, even threats."

Among them was a man who approached Ramboatiana directly. "He had nothing left but the will to begin again. He asked us for food, but we're not an NGO," he said. "So, we offered something else."

That became Kebara, a relocation project on unused state land. Phael Flor arranged transport, built temporary shelters, and provided two hectares each to fifteen pilot families. They were trained in composting, biopesticides, pig farming, and later, dairy, poultry, and fishponds.

"Our goal was food autonomy—and dignity," Ramboatiana said. "The village of Kebara isn't a miracle. There's no fairy-tale ending. Just land, training, and people willing to start again."

Today, the man who first approached him leads the community. He still bears the scars but also embodies what's possible.

Phael Flor's broader model follows the same principle: placing distillation units near farms and supporting long-term, sustainable income. Their key crops—turmeric, ginger, cinnamon, pink peppercorn, and black pepper—grow from Madagascar's soil, and also from the quiet resilience of its people.

The story of Kebara lingered as we continued down the dirt road. The tension in the car softened, but my driver's eyes still darted to the rearview mirror.

After a long silence, he finally said, "Before the pandemic, there were times—rare, but they happened—when the Dahalo would strike tourist cars. Not to harm them, just to take what was valuable. Money, cameras, laptops, phones." He exhaled, as if shaking off the weight of old memories.

Enough to make the trip miserable, I thought. I let that sink in. Even if the risk was small, the consequences could have been severe. And yet, we made it through unscathed.

The immediate sense of danger had passed. We reached the banks of the Manambolo River and boarded another makeshift barge. On the other side, nestled atop a hill, stood L'Olympe du Bemaraha—a boutique hotel offering sweeping views of the surrounding dense forest.

The stillness of the place was a stark contrast to the chaotic road we had just endured.

Stepping into my bungalow, I let out a breath I had not realized I was holding in. The room was basic yet inviting, with wooden beams and a mosquito-netted bed offering a much-needed sense of quiet retreat. A cool, refreshing shower washed away the layers of dust and exhaustion from the nine-hour journey, leaving only the lingering thrill of the adventure behind.

Hunger soon replaced fatigue, and I made my way to the dining hall, where the evening's menu featured zebu—the unavoidable staple in Malagasy cuisine.

Alongside the classic Romazava—a hearty stew of zebu meat and greens—the menu offered a grilled zebu steak, which I chose after starting with a bowl of *lasopy*, a delicate, velvety vegetable soup.

The next day, a local guide picked me up at the hotel for our journey to the Tsingy de Bemaraha National Park. Designated as a UNESCO World Heritage site in 1990, the park is known for its extraordinary geological formations and biodiversity. Often called a "stone forest," this labyrinth of razor-sharp pinnacles, deep canyons, and hidden caves was sculpted over millions of years by erosion. Today, it remains one of Madagascar's most breathtaking destinations for adventure-seekers.

My guide accompanied me the entire way, ensuring I could safely navigate the park's demanding terrain. Outfitted with a harness and double lanyard, I tackled the via *ferratas*—crossing wooden hanging bridges, balancing on razor-edged limestone rocks, and climbing up near-vertical ladders.

The first section of the trail led under the woods, at the foot of the first *tsingy*, before descending into a hidden entrance beneath the massif. With only the glow of our headlamp to guide us, I squeezed through winding rock corridors—some barely wide enough to pass, others so low I had to crouch. A final, narrow passage led to an inner chamber—the last threshold before the ascent.

Emerging from the cave, we faced the final challenge—a series of steep ladders clinging to the limestone wall. Step by step, we climbed, the jagged formations rising around us. Then, at last, the summit came into view, crowned by a solitary wooden watchtower.

Ahead, a narrow suspension bridge swayed between towering limestone peaks, connecting one summit to the next with another wooden watchtower. The path zigzagged between boulders and needles, climbing and dipping while staying on the ridges. The view was nothing short of breathtaking—a 360-degree panorama of stone blades stretching endlessly into the horizon.

And in that moment, the grueling nine-hour journey faded into insignificance. This was a view unlike any other.

The road south to Morondava was no less exhausting than the journey north. But this time, we were not alone. A convoy of twenty-five vehicles followed the dirt road with armed military personnel stationed in three of them. Through the most perilous stretch, their presence was a silent reminder of the risks lurking beyond the bushes and trees.

It wasn't just precaution—it was a response to something deeper: the zebu. More than animals, zebus are a form of wealth, status, and sacrifice here. And with that comes danger. The Dahalo, cattle rustlers turned outlaws, don't steal out of malice. They steal because zebus are power.

I knew then that if I wanted to understand Madagascar, I would have to return. Not just to chase flavors or follow landscapes, but to follow the zebu itself. Southward, where its meaning runs deepest. Among the Bara tribe. The next journey was already calling.

As dusk approached, we stopped at the Avenue of the Baobabs. The baobabs stood unchanged but now bathed in molten gold, painting long shadows across the sandy ground. Pressing my ear against the rough bark, I imagined them whispering a different story—the story of the traveler who had come, seen, and carried their memory forward.

The journey south on Route *Nationale* 7 (RN7) began, as all my great Malagasy adventures seem to—with a traffic jam in Tana. Antananarivo's narrow streets slowed our escape to a crawl, the city holding us in its tangled rhythm of honking cars and zigzagging scooters just a little longer.

I was looking forward to this journey. The goal of my third trip in May 2025 was clear: a deep dive into the world of zebus. Nirina wanted me to witness the largest zebu market on the island, in Ambalavao. The distance from Tana was 287 miles—but as I learned on previous trips, distance in Madagascar means little. It's time that counts. Nirina and his driver estimated ten hours. It turned out to be the longest drive of my life.

Once we finally broke free, the familiar terraced hills rolled out before us, barely vegetated. Cassia trees lined the road, their yellow clusters drooping like chandeliers. I could see why they were called the "golden shower tree." Villages appeared one after the other, each bearing the fingerprints of both global and local commerce: brightly colored signs for World Cola, Vache Qui Rit, and Airtel rose above humble roadside *échoppes*. Poinsettia trees—red and green bursts I'd only ever seen in holiday pots—stood tall and wild along the road. Madagascar's version of Christmas, thriving under the sun.

We passed half-finished brick houses, their skeletal frames exposed, open to the elements, yet full of hope. Some homes were hidden behind cement walls crowned with barbed wire, others more open—sturdier than the homes I'd seen along RN2. As RN7 winds downward, the land exhales.

I rediscovered the emerald rice paddies, opened like green mirrors catching the sky. On the shoulder of the road, children in uniform walked home from school.

We stopped often. One does not travel with Nirina and passes up the chance to eat. "You're here to keep discovering the food of Madagascar," he reminded me. Our lunch stop was an unassuming village outpost only Nirina would know, where the specialty was *magret rossini*—farm-raised roasted duck breast crowned with pan-seared foie gras.

Later, near Sambaina, we pulled over again for thumb-sized pork sausages, grilled on a cast-iron pan set directly over glowing embers.

A few hours on, we stopped at a roadside fruit stand and gathered a still life of Madagascar's bounty: persimmons, pears, green and violet avocados, and the custard-sweet *coeur de boeuf* (Annona reticulata fruit). Nirina showed me how to eat a persimmon Malagasy-style—biting a small hole into the skin and sucking the thick, syrupy flesh directly from the fruit. "Farm to table?" I joked, "This is farm to face."

"A year ago," Nirina said, "we'd have passed hundreds of zebu hooves walking from Ambalavao to the capital. No more. That practice is now banned. Trucks replaced hooves. The meat is more tender, they say. The journey shorter. Efficiency has eclipsed ritual."

Our driver navigated through bikes, carts pulled by zebus, and the occasional wandering goats. Darkness fell fast—sunset comes at 5:30 p.m. in May. We still had miles to go. The road demanded full attention. At most: eighty kilometers per hour—if you dared.

Then came the rough patch. No public lights. Just our high beams catching ghosts of potholes. The headlights revealed fleeting glimpses of the road ahead before the blackness swallowed them whole. Suddenly, the engine belt began to squeal, and a sharp, acrid smell of scorched rubber filled the car. Our driver pulled over, lit a candle stub, and rubbed the wax into the belt—an old trucker's trick. It worked. We pressed on.

I sat in silence behind the driver, listening for more engine trouble. Nirina, unfazed, was watching movies on his laptop, headphones in. Every so often, we were pulled over. Papers requested. Eyes scanning us under flashlight beams. For safety reasons, it's forbidden to drive on the roads at night. But, apparently, those rules didn't apply to us.

We rolled into Ambalavao as the sun rose, after an eighteen-hour drive from the capital. The journey had taken its toll—on mental, on nerves—but in return, it had given us a story.

We slept for just three and a half hours. At breakfast, Nirina was already planning our visit to the zebu market.

But before the long road south to Ambalavao—before the dust, the winding hills, and the rice paddies—I made an important stop in Antananarivo.

I arranged to meet Chef Henintsoa Moretti at Haka Fy, her restaurant nestled within the historic garden of Andohalo, in the capital's upper town. Haka Fy, meaning "to enjoy" or "to taste," is a contemporary Malagasy restaurant that pays homage to the island's culinary roots.

The sun filtered gently through the leaves above our table as I sat across from her. Through her extensive research project, Chef Moretti has traversed across Madagascar's diverse regions, collecting and preserving traditional recipes from local grandmothers. Her mission is to showcase the rich tapestry of Malagasy culinary heritage—not simply as nostalgia, but as a living, evolving tradition. Her work has made her a pivotal figure in the preserving and celebrating of Madagascar's gastronomic identity.

We weren't talking about modern gastronomy or plating aesthetics. We were talking zebu.

"The zebu," she said, pausing to sip from a glass of rosé, "is the animal that unites us all."

I had heard variations of this before during my previous visits but coming from a chef whose menu bridges tradition and modern flair, the sentiment struck a different chord. "Pork, for instance, divides. Lamb divides. Religion, region...but zebu? Zebu is our common ground. It's Madagascar's culinary identity."

She described how zebus—*Bos indicus*, the distinctive humped cattle originating from South Asia—have embedded themselves into Malagasy history, ritual, and cuisine. Their role isn't merely functional; it's cultural, emotional, and spiritual.

"Historically," she noted, "zebu meat was reserved for kings. There's even a story—true or not—about a sovereign who first tasted grilled zebu after lightning struck one in the royal fields. The scent, they say, was so intoxicating that he ordered his cooks to find a way to recreate it."

That anecdote has the flavor of legend, but the reverence persists. Even today, zebu is more than food—it's ritual. It marks death, marriage, sacrifice, and celebration.

I asked how most people buy zebu meat. She smiled. "Supermarkets exist, yes. But ninety percent of Malagasy people still buy from the market." After slaughter, the meat is distributed in quarters or whole to butchers, who then break it down for local sale.

She explained the most common cuts: filet, the most tender; *vodihena*, akin to round steak, and *la bosse*, the prized hump. Rarely sold whole, the hump is typically shared with other cuts, a delicacy in high demand. "It melts on the tongue when grilled over open flame," she said. "The hump is tradition incarnate."

We shifted to traditional preparations. *Varanga*, or *jaka* in the southern dialects, is a confit-style dish once reserved for royalty during *lanonana* ceremonies. Originally preserved in fat and buried in clay jars, today's version still echoes that instinct preservation—long braised, gently shredded, layered with memory. In the south, *varanga* can also mean sun-dried zebu, eaten like a nomadic jerky.

Then there's *maskita*, Madagascar's skewers—two cubes of filet, sandwiching a pearl of hump fat, grilled over coals or directly on embers. Regional sauces bring further complexity: in the northwest, a crushed peanut-tomato-onion blend called sauce *voanjo*; elsewhere, pickled green papaya or inventive glazes with soy and honey. But, she reminded me, "Traditional Malagasy food didn't use spices. Those came later. Our authenticity lies in simplicity—salt, fat, fire."

Chef Moretti mentioned that zebu's meaning transcends cuisine. It's a national identity. Even the country's soccer team bears its name: the Barea.

At Haka Fy, her homage to the zebu is more than symbolic. Her signature dish, *manaramolotra*—loosely translated as "abundant satisfaction"—features four zebu parts: tongue, tripe (blanched and delicately cleaned), ribeye, and tail. "It's a festive plate," she said. "It brings the whole beast to the table—abundance, heritage, pride."

Unlike beef in France or Japan, Malagasy zebu meat is never marbled. "No *persillé* here," she said. The animals graze freely—no grain-finishing, no stalls. Some have experimented with pen-feeding to tenderize the meat, but marbling remains elusive.

For a time during colonization, zebu was dismissed as *viande du pauvre*—a poor man's meat—while turkey and chicken, newly introduced by French and British customs, became holiday fare. The irony? Zebu, which takes years to raise, was cheaper than antibiotic-laced poultry imported en masse.

"When I was little," Henintsoa confided, "eating zebu at Christmas meant we couldn't afford chicken. It meant shame. Now, I say it's time to reclaim it."

We shared a meal under the soft rustle of leaves in Haka Fy's garden. She insisted I try her signature dish, *manaramolotra*. The mix of tongue, tripe, ribeye, and tail—slow-cooked for forty-eight hours—was delicious. The jus had a rich, fatty mouthfeel. A few pink peppercorns added a zingy lift. The dish was also served with Romazava, the traditional leafy broth, and a blend of red and white rice.

Before leaving, I asked her if she thought zebu would ever reach the reverence that Wagyu or Angus enjoy abroad. She laughed—not dismissively, but knowingly. "We're not trying to copy. We're telling a different story."

I thought of her words as the car climbed toward the Ambalavao Zebu market. If Haka Fy was one chapter in the zebu's tale, what awaited us on the cracked earth outside the market was another—louder, dustier, and grounded in centuries of tradition.

The zebu market took place in a vast open-air theater set upon rust-red earth—cracked, sunbaked, and shaped by decades of footsteps and hooves. A dense line of men etched the horizon. As we climbed to the top of the hill, the ground beneath my feet seemed to ripple like parched skin—its hardened surface a testament to drought.

Clusters of men stood in tight circles, while others guided their animals across the open plain toward a wooden enclosure. I would learn later this was the holding pen for zebus already sold, waiting for their new owners to arrive with a truck and haul them to their next destination. The cattle formed a living mosaic: glossy flanks in hues of sand, chestnut, charcoal—thick necks, and all sizes of horns. They waited, seemingly unfazed, as buyers inspected them—touching flanks, checking hooves, and appraising silently.

There was a hum to the place, not loud but constant: the low murmur of bargaining voices, the grunt of zebu resisting the sharp crack of a baton, the occasional sharp whistle or barked command. The smell was unmistakable—damp earth, livestock, and dust.

From this spot, perched high above the plain, the view was staggering—a 360-degree panorama of the surrounding massifs, their shadows rolling slowly across the valley floor like drifting clouds.

My conversation with Chef Moretti in Tana echoed in my mind. In Madagascar, a zebu is not just livestock. It is wealth, ritual, dowry, and sacrifice. To observe a transaction here was to witness something older than modernity—a continuation of customs passed down across generations.

I asked Nirina about prices. He pointed casually to a small group nearby: the largest, older zebus—around fifteen to eighteen years old—sold for roughly 2 million ariary (about $440); medium-sized animals fetched about 1.5 million ariary ($330), while younger ones, just two or three years old, cost closer to 400,000 ariary (eighty-eight dollars). A lot of money, considering the average monthly income per person in Madagascar is around fifty dollars.

Nirina added that zebus are usually rested from labor six months before being sold, allowing them to fatten. These are called *zebus de fosse*—"pit zebus"—a term rooted in older traditions, when zebus were placed in earthen pits to trample and soften soil used in building homes. The animals would compact and knead the earth with their weight, while simultaneously gaining flesh.

After we left the market, but before continuing our route toward Isalo National Park, Nirina suggested a detour. He wanted me to meet one of his longtime friends: Rija Ragon, who is involved with the Anja Reserve and recently opened the Anja Reserve Restaurant and Lodge.

Rija Ragon is a Franco-Malagasy, born and raised in Ambalavao. His father, a Frenchman, settled in Madagascar during the '60s and '70s, shortly after independence. Rija's upbringing was bicultural and deeply tied to Ambalavao, where his mother was from. This dual identity fueled his lifelong attachment to the region, both personally and professionally.

In the 1990s, his family established the first hotel in Ambalavao, Aux Bougainvillées. At the time, Madagascar was still grappling with neo-communist policies and limited tourism. Guests would ask for local attractions, prompting Rija to recommend a nearby forest—what would later become the Anja Reserve. As tourists trickled in, the family helped build trails and infrastructure, laying the groundwork for a community-managed reserve.

In the early days, local villagers hunted lemurs for food. But through persistent education, support, and economic incentive, Rija and his family helped change this mindset. They proved to the villagers that protecting lemurs could bring in sustainable income through tourism. From an initial population of just ten to twenty lemurs, the reserve now shelters around eight hundred, a powerful testament to the long-term impact of conservation.

The Anja Reserve isn't state-run. It's managed by the local villagers through a VOI (village-based organization), covering seven hundred hectares of primary forest. This became a model, gaining international recognition, with villagers responding quickly to fires or illegal logging—demonstrating a deep sense of ownership and pride.

In the beginning, most villagers were illiterate, and the idea of long-term gains from conservation was difficult to grasp. Concepts like "saving for tomorrow" held little relevance. To bridge the gap, Rija's family personally financed the early efforts, including paying villagers monthly to guard the forest—acting as trust builders until the benefits became visible.

Today, the reserve attracts more than fifty thousand visitors annually, generating more than two billion ariary in revenue. Still, Rija admits that challenges remain. Community management of funds has been uneven—there is still no clinic, and reinvestment in education or healthcare remains minimal—revealing gaps between income generation and social infrastructure.

Rija also founded The Anja Reserve Lodge near the reserve—an eco-friendly hotel built and run primarily by locals (90 percent of the staff). It provides jobs, training, and a pathway into the tourism industry, empowering villagers to pursue careers beyond Ambalavao.

But growth brings new risks. With more than one thousand people now part of the guiding association, competition is fierce. Rija fears new members might wait years for a single tour opportunity. He stressed the urgency of vocational training, especially in language skills and hospitality, to prepare youth for a sustainable future in tourism.

Despite the reserve's income, healthcare infrastructure remains nonexistent. Rija is currently building a community dispensary across from his lodge, fully funded by his operations. His plan includes staffing the clinic, securing medical supply donations from travelers, and co-managing it with the village association—an effort to fill a critical social gap left by underfunded public systems.

The lodge sources vegetables from nearby women farmers, strengthening local food systems. But monoculture farming (e.g., only onions or only potatoes in a season) hinders consistent supply. Rija works to educate farmers about crop rotation and the market potential of diverse produce, linking sustainable agriculture with culinary tourism.

The restaurant's menu centers around zebu, the region's cultural and gastronomic staple. Vegetables are bought daily from local women, reinforcing the lodge's economic connection to the village. This culinary anchoring in local produce reinforces the region's identity and keeps money within the community.

Rija is proud of what he's built, but he's far from finished. His mission is clear: to create sustainable systems that empower, educate, and endure.

We said our goodbyes and continued southwest, toward Isalo National Park. As we drove, the landscape changed to vast plains and wind-sculpted outcrops. It was hard not to think about the American Southwest. The terrain evoked something between Utah's Monument Valley and Arizona's red rock deserts—vast, cinematic, humbling. A place that, like Madagascar itself, conveyed a monumental scale with minimal human imprint.

Just as I was settling into the ochre calm of Isalo National Park, Nirina surprised me. With help from the lodge staff at Le Jardin du Roy, he had arranged something unexpected: a meeting with Farracel, the village healer and chief of a nearby Bara community—one of the last men in the region still practicing ancestral rites of astrology and healing.

The Bara people—historically semi-nomadic cattle herders—have long maintained strong ties to zebu cattle, central to their identity, rites of passage, and economy.

A few miles from the lodge, we reached their village, which felt sculpted from the very earth that surrounds it. The modest rectangular homes seemed built from sun-dried clay, their textured facades echoing the red laterite soil beneath. I later learned the walls were made from a traditional mixture of red clay, zebu dung, and soil harvested from termite mounds. The result: sturdy, breathable walls, perfectly suited for the dry climate. Thatched roofs made from local grasses rested lightly atop, shielding residents from the restless sun.

We first saw Farracel from a distance as Nirina launched his drone to capture aerial shots. Dressed in shorts and a t-shirt, the chief greeted us with a nod, asked us to wait, and disappeared. A few minutes later, he reemerged transformed, wearing a full ceremonial outfit—an arresting blend of tradition, symbolism, and personal flair.

He stood tall in a crimson robe trimmed with white, layered over a white shirt. His red headscarf sparkled with sequins and stars. Around his neck, an eclectic necklace of beads, animal teeth, keys, bones, and wooden charms swung with each movement—each likely carrying ancestral or protective meaning. A cane of carved wood rested in his palm. The final touch: oversized sunglasses, slightly askew, offering a wink of modern playfulness to a deeply traditional ensemble.

As we waited, I captured a moment that would stay with me long after the trip: a barefoot child in a red hoodie, standing silently, eyes locked on the drone rising overhead. Still and steady, he watched the blinking creature hum into the sky. A moment suspended between two worlds. I couldn't guess what he was thinking. What stories will this child tell?

Farracel invited us into his home. The single-room structure was small and simple. Beige walls were decorated with children's drawings made from red laterite soil: zebus, suns, stick figures. The floor, covered in worn *vinyl floor*, was powdered with fine dust. A table and two plastic chairs stood at one end, where his healing tools were arranged. Farracel invited us to sit on the floor. On the opposite wall, a small, darkened opening hinted at a

sleeping area. From within that shadowed recess, several children's eyes watched us, curious and silent.

Nirina encouraged me to ask anything. I spoke in French. He translated into the regional Malagasy dialect, and then back again.

"How old are you, and what is your role here?"

"About ninety," Farracel said. "I protect the village. I heal. I prevent misfortunes. I speak to the ancestors." He described rituals using blessed water and, at times, animal sacrifices, particularly during hardship—like drought. He relied on local plants and roots, the village living pharmacopoeia. He also read the *vintana*—a traditional astrological system rooted in Arab influence—to determine auspicious days. He added that his role extends to spiritual meditation for the community's well-being. In both health and ceremony, his presence was central.

"What about the zebu?" I asked. I'd seen the village enclosure was empty.

He explained that the zebus were out grazing with a herder, often a child, from dawn to dusk. They rotated through natural pastures. Fenced fields were uncommon.

Nirina added that zebus were everything here. They plowed fields, transported goods, and replaced vehicles. They even pulled carts carrying the sick. I asked how many zebus the village had, but the only answer I got was a long "ahhh" with a hand gesture. Nirina translated: "A lot." He explained that the chief wouldn't give an exact number—zebu are the village's most important markers of wealth, and ownership is not something disclosed lightly. To reveal how many one has is to reveal one's social standing, and that kind of information is guarded.

Curious about daily life, I asked how meals were shared.

Farracel said food is eaten on the ground, with spoons. Elders eat separately, shielded from the competitive speed of youth. Meals are humble: rice, cassava, sweet potatoes, corn. Meat—zebu, chicken, duck—is for special occasions. Lemur meat was mentioned, rarely.

Respect for elders was non-negotiable. "You must bow at the door when entering. You sit before serving food to a parent."

I turned to rituals involving zebu.

"Zebu are sacrificed," he said. "For births, deaths, droughts, marriages. To call blessings or avert misfortune."

When his adult son joined us, I asked cautiously, "Is stealing a zebu still part of a young man's initiation?"

He nodded. "Yes," he said simply. He had done it himself, years ago.

"But stealing a zebu remains a capital crime," I added.

He didn't answer. The look he gave me said "we know, but this is our tradition."

I asked about relationships with other tribes. The chief and his son said the Bara usually kept to themselves. "Except for school or harvest," the son added. "Though lately, we marry outside. It creates beautiful mixed children."

When I asked about selling their zebus to the market, they mentioned they were sold occasionally, mostly castrated males, prized for their size and meat. Female zebus were kept for milk. The closest markets, like the one we visited in Ambalavao, were far away, so sometimes traders come directly to the villages, collecting cattle from several communities before heading to the market.

Before we left, we offered a few bills as thanks. As we drove away, we passed the village's sacred tree—its base strewn with worn clothes and old bottles. Offerings to ancestors, whispers of gratitude for safe births, good harvests, and restored health.

Over breakfast the next morning, I ordered grilled pieces of zebu. The meat, tender and charred (very similar to burnt ends), carried with it a trace of the village's story. I thought of Farracel, his sunglasses glinting in the sun, and the boy beneath the red hoodie, watching the sky for answers.

From there, we made our way from Tuléar—also known as Toliara—toward Fort-Dauphin, or Tolagnaro, on Madagascar's southeastern shore. On paper, the 387-mile journey should have taken half a day. In reality, it turned into a grueling thirty-hour drive that tested both patience and suspension systems. The road—if it can still be called that—unraveled into a sequence of craters, washouts, and detours that forced us to drive through the night—twelve hours straight without sleep, navigating by headlights and stubborn resolve. At times, it felt less like a drive and more like an off-road pilgrimage. I may have arrived in Fort-Dauphin physically intact, but I'm fairly sure my spine took on a new alignment along the way.

We finally approached the city, nestled between the Indian Ocean and the mountains, with the verdant slopes of Pic Saint-Louis. This place is known for its nature's diversity from golden beaches to lush rainforest.

On the outskirts, we visited BoViMa—short for "Bonne Viande de Madagascar"—a World Bank–backed operation with a bold ambition: to modernize zebu meat production and put Madagascar's beef on the global map.

A local contact of Nirina's had arranged a meeting with PJ, the company's South African operations manager. He welcomed us with a firm handshake and a dose of realism.

"This is the only export-approved abattoir in the country," he said. "We're ISO 22000 certified and recently passed Halal audits. But open a menu in Dubai, and you'll see South African steak—not zebu."

That's just one challenge. The bigger one is cultural. Outside the gates, tradition pushed back. In Madagascar, zebus are more than livestock—they're status symbols, central to rites of passage and ancestral traditions. A public outcry had led to the government to ban zebu meat exports, blindsiding the company.

"When the feasibility study was done, there was no ban," PJ explained. "Then it came in. We had to rethink everything."

Today, the company supplies hotels in Antananarivo with premium cuts like ribeye and fillet while offering more affordable offal and brisket locally. BoViMa slaughters up to 150 zebu a week—well below its one-hundred-a-day capacity—but volume is growing.

To improve quality, BoViMa increasingly relies on its own feedlot. "Market zebus are often old, lean, and poorly grazed," said PJ. "Our feedlot animals get high-protein diets, and the difference is obvious." The goal is to phase out market purchases entirely and raise five thousand zebus under strict standards.

But doing so means challenging long standing traditions. "We aim to slaughter in around two years," PJ said. "That's young by local standards. It's going to take time to shift the mindset."

To bridge that gap, BoViMa is investing in a network of satellite farms. Approved locals are given land, water access, and then pregnant heifers. BoViMa retains ownership but buys back the animals once they're raised. "It's not just contract farming," PJ said. "It's a partnership. We want them to be part of the system, not outside it."

The company handles only primary butchering in Fort-Dauphin. The transformation happens in Antananarivo, where BoViMa's processing partner—led by a former chef from South Africa's Blue Train—turns zebu into sausages, mortadella, and tomahawk steaks for the capital's upscale hotels. "He gives a second life to cuts most Malagasy chefs haven't worked with," PJ said.

Still, much of the local market demands offal—intestines, feet, tongue, tripe. BoViMa caters to that too. "We sell everything," PJ said. "Even hides—sometimes to tanneries, but more often to lobster fishermen who use them as bait."

Local resistance remains, especially around export plans. "People ask, 'Why feed others when we're hungry?'" PJ said. "But exports could mean jobs, infrastructure, and foreign currency. We're trying to show that both can exist."

Zebu meat, in BoViMa's hands, is no longer just about rituals. It's about refrigeration, consistency, and traceability. But it's also a balancing act between modernization and cultural respect.

In Madagascar, the modern story of industrial zebu meat is still being written.

On the long ride back, I replayed the journey: the chef's reverent words, the market's dust, the child staring at the drone, the factory's sterile efficiency. I realized I had seen every version of the zebu—sacred, transactional, ancestral, industrial. Each one real. Each one incomplete on its own. How can one animal carry so much?

I saw how one animal could unify people. Rich or poor, Christian or Muslim, highlander or coastal villager—every Malagasy knows the shape of a horn, the pace of a herd, the gravity of a sacrifice. In a fragmented world, that kind of shared reverence is rare. It's worth honoring.

CHAPTER 7

Beyond the Hive

Madagascar's Honey Odyssey

Tsy ny hosoran-tsakay no ho mangidy;
tsy ny hosoran-tantely no ho mamy;
fa ny atao no mahasoa sy maharatsy.

It's not being rubbed with chili pepper that makes you smell bad,
and it's not being smeared with honey that makes you smell good,
but it's what you do that makes it good or bad.

—TRADITIONAL MALAGASY SAYING

The relentless journey to Ambanja from the rice fields of the north Diana region was a grueling test of patience, each mile stretching interminably as our car lurched and jostled over the treacherous *Route Nationale 6* (RN6). It took two and a half hours to cover just sixty miles. It felt as though the journey might never end. When we finally arrived at Ambanja, I felt relieved.

◀ *In a rural yard near Ambanja, bees turn blossoms into survival—one golden drop at a time.*

As we meandered through the winding roads of town, palm trees along the unpaved road swayed gently in the breeze. Upon reaching the entrance of our hotel, a sense of tranquility washed over me. The signpost, adorned with the name "Palma Nova" in bold blue letters, stood as mark of hospitality. Managed by Chef Farah's mother, the Palma Nova hotel was charming and picturesque. A majestic traveller's palm, or Ravenala, native to the island of Madagascar, lined the driveway as their fronds rustling softly as if in greeting. The traditional thatched roofing structures of the Palma Nova hotel came into view, standing in harmony with the natural surroundings. The pathway, bordered by an array of tropical plants, led toward the inviting thatched-roof buildings that promised a peaceful retreat.

As I stepped out of the car, my body felt as though it had been slowly compressed and then released, like a spring unwinding. It took a few moments to soak in the vibrant ambiance. To my right stood a magnificent cashew tree, its broad, leathery leaves forming a dense, shady canopy. Nearby, the distinctive noni tree, with its large, dark green leaves and bumpy fruit, caught my eye. The unique blend of these trees against the backdrop of the hotel roof created a serene, picturesque setting. It felt as though nature had crafted this spot as a perfect haven.

I was immediately struck by the rustic charm of the open dining area. The high, thatched roofs supported by sturdy wooden beams provided ample shade while allowing the gentle breeze to flow through, emphasizing the hotel's integration with nature. Tables adorned with white tablecloths were neatly arranged, offering a pleasing setting for a meal. Cozy seating areas with cushioned benches invited a moment of relaxation, adding to the overall hospitality of the space. The open design allowed natural light to filter in, creating a warm atmosphere that instantly put me at ease.

There stood Farah's mother, a middle-aged woman with an Asian complexion, reflecting the rich cultural landscape of Madagascar. Her presence commanded attention without uttering a word. She welcomed us with a generous smile, her kindness immediately making us feel at home.

At Palma Nova, the Vietnamese-Malagasy family behind the restaurant brings a distinctive fusion of flavors to every dish. As we settled in for dinner, the menu invited us to start with either a refreshing tomato and basil salad or a vibrant Vietnamese salad bursting with fresh herbs. Next, we could explore the delicate flavors of zebu carpaccio or dive into a rich, comforting crab soup. For the main course, we were tempted by the zebu meat skewers, prepared with a Vietnamese twist, or perhaps the succulent zebu steak, perfectly paired with a green pepper sauce. The Romazava chicken offered us a taste of traditional Malagasy cuisine, while the Thai duck with peanut sauce added an exciting, exotic twist. Each dish at Palma Nova felt like a culinary journey, telling the story of how diverse cultures came together on a single plate, right in front of us.

After a dinner, Farah's sister showed us to our rooms. Mine was on the garden side. Basic, but clean. A bed with a mosquito net and an open shower. Two green geckos, each nearly the length of my hand, clung to the wall, kept me company during the night.

As the first light crept in, a rooster announced the day—louder and less forgiving than any alarm clock. It was too early for breakfast, and the morning sun just begun to paint the sky. Today's agenda included a visit to a local farmer who integrated several hives from a honey company called Beekeeper into his garden. With time on my hands, I decided to revisit my notes and watched the recording from my conversation with Gaël Hankenne, the co-owner of Beekeeper, I had prior to my trip to the island. His insights into sustainable beekeeping practices and the company's mission to support local farmers would be fresh in my mind as I prepared for the day ahead.

At the beginning of our conversation, I asked Gaël about the origins of his adventure and the creation of his honey company. I wanted to learn more about his goals in supporting the local community.

After completing studies in economics, Gaël embarked on a period of travels, which eventually led to a decade-long tenure with Médecins Sans Frontières (Doctors Without Borders). This experience would become a defining chapter in his life, shaping not only his perspective but also the mission that would later drive his honey company. The desire to support local communities grew out of these formative years, where his work with Doctors Without Borders left an indelible mark on his approach to business and social impact.

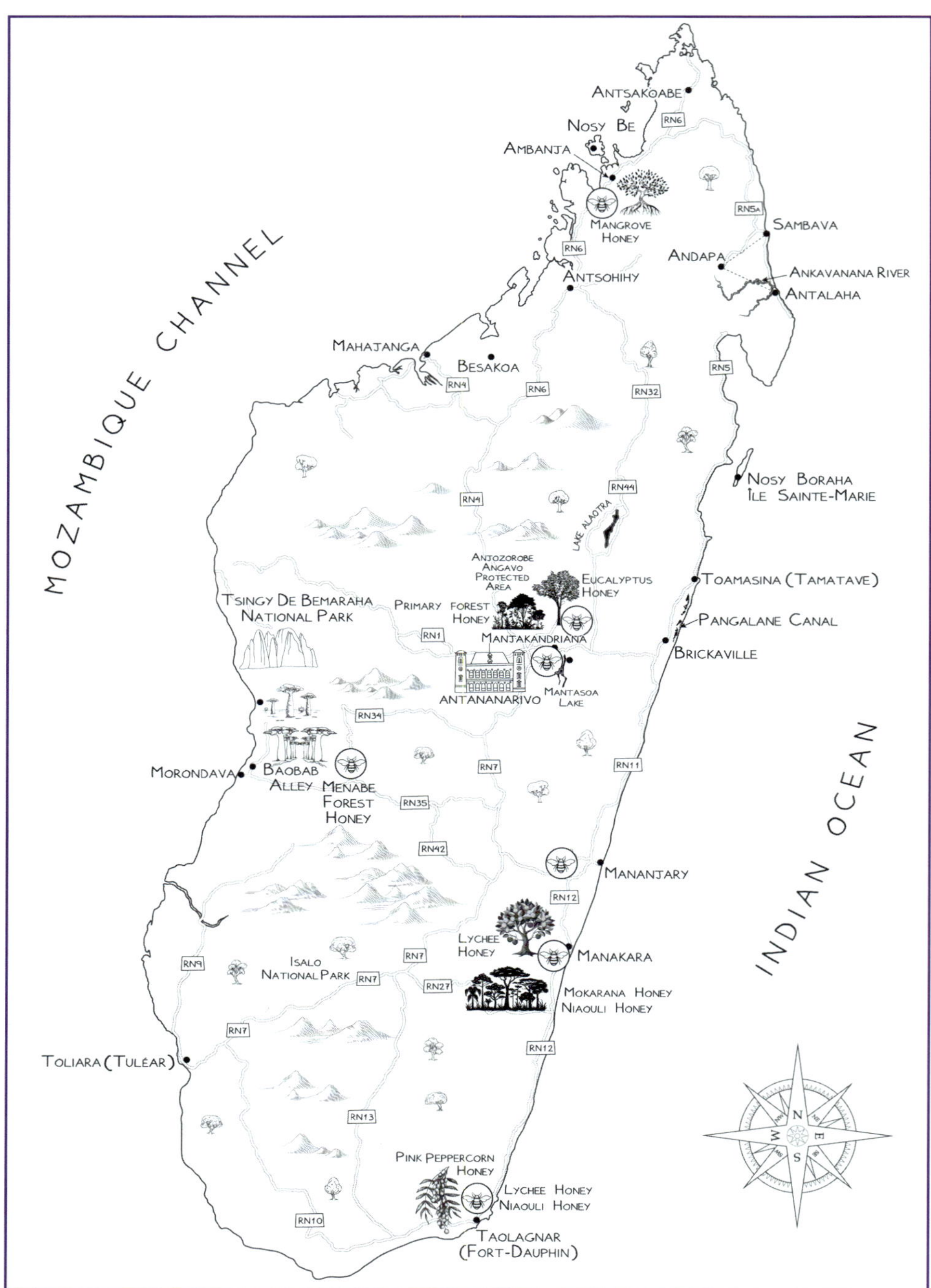

Mapping the blossoms behind beekeeper's unique honey.

In 2015, Gaël and his wife arrived in Madagascar, leaving behind the tumultuous environment of South Sudan, Africa, where he was last based for Doctors Without Borders. Gaël explained how their journey to this beautiful island was fueled by a profound admiration for its breathtaking landscapes and a deep concern for its pervasive poverty.

"Madagascar is the fifth-poorest country in the world. It's hard to stay indifferent. As you've probably seen in Tana, you can be in a beautiful neighborhood and right next to it, there's a family living off the garbage."

Together they began to contemplate the idea of creating something meaningful. They believed firmly that the true pillar of development was business. Gaël's experiences in the NGO world with Doctors Without Borders had shown him that while humanitarian aid is essential in times of crisis, it is business that drives sustainable development. This approach could create a win-win situation—benefiting producers, the company, and the final customer alike.

Gaël recounted a pivotal moment when his brother, an amateur beekeeper, visited Madagascar. Reflecting on the early days, Gaël's brother pointed out the honey in their region, admiring the richness it held. The surrounding biodiversity promised exceptional honey unlike any other. This observation sparked an interest that would soon evolve into a passion for beekeeping. They saw it not just as a business but also as a product of immense value, carrying only positive externalities. It nurtured the environment, offered additional income to local farmers, and provided a wholesome, healthy option for consumers. What began as a simple remark grew into a commitment to harness the natural gifts of the island, with honey becoming a symbol of sustainability and shared prosperity.

I listened intently, fascinated by the journey, and asked how he started the beekeeping venture.

Gaël explained that initially, they learned beekeeping through online courses and hands-on experience. They identified areas in Madagascar suitable for beekeeping and established two operational models. The first involved working with experienced beekeepers, providing pre-financing and training to enhance their production. They formalized these partnerships with five-year contracts. The second model targeted regions where beekeeping was entirely new. They collaborated with organizations focused on environmental conservation, like reforestation of mangroves. They introduced beekeeping to provide alternative income sources for local farmers. Gaël explained that beekeeping offered a sustainable, environmentally friendly way to boost their incomes instead of traditionally relied-upon activities like charcoal production and rice farming.

I was curious about how Beekeeper went about understanding the local flowering calendar, especially in regions where they weren't yet established. Gaël said the process depends largely on the region. In areas where beekeepers were already active, they typically had a good grasp of how the blooming seasons unfold and could share their insights. However, in regions where beekeeping was starting from scratch, the approach required more groundwork. One method involved finding local honey hunters—individuals who engaged in traditional honey collecting. These hunters provided valuable information about when they typically harvested honey, which in turn offered clues about the local flowering periods. To deepen this understanding, it was common to collect honey samples from these hunters or even from local markets. Although market samples weren't always ideal, they still provided a basis for analysis. These analyses helped identify the types of honey being harvested, offering a clearer picture of the nectar sources and flowering seasons in the area. This information was essential for planning and optimizing beekeeping activities in these new regions.

I also asked Gaël to explain how beekeepers rear the queen bees from the wild bee colonies. He said it was a traditional practice that was a vital part of beekeeping on the island, offering a means to enhance the genetic diversity and resilience of managed hives. Gaël said beekeepers, based on the knowledge passed down through generations, venture deep into the forest to locate natural hives, seeking the queen bees.

Gaël emphasized the importance of continuous training and support. They work with external trainers and local production managers to ensure the success of their initiatives. When the time of the harvest comes, they take an active role to ensure the honey meets the highest standards.

The Traditional Process to Rear the Queen Bees in Madagascar

1. The beekeepers search for wild colonies, hidden in hollow trees or nestled within rock crevices. They rely on their understanding of the local environment and the behavior of bees to identify these hives.
2. Once the hives are located, they assess their strength, looking for signs of healthy and productive queens. The process of extracting the queen is intricate and requires careful handling. They use smoke to calm the colony—a technique that pacifies the bees by masking the alarm pheromones they release when threatened.
3. With the bees subdued, they carefully open the hive. The queens, distinct in their size and appearance, are sought out among the worker bees. Once spotted, they are gently captured. Transporting the queen to a managed hive is a crucial next step.
4. The beekeepers place the queen bees in a protective "cage," often accompanied by a few worker bees to tend to their needs. This setup includes a food source, such as sugar water or honey, to sustain the queens during their transition. The goal is to introduce them to a new colony without causing disruption or rejection.
5. The introduction process is meticulous. The "caged" queens are placed within the managed hives, allowing the worker bees to become accustomed to their scent. Over several days, this gradual exposure helps the colonies accept the new queens.
6. As the new queens begin their role, laying eggs and establishing new brood, the cycle of life in the hive continues.

This delicate balance between tradition and innovation is at the heart of beekeeping in Madagascar, where the pursuit of honey is as much about preserving cultural practices as it is about economic necessity. Queen rearing in Madagascar is more than just a practical technique; it is a reflection of the island's rich beekeeping heritage.

I was impressed by the dedication and vision behind the venture. Gaël's journey from economics and humanitarian work to sustainable business in Madagascar was truly inspiring.

Gaël smiled, appreciating the acknowledgment, and concluded that it has been a transformative journey, driven by passion and purpose. They are committed to making a positive impact on the environment and the lives of the local people.

As I replayed the recording, Gaël's words echoed the ideology that underpinned Beekeeper's mission. The sun had now fully risen by the time the video ended. I was ready to see firsthand how Gaël's vision translated into action on the ground. Closing my notebook, I stepped out of my room into garden's crisp morning air, eager to visit the local farmer who had installed Beekeeper's hives and made them a part of his daily routine.

I joined Nirina and Chef Farah for breakfast. Nirina was enjoying his favorite traditional rice soup with beef. My morning stomach was not ready for the experience, and I opted for the fresh soursop juice, an omelette, and a fruit platter with mango, papaya, and the local little sweet bananas—my favorite!

Maroussène Kennedy, an experienced agricultural technician from Beekeeper based in Ambanja, joined us to guide us to the local beekeeper outside the town. Kennedy met Gaël while doing an internship during his studies. As we conversed in French, I quickly recognized his passion for working in rural areas, especially in beekeeping. During our drive to the destination, I took the opportunity to learn more about his experiences and the challenges he faced in his work.

As we left the busy streets of Ambanja behind, the scenery shifted to the quieter environment of the countryside. We crossed the wide Sambirano River, its waters vital to the surrounding fertile lands. The landscape, with its dense greenery near the river, turned into a more barren scenery as we progressed on these winding roads, reflecting the slower pace of life in these rural areas.

Kennedy's passion for working in rural areas was evident in the way he connected with both the land and the community. His interest in beekeeping, or apiculture, went beyond the production of honey; it was about a deeper understanding and respect for nature. The bees, vital to the local ecosystems, represented a delicate balance that he found incredibly rewarding to maintain. His work wasn't confined to a single area; it spanned across Ambanja, where he collaborated with fifty-three beekeepers. In the southern zone, south of the Sambirano River, twenty producers were making strides in their craft, while in the northern zone, north of the river, thirty-three more were doing the same. Each region presented its own set of challenges and opportunities, but with each passing season, progress was being made.

I asked Kennedy about the types of honey primarily produced in the area. As we passed through landscapes dotted with unique flora, he explained that the main types of honey were mangrove and *Leptolaena*, an endemic honey-producing plant from the island, known locally as *zahana*. He emphasized that these honeys are highly valued for their distinctive flavors and beneficial properties.

I asked Kennedy to explain the tradition of honey hunting. He pointed out that it was a practice deeply embedded in the local culture, providing both sustenance and income for rural villages.

The process begins with experienced hunters searching for wild bee colonies hidden in the forest. These hunters rely on their knowledge of the environment and bee behavior, often trekking miles to find the elusive nests. Once a hive is located, hunters use minimal protective gear and smoke to help pacify the bees. They cut away the honeycomb using knives and other tools. The harvested honeycomb is often pressed to extract the honey, which is then strained to remove impurities like wax and bee parts. The honey is stored in containers for consumption or sale—often plastic water bottles that children have collected from tourists' cars passing through villages. However, Kennedy pointed out that traditional beekeeping methods are often far less sustainable, as they typically involve harvesting most or all of the honeycomb, sometimes destroying the hive in the process.

He added that although a large number of farmers were initially motivated to adopt modern beekeeping, many dropped out after the first year due to the hard work involved and the unexpected challenges. Traditional honey hunting methods are deeply rooted in the region, making it difficult to change long-standing practices. But he noted that those who have embraced modern beekeeping techniques have experienced significant benefits, highlighting the potential for progress despite the challenges.

He mentioned that in the southern zone, beekeepers were able to produce 735 kilograms (1,600 pounds) of mangrove honey between December and January.

The car came to a stop along the road, right in front of a vibrant blue house. We made our way down the path beside it, leading to an open area surrounded by other small dwellings. Behind the buddings. I could distinguish visible parts of a few blue beehives in a large and unmaintained garden. The ground of the open area was unpaved, and chickens roamed freely around us. With no one in sight, we chose to sit on large logs of wood arranged in a circle beneath a magnificent cashew tree.

As we settled into one of the cozy seating areas, I turned to Kennedy with a question that had been on my mind. "What are some of the main challenges you face in working with these beekeepers?" I asked.

Kennedy took a moment before responding. "One of the biggest challenges is the distance between the beekeeping sites. Traveling between them isn't easy, especially during the rainy season when the roads become nearly impassable. Additionally, convincing the beekeepers to shift from traditional methods to modern practices requires a lot of time and effort. But seeing the positive impact on their lives and the environment, like where we are today, makes it all worthwhile," he said thoughtfully.

The farmer emerged from the main blue house, greeted us with a warm smile, and joined us. He spoke only Malagasy, so Kennedy served as our translator, seamlessly conveying my questions and the farmer's responses. I was eager to learn about his life before he took up beekeeping. He shared that he previously raised and sold chickens, but honey production had become a valuable source of additional income. Despite the benefits, he acknowledged that the work was demanding, and many local farmers were still hesitant to commit to it.

We followed the farmer into the garden, where he proudly showed us his beehives. He explained that he maintained around twelve hives, producing an average of one hundred kilograms—approximately 220 pounds—of organic certified honey each month. The hives were nestled among tall grasses, wildflowers, and bushes that thrived in the sandy soil, partially hidden from view. I noticed all the hives were oriented in the same direction, their entrances facing the sunrise. The farmer explained this positioning encouraged the bees to start their work earlier each day.

At Kennedy's request, the farmer agreed to open one of the hives for us. He disappeared briefly into one of the dwellings and returned wearing a well-worn veil of fine mesh and gloves that weathered many seasons. With practiced precision, he gently puffed smoke from a small, handmade smoker into the hive's entrance. The dark bees, sensing the smoke, instinctively calmed and retreated deeper into their home.

With care, the farmer pried open the hive, the wooden lid lifting with a soft creak. Inside, the hive buzzed with life. The combs, rich and thick with honey, glistened in the soft light. As the farmer inspected the frames, I admired the intricate patterns of the comb, each cell meticulously filled with honey. When I asked how often he visited the hives, he replied that he checked on them every two weeks. With a gentle touch, he replaced the frame and carefully secured the lid. Kennedy explained this honey was now all-flowers, as the season for mangrove honey was over.

After removing his equipment, we returned to our seats under the shade of a cashew tree. I inquired about the main challenges he faced as a beekeeper. He explained when the flowers were abundant during the season, he could achieve excellent honey production in just three months. However, his primary concern was deforestation, which threatened the availability of honey-producing plants and, consequently, reduced his yield.

As we drove back to Ambanja, my thoughts drifted to some articles I read before my journey to the island. Curious to delve deeper, I asked Kennedy to share more about the connection between the Malagasy people and honey.

Beekeeping has long been a vital part of Madagascar's heritage, with a history as diverse and complex as the island's flora. In the early twentieth century, Madagascar emerged as a significant player on the global honey stage. Between the 1920s and 1940s, the island was the world's third-largest honey producer, yielding an impressive thirty-eight thousand tons annually. More than 65 percent of this golden harvest was exported to Europe, establishing Madagascar as a key supplier to the international market. However, the honey industry faced a significant setback in the early 1950s when European countries imposed an embargo due to concerns about added sugar and water that did not meet their stringent standards. This blow was compounded by a broader embargo on animal products in the mid-'90s, which further crippled the industry. It wasn't until 2011 that the European Union lifted these restrictions, allowing Madagascar to cautiously reenter the market. By 2015, honey exports had resumed, though on a much smaller scale, with the island exporting fifty-four tons.

Yet, honey in Madagascar is far more than just an export commodity; it is a cultural cornerstone. Beyond its role as a sweetener, honey is revered in rituals and ceremonies, often used as a sacred offering to honor ancestors and deities. The Malagasy language reflects this deep cultural connection—words like *tantely* (honey) symbolize sweetness and affection. Even place names, such as Ambohitantely (honey mountain), north of Antananarivo, highlight the centrality of honey in the island's collective memory.

In the daily lives of the Malagasy people, honey is a staple. With an average consumption of nearly four kilograms (8.8 pounds) per person annually (in comparison, the average consumption per capita in the US is 1.3 pounds), honey is an essential part of life, despite the country's economic challenges. It is a beloved ingredient in traditional dishes and a trusted remedy for ailments like colds and respiratory issues, valued not only for its flavor but also for its healing properties.

The revival of honey exports in the 2010s has been a story of resilience and adaptation. Today, modern beekeeping practices are being harmonized with traditional knowledge to boost production and ensure sustainability. Initiatives such as Beekeeper training programs and the introduction of modern hives have significantly improved yields. This renaissance in the honey industry not only strengthens Madagascar's economy but also contributes to the conservation of its unique biodiversity, serving as a model of sustainable development.

Back to the Palma Nova hotel in Ambanja, after saying goodbye to Kennedy, I asked Chef Farah to share her thoughts, as I was curious to learn more about traditional recipes that use honey.

After our journey through the island, Farah, Nirina, and I went back to see Gaël at Beekeeper in Antananarivo. As we entered their honey production space, Gaël greeted us with welcoming smile. He inquired about our tour around the island, setting the stage for the honey tasting that awaited

Malagasy Traditional Recipe with Honey

Koba Akondro: A popular dessert made from mashed bananas, peanuts, rice flour, and honey, all wrapped in banana leaves and steamed. It's often found at local markets and gas stations across Madagascar.

Bonbon Voanio: These coconut balls are made with grated coconut, honey, and sometimes vanilla. They're a popular sweet treat on the island.

Mofo Gasy: These traditional Malagasy pancakes are made with rice flour, sugar, and sometimes honey. It's one of the popular street foods and is typically eaten for breakfast or as a snack.

Ravitoto: Made from crushed cassava leaves, this dish is sometimes flavored with honey, especially when served with pork, to add a touch of sweetness.

Farah also mentioned that people make baobab juice infused with niaouli honey. She described the process, which requires a hammer due to the baobab fruit's hard shell. After carefully cracking open the shells, people extract the dehydrated pulp and place it into a large bowl. They pour hot water over the pulp, ensuring it's fully covered, and they let it soak for about twenty minutes. After soaking, they use their hands to gently knead the mixture, helping the pulp separate from the seeds. Once the seeds are clean, they strain the mixture, keeping only the juice. Finally, they add some niaouli honey to the juice and stir thoroughly.

us. We all anticipated to sample the unique flavors of Madagascar's honey, but before diving in, my curiosity couldn't wait. I asked what made the bees of Madagascar distinct from others around the world. This query hinted at the rich biodiversity of the island, suggesting that even the bees here might carry a unique character, reflective of their environment.

Gaël shared that the bees on the island are an endemic variety of bee from Madagascar: the *Apis mellifera unicolor*. He added that there are more than twenty thousand types of bees, but the honeybee *Apis mellifera*, which are found on every continent except Antarctica, is the single most important pollinator. These highly adaptive honeybees easily settle into other colonies or in a variety of man-made hives.

The honey tasting session at Beekeeper was organized like a wine tasting. Gaël arranged the various types of honey on the table, starting with the lighter varieties and progressing to the more robust ones. The tasting was designed not only to savor the different flavors but also to highlight the unique floral origins and regions from which the honey was harvested. Gaël explained that some honeys make the transition from one period to another.

"In the Manakara region, for example, we have four different types of honey. We start with lychee in September, move on to *mokarana* in October to November, niaouli in December to February, and then we finish the calendar with all-flower. That's all in the same area with the same hives."

Our discussions frequently delved into the intricacies of classifying and naming honey, especially regarding its floral origins and the difficulties in ensuring consistency across various harvests. At the Beekeeper's site, we received an immersive educational and sensory experience, where Farah, Nirina, and I could fully appreciate the subtleties of each honey variety. It also served as a backdrop for broader conversations about the environmental and cultural significance of honey production in Madagascar.

Gaël commented that the island's diverse and unique flora produces honey with unparalleled qualities. With thousands of endemic species among the nineteen thousand botanical varieties cataloged, this rich biodiversity, from the coastal mangroves to the highland forests, is not only a haven for wildlife but also the uniqueness behind the island's exquisite honey varieties. In a world increasingly enamored with artisanal and organic products, Madagascar stands at the threshold of a golden opportunity—one that promises not just economic growth, but also a pathway to sustainable livelihoods for its rural communities.

Eager to translate our discussions into sensory experience, we began sampling the honeys one by one, ready to experience firsthand the essence of Madagascar's diverse flora. Gaël explained that the honeys have different colors, different tastes, depending on the foraging area, but also on the floral agenda of a certain zone.

We started the tasting with mangrove honey.

Gaël pointed out that in the northwestern region of Antsohihy, mangroves thrive along the coastal edges and river's estuaries, offering a unique floral source for local bees. It is there, in the Diana region, where bees produce mangrove honey, harvested between December and January.

Madagascar Honey Variety				
Honey Type	**Region**	**Season**	**Flavor Profile**	**Application**
Mangrove	Antsohihy	December-January	Complex	Savoy dishes like meats, foie gras, lamb, spareribs
Pink Peppercorn	Fort-Dauphin	April–May	Smooth with subtle peppery note	Signature savory dishes
Mokarana	Manakara	October	Slightly tangy notes and brown notes	Cooking and smoothies
Lychee	Manakara	October	Aromatic and rose (blossom)	Cooking and baking
Menabe Forest	Menabe	May	Delicate blend of jujube sweetness with smoky notes	Alone or in cooking
Tropical Forest	Manakara	March–June	Blend of slightly bitter notes with light floral notes	Breakfast spreads or to sweeten beverages
Primary Forest	Anjozorobe	November	Sweet to slightly tangy flavors	Signature savory dishes
Eucalyptus	North of Antananarivo	June-September	Subtle notes of salted caramel	Breakfast spreads and drizzling over ice cream

This honey is a reflection of its surroundings: bold and powerful. It is praised for its rich, complex flavor. Gaël revealed the complex flavor profile makes it a perfect match for savory dishes, especially when paired with meats, foie gras, lamb, and spareribs, or used in frozen desserts to add a unique twist. He added that it is also suggested for use in barbecues, couscous, and even yogurts.

Gaël mentioned, with its distinct terroir, this honey appeals to gourmet markets, and it could be interesting for the United States, where demand for exotic and organic honey is surging.

I recalled our farmer outside of Ambanja who was producing mangrove honey, and I noted the production of this honey is tied to the unique mangrove ecosystems in Madagascar, adding an environmental aspect to its story.

Our second tasting was pink peppercorn honey.

Gaël stated it comes from the southeastern region of Madagascar, near Fort-Dauphin, where bees gather nectar from the pink peppercorn trees that thrive along the coast. Harvested once a year in April and May, this honey reflects the unique environment of the area.

The flavor began with a smooth sweetness, but what set this honey apart was the subtle peppery note that emerged afterward. It was a hint of spice that added depth without overpowering the palate.

Pink peppercorn honey became a favorite of mine. Gaël added that the delicate and nuanced flavors appeal not only to adventurous foodies but also to chefs seeking unique ingredients for their signature culinary creations.

Our third sample was *mokarana* honey.

Gaël clarified that the *mokarana* tree is not endemic to Madagascar but is believed to have originated from Oceania. It provides a unique nectar source for local bees. The result is *mokarana* honey, harvested in October in the Manakara region, known for its bright, fruity flavor.

This honey is distinctive, with its slightly tangy notes reminiscent of lemon and grapefruit and an additional brown note that reminded me of caramel or sweet almond. Gaël suggested this honey captures the vibrant, tropical essence of Madagascar's southeast. It is a honey for those who appreciate a lively, citrus-like flavor that adds a special touch to any culinary creation.

When I pointed to a beginning of crystallization of the honey in the jar, Gaël explained the honey's crystallization process is a natural one, which some consumers mistakenly view as a sign of poor quality, although it is a mark of authenticity and high sugar content.

Crystallized honey develops a grainy or gritty texture, which some people find less appealing compared to the smooth, liquid consistency that is often preferred for spreading on toast, mixing into a beverage, or using in recipes. The crystallization also makes the honey appear cloudy or opaque, which can be off-putting to those who prefer the aesthetic appeal of clear, liquid honey.

"To understand why honey crystallizes," said Gaël, "it's important to know that honey is composed mainly of sugar and water. The sugar is dissolved in the water, but honey contains more sugar than the water can permanently hold. Over time, the sugar will begin to separate from the water, leading to the formation of crystals. This process, known as crystallization, occurs naturally and is influenced by the specific variety of honey. Some types of honey crystallize quickly, while others may remain liquid for a longer period."

Gaël stated that contrary to popular belief, the crystallization of honey is not a sign of poor quality or adulteration. In fact, it's quite the opposite. Crystallization indicates that the honey is natural and 100 percent pure. This is especially true for raw and less processed honeys, which are more prone to crystallization because they retain more of their natural components.

Gaël added in Europe and other parts of the world, including Japan, the United Arab Emirates, and the United States, there is often a misconception among consumers that crystallized honey is inferior or even fake. This has led the honey industry to produce honey that remains perpetually liquid, maintaining a consistent color, odor, and taste. However, this uniformity is not a natural characteristic of authentic honey.

"For instance," said Gaël, "If you compare *Litchi* honey from different years, you will notice variations in taste, color, and crystallization patterns. These differences arise due to factors like changes in the environment, the timing of flowering, and even the methods of honey extraction."

He emphasized that crystallization rates vary depending on the balance of glucose and fructose in the honey. Honey with a higher glucose content tends to crystallize faster, while those with more fructose remain liquid longer. Over time, all honey will crystallize; it's simply a matter of when, not if. He gave an example of honey produced in April 2023 that might begin to crystallize within a few months, while honey from 2022 could still remain liquid after a year. This variation is a natural characteristic of honey and serves as an indicator of its purity and authenticity.

In essence, I gathered that although crystallization may alter the texture and appearance of honey, it is a hallmark of its natural quality. Understanding this process allows consumers to appreciate the true nature of honey and the craftsmanship involved in producing it.

As we just talked about lychee honey, Gaël decided to change slightly the flow of the tasting as he was grabbing the jar of lychee honey.

Gaël said the air in the Manakara region, in the southeast of the island, is filled with the scent of blooming lychee trees, and the bees create a honey that captures the essence of these fragrant flowers.

"Harvested in October, lychee honey is a sweet, aromatic delight that's become a best-seller in the region," said Gaël.

This honey is very floral, with notes reminiscent of the lychee fruit itself, with a hint of rose that adds to its complexity. It has a long-lasting flavor. Gaël commented that this honey is a versatile choice for cooking, baking, or simply spreading on toast.

Gaël highlighted this honey, which has won a gold medal in France, is particularly popular across the globe. He added that despite its floral nature, some describe it as reminiscent of a bouquet of roses, making it a best-seller, especially among children, who enjoy it straight from the jar. This honey is produced in large quantities in Madagascar, and its distinctive taste has made it a favorite in various markets.

Next in our tasting journey was the Menabe forest honey.

In the sun-soaked plains of western Madagascar lies the Menabe region, known for its vast landscapes and unique flora. It is here, in May, that Menabe forest honey is harvested, capturing the essence of this warm and arid environment.

Gaël emphasized the honey from these areas carries the earthy, aromatic notes of the endemic plant species. Its profile is a delicate blend of jujube's subtle sweetness, intertwined with a smoky note reminiscent of the tall grasses that characterize the area.

He added it is a versatile honey that can be enjoyed on its own or used to enhance a variety of dishes, bringing a taste of Madagascar's wild west to your kitchen. He also mentioned this honey is known for its rapid crystallization, which is attributed to its glucose content. As Madagascar looks to expand its honey exports, the unique qualities of the Menabe's forest honeys offer a distinctive profile.

While opening the jar of our next tasting of the tropical forest honey, Gaël mentioned we were back in the humid forests of the southeast, near Manakara. In this region, the bees work through the transitional period from the end of the rainy season to the bloom of spring, resulting in tropical forest honey, harvested between March and June.

This honey is mild, with a lingering flavor profile, combining slight bitterness with the light, floral notes from the early spring. Gaël said it is an ideal honey for breakfast spreads or for adding a subtle sweetness to beverages.

Tropical forest honey embodies the changing seasons of Madagascar's southeast, offering a taste that is both complex and balanced, perfect for those who appreciate the natural variations in flavor that different times of the year can bring.

Next was an intriguing honey: the primary forest honey.

Gaël pointed out this honey comes from the Andranomay Forest, and is also known as "primary forest honey." It is a product of the forest corridor near Anjozorobe and the Saha Forest Camp. It is one of the last remaining primary forests in the highlands. This protected area, part of the Anjozorobe Forest, is not just a haven for wildlife but also the source of an exceptional honey, harvested each November.

There were more emotions in Gaël's voice when he was talking about this honey. He said the primary forest honey is a vibrant reflection of its origin. The bees here collect nectar from a diverse array of flora, resulting in a honey that bursts with a symphony of flavors. I closed my eyes and let the drops of honey sit on my tongue. It was a taste of Madagascar's rich biodiversity, with a complex profile. Gaël said the taste can range from sweet to slightly tangy, depending on the year's bloom. It was more than just a delicious treat; it was a product of the forest's preservation efforts, supporting the local communities that protect this precious ecosystem.

Gaël admitted this honey is a source of pride for Beekeeper. His passion for the Anjozorobe-Angavo Forest corridor became unmistakable. He spoke with conviction about the importance of this biodiversity hotspot, stressing that its protection is essential not only for the bees but also for the entire ecosystem. The work being done in the region is a vital effort to maintain ecological balance and support the unique species that call this area home.

When asked to highlight a project that filled him with the most pride, Gaël immediately mentioned Lovasoa Rakotanaivo, a local beekeeper from the northern part of the Anjozorobe-Angavo forest corridor. Lovasoa's story was one of transformation and resilience. Once a charcoal maker, he shifted to beekeeping—a choice that proved to be more profitable and sustainable. Despite the ongoing challenges posed by deforestation, Lovasoa remained dedicated to the beekeeping project. In 2022, Gaël witnessed a poignant milestone in Lovasoa's journey: He built his own house and completely stopped making charcoal. Recently, Lovasoa added ten new hives, a testament to his commitment and the success of the initiative. For Gaël, this represented more than just a personal victory; it was a small yet significant triumph for the entire forest. What made it even more meaningful was that seven others expressed a desire to follow in Lovasoa's footsteps.

Gaël expressed regret that I hadn't had the opportunity to visit Lovasoa during my trip to Madagascar. The journey would have required a turbulent two-hour car ride followed by a two-hour walk across paddy fields and mountains—a daunting trek I had reluctantly declined. While the visit didn't fit into this trip, the story of Lovasoa and the work being done in the Anjozorobe-Angavo forest corridor left a lasting impression. *Perhaps another time*, I thought, *the chance to witness this remarkable project firsthand would come*.

The second-to-last honey of our tasting was the eucalyptus honey.

During my two trips to Madagascar, I noticed in the highlands, near Tana, plantations of eucalyptus trees doting the landscape. Gaël elaborated that their tall, fragrant branches provide a unique source of nectar. Between June and September, bees gather this nectar, producing eucalyptus honey.

Gaël emphasized this honey is nearly 100 percent eucalyptus, with a purity level of around 98 percent. This honey melted in our mouth with a distinctive flavor. It revealed its character as it dissolved on our tongue, offering subtle notes of salted caramel. Gaël mentioned this honey is a versatile addition to people's kitchen, excellent for drizzling over ice cream or enhancing your morning breakfast. Eucalyptus honey is not only a popular sweetener but also valued for its health benefits, making it a versatile product for both culinary and wellness markets, especially for respiratory health, and is used locally in Madagascar for these purposes. The natural crystallization of this honey is seen as a mark of its authenticity. Gaël noted that for American consumers, who are increasingly interested in functional foods, Manjakandriana's eucalyptus honey presents a promising opportunity. It aligns with trends toward natural remedies and wellness-focused diets, positioning it as a valuable export.

We ended our tasting with niaouli honey.

Gaël commented that we were back in the Manakara region, where niaouli trees thrive, offering a unique source of nectar for local bees. Harvested between February and March, niaouli honey is not your typical honey—it's an experience for those who appreciate bold and unexpected flavors.

Gaël emphasized that this honey is high in niaouli content, up to 90 percent. It made it easily identifiable and particularly potent. Indeed, this honey was highly aromatic, and it delivered a powerful sensory impact that surprised me. Its flavor profile was complex and intriguing, with notes that reminded me of licorice, coffee, or even earthy vegetables. Gaël said Niaouli honey is a highly divisive variety, loved or hated by those who taste it. This is the honey for epicureans and chefs who seek to add a distinctive touch to their creations. Niaouli honey is perfect for those who enjoy exploring new and unconventional flavors.

When the tasting was over, I asked Gaël if they ever attempted to produce baobab honey, given Madagascar's fame for its baobab trees. The island is famous for the iconic Avenue of the Baobabs, located near the town of Morondava on the west coast. This majestic avenue features towering baobab trees, locally called *reniala* or "mother of the forest," which can reach up to thirty meters in height. These ancient giants, some more than eight hundred years old, create a surreal landscape with their massive, bottle-shaped trunks and sparse, spindly branches reaching toward the sky. It seemed logical to me that Madagascar would produce baobab honey.

Before answering my question, Gaël explained that to label honey as a specific "unifloral" or "monofloral" type, it is generally accepted that at least 45 percent of the pollen content should come from the named flower source. This standard is not enforced by law but is recommended by international guidelines, such as those from the International Honey Commission.

"For example," added Gaël, "honey labeled as 'orange blossom honey' should contain at least forty-five percent of pollen from orange blossoms to be considered authentic." He specified that these guidelines help maintain consistency and authenticity in honey labeling, ensuring consumers receive the product as advertised. He added that Beekeepers follows this international standard, even if it isn't mandatory.

Gaël shared we might indeed find "baobab honey" in stores, but it was not real. He explained there's no such thing as true baobab honey. People can't label honey as "baobab honey" just because they placed a beehive near a baobab tree.

"It's incredibly rare to produce real baobab honey," said Gaël. "It's very complicated, because some baobabs bloom at night, and you would need an entire forest of baobabs. To produce one kilogram of honey, approximately four million flowers must be visited by bees, which is enormous."

From this story of baobab honey, Gaël transitioned into the fact that people need to be cautious, as there are unique markers in these flowers, and a hint of baobab can be found in some wildflower honeys, for instance.

As a side story, Gaël explained Beekeeper has done a lot of research, and their most ambitious project was to try to produce baobab honey. They worked with a researcher from CIRAD (that translates to "French Agricultural Research Center for International Development") in Tana, who showed them the only two remaining baobab forests on the island, one located south of Morondava, between Morondava and Andavadoaka, and the other one along the Mangoky River. Beekeepers targeted both these areas and placed fifteen hives.

"You have to understand the context in Madagascar," added Gaël. "We are in the middle of a dry forest, fourteen kilometers, or eight and a half miles, from the nearest water source. The beekeeper had to make a round trip to bring water to the bees, as they needed to drink, as there wasn't water nearby. We managed to obtain a little bit of honey. The professor at the University of Antananarivo was overjoyed. She said that she had never seen this and asked me to immediately come to the laboratory. 'Swear to me you didn't add baobab pollen,' she said. 'This is an incredible honey! It's unheard of!'"

Gaël stood up and stepped away for a moment and returned with a glass jar containing a small amount of honey at the bottom.

"We have a small amount left, which I had to part with because people at the office started eating it, but that's all that was left. It's the only honey we can confidently say contains about fifty-six percent of baobab pollen!"

Gaël cautioned us to be vigilant about certain honey types being misrepresented on the market or sold on Facebook. He pointed out that some honeys are incorrectly labeled, such as "mango honey," which doesn't exist, since mango trees are not melliferous (honey-producing plant or tree).

Having explored the intricate flavors of each honey, our conversation naturally shifted to the broader economic impact these unique varieties could have on Madagascar's future. As Beekeeper explores these diverse honey varieties and as Madagascar's honey industry grows, the economic implications are profound in the country's rural areas. In several rural regions, beekeeping is increasingly seen as more than just a supplementary income—it's a pathway to financial stability. Madagascar's honey, known for its unique flavors, has significant export potential. While Africa contributes 10 percent of the world's honey production, Madagascar is only beginning to tap into its potential in global markets. The demand for organic and specialty honeys is particularly high in the United States, where annual needs reach two hundred thousand tons. This presents a considerable opportunity for Malagasy honey producers.

However, there are challenges to overcome. Meeting international honey standards is a significant barrier for many small-scale producers. Despite these hurdles, beekeeping could become a primary livelihood for many, offering a way out of poverty for rural families.

What Gaël was covering echoed what Kennedy already shared with us. Economic thresholds are clear: with twenty hives, a beekeeper can live above the poverty line; with fifty hives, they can enter the middle class. These figures highlight the real impact that honey production can have on improving livelihoods.

By establishing robust systems for quality assurance, Madagascar can not only secure its place in the global market but also ensure that its beekeepers receive fair compensation for their work. The ripple effects of such economic empowerment are manifold, from improved living standards to enhanced educational opportunities for beekeepers' children. By unlocking the economic and social benefits of this natural resource, Madagascar can pave the way for a sweeter, more prosperous future. The journey from hive to market may be complex, but the rewards—both for the beekeepers and the global consumers—are undeniably worth the effort.

Beekeeping in Madagascar has the potential to evolve from a small-scale activity into a key driver of economic development. With targeted investments and a focus on quality, the industry could generate significant export revenue and provide a sustainable source of income for rural families.

Gaël asked if I visited the forests during our tour. I nodded, recalling the landscapes we encountered. However, amidst the beauty, the sight of deforestation left a lingering concern, particularly in the Anjozorobe-Angavo forest corridor.

Gaël's demeanor shifted as the gravity of the situation became apparent. Deforestation, he explained, is a significant and growing threat in the region, with far-reaching consequences for bee habitats. The loss of trees and bushes isn't just about the wood; it means the destruction of native vegetation that bees depend on for nectar and pollen.

His concern was evident as he spoke about the bees, essential pollinators whose survival is intrinsically linked to the health of the forest. Without a diverse range of plants, bees are forced to travel greater distances in search of food, a stressor that diminishes their efficiency. The ripple effects were clear—reduced nectar availability directly impacted honey production.

I was curious about how climate change was affecting his business.

Gaël sighed. "Climate change is another challenge. It disrupts flowering patterns—sometimes flowers bloom too early, sometimes too late. This unpredictability can leave bees without food at critical times. It the long run, it could impact honey yields."

As we continued our conversation, Gaël explained how deforestation also affects the quality of honey. "When the diversity of plants decreases," he said, "the honey loses its unique flavor and nutritional properties. Monocultures, which are common after deforestation, produce honey that's bland and less nutritious."

He continued talking about Madagascar's isolation through time that has led to the evolution of unique plant species, many of which are crucial for local bee populations. He blamed deforestation, which threatens these endemic species, reducing the diversity of plants available for bees. By focusing on beekeeping, companies like Beekeeper help conserve these native species, and indirectly contribute to reducing the risk of bushfires, as diverse forests are generally more resilient to fire.

He paused, reflecting on the broader impact of his work. "Beekeeping is not just about producing honey; it's a way to protect our forests. By providing an alternative livelihood to slash-and-burn agriculture, we can reduce the pressure on these ecosystems. People can earn a living without resorting to destructive practices. Now we are struggling because the forest is retreating faster than the bees can work! The bees have less flowers to pollinate as the forest is destroyed."

The discussion shifted to the collaborative efforts shaping the region's beekeeping industry. The role of NGOs and honey companies emerged as a point in the conversation. Gaël, reflecting on their impact, acknowledged their crucial contributions. NGOs not only provide essential training and resources to local communities but also empower them to establish their own beekeeping ventures. By linking these small-scale producers to both national and international markets, they ensure that the honey fetches fair prices, promoting fair-trade practices and ethical sourcing.

Leaving Beekeeper, I felt inspired by Gaël's commitment to beekeeping and conservation. Their efforts were not just about producing honey but about preserving the rich biodiversity of Madagascar. It was a powerful reminder of the interconnectedness of nature and the importance of sustainable practices in protecting our planet.

The honey market faces significant challenges due to the prevalence of adulterated honey, a problem far more widespread than initially anticipated. While there was always an awareness of the complexities within the honey industry, the expectation was that there would be a strong demand for authentic, pure honey. However, it has become evident that even consumers are being misled by the industry, often purchasing adulterated or entirely fake honey without realizing it.

Gaël shared that a recent study by the European Union, released a month prior to our first conversation, revealed startling findings: 46 percent of the honey sold in European supermarkets was either adulterated or could not legally be labeled as honey. The report mentioned that just in the UK alone, ten honey samples were tested, and all ten failed to meet the standards required to be called honey. This situation has exposed a critical issue that was not given enough consideration—the extent to which consumers are being deceived and the impact this has on the market for genuine honey.

Gaël added that despite the challenges, there is a segment of the population, both consumers and distributors, that strongly supports initiatives focused on providing authentic honey. However, most consumers are swayed by lower prices, often opting for cheaper, mass-produced honey from places like Argentina, which often serves as a front for honey originating from China. These products are designed to meet consumer preferences for honey that remains liquid, with a consistent taste and smell, but they lack the authenticity of true honey.

He pointed out the issue is further compounded by the pricing structure within the industry.

"To support local producers and ensure a fair-trade model, Beekeeper purchases honey at a higher price, reflecting the quality and stringent standards we require. This approach aims to create a win-win situation: a fair price for producers, a sustainable business model for us, and a high-quality product for consumers. However, this often means our honey is more expensive than the cheaper, adulterated honey flooding the market, particularly from China!"

Gaël wanted me to capture that this price disparity creates a significant hurdle, as many consumers prioritize cost over quality, unknowingly choosing a product that is far removed from what honey is meant to be.

The challenge, therefore, is not just in producing authentic honey, but in educating consumers about the value of purity and quality, and in overcoming the deeply entrenched preference for uniform, inexpensive products that dominate the market.

More than just a natural sweetener, honey tells a tale and connects people, land, and the tiniest but most vital members of our ecosystems. Tasting honey in Madagascar, I was reminded that its flavor carries the imprint of its surroundings: the wildflowers of the highlands, the mangrove blossoms of the northwest, or the lychee blooms of the southwest. Each spoonful reflects place, season, and the beekeepers who carefully tend to their hives.

Meeting local beekeepers on the Red Island reinforced something I had long known but had never felt so acutely: To enjoy honey is to take part in a responsibility. It means choosing honey that sustains not only our palates but also the people and pollinators behind it. It means ensuring that in the process of harvesting, enough is always left for the bees themselves—because without them, there is no future harvest.

Lychee Ganache with Madagascar Honey and Chocolate from *Chocolaterie Robert*

Recipe by Chef Guy Krenzer (Directeur de la Création—Chef Exécutif at Lenôtre, France)

INGREDIENTS

10.8 oz. (1⅓ cups) lychee purée (307 g)
3.2 oz. (6½ tbsp.) high-quality unsalted butter (91 g)
4.7 oz. (⅓ cup + 1 tablespoon) Madagascar lychee honey (133 g)
7.6 oz. (1¼ cups) Madagascar 70% dark chocolate couverture (Maison "Robert") (215 g)
7.6 oz. (1¼ cups) Madagascar 58% dark ganache couverture (215 g)

(Note: If the exact Madagascar couvertures aren't available, you may substitute with high-quality dark chocolates with similar cacao percentages for a comparable result.)

PREPARATION

1. Steam the honey at 95°F (35°C) to achieve a smooth, homogeneous texture. Stir gently with a spatula.
2. Heat the lychee purée to 212°F (100°C), then add the butter and warmed honey. Mix well until fully combined.
3. Cool the mixture down to 149°F (65°C), then add the melted chocolate couvertures, which should be at 113°F (45°C). Stir until smooth and glossy.

SERVING SUGGESTIONS

Garnish chocolate bonbons, poach on shortbread, or serve with fruit such as lychee, etc.

Malagasy Coconut Chicken with Honey

Traditional Malagasy Recipe

Serves 4 people

INGREDIENTS

2 ¼ pounds bone-in chicken, cut into pieces
1 medium onion, thinly sliced
2 garlic cloves, minced
1 piece fresh ginger, about ¾ inch, grated
3 ripe tomatoes, chopped (or 2 tablespoons tomato paste)
1 can of coconut milk
2 tablespoons Mokarana honey (or a floral honey as a substitute)
2 tablespoons peanut or sunflower oil
Salt and freshly ground black pepper, to taste
Chili pepper (optional, to taste)

PREPARATION

1. Heat the oil in a large pan over medium heat. Sauté the onion, garlic, and ginger until the onion becomes translucent.
2. Add the chicken pieces and brown them lightly on all sides.
3. Stir in the chopped tomatoes (or tomato paste) and mix well. Let simmer for about 5 minutes.
4. Pour in the coconut milk and add the mokarana honey. Season with salt and pepper. If you enjoy a bit of heat, add a whole chili pepper (remove it before serving).
5. Cover and simmer gently over low heat for 30 to 40 minutes, until the sauce is rich and the chicken is tender.
6. Adjust seasoning if needed and serve hot.

CHAPTER 8

The Fragrant Rice of Madame Rose

Ny vary no aina.

Rice is life.

—TRADITIONAL MALAGASY SAYING

How did a grain from Madagascar come to define Southern cuisine in America? In *Carolina Gold Rice: The Ebb and Flow History of a Lowcountry Cash Crop*, Richard Schulze traces its unexpected journey—not from a kitchen, but from the deck of a storm-battered brigantine captained by John Thurber. In the late seventeenth century, Thurber's Liverpool-bound ship sought shelter in Charleston Harbor after being caught in a tropical storm. Among its cargo were rice seeds from Madagascar—a gift of chance that would reshape agriculture in the region.

◄ *Rice field outside of Antananarivo.*

Local planter Henry Woodward, one of the area's earliest English settlers, befriended the captain and became interested in the seeds. He cultivated the rice and shared it with neighboring farmers. In the rich Carolina soil, it flourished. Season after season, the crop grew more prominent, eventually becoming the region's primary cash crop. This rice, later known as Carolina Gold, helped transform Charleston into one of America's wealthiest cities.

Its influence extended far beyond the fields. Carolina Gold's success was intertwined with the economic rise of the South and the harsh realities of slavery and exploitation. Rice dominated South Carolina's coastal plantations until the Civil War. Afterward, production sharply declined due to labor shortages, financial instability, and damage from powerful storms.

By the late nineteenth century, the fields of Carolina Gold were abandoned, and the crop's presence in the South gradually faded, along with its historical ties to Madagascar. For decades, it seemed destined to disappear from memory. But history has a way of resurfacing. Driven by a dedication to preservation and pride, a new generation of growers and historians revived the legacy of Carolina Gold. Today, the grain—and the story it carries—has reclaimed its place on Southern tables and within the broader narrative of American cuisine.

Centuries later, the legacy of Carolina Gold Rice found passionate advocates in individuals like Chef Sean Brock and Glenn Robert, founder of Anson Mills. Together, they spent years rediscovering and re-establishing heritage crops, pluses, and legumes in the Lowcountry region.

Chef Sean Brock is renowned for his profound appreciation of and dedication to reviving Southern cuisine, particularly through traditional ingredients like Carolina Gold Rice. His 2014 cookbook, *Heritage*, weaves the narrative of Lowcountry cooking with his unwavering commitment to preserving the unique culinary history of the South. Brock's approach seamlessly blends modern culinary techniques with traditional practices, demonstrating how ancient grains like Carolina Gold Rice can play a pivotal role in contemporary dishes while honoring their historical significance. Raised with the Southern soil under his fingernails, Brock transcends the role of a chef; he is a custodian of Southern heritage, dedicated to restoring the integrity and authenticity of regional cuisine.

Glenn Roberts, founder of Anson Mills and former president of the Carolina Gold Rice Foundation, has been a driving force in the revival of Carolina Gold Rice. His journey began in the 1990s, when he became frustrated by the scarcity and poor quality of heirloom grains. Determined to restore this iconic Southern staple, Roberts collaborated with rice geneticists and local farmers to reinvigorate the Carolina Gold strain, ensuring its purity and viability. Since founding Anson Mills in 1998, he has reintroduced Carolina Gold Rice and other nearly extinct heirloom grains, enriching the Southern culinary landscape while preserving its agricultural heritage.

My introduction to Carolina Gold Rice happened far from its Southern origins—at the 2009 StarChefs International Chef Congress (ICC) in Manhattan's Armory building. The venue, rich in history, buzzed with culinary energy each year until the event's unfortunate halt due to COVID. That year, the grand halls on Park Avenue were filled with chefs and food enthusiasts exchanging ideas, techniques, and flavors from around the world.

Among the workshops, one session caught my attention—a demonstration on Lowcountry cooking led by Chef Sean Brock, then the chef at McCrady's in Charleston. His focus on heirloom ingredients, including Carolina Gold Rice, aligned with my growing interest in Southern culinary heritage. Brock's passion for preserving heirloom grains and vegetables was evident as he spoke about the importance of safeguarding these foods—not only in the South but across all of America's regional culinary traditions.

During the demonstration, Brock prepared his version of shrimp and grits, showcasing heirloom corn and South Carolina shrimp. In small groups, we used liquid nitrogen to grind Jimmy Red Corn and shrimp into a fine texture. The final dish was a revelation: shrimp stock gel, fresh herbs, and crisp shrimp toast alongside the mixture. Each bite felt like stepping into a living piece of culinary history.

That experience left a lasting impression. Visiting McCrady's had long been on my list, but after hearing Brock speak and sampling his work, it became a priority. Inspired by his dedication to reviving traditional Lowcountry flavors, I traveled to Charleston. Brock's dishes told the story of the region—highlighting local seafood, rice, and greens while blending elements of innovation and global influence. Charleston's food scene, shaped by chefs like Brock, celebrated the deep roots of Southern cuisine while embracing a forward-looking approach.

A few weeks before my trip, I reached out to Chef Sean Brock to confirm he'd be at McCrady's the night I planned to dine there. I had long admired his work, considering him one of the most brilliant chefs in the country. The visit wasn't just another stop—it was the reason for my trip. I hoped for a brief greeting or perhaps a glimpse of him in the kitchen. To my surprise, Chef Brock personally greeted me at my table.

That night was unforgettable. Not only did Brock welcome me, but he also prepared each dish from the tasting menu tableside, an unexpected and extraordinary gesture. Watching him cook felt like witnessing an artist at work, blending tradition and innovation with every plate. The evening remains a cherished memory. I even framed the menu—signed by Brock—where it hangs in my home as a reminder of that remarkable night.

I can still taste the flavors—South Carolina crawfish paired with sweetbreads, sweet onions, and tomato; pork with pine, morels, and green garlic; and his celebrated Hoppin' John. Tasting Brock's version of Hoppin' John was especially meaningful. For him, the disconnect between the Southern classics he read about and the bland, uninspired versions he encountered in restaurants fueled his quest to rediscover the dish's original form. The bland, uninspired versions of Hoppin' John he found—stripped of their essence and crafted with generic ingredients—stood in stark contrast to the vibrant, soulful meal it once was.

That journey led Brock to Carolina Gold Rice and Sea Island Red Peas, the foundational components of Hoppin' John. This pursuit brought him into collaboration with Glenn Roberts, sparking a broader effort to revive the grains that once defined Southern cuisine. Carolina Gold Rice, once the backbone of South Carolina's agricultural wealth, vanished by the early twentieth century. But, through the efforts of people like Brock and Roberts, its legacy returned—it found its way back to Southern kitchens—and, on that unforgettable evening, to my table.

My research into the rich culinary heritage of Madagascar uncovered the historical link between Carolina Gold Rice and the rice fields of the Red Island. This connection reframed my understanding of rice—not just as a crop, but as a living thread that ties together continents, histories, and cultures. The journey of rice from Madagascar to the Carolinas was more than a story of agricultural adaptation; it was part of a larger, intricate web of migration, trade, and survival. Food rarely travels alone. It moves with people—through forced migration, exploration, and the unpredictable paths of history. Sometimes it follows the contours of war and displacement; at other times, it spreads quietly along the edges of trade routes or finds new lands by chance. Each grain, spice, or plant carries within it the echoes of the hands that once sowed and harvested it, as well as the larger forces that dictate its movement across oceans and borders.

When I landed in Antananarivo for the second time, a sense of familiarity sharpened my anticipation. The rice paddies lining the road from the airport to the capital no longer surprised me, but they still commanded my attention. Their shimmering expanse, glowing in the sunlight, hinted at the enduring connection between land, tradition, and sustenance. Workers, their heads bent beneath wide straw hats, moved methodically across the flooded fields—an unspoken rhythm passed down through generations.

Returning to the Grand Hotel Urban felt natural. Perched above the city near Ambohijatovo Garden, it offered a vantage point that grounded me after the long journey. As dusk fell, I watched from my room as the lights of Antananarivo flickered to life over the streets and houses below. The glow revealed the city's layered reality, where beauty and hardship intertwined in quiet coexistence.

The next morning, I found a corner on the hotel's deck, waiting for my guide and friend, Nirina. The air carried the distant hum of daily life—dogs barking and the occasional burst of laughter from the streets below. Nirina arrived in jeans and a thick green jacket, grinning at the sight of my light linen shirt. "Aren't you cold?" he teased. "It's twenty-five degrees"—seventy-seven degrees Fahrenheit—I shot back, laughing. "Perfectly warm." His easy laugh pulled me indoors, where we found a table near the bar. I had momentarily forgotten it was June, the fall season in the southern hemisphere.

Over coffee, we retraced our last conversations and outlined plans for the days ahead. "I want to focus on rice," I said, eager to dive deeper into its significance in Malagasy culture. Nirina nodded knowingly. Rice, I had come to realize, was more than just a staple here—it was a cultural anchor, shaping daily rituals and connecting the Malagasy people to their land and ancestors.

"Rice is everything," Nirina began, leaning into the conversation. "Traditionally, we eat it three times a day." His voice warmed with nostalgia as he described the morning ritual of *vary sosoa*—a simple rice porridge, light yet comforting. As he spoke, I sipped a glass of *corossol* juice. Its citrusy flavor, with hints of pineapple and banana, and creamy texture had become a quiet indulgence of mine during each visit to Madagascar—a small ritual of my own.

Nirina explained how lunch and dinner revolved around well-cooked rice, often accompanied by Romazava, a broth made with *brèdes mafanes* (greens), tomatoes, onions, and zebu or other meats. "Romazava is our national dish," he said. "It changes a little depending on the day, but the rice is constant." As he spoke, I could see how these meals—rooted in repetition and modest ingredients—formed the foundation of daily life.

Yet, not all traditions endured untouched. Nirina's expression shifted as he described how economic shifts altered the landscape. "Nowadays, many families start the day with bread and coffee," he said, pointing out the vendors who carried large thermoses of steaming coffee through the streets. "It's faster, cheaper." But despite these changes, rice still found its way to the table in other forms. *Mofo gasy*, beloved rice cakes fried in specific molds and often enriched with coconut milk, remained a staple of Malagasy mornings. The variations of recipes occur based on the regions of Madagascar.

Months later, this understanding of *mofo gasy* deepened during a visit to the restaurant Haka Fy in Tana, where Chef Henintsoa Moretti added another layer to its narrative.

"*Mofo gasy* is a rice-flour fritter," Moretti explained, "sold in the little cafés that line the streets across the island. There's also a salted version, *ramanonaka*, which is baked on one side." She emphasized that the batter contained salt, black pepper, *voatsiperifery* pepper, and pink peppercorn. Continuing, she added that in other regions, especially in the north of the island, *mofo gasy* was called *mokary*, and was sometimes topped with grated coconut and coconut milk, or flavored with vanilla and cinnamon.

The nuances of *mofo gasy*, from Henintsoa's kitchen to the bustling streets, revealed the many layers of regional tradition. Yet, as I sat across from Nirina, I was eager to trace these threads even further back. I returned to our conversation, asking if any legends or stories were woven into the fabric of Malagasy rice culture. He smiled, sharing the saying "*toa ny rano sy vary*" or, "like water and rice." The phrase symbolizes inseparable elements, reflecting the importance of rice in the Malagasy identity. "There's a legend too," Nirina added, leaning forward slightly. "It's said that rice first came to Madagascar from the daughter of Zanahary, the supreme deity. She descended to Ankaratra, bringing with her a rooster and hen that had eaten rice from the paddy. After they were cooked and eaten, undigested grains of rice scattered on the land, sprouting and spreading across the island. This marks the beginning of rice cultivation on the island, which explains why the rice harvest is considered sacred and celebrated with ritual ceremonies."

As our conversation shifted to the economic realities of rice, Nirina's tone grew more serious. "Rice is essential here, but the industry remains fragile," he explained. "At one point, a president nearly lost power over a rice importation crisis. Most rice farming is still subsistence-based. The market mainly serves urban areas and a handful of farmers who manage to produce a surplus."

We discussed the potential of rice farming. Nirina was hopeful yet pragmatic. "If we want to secure our future, we have to move beyond survival. We need sustainable solutions that can support both our people and the economy," he said, acknowledging that without better infrastructure to connect regions, Madagascar's dependence on imports would persist. "Madagascar could become the breadbasket of the Indian Ocean, but that future feels distant without the right investments to strengthen local production."

Curious about the role of rice beyond the local market, I pressed further. When the conversation shifted to exports, Nirina explained that Madagascar focused on cultivating aromatic, high-quality varieties—grains prized internationally but less favored domestically. These fragrant varieties, while exceptional, don't swell as much during cooking, making them less practical for the average Malagasy family, where filling portions matter more than nuanced flavor.

I asked about the rising popularity of aromatic rice, like Madame Rose, which I had enjoyed in local restaurants during my initial trip to the island. Nirina's face lit up. "It started in the northern cities," he said, "the origin of Madame Rose rice. The unique flavor amazed local tourists, sparking inter-regional demand."

As we prepared for the journey north to visit the COFAMADI cooperative, Nirina's enthusiasm was contagious. He spoke passionately about the cooperative's vital role in cultivating Madame Rose rice, a variety known for its delicate fragrance and unique flavor. "The cooperative ensures the quality and authenticity of Madame Rose," he explained. "Some try to mix in other varieties, but this is about preserving heritage. It's also about the rice's enhanced market value."

The next leg of the trip felt like a natural progression—a step deeper into Madagascar's identity, seen through the lens of its beloved rice fields. After exploring vanilla golden triangle in the SAVA region, cruising the Pangalanes Canal near Toamasina, and visiting sturgeon farms east of the capital, this visit to the rice cooperative COFAMADI offered a firsthand look at how local farmers were safeguarding one of the island's most esteemed rice crops.

Heading north along the Route *Nationale* 5a (RN5a), the drive unveiled a new side of Madagascar. The freshly paved road cut through rolling hills, tracing the land's curves with precision. The absence of potholes allowed the car to glide forward, carving through the landscape like a dart. The sky was wide, often scattered with clouds that promised rain but held back just enough to let the sun through. Mountains layered in the distance, their outlines blurred by the afternoon heat.

This stretch of road felt different—no palm trees lining the route, no thick tropical vegetation. Instead, dry slopes of brown and green unfolded before us, reflecting the island's striking geographical contrasts. Zebus, the iconic humped cattle of Madagascar, wandered onto the road without urgency, their calm presence frequently forcing us to stop. The interruptions felt less like inconveniences and more like reminders that life here moved at its own steady rhythm.

In the villages we passed, children waved at our car as smoke from cooking fires curled into the sky. The journey stretched on, unhurried, revealing both the sparse and lush dimensions of Madagascar's landscape. The zebus passed by, close enough to see the dust on their hides and the calm in their eyes.

As we left the hills behind, the land flattened into sunlit savannah. The open expanse, dotted with low shrubs and the occasional lone tree, felt stark yet captivating. The air was dry, and the earth beneath the bright sky shifted between gold and ochre. There was a quiet beauty that filled the landscape—unforgiving yet alive with subtle movement. There was no rush here, only the eternal pace of nature's subtle cycles. Shadows crawled slowly over the earth as the sun moved across the sky, marking time in a place that felt timeless.

When the car turned north onto RN6 toward Diego-Suarez Bay, cultivated fields reappeared. By the time we reached the village of Antsakoabe, the landscape had transformed once again—this time into a patchwork of vibrant rice paddies. These fields were the domain of Madame Rose, carefully tended by the farmers of the rice cooperative. Stretching across the valley, the bright green stalks rippled gently in the breeze. We were in the Diana region, known for its rice cultivation. These fields, well-maintained and neatly demarcated, illustrated the collective efforts of farmers working together to produce this valued crop. This route through northern Madagascar offered a glimpse into the agricultural practices of the region, where farming was both a livelihood and a tradition.

Lucien, a key figure in the COFAMADI cooperative, met us by the roadside and led us along a narrow path toward the paddies. We followed him through the woods and across rills of water, each step revealing more of the intricate landscape and the care taken in nurturing these precious crops.

When we reached the edge of a field, I settled on a tree stump, unpacking my recorder and microphone.

"Good evening, Lucien," I greeted, initiating our conversation against the backdrop of rice fields. Lucien, who oversaw operations across four communes, was an integral figure in the cultivation of this hero variety.

"I oversee operations here at COFAMADI," he said. "Our primary focus is Madame Rose, but we cultivate other varieties too."

He spoke proudly of the rice's fragrant qualities, explaining how it differed from other local varieties, such as Mogodro and Makalioka. Madame Rose, he explained, wasn't just a crop; it carried a legacy tied to the land and the farmers who nurtured it.

I asked Lucien to walk me through the cultivation process. "It all starts with traditional plowing," he began. "We use oxen to prepare the land. After flooding the fields, we sow the seeds carefully. Managing water levels is essential—especially with the unpredictable rainfall we face. We monitor the fields constantly to ensure the rice matures properly."

The conversation turned to the cooperative's ongoing challenges. Lucien acknowledged climate change brought erratic weather patterns and increased pest issues. "Maintaining the quality of Madame Rose is critical as demand grows," he admitted. "We're committed to sustainable practices, but it's a constant effort."

Curious about their expansion plans, I asked about export potential. Lucien shook his head slightly. "For now, our focus is on the local market—mainly Antananarivo," he said. "Madame Rose is more expensive, but it has a loyal following among restaurants and urban buyers. Exporting could come later, once we strengthen our local footprint."

Before we left the fields, I inquired about the origins of Madame Rose's name. Lucien smiled. "It comes from a local legend," he said. "Rose was a woman who planted the first seeds of this variety. Her harvest was so fragrant that the rice was named after her. A local mayor helped spread its fame during a community festival, and the name stuck."

I thanked Lucien for his time, and as I packed my equipment, I reflected on the profound story of resilience and community embedded in the fields of COFAMADI. The Madame Rose rice variety stands out in Madagascar for its unique characteristics. Highly prized for its fragrant aroma and exceptional flavor profile, Madame Rose is akin to Jasmine or Basmati rice but holds a special place in Malagasy cuisine because of its local cultivation and distinctive attributes. This prompted the question: Could the Madame Rose variety play a role in Malagasy cuisine similar to that of Basmati in Indian and Pakistani dishes, or Jasmine in Thai and Vietnamese recipes?

Varieties of Rice

Rice varieties around the world significantly shape regional cuisines by forming the foundation for traditional dishes and fostering culinary innovation. Here's a closer look at how this integration manifests across different cultures.

Basmati Rice in South Asian Cuisine: Known for its fragrant aroma and long, slender grains, Basmati rice is a staple in Indian and Pakistani kitchens. Essential for biryanis and pilafs, it is also commonly served with curries. The grains remain distinct when cooked, perfectly absorbing the rich spices typical of South Asian fare.

Arborio Rice in Italian Cuisine: Arborio's short grains are pivotal in risotto preparation. Its high amylopectin content helps absorb liquids and release starch, creating risotto's signature creamy texture. This variety epitomizes the Italian flair for dishes that are both hearty and refined.

Jasmine Rice in Southeast Asian Cuisine: With a slightly sticky texture and a subtle floral aroma, Jasmine rice is ideal for holding the rich sauces of Thai curries and Vietnamese stir-fries. It complements the bold flavors typical of Southeast Asia, such as lime, cilantro, and lemongrass.

Sticky Rice in East Asian Cuisine: Known as glutinous rice, it is central to Chinese, Japanese, and Korean dishes. Used in zongzi (rice dumplings) in China, as the base for sushi in Japan, and in traditional Korean desserts like tteok, sticky rice holds cultural importance, particularly during festivals and celebrations.

Koshihikari Rice in Japanese Cuisine: The slightly sticky texture of Koshihikari makes it perfect for sushi, aiding in its shape retention, whether it's hand-pressed for nigiri or rolled into sushi rolls. Its inherent sweetness also enhances the flavor of raw fish in sashimi and sushi.

Carolina Gold Rice in Southern US Cuisine: This heirloom variety is essential to the Lowcountry cooking of South Carolina and Georgia. Known for its rich, nutty flavor and chewy texture, it serves as the preferred base for dishes like Hoppin' John and Lowcountry boil, connecting it deeply to the culinary traditions of the African diaspora in the southern United States.

Despite its exceptional qualities, Madame Rose rice is not as widely produced as other varieties in Madagascar. Its cultivation is labor-intensive, relying on specific climatic and soil conditions to maintain its high quality and fragrance.

As a premium product, Madame Rose rice carries significant cultural and economic value. For local farmers, it is a source of pride, commanding higher prices in both local and potentially international markets, reflecting its status as a luxury good.

Nestled in the heart of a quaint Malagasy village, we stopped at a small inn, lured by the promise of a traditional meal—*vary sy laoka* (literally "rice with side dish" in Malagasy). There was nothing extravagant about the setting, but the simplicity felt intentional, a reflection of the essence of Malagasy cuisine. Seated at a modest wooden table, I watched as the innkeeper began preparing the rice for the meal. She carefully measured around one hundred grams per person—no bread filled the gaps here, so the rice needed to satisfy. After a meticulous rinse, the grains were placed in a saucepan with one and a half times their volume in water. The pot came to a rolling boil over a strong flame, steam curling into the open air. Once the heat was lowered, she skimmed the surface with a practiced gesture that felt both deliberate and instinctive. The result was fragrant and golden, filling the room with a scent that signaled more than just readiness—it was the scent of home, comfort, and something fundamental to life here.

The innkeeper placed a generous plate of steaming white rice in front of me. Surrounding it were small dishes, each offering a distinct yet interconnected flavor.

The first was *laoka*, or *ro* as they say in the east of the country, a comforting stew of vegetables and meat gently simmered in water. Beside it sat *lasary*, a bright, fresh medley of chopped tomatoes, onions, and pimentos that added a burst of color and tang. Fruit was available, but, as I learned, was typically enjoyed between meals as a snack, a quiet defiance of the Western notion of dessert.

The meal ended with a simple yet captivating drink—*ranon'apango*. Made from grilled rice steeped in hot water, it's also known locally as *ranovola*, or "golden water." I had heard of this drink before, but tasting it firsthand brought a new level of appreciation. Served hot, its earthy flavor lingered, grounding the meal in a sense of place and tradition.

As I sipped the last of my *ranon'apango*, I realized that through something as humble as rice, I had been offered a window into the heart of Madagascar.

Leaving the rice fields of northern Madagascar behind, I made my way back to the bustling capital. A short flight from the northwest spared me the exhausting twelve-hour drive through the countryside. Back in Antananarivo, I had planned two reunions tied to my first visit. The second, later that afternoon, was with mixologist K-Mëc at La Teinturerie. But first, I was set to meet Chef Lalaina at his restaurant, Marais.

As we sat in a quiet corner of the restaurant, the ambient sounds of the kitchen provided a comforting backdrop. Chef Lalaina, with his warm and engaging smile, began to describe the foundational role of rice in Malagasy culture. "Rice is not just our staple food; it's a core part of our identity," he explained, pausing briefly to let the weight of his words settle. "In Madagascar, you don't simply invite someone to lunch; you invite them to share your rice. That's the essence of *manasa hihinam-bary*, or 'come eat rice.'"

His reflection on the social and economic importance of rice naturally led us to discuss the vast varieties cultivated across the island. As he described them, his enthusiasm became evident. "Each type carries its own story—its own flavor, aroma, and tradition."

I mentioned the fragrant Madame Rose rice I had learned about during my visit to the northern rice fields.

"Madame Rose rice is exceptionally fragrant and distinct in both taste and texture," he noted. "It's the star in dishes like *vary sosoa*, a kind of rice soup that showcases its bright white color and exceptional aroma."

Curious, I asked what distinguishes Madame Rose from other fragrant varieties. "It has long, fine grains that become highly aromatic during cooking and eating," answered Lalaina. "It's a sensory delight."

Our discussion naturally shifted to how Lalaina integrates traditional Malagasy ingredients into modern culinary techniques, blurring the line between the familiar and the innovative. "Rice is often seen as a base or a side, but I like to reimagine it—giving it a starring role," he says. "I work it into tuiles, croquettes, even thin rice veils. Sometimes I'll use Madame Rose rice to bind ingredients for refined stuffings or to enhance veloutés."

I asked him how these ideas translate into the dishes at Marais. Lalaina began listing creations that reflect both his respect for tradition and his drive to experiment. "I've made *cromesquis* breaded with panko in pecorino *espuma*, a risotto with asparagus and wild pepper condiments, and a sweet Madagascar spice and honey rice pudding."

As our conversation shifted from fine dining to the broader role of rice in Madagascar's economy and daily life, Chef Lalaina highlighted the growing challenges posed by climate change. Erratic rains and increasing pest invasions, he explained, are threatening a crop central to the nation's identity and culture.

To illustrate rice's versatility in Malagasy cuisine, Lalaina introduced me to *vary sosoa*, a traditional breakfast dish often made with red rice. "For a typical Malagasy breakfast, we might prepare *vary sosoa* with red rice," he said." It's cooked with more water than dry rice, giving it a tender, creamy texture—like a porridge, somewhat similar to European risotto but juicier." When leafy greens, known as *brèdes*, are added, this dish becomes *vary amin'anana*, a heartier version rich in nutrients.

Lalaina also shared the practice of making *vary maina* and *ranovola*, underscoring how deeply intertwined rice is with daily life and traditional practices. "We cook rice slowly, adding water in stages until it's fully absorbed. At the bottom of the pot, a crust forms—fragrant and slightly burnt. That's *vary maina*, or dry rice. After the meal, we pour water over the crust to create *ranovola*, a smoky, amber-hued drink," he says. This transformation of humble ingredients reflects the resourcefulness embedded in Malagasy culinary tradition.

Before we finished, I asked Lalaina about the place of rice in the Malagasy diet today. His response was direct and heartfelt. "It's our daily bread. We eat it three times a day. It's what sustains us," he said. But his words carried a sobering reality. "For some, rice is becoming harder to afford. Economic hardship forces many families to substitute it with *manioc* or corn."

Months later, I recalled this conversation during a visit to Haka Fy restaurant in Antananarivo, where Chef Henintsoa Moretti echoed a similar sentiment about rice's role in Malagasy meals. "Rice is always the preferred accompaniment—more abundant on the plate than the meat or fish it's served with," she explained. Yet, this wasn't universal across the island. In some regions, staple foods like *manioc* or sweet potato replace rice, depending on availability and economic conditions.

When I talked to her about Madame Rose rice, she elaborated on the significance of *vary magnitra* (fragrant rice). "As its name suggests, it has a light fragrance that enhances meat and fish dishes. It grows in the north of the island. Its delicate aroma enhances dishes but comes at a price—twice that of standard rice," she said.

"I use it for buffets, but not for everyday service," she admitted. Procuring quality rice in Antananarivo can be challenging, with counterfeit varieties sometimes passed off as the prized Madame Rose. "Finding a reliable supplier is complicated," she added with a sigh.

These conversations—with Chef Lalaina, in the rice fields and with my friend Nirina—painted a vivid picture of rice's significance in Madagascar. Whether showcased in the refined creations at Marais or embodied in the comforting simplicity of *vary sosoa*, rice remains an anchor of Malagasy daily life, connecting the past to the present and the fields to the table.

After a delicious lunch with Chef Lalaina at Marais, I returned to La Teinturerie—a nexus of creativity where the innovative spirit of Madagascar came alive through art, music, and mixology Here, local pride was distilled into every cocktail, as visionary bartenders reimagined traditional flavors with modern flair. The atmosphere, reminiscent of Brooklyn or Miami's Wynwood, pulsed with youthful energy. Vivid graffiti splashed across the walls alongside curated gallery pieces, reflecting Madagascar's dynamic blend of tradition and innovation. Green foliage draped over eclectic bar setups and cozy outdoor seating areas, creating a lively yet relaxed ambiance that harmonized natural and urban elements.

At the heart of this creative whirlwind was Randrianarisoa Mahery Tiana, or K-Mëc, a visionary mixologist who had pioneered Madagascar's craft cocktail movement. I first met him in October 2022, during a cultural exchange trip with mixologist Shannon Tebay, Chef Elizabeth Falkner, and Chef Michael Gulotta. One of our objectives had been to explore the emerging cocktail scene in Antananarivo, and K-Mëc had invited us to judge Madagascar's inaugural craft cocktail competition.

Held at La Teinturerie, the competition was a vibrant showcase of ingenuity and passion, featuring local bartenders from bars and hotels across the city. Each participant aimed to redefine what Malagasy mixology could be, drawing on local ingredients and traditions to create bold, inventive drinks. The event was a landmark moment, celebrating the creativity of Madagascar's emerging cocktail culture.

Before leaving that year, I had challenged K-Mëc to draw inspiration from *ranon'apango*, the traditional Malagasy drink made by adding hot water to toasted rice remnants. This everyday staple, born of resourcefulness, epitomized Malagasy culture—transforming simplicity into something nourishing and comforting.

Seven months later, stepping back into La Teinturerie and seeing K-Mëc again, I felt a renewed energy in the air. The success of the first cocktail competition sparked a movement, inspiring local establishments to experiment with craft creations of their own. The enthusiasm even led to a second competition, solidifying this exchange of ideas and traditions.

"It was a dream come true," K-Mëc said, his excitement palpable as we reminisced about our collaboration. "Last year marked the start of a new chapter for Malagasy mixology, thanks to your efforts and the involvement of the chefs."

With a knowing smile, K-Mëc excused himself and slipped behind the bar. Moments later, he returned, holding a mason jar that gleamed with promise. "I've been working on this ever since your challenge," he said, presenting his creation with pride.

He called it Apango—a cocktail crafted from local rum, bitters, simple syrup, and water infused with toasted rice. Finished with a delicate layer of cream and garnished with a stalk of rice, the drink paid homage to a childhood treat. K-Mëc explained, "Traditionally, Malagasy parents make a 'dessert' for their children by sweetening the leftover toasted rice with sugar and milk."

As I sipped the creamy concoction, the flavors told a story both familiar and inventive. The toasted rice's earthy warmth merged with the brightness of local ingredients, creating something entirely new yet deeply rooted in tradition. It was a testament to how Malagasy culture, like its cuisine, adapts and thrives without losing its essence.

"This is more than a drink," K-Mëc continued. "It's a toast to our heritage—and to where we're heading."

In that moment, I was reminded of the saying "*Ny vary no aina*," or "Rice is life." Just as rice had traveled from the fields to the table, inspiring traditions and transformations, it had now found its way into a cocktail. APANGO was not just a drink; it was an evolution—a bridge from history to modernity, carrying the spirit of a culture that continues to innovate while honoring its roots.

La Teinturerie, with its buzzing energy and endless creativity, felt like the perfect place to conclude my journey through Madagascar's rice culture. The grains of tradition—whether served as a soup, shaped into cakes, or stirred into a cocktail—had woven their way through every experience, reminding me that rice truly is life.

Apango

Recipe by Mixologist K-Mëc (La Teinturerie in Antananarivo, Madagascar)

Yields 1 cocktail

INGREDIENTS

Burnt Rice Infusion *(make in advance)*

10 tbsp. cooked white rice
50 cl. water (500 ml.)

TO ASSEMBLE AND SERVE

2 oz. dark rum (6 cl. → 2 oz. → 1 jigger + ½ jigger)
1⅓ oz. burnt rice infusion (4 cl. → 1 ⅓ oz. → 1 pony jigger + ⅓ pony jigger)
⅔ oz. sugar cane (2 cl. → ⅔ oz. → 1 pony jigger)
½ oz. sour cream
2 drops Peychaud's Aromatic Bitters

PREPARATION

For the Burnt Rice Infusion

1. In a dry saucepan, toast the cooked rice over medium heat until it becomes dark and aromatic—nearly burnt, but not turned to ash.
2. Add the water to the pan and bring to a boil.
3. Reduce heat and simmer for 20 minutes.
4. Strain the liquid through a fine mesh sieve or cheesecloth and let cool.
5. Store the infusion in a sealed container in the refrigerator. Use within 3 days for best flavor.

Recipe continues →

TO ASSEMBLE AND SERVE

1. Add all ingredients to a shaker with ice: dark rum, burnt rice infusion, sugar cane syrup, sour cream, and bitters.
2. Shake vigorously until well chilled and creamy.
3. Strain into a chilled cocktail glass or serve over a large ice cube in a rocks glass.

SERVING SUGGESTION

1. Serve in a rock glass.
2. Place an ear of rice in the glass.

CHAPTER 9

In Search of Essence

Madagascar's Influence on Modern Perfumery

Aza mandinika ny voninkazo
fa ny hanitra no mamerovero azy.

Do not just look at the flower;
it is its fragrance that enchants.

—TRADITIONAL MALAGASY SAYING

The first thing that struck me about Madagascar was the air, filled with scents as diverse as the landscapes it drifted through. In the capital, a peculiar mixture of aromas greet you—the unmistakable smell of vehicle exhaust winding its way through the streets and clinging to the buildings, mingling with the earthy smoke from coal-burning stoves. It's a city struggling with air quality, where the weight of pollution lingers, casting a haze that speaks to both growth and hardship.

◀ *Nosy Be's gift to the world: Ylang-Ylang.*

Outside the city, though, the air changes. In the countryside, it feels fresher, lighter—a breeze carrying the faint notes of wild plants and fertile soil, as if nature itself has drawn a line separating rural life from the urban hustle. Still, there are moments, particularly in the dry season, when the familiar, smoky scent of slash-and-burn agriculture drifts through the fields, a reminder of the deep-rooted, complex relationship between the land and the people who rely on it.

Across every corner of the Red Island, the air seemed to carry its own distinct memory for me. The immersive scents along forest trails near Andasibe held a blend of damp earth and foliage; by the Ankavanana River, the air was sweet with the ginger and citrusy fragrance of torch ginger flowers. In Antalaha, the thick, dark aroma of vanilla curing facilities lingered heavily, while in Nosy Be, the heady scent of ylang-ylang flowers filled the air. In Toamasina, the smell of grilled meat skewers mixed with the scent of fried bananas lingered over the bustling streets and along the beachfront. Each scent held a fragment of Madagascar's spirit, a sensory bookmark along my journey.

On my first trip to the island, I encountered unique raw materials used in fragrances: patchouli, vetiver, and ylang-ylang. The experience was unexpected and sparked a curiosity I knew I had to pursue further. Once back in the US, I arranged a meeting in Manhattan with two perfumers from my company who explored the island years before my visit. I wanted to revisit the scents of patchouli, vetiver, and ylang-ylang with them, exchanging insights from our separate journeys through Madagascar's aromatic landscapes.

I drove from New Jersey into Manhattan for a meeting with two Symrise perfumers, Christelle Laprade and David Apel, who had both participated in a fragrance expedition to Madagascar back in 2015.

Christelle Laprade's passion for scent began in her childhood in the south of France. She recalls her parents capturing her on Super 8 film, surrounded by flowers, while her brother rode circles around her on his bike. Unfazed, she focused on picking and smelling blooms. Her family fed her curiosity, handing her different things to smell. Living in Provence gave her a bounty to explore—rose bushes, carnations, jasmine, and even mimosa in winter. Toward the end of high school, a visit to a local career center led her to ISIPCA, the International Institute of Perfumery, Cosmetics & Fragrances, in Versailles. She joined Symrise nearly eighteen years ago and has worked with brands across the spectrum, from small niche names to major luxury fragrance houses, always bringing her distinct style and perspective to the table.

David Apel's journey was completely different. Growing up in New Jersey, he stumbled into perfumery almost by accident. With a background in environmental chemistry, he took an entry-level role at Givaudan, initially expecting to work in their environmental department. But when he was offered a spot in the perfume labs, curiosity pulled him in. There, he encountered raw materials with exotic names and captivating aromas, sparking an unexpected passion for scent. Since then, he's spent more than sixteen years at Symrise, but his career spans more than forty-five years in the fragrance industry.

It was clear to me they were the right people to talk to, and at a walking distance from the Plaza Hotel, at the southeast corner of Central Park, I entered the newly renovated Symrise offices on Park Avenue.

Christelle and David invited me to take a seat at a long glass table, each with their leather-bound notebooks in hand, ready to evaluate some of the raw materials and essential oils coming from Madagascar. On the table, arranged with precision, lay trays of freshly prepared blotters, each strip ready to be hand-dipped and briefly left to evaporate. Perfumers refer to these strips as "*mouillettes*," and they are handled with utmost care. They serve as tools of translation, each one absorbing and releasing the intricate structure of a scent.

We started looking at pictures from our respective trips on our phones, as David and Christelle recalled their lasting memories from their journeys. David spoke of the scent of smoke from wood fires and roasted coffee, or dark vanilla notes in the vanilla curing facility. Christelle, on the other hand, was remembering the people. "The most memorable parts for me weren't just the things I saw—they were more about the sounds." She recalled when they were in the jungle and stumbled upon locals singing. They were invited to join in, and the community welcomed them into their church. For

Christelle, that was a deeply moving moment—a moment of genuine connection that left a lasting impression.

The first essential oil we evaluated was patchouli. Patchouli comes from the leaves of a perennial shrub in the mint family, cultivated in the humid climate of tropical regions like Indonesia, India, and Madagascar.

The perfumers opened a sample vial containing the patchouli extract and dipped the blotters into the liquid. Christelle invited me to gently lift the smelling strip and bring it close to my nose, observing the initial top notes before allowing the fragrance to settle. I smelled a richly layered, complex scent that defied simple classification. The perfumers explained that on the first inhale, there was an immediate earthy quality often described as damp soil or a forest floor, carrying a natural, grounding depth. David commented that this characteristic earthiness was softened by a slightly sweet, almost balsamic warmth that lingers, adding a comforting, resinous base note. Patchouli had an unmistakable woody-spicy character, reminiscent of dark woods and even hints of camphor, giving it an almost medicinal edge. David explained when aged, patchouli develops a smoother, more rounded profile, with softened edges that reveal subtle chocolatey or tobacco-like undertones. This maturity lends a softness to its initial intensity, transforming it into a scent that sits more subtly on the skin, blending seamlessly with other ingredients in the fragrance.

He explained patchouli's intensity makes it a foundation note for many perfumers. Some have to start with it at the beginning of a composition; even the smallest addition later on can alter the entire fragrance, transforming it into something entirely new.

"Patchouli has that kind of influence," said David. "It is pervasive, incredibly long-lasting, and has an overwhelming presence. Yet, despite its strength, it can be shaped in remarkable ways, becoming an essential ingredient in some of the most successful women's fragrances ever created."

I asked them to share a few examples of fragrances on the market that highlight patchouli. They mentioned several Mugler fragrances, where Patchouli is blended with various notes. The first, Angel, launched in 1992, pairs Patchouli with sweet notes, while A*Men Fantasm, released in 2024, combines patchouli with warm, spicy accords. Another classic,

Coco Mademoiselle from Chanel, balances patchouli with citrus and woody elements. Each of these compositions showcases patchouli's versatility in different olfactory contexts.

I shared my memory of seeing patchouli shrubs for the first time and showed them a photo I had taken at a cocoa farm nestled along the Ankavanana River, north of Antalaha in the SAVA region. The image showed rows of patchouli bushes growing in the cool shade beneath the cocoa trees—a dual-crop strategy to sustain the farmers' income. Our Symrise hosts explained how cocoa trees take about five years to mature and produce pods, which were harvested twice a year. This waiting period created a challenging gap in income for the farmers. To bridge that gap, they planted patchouli between the young cocoa trees. Unlike cocoa, Patchouli can be harvested two to three times a year, providing a more frequent income stream and supporting farmers during the waiting period for the cocoa trees to reach full production. This intercropping approach not only offers a sustainable livelihood but also maximizes the productive use of the land.

"Under the shade of the cocoa trees," I recall, "the patchouli spread like an ocean of emerald foliage."

Patchouli

Origin: Philippines, India, and Malaysia.

Sources: Indonesia—Sumatra and Java, Madagascar.

Fun fact: Scent of the '60s—Patchouli became a symbol of the counterculture movement in the 1960s and '70s, where its earthy, musky scent was embraced by hippies as a natural alternative to synthetic perfumes. It became associated with freedom, peace, and spirituality, and its popularity endures today.

Profile: Sweet, dark, earthy, and woody,

Gender: Used in both female and male fragrances.

Perfume examples: Ralph Lauren for Men, Cabochard by Grès for Women, Bandit by Robert Piguet for Women, Paloma Picasso for Women, Angel by Mugler, A*Men Fantasm by Mugler, and Coco Mademoiselle by Chanel.

David nodded. "It's intentional. Patchouli thrives in the shade, and keeping it out of direct sunlight helps retain the plant's moisture, which boosts the essential oil yield," he explained.

I presented a second picture on my phone of a nearby vast, open shed, where harvested patchouli shrubs had been hung upside down to dry. I remembered their scent filling the air. The farmers used a traditional drying method, allowing the air to circulate around each plant to prevent mold and to preserve the oil-rich cells within the leaves.

"That drying technique is key," David said, looking at the oil in the bottle. "By letting the leaves dry slowly, the farmers are preserving the natural potency and quality of the patchouli. It's what makes Madagascar's variety so unique—broad, soft, with a hint of smokiness from the distillation process."

I shared how, during my trip, trailers laden with patchouli shrubs would rumble past, pulled by tractors heading to distillation. Even before processing, the air carried a subtle, warm fragrance, a preview of the rich scent concentrated in the oil—a hint of the very scent now lingering between us in this room on Park Avenue.

"It's unmistakable," David said, taking another whiff of the oil. "Madagascar's patchouli captures a depth and complexity you just don't find elsewhere."

David and Christelle shared insights into the unique qualities of Madagascar's patchouli, an ingredient that had drawn each of us back to the essence of the island in different ways.

David commented that unlike other varieties, the Madagascar-sourced patchouli was lower in *patchoulol*, the compound that gives the oil's often intense and pointed profile. He explained that the high-*patchoulol* variety, which dominates the market, has a sharp, camphor-like quality—almost aggressively so, which masks the natural, earthy warmth he associates with patchouli. In contrast, the Madagascar quality reminded him of the first time he encountered the oil—a rich, expansive scent of soft earth, like a cloud that diffuses gently yet carries a depth of warmth and power. The patchouli sourced from Madagascar stood out with its balanced, broad aroma, retaining a hint of smokiness from the distillation process. This subtle touch added character and made it easy to work with in various formulations.

For Christelle, Madagascar's patchouli also had a unique versatility. She noted a subtle animalic hint to it, a quality that made it adaptable across fragrance profiles. Depending on the fragrance's top notes, Christelle might test a few different sources of patchouli to see how each one impacts or complements the composition. Madagascar's patchouli added an intriguing depth without overpowering, allowing her to refine a fragrance's complexity based on the client's vision or the specific olfactory profile she wanted to achieve.

They both commented that beyond its olfactory qualities, Madagascar's patchouli is economically advantageous—a rare benefit in an industry often affected by fluctuations in material availability and price. With control over crop cultivation and production, our company could maintain both quality and supply stability. At a time when patchouli was in high demand and costs were rising, this level of control provided security, ensuring they could continue to use this remarkable ingredient while managing costs effectively. In the world of fragrance, where consistency and quality are paramount, Madagascar's patchouli was offering both—a scent and a strategy.

During our conversation, I found myself curious about the creative journey behind a fragrance. What shapes and influences their vision? I wanted to understand the sources that inspire them when crafting a scent—the memories, places, and details that come together to create something unique.

David leaned back, reflecting. "For me, it's complicated, in a way," he said. "It depends on so many factors, but most of all, I always go back to nature."

He shared a story from early in his career, a time when he'd felt driven to capture his own surroundings. "My first success—if you want to call it that—came from trying to recreate a moment from Acadia National Park in

Maine. I'd taken a trip there and was struck by the ruggedness of the coast, the crashing surf, the scent of pine trees mingling with the salt air. I wanted to bottle that exact feeling."

David shared how he'd crafted an accord, blending different elements to mirror that coastal scene, and presented it to a client on a clear, blue-sky day. "I hadn't even explained it, but he took one whiff and said, 'I smell pine trees and birch leaves crashing on the surf.' I was floored. That moment hooked me on the idea of translating my own experiences into fragrance. It's like connecting on a deeper level, where scent bridges memories," he reflected.

There was a hint of nostalgia in his voice as he continued. "It was a very American perspective, if you will. I didn't grow up like Christelle, in the lavender fields of southern France. I wasn't surrounded by mimosa, jasmine, orange flowers...all those Mediterranean scents. They were mysteries to me. But I did have my own memories—my own world of scents."

He smiled, glancing at the sample bottles on the table. "Inspiration comes in so many forms," he said, almost to himself. "I've been inspired by music, even by a mathematical equation once—it made me think about how to structure a scent. But mostly, it's personal. It always seems to come back to something I've experienced."

As he spoke, I could imagine the layers behind each fragrance he crafted—a blend of memory, place, and curiosity, all distilled into something you could hold in a bottle.

I asked him to explain the word "accord" in the context of fragrance creation.

"An 'accord,' in perfumery," described David, "is similar to a chord in music. Just as individual musical notes combine to create a chord, a few carefully chosen fragrance notes blend together to form an accord. A perfume might be built around one strong, dominant accord with softer notes enhancing it, or it could be a composition of several distinct accords working together to create a layered scent."

Christelle smiled as she considered the question about her sources of inspiration, leaning forward slightly, as if ready to share a few secrets. "For me, inspiration can come from so many places," she began, glancing over at David. "I know you can relate to this, David—we have talked about it before.

It can be anything from a unique food pairing to the layers of culture in cuisine. Remember when we talked about preserved lemons? That tangy, almost fermented scent from Moroccan food?" She paused, her eyes lighting up at the memory. "It's the kind of thing that stays with you, something you can build on."

She tapped her fingers on the table thoughtfully. "And fashion," she added, her face breaking into a soft smile. "I think a lot about fashion design. It moves me in a way that's hard to describe. Once, I created a fragrance for Christian Siriano, and the brief was so vague, I had to reach for something concrete. I picked one of his dresses from his latest show and just...let my imagination go. I started thinking about the dress's texture, the layering, the colors. I imagined ingredients that could convey those same qualities in scent."

She gestured as if layering invisible fabrics in the air. "It's like translating something visual into scent—finding notes that echo the richness or subtlety of a design. It's the same with architecture or interior design—colors, textures, the way materials are layered, all of that can influence how I build a fragrance."

She continued and said that places, too, could be sources of inspiration. She recalled past journeys to Madagascar or Oman, as those trips left such an impression on her. "You're surrounded by different scents, like incense, mingling with the sea breeze in Oman. It's a different world, and you come back with this sensory catalog you didn't have before."

David nodded in agreement, but she continued, her voice growing warmer. "Then, of course, there are the raw materials our company develops. Each new one feels like adding someone new to the team. They bring a fresh perspective to our palette, giving us new ways to express ourselves." She laughed softly, clearly amused by the thought. "It's like welcoming a new colleague—you want to get to know them, understand what they can bring into the mix.

"And then," she added, "there are those raw materials that make everyone wince—the ones evaluators react to with a big, 'Oh, no, please don't.'" She grinned, delighted by the challenge. "Those are my favorites. I love working with the 'ugly ducklings,' the materials no one wants to touch. There's something incredibly satisfying about hiding them within a fragrance, finding a way to make them palatable, even beautiful. Nobody uses them, so if you can create something remarkable with those rougher, more challenging notes…it's a victory."

As Christelle shared her sources of inspiration, I could see the depth of her creative process, each experience layered and interwoven. Her process was not just about capturing beauty; it was about finding it in places others might overlook.

As they prepared the next essential oil for us to smell, I asked if any memory came to mind when I mentioned Madagascar.

"For me," said Christelle, "it would be the mandarin. The first time I smelled it…it was unforgettable. They brought fresh mandarin leaves to the house where we were staying, right near the sea. I remember inhaling that incredible mix—the scent of the leaves, the citrus of the fruit, and the salty air drifting in from the ocean."

She paused, almost as if she were back in that moment, savoring the memory. "It was raw, untouched—straight from the tree. I couldn't tell if it was the mandarin itself or the way it blended with the sea air. But there was something so powerful about it, something I couldn't quite capture in a single note."

David chimed in, nodding as he recalled the moment. "Yes, I remember that" he said, glancing at Christelle with a smile. "You were so taken with it—keyed into it so strongly. I think it was the very next day we were already setting up distillations. It was pretty wild."

He paused, clearly impressed with how that initial spark had evolved. "And now? It's actually one of our most successful products. All from that first encounter."

Almost as if he could still smell the memory, David said, "For me, coffee was unforgettable the very first time I went to Madagascar. You wouldn't necessarily think of coffee as something extraordinary, but every night, I would sit in the food space we had put together on the coast—a simple wooden structure with a thatched roof. The team would roast coffee beans for the next morning's brew, and the air would fill with the scents of the sea, wood, smoke, and the rich, earthy aroma of coffee." He paused, the memory

vivid. "I would sit there, writing in my journal, surrounded by those smells, and it struck me in a way I had never experienced before. It was more than just coffee; it was the whole setting, the immersion in that moment. Coffee is unique in that way—each culture brings its own tradition to it. It's different in Italy, different in France, different in the US But this—this was something entirely new for me."

He shook his head, smiling, and said that all things considered, coffee ended up being one of his most important sensory experiences from that trip.

"One of the most fascinating experiences for me," he added, "was when we first encountered *longoza*. You might know it by its scientific name, *Aframomum angustifolium*, part of the ginger family. Locally, they use it for all sorts of things, and it's a striking plant, almost like a bird of paradise with its bulb shape."

I nodded, adding, "Yes, I remember those incredibly fragrant leaves, growing everywhere on the side of the roads or pathways. Many Malagasy consider it an 'invasive' plant, but it has so many uses. I saw locals using the leaves to wrap food, almost as a substitute for banana leaves."

David smiled, picking up the thread of the memory. "One night, Christelle, I, and a few other perfumers had gathered some longoza we had picked earlier in the day. We cut it open, and the sight was remarkable—white pulp around the outside, with these vibrant black seeds inside. When we crushed the seeds, the aroma that burst out was something else entirely. It was this incredible blend of spicy, zesty, peppery notes—almost like cardamom, but layered with so much complexity."

He paused, savoring the memory. "We even tasted some, just to understand it fully. From that moment, we knew it was something special, and that experience sparked a whole development process. Today, *longoza* is one of the ingredients Symrise is actively promoting from Madagascar."

David glanced down at his hands, as if he could still feel the plant's strange effect. "What I found fascinating was the way it reacted with the skin. Do you remember that sensation, Christelle? It was like our hands were suddenly wrapped in plastic, this tightening effect. Later, I learned that *longoza* was used in some Dior products for skin tightening."

He laughed softly, shaking his head. "It's those serendipitous moments—trying things out, experimenting, letting curiosity lead the way. You never know what you'll discover."

Reflecting on their trip, David and Christelle spoke about its objectives, which went far beyond discovering new scents. The primary objective was to identify potential plants and flowers that could be distilled and used in fragrance creation. But just as important was the commitment to supporting the farmers who grew vanilla and sold it to Symrise. Vanilla harvesting lasted only a few months each year, leaving farmers with limited income for the remainder of the year. By diversifying crops, the team aimed to provide additional sources of income, allowing these farmers to sustain themselves without needing to migrate back to urban areas.

Before their trip, the farmers were already cultivating vetiver, a familiar ingredient in perfumery. David recalled uprooting vetiver in the field himself, connecting with the plant from its roots. "It's such a great synergy," he said with a smile. "A win-win for everyone. The company sent perfumers out there to explore because we are endlessly curious people—there's nothing we won't crack open, bite, sniff, or tear apart just to catch the scent. And so many of these materials are readily available and locally valued, making them a natural fit for our work."

Christelle added that it was more than just discovering new ingredients. They wanted to promote the raw materials that were already so important to these communities. Witnessing firsthand the impact of their work on local schools, healthcare, and more, changed how they viewed those ingredients. They became genuinely proud to use them, knowing they contributed directly to the well-being of the people living on the island.

David nodded in agreement. "Living among them, even briefly, meant a lot. Making connections, experiencing their daily lives, eating their food, and learning about their culture—it was pretty amazing. We were not just observers; we were participants, if only for a little while."

He reflected quietly, his voice carrying a note of sincerity. "I don't think I ever truly appreciated the raw materials in the way I did after visiting Madagascar," he admitted. There was a depth to his words, a sense that the trip had shifted something fundamental in his perspective.

As I listened to Christelle and David recount their experiences, I felt that familiar tug—a sense of a journey that goes beyond geography, one that reshapes how you see the world and the work you do within it. Their words reminded me of my own return from Madagascar and how those trips left a lasting mark on me, just as they had on the three American chefs who traveled with me. We each came back with more than memories; we returned with a deeper understanding, a respect for the people and the land that had welcomed us, and a new layer to our craft. Listening to David and Christelle, I realized we were all bound by that shared experience—an exploration that became a personal transformation.

Christelle reached out for the next essential oil sample to evaluate, vetiver.

Vetiver is more than just an essential oil; it embodies a memory of the island, intertwined with its very landscape. Madagascar is recognized as one of the nations facing particularly severe issues related to soil erosion. In rural areas, vetiver is primarily used for stabilizing soils, serving as an anti-erosion barrier on the hillsides. But I wanted to go deeper, to understand why perfumers value this ingredient so highly. What makes vetiver stand out to them? What role does it play in a fragrance, and what qualities draw them to it again and again?

With that in mind, I turned to the perfumers, hoping to gain a clearer perspective. As we examined the scent, David said, "I bet you're going to get two different answers from two perfumers. I'm going to let Christelle go first!"

"It really ties back to what you asked about how these experiences change our perspective," she began. "Most of the time, we know raw materials through a bottle—a small vial we dip into, each filled with an oil from a different part of the world. For vetiver, for instance, I was used to smelling versions from Java (Indonesia) or Haiti, each with its own characteristics.

"But when you're out in the fields in Madagascar and you smell vetiver fresh from the ground, it's different. Suddenly, you're not just smelling it as an oil—you're smelling the root, the earth, and the air around it. That's when I realized how much more there is to vetiver than what we get in the lab."

Christelle described the layers she found within the scent of vetiver. "It's woody, but it's actually a root, so it has this warm, almost citrusy, grapefruit-like top note—something you'd never expect. It's a clean woodiness, not sharp like cedarwood, but more refined, with a subtle earthiness. Depending on its origin, sometimes you get a hint of smokiness, but for me, the vetiver from Madagascar is the cleanest, the least smoky, with this freshness that I love."

Vetiver

Origin: Native to the Indian subcontinent.

Sources: Haiti, Indonesia—Java, India, Madagascar.

Fun Fact: Eco-Warrior—With one of the most robust root systems in the plant kingdom, vetiver is famous for preventing soil erosion. Its roots can grow as deep as ten to thirteen feet (or three to four meters), which helps stabilize soil and prevent landslides, especially in tropical regions.

Profile: Vetivers from different parts of the world differ a lot. Haitian vetiver is clean and ethereal, while the Javanese one is smoky and dusty.

Gender: Mainly used in male fragrances.

Perfume examples: Most designer brands have a fragrance based on vetiver (Guerlain, Dolce & Gabbana, Tom Ford, Terre d'Hermès, Vétiver by Guerlain, Spade of Vetiver by Regalien, and Kenzo Air for Men).

Now, when Christelle works with vetiver, she no longer sees it as just an oil in a bottle. Her mind travels back to Madagascar, to the warmth of the earth and the humid air, to the rich ochre-toned soil that cradled the roots. This connection gives her a deeper, more layered understanding of the material. Each time she incorporates vetiver into a fragrance, she brings with it a piece of Madagascar's landscape, a tangible memory of the place where the scent was born. Madagascar, she explained, had shown her a different way to see these raw materials—grounded in their environment, layered with the natural world around them.

Listening to them, I found it fascinating to realize something I never considered before: they don't just view these elements as isolated ingredients. Instead, they approach each one in the broader context of its origin—how it exists within its natural surroundings. Whether it is the mandarin experience from Christelle, infused with the nearby sea breeze, or the coffee episode from David, whose aroma mingled with the coastal air and earthy scents, their approach reveals layers that go beyond the raw material itself.

David had a different take on vetiver. He reflected on his early understanding of the product. "I didn't know these materials firsthand—I learned about them from books, where they were categorized simply as woody notes. Vetiver was labeled as a 'wood note.' But for me, experiencing the crashing surf, the driftwood soaked in salt—that was what vetiver felt like. The way salt and sea air infuse the driftwood with a smoky, briny quality reminded me of vetiver's character."

He explained how vetiver always brought him back to the sea—a woody, salty, almost oceanic scent that captured the essence of driftwood and the ozone-filled air. However, hearing Christelle's description, he began to see vetiver in a new light after their time in Madagascar. There, he had come to understand the earthier side of it, recognizing how vetiver's unique qualities were deeply connected to the land where it grows. This fresh perspective made him realize even something as seemingly straightforward as vetiver could be multilayered, its essence shaped by its environment and origins.

I asked them if the vetiver was a unisex note. David reflected on how vetiver has traditionally found its place in masculine scents. Though it's frequently used in women's fragrances as well, it often plays a subtler background role in those compositions. "We've all experimented with pushing its boundaries," he thought, recalling past attempts. The idea of "overdosing" vetiver in a feminine fragrance—bringing it to the forefront—was something he found intriguing, even though his previous efforts hadn't quite achieved the effect he'd envisioned. Despite his attempts, vetiver still seemed to resonate more naturally within the masculine realm.

Christelle mentioned a few examples, noting that Terre d'Hermès, Vétiver by Guerlain, and Spade of Vetiver by Regalien each showcase different profiles of vetiver in men's fragrances. Each fragrance offers its own unique take on vetiver, illustrating the origin and versatility of this note in the realm of masculine scents.

As we finished exploring the layers of the vetiver essential oil, I reached for my phone, eager to show Christelle and David a series of photos from my trip to Nosy Be, where I had visited a ylang-ylang plantation. The images brought back a clear sense of the place—the rows of ylang-ylang trees, the distillation tanks, the characteristic golden flowers. With each picture, I felt myself pulled back to the island, its rich, humid air thick with the floral fragrance of ylang-ylang.

As I began flipping through the photos, memories of my time there came rushing back—the details of the plantation, the harvesting process, and the people who tended the trees with such care. Each image seemed to transport me back to Nosy Be, immersing me once again in the sensory world of ylang-ylang. Sitting at the table with Christelle and David, I let myself slip into that memory, recalling the island's intoxicating blend of colors and scents. The photo was a selfie I had taken on the boat ride to the island, with Nirina and Chef Farah smiling beside me and the lush hills of Madagascar's east coast in the background.

We left the Palma Nova hotel in Ambanja that morning and drove to the harbor of Ankify to take a small boat to the island of Nosy Be. The waters of the Mozambique Channel were glistening under the bright morning sun. The harbor was alive, pulsing with the energy of people moving in various directions. Walking toward the pier, I saw a lineup of fishing boats bobbing gently, the clear water mirroring the boats under a bright and flawless sky.

I jumped in the front of the boat, while Nirina and Farah sat behind me. The crossing took about forty minutes—the island of Nosy Be is located five miles from the coast of Madagascar. Along the way, we crossed paths with sailing vessels used by fishermen navigating the waters between the mainland and the nearby islands. Their designs were simple with their tall, triangular sails. As they glided over the shimmering blue water, the boats appeared almost timeless, embodying a way of life that had likely persisted here for generations, untouched by the rush of modernization.

On Nosy Be, groups of people were making their way out of the harbor to the nearby city. Men were carrying large suitcases on their heads, while others held baskets and bags filled with goods purchased from Madagascar. The breathtaking backdrop of the ocean and the rolling hills of Nosy Be framed the harbor, highlighting its role as a central hub where locals and visitors come together. As I made my way to the small pickup vehicle Nirina had arranged for us, I passed a man walking with a large bundle of green bananas skillfully balanced on his head.

The three of us climbed into the front row seats and drove into a street lined with small, bright yellow tuk-tuks. The street was framed by a mix of small shops, palm trees, and utility poles. Pedestrians in vibrant clothing walked along the sidewalk and crossed the street from all directions. In the distance, the pointed steeple of a church peeked over the rooftops, hinting at the blend of local culture and colonial influences that characterize this island town.

Nirina took *La Route de L'Est* (the East Road). Basically, two main roads led people outside of the harbor of Nosy Be: the road toward the east and the road toward the west of the island. The island is only about 120 square miles.

Nosy Be is famous for its touristic snorkeling and diving activities. But on this little island—even if its name means big island—lies a worldwide coveted oil from the *Cananga odorata genuina*, commonly known as ylang-ylang. The flower's sweet, flowery notes are used in fine fragrances, cosmetics, soaps, and aromatherapy, earning Nosy Be the nickname "*l'île aux parfums*," or "the fragrant island." Ylang-ylang essential oil is a key component of Chanel's renowned No. 5 perfume.

The tree originated from the Philippines. French traders returned to the colonial territories of Mauritius and Réunion with the tree's seeds at the end of the eighteenth century. By the end of the 1800s, the French had built sizable plantations on their colonized territories. French missionaries brought the tree to Nosy Be and other regions of northern Madagascar in the 1920s. The world's two biggest producers of the essential oil are Madagascar, specifically Nosy Be, and the Comoro Islands.

Nirina was bringing me to one of the large companies that had a direct hand in every stage of the process, from growing the flower to exporting the essential oil of ylang-ylang. It was part of his family business.

As we came closer to the entrance of the plantation, Nirina pointed my awareness to slightly bizarre-shaped trees. The trees swayed and curled as if sculpted by a whimsical wind, forever caught in a slow-motion dance. I learned later, while walking through the pathways of the plantation, that the trees were trimmed at one and a half years old to maximize flowering and also facilitate the picking of the flowers.

We parked the car next to a colonial house and met with Madame Camara, who had been the administrative assistant for fourteen years on the plantation owned by the group Ramanandraibe, but the plantation dated back from the French colonial time.

Madame Camara invited us for a light lunch under the porch of the colonial house. Surrounded by pink anthuriums and red passion flowers, she treated us with a glass of *ranovola*, fried shrimps, steamed green beans and carrots, and finished the meal with slices of fresh picked oranges, small fragrant bananas (my favorite!), and chocolate flan (using the chocolate from Chocolaterie Robert).

After lunch, we toured the distillery and strolled through the plantation, passing rows after rows of ylang-ylang trees. The twisted limbs of each tree resembled dancers frozen mid-pose as if captured in an eerie, ethereal ballet. It struck me that the scene could serve as the perfect backdrop for a horror movie at night. Alongside ylang-ylang, the plantation cultivates other species for essential oil production, including bay leaves, cinnamon, and *combava*, though ylang-ylang remains the main crop, yielding around 150 metric tons of flowers each year. I also learned that ylang-ylang is a perennial plant, continuously blooming, with its peak season between March and May. Madame Camara mentioned that ylang-ylang trees produce flowers after three to four years, and there are still a few huge, uncut trees that germinated more than fifty years ago and still give flowers.

Flower harvesting at the plantation happens mostly in the early morning. Around eighty local women gather in the fields to begin their work, spending two to three hours collecting the delicate blooms. During peak season, they can collect more than twenty kilos of flowers daily, but in the dry season, their yield drops to just two or three kilos. The harvested flowers are placed in baskets and then carried by men to the stills, where they begin the process of distillation.

We stopped in front of a tree with a few yellow ylang-ylang flowers still hanging—likely missed by the morning harvesters. The petals curled outward in gentle arcs, reaching in different directions, their colors shifting from chartreuse to bright yellow, with hints of lime green in the less mature blossoms. Madame Camara picked a few flowers and placed them in my hands. The petals were soft and almost weightless, yet their scent was anything but subtle. Ylang-ylang's fragrance is unmistakable—rich and layered, with notes that suggest creamy vanilla, ripe banana, and a touch of honeyed jasmine.

During our tour of the plantation, I noticed wooden panels laid into the earth, each bearing the name of a well-known figure from the worlds of fashion and fine fragrance. Many of these names belonged to people who had come here to plant their own ylang-ylang or *combava* tree—a tradition that marked their visit and left a lasting connection to the plantation. Nirina explained the significance of this ritual, and then Madame Camara turned to me and said it was now my turn.

Honored, I chose to plant a young ylang-ylang tree, knowing it would take root on this island alongside those planted by others who had come before me. Photos captured the moment, and I could already picture the small wooden sign, etched with my name, marking the future tree. Weeks after I returned to the US, Nirina sent me a picture of the sign itself—a reminder of this meaningful connection to Nosy Be and the heritage of the plantation.

Walking back to the colonial house at the end of the afternoon, I tried to savor the intoxicating experience. The air was thick with the heavy aroma of ylang-ylang, a scent that deepened as the end of the day progressed. The fragrance enveloped me—a rich, sweet, and slightly spicy bouquet that evoked notes of jasmine and neroli. It was a heady perfume, both calming and euphoric. The scent was so potent that it seemed to hang visibly in the air. It was, for me, an unforgettable sensory experience that was both mystical and otherworldly.

As Christelle and David looked through my photos of the ylang-ylang plantation—images of the trees and their blossoms—I could see a hint of envy in their expressions. For them, as perfumers, experiencing the source of this raw material firsthand would have held an even deeper significance.

They handed me the scent strip dipped in Madagascar ylang-ylang essential oil. The fragrance was unmistakable—rich, tropical, and deeply intoxicating. I closed my eyes, and for a moment, I felt as though I might open them to find myself back among the rows of ylang-ylang trees atop the plantation in Nosy Be.

David inhaled deeply from the scent strip, then paused, as if gathering his thoughts. "It's overwhelming," he said, "but in a way that just pulls you in completely. You can almost feel the humidity in it…like you're right there on an island." He looked at me with a glimmer of recognition in his eyes. "This scent doesn't just hit you—it surrounds you. You feel it as much as you smell it."

Christelle added, "It's an intoxicating scent!"

David reflected that smelling ylang-ylang in its natural environment was a completely different experience, especially for a perfumer who is used to encountering it only in a lab. Over time, ylang-ylang has become so prevalent in various products that its unique beauty has, in some ways, been diluted. It is often found in everyday items—even something like furniture polish or hairspray. While this highlights its versatility, it has also given ylang-ylang a functional, almost utilitarian aspect due to its long history.

"But experiencing it in nature, like you did," added David, "carried on by a warm breeze, you encountered the true character of ylang-ylang. Its fragrance became something richer, more alive—a reminder of its origins

Ylang-Ylang

Origin: Native from the Philippines, though many of these plantations were severely damaged or destroyed during World War II.

Sources: Comoro Islands and Madagascar.

Fun fact: Multiple Grades of Oil—Ylang-ylang oil is distilled in stages, producing up to five different grades. The first distillation, called "ylang-ylang extra," is the most prized in perfumery for its intense, complex aroma, while later distillations are often used in cosmetics and aromatherapy.

Profile: The profile depends on the fractions from the distillation. The first series of fractions are "Extra Superior" and "Extra," and then come, in order, "First," "Second," and "Third." Rich, floral, sweet notes combine with a fruity note of banana (bubble gum) and can have woody, dirty, and sour nuances.

Gender: Mainly used in female fragrances.

Perfume examples: Channel No. 5, Arpège by Lanvin for Women, Samsara Eau de Parfum by Guerlain for Women, and J'Adore Extrait de Parfum by Dior.

beyond the confines of commercial use. I understand that the experience was profound, almost transformative."

Christelle and David commented that seeing ylang-ylang in its natural setting on the island shifted their perspective, taking them beyond the familiar, almost conventional idea of the scent. It opened new possibilities, inspiring them to consider fresh ways to work with it.

"Honestly," said David, "I might not have thought to use it otherwise—it's often seen as a somewhat dated material."

He reflected on how his approach to working with raw materials had evolved. "These days, we are trying to incorporate materials as they exist in their natural element," he said thoughtfully. "For me, that means bringing in the environment as much as the ingredient itself."

He explained how this approach transformed his experience with vanilla in Madagascar. "Smelling it there, with that infusion of smokiness from the curing process, was something entirely different. It wasn't just vanilla—it was the air, the warmth, the whole atmosphere around it." He paused as if remembering the scene. "Everything had this ambiance. It was almost like stepping into a moment, capturing that feeling of being on the island."

David gestured with his hands, trying to convey the sensory immersion. "It reminded me of when you get off a plane somewhere tropical, and the warm air hits you with this rush of new scents. You think, 'I want to bottle this feeling.' That's what it felt like."

Reflecting on how he had worked with vanilla after that experience, he admitted, "It's a different approach now. Before, I would have thought of vanilla as just an isolated note. But now, I try to bring in that whole sense of place, that warmth, that atmosphere. It's about recreating that moment in the fragrance, not just the ingredient."

"But trends are cyclical," added Christelle. "Ylang-ylang might make a comeback. With a more modern interpretation."

Christelle uses the rose scent as an example. She said that the new generations have rediscovered it. "Rose was old fashioned. It smelt like grandma to us. It became cheap and was used in products like toilet paper!"

But, she said, it has been reinvented and appreciated by Gen Z, and it is a big trend right now. Perfumers have reinvented it by combining the rose scent with amberwood, for instance, like in Dina by Verset Parfums.

As we wrapped up our evaluation with the perfumers, I took some chocolate tablets I brought back from my trip to Madagascar. I wanted to conclude with a tasting of Chocolaterie Robert's ylang-ylang white chocolate—a creation renowned for celebrating Madagascar's local ingredients. The experience began with top notes that unfolded immediately upon opening the packaging, filling the air with the intense floral aroma of ylang-ylang. In the heart notes, the delicate sweetness of white chocolate emerged, releasing a creamy, milky taste. This balanced partnership between the creamy richness of chocolate and the lightly spicy floral complexity of ylang-ylang created a harmonious contrast that felt indulgent and refined. Finally, the base notes introduced subtle, comforting hints of vanilla and cocoa butter, bringing a sense of warmth and roundness that lingered on the palate. Throughout, ylang-ylang remained as an enchanting, soothing undercurrent, concluding the tasting with a lasting impression of Madagascar's unique olfactory landscape.

As my meeting with the perfumers ended, I reflected on how much deeper the story of Madagascar's search for essential oils had become. What began as an exploration for new ingredients—plants, flowers, and roots to serve as fresh raw materials for perfumery—transformed into something much richer. For Symrise, sourcing directly from Madagascar held clear economic advantages, allowing them to control costs and ensure a steady supply of these rare, high-quality materials, compared to sourcing it from other parts of the world. But the impact went far beyond the financial.

By supporting local communities in cultivating crops like ylang-ylang, vetiver, cinnamon, or ginger, the company was helping farmers diversify their sources of income, thereby creating a more sustainable livelihood. This collaboration also promoted the preservation of Madagascar's unique botanical heritage. With its diverse climates and soils, the island provides an environment where an extraordinary range of species can thrive. By investing in these local crops, companies contribute to the conservation of these species and the landscapes they inhabit.

But perhaps the most significant outcome of this journey to Madagascar was less tangible—a human experience that left a lasting mark on everyone involved. The perfumers returned not only with new raw materials but with stories of a place that felt like paradise, where they were welcomed by people whose kindness and warmth were as remarkable as the landscapes around them. What began as a search for ingredients became a journey into the heart of a culture, a connection between craft and community that now shapes the very way the perfumers create. Their experiences in Madagascar—the sights, scents, and warmth of the people—are woven into each new fragrance, influencing their approach and deepening their understanding. The journey left them with more than memories; it redefined their craft, grounding it in a respect for the origins of the ingredient and a commitment to honoring the people behind them.

RABEKIJANA Farah

CHAPTER 10

Reimagining Roots

The Contemporary Culinary Voices of Madagascar

Ny mahay miova no mahavita mandroso.

Those who know how to change can move forward.

—TRADITIONAL MALAGASY SAYING

Madagascar's culinary landscape stands at a turning point. For far too long, it has been entirely ignored on the global stage, overshadowing a culinary heritage that deserves far broader recognition.

Today, a new generation of chefs, mixologists, and culinary innovators is emerging, identifying and documenting regional culinary recipes and reinterpreting local traditions in creative manners. This movement mirrors a broader global trend that values and incorporates indigenous knowledge and heritage-based culinary practices.

◀ *Top left: Chef Lalaina Ravelomanana; Top right: Chef Henintsoa Moretti; Bottom left: Mixologist K-Mëc; Bottom right: Chef Farah Rabekijana.*

The significance of these emerging voices lies in their ability to confront outdated beliefs that have relegated Malagasy cuisine to the periphery of culinary discussions. As global interest in genuine food experiences continues to rise, the efforts of these modern pioneers—whether they are passionate custodians of traditional recipes or innovative fusion creators—provide a dual perspective that honors historical culinary practices while embracing the excitement of new possibilities.

This chapter unfolds like a culinary journey through Madagascar's evolving gastronomic landscape, beginning with the deep-rooted traditions of late Mariette Andrianjaka, expanding into regional flavors with Chef Henintsoa Moretti from restaurant Haka Fy, venturing into bold, adventurous territory with Chef Farah Rabekijana, embracing innovative fusion led by Chef Gilbert Kakulé, and culminating in the refined artistry of modern gastronomy from Chef Lalaina of the Marais restaurant, with a final toast to the island's burgeoning craft cocktail scene by mixologist K-Mëc.

Traditional Roots: Chef Mariette Andrianjaka

Mariette Andrianjaka transcended the role of a typical chef; she embodied the essence of Madagascar's culinary heritage. Her life and contributions serve as a fundamental pillar of the nation's gastronomic identity, influenced by indigenous practices, colonial legacies, and her relentless vision.

I was not able to meet Mariette during my first trip to the island, and she passed away in November 2023, but I was able to remember her life and legacy with people who knew her well.

Born near Antananarivo, she grew up in a household where it was all about authentic, heartfelt cooking, and where local markets defined the rhythm of each day. In the early morning hours, she used to accompany her grandmother through meandering streets to vibrant stalls filled with ginger, fresh cut meat, and the soft green leaves used in classic dishes like *ravitoto*. These market visits were instrumental in shaping her culinary philosophy: honoring the land, prioritizing seasonal ingredients, and appreciating the nuances of each component.

From an early age, she sensed that the heart of Malagasy cuisine resided not merely in its methods but also in its gentle pace—an almost meditative respect for the slow cooking of broths and the meticulous preparation of meats. She often shared how her grandmother held the belief that "patience in the kitchen reflects patience in life," emphasizing that each ingredient has its moment to unveil its finest flavor. During those formative years, she came to regard even the simplest roots and tubers—such as cassava, taro, and sweet potatoes—as culinary treasures with immense potential.

Mariette's departure from Madagascar to France in the late 1960s marked a significant turning point in her culinary journey, as her reputation among local food enthusiasts had begun to grow, although she remained largely oblivious to the admiration she inspired. This transition was prompted by an extraordinary opportunity: an apprenticeship with Charles Barrier, a Michelin three-star chef based in Tours (a city in the central-western part of France, considered the "gateway" to the Loire Valley). While her grandmother taught her the art of home cooking, Barrier's kitchen introduced her to the meticulous nature of haute cuisine. She immersed herself in the complexities of French sauce preparation, honing her skills in reductions and grasping and understanding the science behind browning. Where the French might finish with a swirl of butter, she began imagining ways to incorporate the coconut milk or zebu butter of her homeland. She would later recall how Barrier's insistence on discipline sharpened her culinary instincts: "He made me weigh each gram of flour, each drop of stock, ensuring I understood the true cost of each error. But the lessons I cherished most were the ones about letting flavors speak rather than forcing them."

Upon returning to Madagascar in the early 1970s, Mariette brought back with her enhanced technical expertise and a revitalized dedication to promoting her nation's culinary traditions. Her time in France instilled in her the belief that Malagasy cuisine, characterized by its rich array of aromatic spices, zesty ginger-infused broths, and fresh ingredients, warranted a place of honor on the global culinary map. This conviction led her to open Chez Mariette in Antananarivo, a restaurant often described as a seamless blend of homey warmth and sophisticated elegance. Although the establishment was modestly sized and located in a neighborhood renowned for its historic colonial architecture, news quickly spread that Mariette's three-course tasting menu was unparalleled in its authenticity and craft.

Diners at Chez Mariette experienced not just a meal, but an exemplary demonstration of successful fusion cuisine. She structured each course around a singular, defining ingredient—be it goose, zebu, or freshwater prawns—while highlighting complex layers of flavor sourced from local spices such as *voatsiperifery* and cloves. A typical dining experience might begin with a delicate chicken and ginger broth, infused with vibrant, herbal undertones. Next came a main course that married the heartiness of traditional Malagasy stews with the elegant presentation refined in France—such as a rare zebu filet, adorned with a sauce enriched by slowly caramelized shallots, a hint of local rum, and a touch of cream. Desserts frequently showcased the exquisite vanilla for which Madagascar is renowned, featuring either a classic vanilla flan or flambéed bananas in sugarcane spirits, paying homage to her grandmother's time-honored techniques for extracting sweetness from local fruits.

Through her diligent and innovative approach, Mariette earned the esteemed title of the "Queen of Malagasy Gastronomy." Her culinary creations attracted royalty, celebrities, and dignitaries, effectively placing Madagascar on the international culinary stage in an unprecedented manner. Among her most illustrious guests were Paloma Picasso and Prince Albert of Monaco, captivated by the unique native Malagasy flavors skillfully combined with French culinary techniques. It was rumored that African heads of state, gathering in Antananarivo for diplomatic meetings, would discreetly visit her restaurant, often requesting her signature goose dish. By hosting extravagant banquets that honored local traditions, Mariette garnered admiration from both the global elite and everyday Malagasy diners, who appreciated the recognition of their traditional dishes at the highest gastronomic levels.

Even as her name became a symbol of sophistication, she never wavered from the grounding principles she inherited. She was often found wearing a practical apron in the restaurant's bustling kitchen, personally tasting the stocks and adjusting their seasoning by instinct rather than relying on a timer. Staff members recall that no pot was too large or too modest for her care, and every garnish—whether a sprinkle of scallions or a dash of local pepper—was applied with purpose. Her global recognition and the fierce love for her

homeland's cooking traditions propelled her to an almost legendary status among her contemporaries. Younger Malagasy chefs speak of her with great respect, highlighting her unique combination of humility and excellence as the standard they aspire to achieve.

In 2015, Mariette's culinary talents were showcased to a global audience when Anthony Bourdain featured her in an episode of *Parts Unknown*. Bourdain's quest for authentic narratives and flavors aligned with Mariette's ethos of honest cooking. That episode highlighted two of her standout dishes: a richly aromatic goose special, renowned for its marinade of ginger, onions, and occasionally a hint of local sugarcane rum, and a restorative chicken and ginger broth. Bourdain's genuine admiration on screen further served as another testament to Mariette's uncanny ability to fuse rustic simplicity with nuanced flavors. For many viewers around the world, this was their first encounter with Malagasy cuisine, extending beyond the usual references to vanilla exports or tropical beaches.

Her legacy was fundamentally anchored in her remarkable ability to salvage recipes and techniques that were on the verge of being forgotten. Madagascar is an island whose culinary identity was shaped by waves of migration from Austronesian peoples to Arab and European traders. This diverse heritage has led to the creation of a wide array of dishes—some characterized by bold spices, while others are more subdued yet earthy in flavor. Over the years, colonial influences have introduced French culinary methods; however, many Malagasy households continue to utilize open-fire cooking and basic equipment. Mariette, in her role as cultural ambassador, collected these techniques and stories. She meticulously documented practices such as the incorporation of dried fish in vegetable stews by certain inland communities and the smoking of shellfish by coastal families. By writing down and practicing these methods alongside her French-inspired innovations, she started building a living archive of Madagascar's culinary DNA—one that not only preserved tradition but also enhanced it.

Her creative contributions had practical ripple effects too. As she gained renown, she advocated for higher-quality local produce. Her early morning trips to the markets turned into broader campaigns for local farmers to cultivate stronger, more sustainable harvests. Additionally, she offered training to her staff—many of whom were inexperienced individuals from rural areas—who subsequently established their own restaurants throughout the island. For Mariette, mentoring was not a charitable side project; it was integral to her vision of advancing Malagasy cuisine through the skills of the upcoming generation. By encouraging her mentees to explore new ideas while remaining faithful to traditional practices, she guaranteed her impact would persist long after the closure of Chez Mariette.

Mariette Andrianjaka may no longer be present, yet her influence continues to resonate in kitchens throughout Madagascar. The layered broths, the delicate balance of ginger and onion in slow-simmered stews, and the delightful combination of freshly ground local spices with traditional French sauces have all fostered a vibrant dialogue among modern chefs. Her recipes may live on handwritten in notebooks or on chalkboards in bistros, but the sense of possibility she instilled is intangible and immeasurable. Each time a young chef enhances a dish of *ravitoto* with a touch of cream or creates a flambé using local fruits, they pay homage to the legacy she tirelessly cultivated.

She was a woman who mastered both the traditional village kitchen and the high-end culinary world, bridging old and new with each thoughtful dish. For Madagascar, she was a beacon who served as a poignant reminder that "modern" does not have to forsake the past; rather, in her capable hands, the past became the essential element that transformed every dish into a timeless homage to Malagasy culture.

Regional Exploration: Chef Henintsoa Moretti

Chef Henintsoa Moretti grew up in Toamasina on Madagascar's east coast. When speaking with me, she vividly recalled the potent aroma of cloves wafting from the local warehouses in her hometown, where women sorted the spice after harvest. For her, that scent has remained an iconic memory and something she always seeks out when she returns to Tamatave.

"For me, Tamatave is the smell of cloves," she concluded, punctuating the recollection with a smile.

She also described how, as a young girl, she would head to the nearby *bazarbè* (market) to buy lychees, reminiscing about the affordability and abundance of local produce in those days.

"When you bite into a lychee," she said, "the aroma shoots straight up into your nose before the taste even hits your tongue."

Today, Madagascar exports a significant share of the world's lychees, and the region of Tamatave is well-known for its high-quality harvest. "We are among the world's top lychee exporters, but in Tamatave, it's first and foremost an everyday fruit." These early experiences shaped her connection to Madagascar's unique sensory palette.

Initially, she never planned to become a chef. Over the years, she worked in various fields—ranging from managing an orphanage's legal department to assisting with accounting for a boat-manufacturing company, working in logistics for an American firm, and even directing a four-star hotel. These varied roles honed her managerial skills and adaptability, ultimately shaping her approach to running a restaurant.

Chef Moretti's husband is Italian, and I was eager to learn the story of how he first arrived on the island. She explained he initially came to Madagascar for volunteer work. "With my husband, we opened the very first real pizzeria in Tana, Chez Lorenzo. He introduced Neapolitan pizza, which didn't exist here before." Occasionally, she found herself in the kitchen out of necessity.

Over time, though, she fell in love with authentic Malagasy cuisine and made it her life's passion. That shift transformed her from an incidental cook into a dedicated chef, driven by her desire to promote traditional Malagasy dishes. Today, she runs Haka Fy, located near the Queen's Palace (Rova). In Malagasy, "*haka fy*" literally means "to take pleasure."

Her menu features authentic, regionally inspired recipes, alongside Italian classics. Among her signature preparations are slow-cooked zebu (including a forty-eight-hour version), fish with coconut sauce, and a whimsical pizza topped with *ravitoto* (cassava leaves), reflecting a creative fusion of local staples with international influences.

She focuses on preserving the authentic "identity" of Malagasy dishes, while refining presentation through modern plating techniques. By working with fresh ingredients, respecting original recipes, and introducing subtle twists, she offers a dynamic culinary experience that bridges heritage cooking and contemporary expectations.

To her, Malagasy cuisine is central to Madagascar's cultural and touristic identity. She believes that the cuisine—characterized by its diversity, fresh ingredients, and vibrant flavors—has untapped potential to delight local and global audiences alike, much as Madagascar's flora, fauna, and landscapes fascinate visitors.

Our conversation turned to her journey, which began by offering mostly familiar local fare and Italian dishes, but gradually shifted toward rediscovering and showcasing Malagasy culinary heritage.

"In the national archives, I found no written record of Malagasy dishes. It's as though our cuisine didn't exist in writing! I found the journal of a former prime minister listing only French dishes for his son's wedding translated into Malagasy. We had already neglected our own culinary art."

Motivated to unearth these lost traditions, she traveled throughout the country (after 2021) to meet elders and guardians of oral knowledge and traditions. "I was convinced there were still women of my generation holding on to their ancestors' recipes, and I wanted to meet them before it was too late." Through these encounters, she collected a variety of cooking methods and recipes linked to Madagascar's many regions.

"When people travel to Tamatave, they only talk about the Chinese soup, whereas dishes like Saliboaka (smoked fish prepared with moringa leaves) and Ravikazaha (dish based on cassava leaves) exist—but no one mentions them."

Chef Moretti highlighted three emblematic Malagasy ingredients. Zebu, she explained, is universally eaten across Madagascar; *brèdes mafanes*, an herb with a slight numbing, peppery quality, commonly appears in soups and stews—Romazava being a prime example. And then there is vanilla, one of Madagascar's most famous exports worldwide.

"Here, we don't traditionally cook much with spices like vanilla or cinnamon. We mainly exported them, but now we're rediscovering them in our own dishes, like vanilla-flavored shrimp or *canard aux épices*. I love cooking Label Rouge shrimp with vanilla. It's absolutely delicious—truly a dish that pleasantly surprises people."

A pivotal example of this evolving identity is zebu's place in Malagasy culture.

"In the days of the monarchs, zebu was eaten at all ceremonial events. Today, it has become a commonplace meat, even seen as 'less chic,'" she continued, noting though it was historically a noble meat associated with royal feasts, zebu now competes with imported poultry traditions introduced by foreigners.

"Could you tell me more about the seven royal dishes? They were part of royal banquets, right?" I asked.

"Yes, exactly. The term '*hanim-pitoloha*' is used to describe them," she said, explaining that the word signifies abundance. "It literally refers to the seven royal dishes we talk about. But in our culinary culture, we don't have a separate 'starter' course—it's a bit like Asian customs. Everything is served at once: fish, eel, turkey, zebu, and pork. Altogether, these make up the seven royal dishes. We also count sides like rice and Romazava. That's what people mean when they refer to the seven royal dishes." Chef Moretti pointed out that this cultural shift reflects an "acculturation" process, where many Malagasies adopted foreign customs and began overlooking local gastronomic heritage.

The discussion turned to the obstacles of popularizing authentic Malagasy dishes in a market that sometimes prefers foreign cuisines.

"Sometimes, I feel we Malagasies are acculturated. We too quickly embraced foreign celebrations, sometimes neglecting our own culinary traditions."

Chef Moretti recounted how certain dishes—like *crevettes* sautéed with fresh *manioc* leaves—initially puzzled diners because they were swiftly cooked rather than boiled for hours. Yet she observed that with persistence and a bit of education, people grew to appreciate the distinct flavor and texture. Her personal adaptations of *manaramolotra* (a slow-cooked zebu dish) and "*pizza au ravitoto*," a playful creation by her husband, represented how deeply she merges personal taste with cultural pride. She admitted, however, there is one dish she could not bring herself to eat (*anguille au porc*, or eel with pork) because of her aversion to eel. Nonetheless, she said, many patrons enjoy it, proving the power of combining personal flair with local traditions.

Having self-published her first Malagasy cookbook, Chef Moretti is already contemplating a second volume focusing on regional ingredients like cacao and vanilla. Though some local institutions were initially skeptical, she remains dedicated to documenting and promoting Madagascar's gastronomic heritage. She occasionally organizes buffets at her restaurant to spotlight traditional dishes.

A significant hurdle in her transition from Italian to Malagasy fare was convincing local and expatriate communities to appreciate genuine Malagasy cuisine—along with managing the financial strain that came with rebranding her restaurant. Strategic partnerships with organizations like Vitogaz and Madagascar Airlines have proven essential. These collaborations underscore the broader cultural impact of Malagasy cuisine and hint at its boundless potential on the global stage.

As her career moves forward, her dream is to document and preserve regional dishes for younger generations, ensuring these recipes don't vanish from memory. One day, she hopes to find a passionate successor to expand Haka Fy beyond Madagascar and continue elevating Malagasy gastronomy internationally.

"The simplest dish can sometimes be the most remarkable," she told me, "like cassava cooked with milk and smoked zebu."

Fish Filets with Curry, Madagascar Vanilla, Coconut Milk, and Red Label Prawns

Recipes by Chef Henintsoa Moretti (Chef-Owner at Haka Fy in Antananarivo, Madagascar)

Serves 4 people

INGREDIENTS

1 onion
4 stalks lemongrass
2 tbsp. oil, divided
Five-spice, to taste
¾ cup coconut milk (6.8 fl. oz. or 20 cl.)
4 fillets of vivaneau bourgeois (red snapper), 7 oz. each (200 g per fillet)
2 Madagascar vanilla beans
4 Red Label shrimp
Salt, to taste

PREPARATION

1. Peel and finely chop the onion and lemongrass stalks.
2. In a wok or casserole dish, fry the onion in 1 tablespoon of olive oil for 5 minutes. Then add the five-spice, the salt, and lemongrass and stir for a further 2 minutes.
3. Gently stir in half the coconut milk. Once the sauce begins to simmer, add the fish. Halve the vanilla pods, scrape out the seeds, and stir into the sauce, then add the remaining coconut milk.
4. Trim the back of each prawn and remove the black vein running down the back. Do not shell them.
5. Simmer for 10 minutes, turning the fish every 5 minutes. Check with the tip of a knife. Place each filet on a plate, top with a prawn and drizzle with the sauce.
6. Serve hot with white rice.

Spicy Duck and Sweet Potato Arancini

Serves 6 people

INGREDIENTS

Spicy Duck

0.7 oz. Four-spice blend
1.7 fl. oz. (⅓ cup) honey (5 cl.)
1 cup (8.5 fl. oz. / 250 cl.) sunflower oil, divided
6 duck legs

Sweet Potato Arancini

4¼ cups water (34 fl. oz. / 1 L)
2.2 lbs. (1 kg.) sweet potatoes
1 star anise
1.75 oz. (¼ cup) grated Emmental cheese (50 g)
Salt, to taste
2 egg whites
3.5 oz. (1 cup) breadcrumbs (100 g)

PREPARATION

For the Spicy Duck

1. In a bowl, mix the four-spice blend, the star anis, and honey with 2 tablespoons of oil. Coat each duck leg with this mixture, massaging the flesh to allow the flavors and aromas to penetrate.
2. Return the duck legs to the bowl with the remaining sauce and leave to marinate for at least six hours (you can prepare the duck legs the day before and leave to marinate overnight, which will make them even better).
3. In a large frying pan, pour 4 tablespoons of oil and brown the duck legs. Cover with water and leave to simmer and reduce.

For the Sweet Potato Arancini

1. In another pot, place the whole sweet potatoes on the bottom, cover with water, and cook for 30 minutes over a high heat.
2. Peel the sweet potatoes and mash to a fine purée using a potato masher. Add the grated Emmental cheese and mix well. Season with salt.
3. Shape into balls 2 inches in diameter.
4. Whisk the egg whites and dip each dumpling in them, then dip in the breadcrumbs.
5. Fry, and serve with the duck legs.

Culinary Adventurer: Chef Farah Rabekijana

Chef Farah always made a point of taking me along when she explored Madagascar's vibrant street food scene or visited local markets. "You can't truly understand the food without understanding where it comes from," she often said. That morning in Antalaha, in the SAVA region, was no different.

She was gearing up to cook dinner at Domaine d'Ambohimanitra later that day, eager to showcase local ingredients in her dishes. Her cooking style seamlessly blends traditional Malagasy flavors with modern culinary techniques—skills she first acquired at a cooking school in Tana and polished through stints at several of the city's top restaurants.

When I first met Farah, she explained her role as a private chef catering to a high-profile clientele. "I cook for ambassadors and ministers. It's all very VIP," she said with a playful smile. In addition to her private chef work, she manages an organic farm in the Ambanja region, growing vegetables and raising livestock.

It was Nirina who introduced us a few months before my second visit to the island. "She's the perfect addition to your journey around Madagascar," he had told me. "Farah travels the island's roads in search of local cuisines, authentic farms, and fishermen. She can introduce you to a wealth of local ingredients you'll want to feature in your book."

But Farah's reach extended beyond her culinary skills—she is also a local influencer, with seventy-five thousand followers on her Facebook page, Mon Road Trip Culinaire (My Culinary Road Trip). She has merged her passions for cooking and motorcycles in this unique project, traversing Madagascar's national roads to highlight major tourist sites, participate in community events, and cook with regional ingredients. Her journeys also serve to educate visitors about local customs and traditions.

As we made our way to the market, I asked her more about her background. Farah was born around thirty years ago on the island of Nosy Be. "My parents decided to move the family to Tana," she explained. "Nosy Be wasn't the best environment for girls." Later, I would learn that the Malagasy government had been actively combating the issue of sexual tourism on the island.

"In Tana, my sisters and I continued our studies. I focused on tourism, specifically the hotel industry," she said. While studying, she began working as an extra at the Carlton Hotel at just seventeen. After six years there, she gained further experience at Chef Lalaina's Canela restaurant, then at La Compagnie des Voyageurs, and finally co-founded the Badass Motorcycle Community Pub. Despite these accomplishments, Farah decided she needed a more transformative path.

"That's when I created Mon Road Trip Culinaire," she said. "I started with a solo motorcycle journey of over six hundred miles from Tana to Tuléar. It created a major buzz!" A young woman traveling alone on a motorcycle, exploring Madagascar's culture and culinary arts—it was a bold move that captured the imaginations of many and solidified her reputation as a true trailblazer.

Stepping onto the paved pathway that cut through the busy market, I was instantly drawn into the vibrant energy of the place. The market was a mosaic of sights and sounds, with stalls covered by colorful umbrellas—red, orange, and purple—each shielding piles of fresh vegetables and fruit. Vendors, mostly women, called out to passing customers or chatted amongst themselves. Their stalls displayed everything from squash and greens to freshly ground spices.

Farah moved deliberately between the stands, scouting for the best produce. She stopped often to engage vendors, inquiring about their goods. At one stall, a young girl held out a bundle of greens—*brède mafane*. Farah inspected them with a practiced eye. "These will do," she said softly, handing the girl a few ariary.

The air was rich with aromas: fresh vegetables, the tang of *combava*, the subtle spice of dried chilies from a nearby stall. We paused at a stand displaying small, tomatillo-shaped vegetables, and Farah gently tapped their skins before selecting a few.

Further on, a vendor's spice offerings drew her attention. Farah spotted bags of pink peppercorn and purchased a small packet. "This will go perfectly with the fish skewers I'm planning, and with the *combava* salad," she noted, already mentally composing her menu.

For me, the market was a fascinating window into local life of Antalaha. Some shoppers lingered to bargain, while others simply caught up on neighborhood news. A woman wrapped in a striking red *lamba* passed by, her vivid attire standing out amid the swirl of colors around us.

Following the scent of salt and sea, we arrived at a concrete structure that housed the seafood section. The first stall, shaded by a bright green tarp, showcased neat piles of shrimp. Farah picked up a handful, evaluating their firmness and sniffing for freshness. "These are perfect," she said, motioning for the vendor to bag her selection.

A few steps ahead, a woman brandished a massive crab, its claws outstretched in protest. She beamed with pride at her catch. "You don't see crabs like this every day," Farah remarked, leaning in to admire it. "We'll need to cook this in a way that highlights its natural sweetness." Nearby, smaller fish were meticulously displayed on banana leaves.

As we continued through the seafood stalls, Farah's gaze lit up at the sight of *carangue jaune* (golden trevally). Their silvery scales caught the diffused light, and the yellow tips of their fins and tails shone vividly. "This is a real find," she said, crouching to pick one up. She examined its firm body with a chef's practiced precision. "Look at that color," she murmured, more to herself than anyone else. "These will be perfect for tonight." Signaling the vendor to prepare two, she suddenly turned to me with a playful grin

"Here," she said, handing me two large fish. "Hold them out at arm's length. I need to send a picture to Nirina—he'll love this!" I followed her instructions, arms extended, feeling a bit ridiculous while she snapped a few photos in the middle of the seafood stalls and all the vendors smiling. "Perfect!" she exclaimed, laughing as she took the fish back.

On our way out, I asked Farah what being a chef meant to her. She fell quiet, pondering. "At first, I was driven by a need to do something meaningful,"

she said. "I wanted to be a chef, to compete in culinary competitions, to travel internationally. It became an obsession—leaving the country and proving myself. But the opportunity never came." Her voice grew softer as she recounted a particularly painful disappointment. "I was once selected for a competition that took place in the Indian Ocean region. I was so excited, but then my visa was refused. I cried so much that day. It felt like the dream was slipping away. Still, I told myself, 'Maybe one day, I'll get another chance.'"

She concluded that, with Mon Road Trip Culinaire, she now had the opportunity to have another vision of culinary travel.

She looked off into the distance, momentarily lost in thought. "I miss it," she admitted, her voice quiet. "Being in the kitchen, leading a brigade, feeling the rush of lunch and dinner service. I miss it so much. But at some point, I had to accept that I couldn't do everything. I had to choose what I really wanted in life."

Her honesty took me by surprise; it wasn't often she showed this vulnerable side. Offering a faint smile, she explained, "I'm at a stage where stability in my career comes first. My dream of having my own restaurant is still close to my heart, but I've realized it doesn't have to happen all at once. I want to give myself time, let my ideas mature. Before, I thought I'd just be a chef, open a restaurant, and that would be the end of it. But now, I see a bigger picture—I want a ranch, I want to explore other ventures. My travels are helping me refine my plans. I don't want to rush. Once I finish my tour of Madagascar, I'll settle down and think about what's next. But," she added firmly, "cooking will always be at the heart of who I am."

When we returned to Domaine d'Ambohimanitra, Farah disappeared into the kitchen with her market haul, while I joined Dina and Nirina to talk about vanilla. By dinnertime, everyone reconvened, eager to see what Farah had created. Standing at the head of the table, she introduced each dish with excited gestures, her enthusiasm contagious.

"We're starting with a bright orange salad, dressed with *combava* and pink peppercorn," she said, her voice warm and inviting. "It's zesty and a perfect palate-awakener."

She indicated a plate of skewers. "Next, fish skewers flavored with lemongrass, *combava*, and pink peppercorn. The flavors are simple but layered, bringing out the freshness of the fish."

Her eyes lit up as she pointed to a dish of deep, smoky hues. "These are smoked shrimps paired with eggplant—bold, earthy, and one of my personal favorites."

Turning to the centerpiece, she presented a beautifully grilled golden eye snapper. "The *carangue jaune* was just for your picture," she teased. "This snapper is seasoned with lemongrass and grilled to perfection. The hint of char underscores its natural sweetness."

She grinned as she introduced the next dish. "And for those who like a bit of heat, we have spicy crabs. The sauce packs a punch, but it's balanced with the sweetness of the crabmeat."

Pointing to another vibrant plate, she said, "These are shrimps with *combava* and avocado. Creamy, tangy, and rich—an unexpected but perfect combination."

Her tone shifted slightly as she motioned to a dish at the end of the table that carried the warmth of tradition. "Here we have *salade de brèdes mafanes*—a warm salad made with *brèdes*, our leafy greens, and aromatic herbs. This is a taste of home for me."

Finally, she introduced dessert. "And to finish, we have breadfruit with banana and vanilla, served with fresh coconut milk. It's simple, comforting, and showcases the flavors of Madagascar."

That dinner was a symphony of freshness, a journey through local produce, and an exploration of new flavor combinations that I hadn't encountered before. The orange salad with *combava* and pink peppercorn was a standout, its zesty brightness perfectly balanced by the subtle warmth of the peppercorn. The smoked shrimps had an incredible depth, their smokiness

pairing beautifully with the eggplants. And the spicy crabs—bold, fiery, and irresistibly sweet—were unforgettable.

The dessert was a revelation in itself. I never tried a sweet dish made with breadfruit before, and the creamy blend of banana, vanilla, and coconut milk was unexpectedly delightful, lingering on my palate long after the final bite.

Once the plates were cleared and the conversation died down to a pleasant hum, I asked Farah about her deeper motivations. "What does Madagascar's culinary culture mean to you?"

"For me, it's truly an art," she said. "Not necessarily in the French gastronomic sense, but an art deeply rooted in Malagasy culture. It's already a powerful asset for Madagascar, though it hasn't been fully recognized yet."

She explained that part of her decision to leave the traditional kitchen setting was her fatigue with routine. "I wanted something different. I told myself, 'This isn't the kind of cooking I want to do anymore.' I wanted to learn from my own country and my own heritage."

Her voice gained strength as she went on. "Now, I'm at peace with calling Malagasy cuisine what it is—an art. It's not modern cuisine as seen in high-end restaurants, but it has its own unique charm and beauty. That's what I want to share with the world."

It is clear Farah that isn't just cooking; she is redefining Malagasy cuisine for both Madagascar and beyond. Through her Facebook platform, Mon Road Trip Culinaire, she is wholeheartedly embracing her role as an influencer, inviting thousands of young followers to discover Madagascar's culinary traditions. Every post, every story, is an open invitation to experience the island's rich flavors—a blend of tradition and Farah's personal creativity. More than just a chef, Farah is a storyteller, a cultural ambassador, and a proud champion for the unique flavors of Madagascar.

Lemongrass Fish Skewers with Combava Zest

Recipe from Chef Farah Rabekijana (Mon Road Trip Culinaire)

INGREDIENTS

Fish Skewers

2.2 lbs. fish fillet(s) (about 4–6 fillets depending on type)
6 cloves of garlic, minced
2 medium onions, sliced
Zest of 1 Makrut lime, or combava
Salt and pepper, to taste
4 lemongrass stalks, bruised or chopped
½ cup sunflower oil

Mint-Lemon Green Sauce

1 small bunch medium-sized basil
1 small bunch cilantro
1 small bunch kale
1 small bunch mint
4 garlic cloves
3 lemons
6 tbsp. olive oil
Salt and pepper, to taste

PREPARATION

For the Fish Skewers

1. Clean and coarsely chop the fish fillets. Mix in a bowl with the garlic, onions and combava zest. Season with salt and pepper, then knead by hand.
2. Cut the lemongrass stalks into thirds and shape fish paste into balls, rolling them gently with the lemongrass stalk.
3. Brown in a frying pan with hot oil, about 5 minutes, in batches if necessary.

For the Mint-Lemon Green Sauce

1. Wash the bunches of mint, kale, basil and coriander and cut off the stems.
2. Peel the garlic and add the herbs (mint, basil, kale, coriander) to the bowl of a blender.
3. Cut the lemons in half, squeeze firmly to release all the juice into the blender.
4. Blend and season with salt and pepper.
5. Add the olive oil at the end and blend to combine.

PLATING

Serve with a mint-lemon green sauce and pink peppercorn.

Innovative Fusion: Chef Gilbert Kakulé

I first met Chef Gilbert Kakulé in 2022, during an evening at Akiba Lodge. Gathered around a large square table with three American chefs and the Symrise team, I felt a quiet anticipation settle over our group—knowing that, in this unassuming lodge, we were about to encounter a culinary philosophy unlike any other. Though not from Madagascar—he was born in Goma, trained in Kinshasa, and had only temporarily relocated to the island—Chef Kakulé brought an outsider's eye and deep respect to the country's culinary heritage. At the time, Akiba Lodge prided itself on sourcing organic products from Madagascar's fertile northeast: ginger, wild pepper, black pepper, cashew nuts, pink berries, cinnamon, corn, fragrant rice, red rice, mango, and vanilla. Surrounded by this abundance of raw ingredients, Chef Kakulé introduced us to his concept of *Afro-gastronomie essentielle*. His creative and delicious interpretations of Malagasy classics made a lasting impression—so much so that, despite the lodge's current closure and his return to his home country, I knew his work belonged in this book.

That evening, each course revealed how seamlessly Chef Kakulé's Congolese heritage could intermingle with Madagascar's local produce. Each course felt like a conversation between place and person—an exploration of traditional techniques, bold flavors, and a quiet, reverent approach to the ingredients themselves. By the time I returned to Madagascar again, Chef Kakulé was already on his way back to Congo. Yet the memory of that evening at Akiba Lodge remains vivid in my mind, a testament to how one encounter, one shared meal, can illuminate entire culinary worlds.

When we finally opened our menus, Chef Gilbert Kakulé emerged from the kitchen. His crisp chef's jacket and welcoming demeanor radiated a quiet confidence—a reflection of someone deeply connected to their craft. I waved him over, eager to learn about the man behind the inspired dishes we were about to enjoy.

"Chef Gilbert, your reputation precedes you. Could you tell us how your path led you from Goma to Madagascar?" I asked.

He smiled and answered, "I grew up in Goma, in the North Kivu province of the Democratic Republic of Congo. My parents were restaurateurs,

so my childhood was steeped in the aromas of morning coffee and the fiery scent of chili peppers. Cooking has been part of my life for as long as I can remember. Later, I studied tourism and hospitality in Kinshasa, and those studies opened the door to Madagascar—a land whose culinary heritage is as rich as its natural beauty."

At that moment, the first course arrived, called "Romatsatso"—a refined take on the traditional Romazava bouillon, reimagined with Thai eggplant, watercress, and delicate watercress blossoms. We paused to savor its earthy simplicity. Chef Gilbert explained that this dish was a nod to Madagascar's culinary tradition, much like the dashi of Japan. "It's humble yet deeply nourishing, much like the Malagasy people themselves."

The conversation meandered through the evening, much like the journey that had brought Chef Gilbert to this table. He spoke passionately about *Afro-gastronomie essentielle*, his philosophy of honoring Africa's culinary heritage by elevating traditional dishes and local ingredients.

"It goes beyond a simple concept—it's part of my identity. The challenge is to respect the simplicity of these ingredients while transforming them into something extraordinary. To me, it's both an art form and a responsibility."

Our plates were cleared, and the next course, *Voanjobory*, arrived—a symphony of textures and flavors featuring Bambara groundnut, cashew mayonnaise, and a vinaigrette of vanilla and citrus. "*Voanjobory* is a staple legume in Madagascar," said Kakulé. "Its richness in protein makes it indispensable. In this dish, I've opted for a vegan twist, letting *voanjobory's* natural richness shine."

Soon, the star of the evening arrived: Hena Kisoa, a dish inspired by the *hanim-pitoloha*, the royal series of dishes of Madagascar. A pork paupiette rested in a creamy sauce of eel and *combava*, paired with *rougail* sauce (a rich, flavorful, tomato-based sauce with onions, garlic, ginger, thyme, chilies, coriander, and other spices, a dish that originated in the French-based creoles of the Indian Ocean), and fragrant rice. The flavors were bold yet balanced, a testament to Chef Gilbert's mastery. "This dish is my homage to Madagascar's culinary royalty," he explained. "It bridges the old and the new, tradition and innovation."

We lingered over dessert, Mahabibo, a creation inspired by the traditional *ranon'apango*, elevated with the nutty richness of cashews and a touch of sweetness—we found ourselves in awe. Chef Gilbert described the inspiration behind the dish: "*Ranon'apango* is a drink made from the burnt rice crust left at the bottom of a pot. It's a symbol of resourcefulness and resilience, much like Madagascar itself."

We noted that *ranon'apango* is much like Korea's *sungnyung*—rice tea made from the scorched grains at the bottom of the pot. Different lands, same spirit: nothing wasted, everything honored.

Chef Gilbert spoke of the farmers and producers he worked with, his admiration evident. "The products of Madagascar have not lost their identity," he said. "In a world obsessed with trends, they remain authentic and traceable. When you know where your food comes from, it creates an impact beyond the plate."

When we finally rose from the table, we left inspired. Chef Gilbert Kakulé had done more than simply serve us a meal—he had taken traditional Malagasy dishes, deconstructed and reinvented them, and infused each bite with his own artistic interpretation. In so doing, he had guided us through the soul of Madagascar while also revealing his own. His dedication to preserving the essence of *Afro-gastronomie essentielle* was evident in every course, reminding us that the power of food lies not only in flavor but in honoring heritage and community.

Voanjobory

Recipes from Chef Gilbert Kakulé (former chef at Akiba Lodge in Antananarivo, Madagascar)

Serves 2 people

INGREDIENTS

Bambara Groundnuts

150 g (5.3 oz.) fresh Bambara groundnuts, or substitute with black-eyed peas
6 cups water (48 fl. oz. or 1.5 L)
2.5 tsp. (15 g) of salt (10 g/L of water)
50 g (1.75 oz.) cashew nuts, crushed
⅔ tbsp. (⅓ fl. oz.) olive oil (1 cl.)
2 vanilla beans
1 lemon
2 garlic cloves, minced
1 onion, chopped
2 vanilla beans
Pepper, to taste

Cashew Mayonnaise

100 g (3.5 oz.) cashew nuts
2 tbsp. + 2 tsp. (1⅓ fl. oz.) olive oil (4 cl. → ~¼ cup)
100 g (3.5 oz.) watercress
100 g (3.5 oz.) *brèdes mafane*, or substitute with arugula

PREPARATION

For the Bambara Groundnuts

1. Sort and rinse the Bambara groundnuts.
2. Place them in a large pot with water, using approximately 1 liter of water for every 100 grams of groundnuts.
3. Bring to a boil, then reduce to medium heat and simmer for 25 to 30 minutes, or until the groundnuts are tender.
4. About 5 minutes before the end of cooking, add 15 grams of salt (adjust based on the total volume).

Recipe continues ⟶

5. Once cooked, drain the groundnuts and allow them to cool. You may adjust the seasoning to taste after cooking.
6. In a bowl, combine the cooked Bambara groundnuts with salt, pepper, vanilla beans (sliced and scraped the beans and collect the caviar), lemon zest and juice, olive oil, 1 minced garlic clove, the crushed cashew nuts, and chopped onion. Mix well, and let marinate in the refrigerator.

For the Cashew Mayonnaise

1. Boil the cashew nuts in a saucepan until they become very tender.
2. Blend the boiled cashews, gradually adding olive oil, until you achieve a smooth, mayonnaise-like texture.

PLATING

1. Thoroughly wash the leafy greens and set them aside.
2. Spread the cashew mayonnaise on a plate, add the marinated Bambara groundnuts on top, and garnish with leafy greens. Serve chilled, and enjoy!

Hen'omby Ritra

Serves 4 people

INGREDIENTS

1.75 lbs. (800 g) beef (shank, chuck, or another tender cut)
4 garlic cloves
1 piece of ginger (about 1 in. or 3 cm.)
2 tbsp. oil
1 tsp. salt
Black pepper, to taste
2 cups (16 fl. oz. or 500 ml.) water

PREPARATION

1. Cut the beef into medium-sized pieces.
2. Mince or finely chop the garlic and ginger.
3. Brown the meat. Heat the oil in a saucepan. Add the beef and brown on all sides.
4. Season to taste. Add the crushed garlic and ginger. Mix well to coat the meat. Season to taste with salt and pepper.
5. Simmer slowly. Pour in the water and cook over a low heat for 1.5 to 2 hours, until the meat is tender and the liquid has reduced almost completely. Stir occasionally and add a little water if necessary.
6. Serve hot with white rice.

Modern Gastronomy: Chef Lalaina Ravelomanana

Chef Lalaina Ravelomanana is at the forefront of Madagascar's culinary evolution. He is the executive chef at Marais, the restaurant owned by Delphyne, Christophe, and Alex (the same owners of the sturgeon farm in Acipenser) on Rue Ravoninahitriniarivo in Tana. On my first visit to Marais, I took the elevator to the fifth floor of the ATRIUM building to a modern restaurant with its open kitchen visible behind glass walls. I stepped through a discreet bookshelf door and inside was a softly lit bar where I found Chef Lalaina chatting with two bartenders.

Catching sight of me, he greeted me with a bright smile. "Welcome to the bar of Marais," he said, his eyes sweeping across the room with evident pride. "I'm glad you could join us in this secret hideaway."

"Thank you, Chef," I replied, placing my recorder on the bar. I was eager to learn more about his unique approach to Malagasy ingredients.

"I never dreamed of becoming a chef. I studied law, computer science, and a bit of architecture, but I needed pocket money and started out as a dishwasher."

The dishwashing job was at Arotel in Antsirabe. After a week of training, hotel managers moved him to the kitchen as a commis chef, where he first discovered his enjoyment of cooking.

"I learned everything on the job. I never went to culinary school; instead, I worked under great chefs who taught me discipline and technique." He mentioned the Tana Plaza, under Chef Philippe Gourio, a French chef with experience under Troisgros, where he learned the fundamentals of cooking.

After Arotel, Lalaina moved through a series of hotels and restaurants in Madagascar—Vakôna, Colbert, Petit Verdot—gaining more responsibility and honing his skills. His significant career development took place at La Varangue, where he stayed eleven years, was given the freedom to create, and truly began his journey as a head chef. Later, he took on an opening project in Nosy Be, then returned to Tana to open his first restaurant: Côté Saveurs. Eventually, through catering work and connections, he found Delphyne, Christophe, and Alex, who financed his dream: the creation of Marais.

Opened in May 2019, Marais sits near the Masay Marsh, which inspired its name. The entire kitchen is on display behind glass walls, allowing diners to see every aspect of meal preparation. Lalaina insists that this transparency is not just for show.

"There's no hiding in an open kitchen," he said. "Successes, slip-ups—it's all out there. It pushes us to remain organized and disciplined, and I think our guests appreciate seeing the real work behind their meal."

While the cuisine incorporates classic French techniques, local ingredients—from cassava and sweet potatoes to exotic Malagasy greens—play a starring role. He also collaborates with farmers and small producers—some of whom grow exotic or rare produce—so he can experiment with fresh, local fruits and vegetables. Yet Lalaina also highlights premium products like shrimp, chocolate, and especially Rova Caviar, the first African caviar brand from the Indian Ocean.

"I'm an Ambassador for Rova Caviar," he explained proudly, "and it's more than just a title. I've developed more than three hundred recipes featuring it. Caviar has a subtle, buttery taste that needs to be respected, not overpowered."

Chef Lalaina grew up partly in Tananarive (Antananarivo) and partly in Antsirabe, where his grandparents were from. Raised by a strict but supportive father who served as a *gendarme* (national police force), he learned discipline at an early age. His creativity blossomed in the kitchen, where he rotated meal duties with his siblings and helped his mother prepare daily family meals. He recalls using bottle caps as cake molds, heating them over sand and charcoal in place of an oven. This resourceful experience of baking with improvised tools foreshadowed his inventive approach to food.

This inventive streak continues in his cooking philosophy. Everyday life, street foods, art, and music all spark new dishes. Yet fundamentals like classic sauces or proper slow cooking remain crucial. "You need a solid base," he said, "before you can transform or 'elevate' a traditional recipe."

Among Madagascar's iconic dishes, Lalaina cited Romazava (a broth with *brède mafane* leaves and zebu meat) and *ravitoto* (cassava leaves cooked with pork or other meats). He enjoys reimagining these dishes in a gourmet fashion.

He illustrated this with an example of deconstructing Romazava. "I transform Romazava by slow-cooking the beef, making an emulsion with *brède mafane* flowers, and turning tomato *rougail* into a sorbet or molecular spheres—presenting it in a gourmet style. It retains the essence of the original but becomes something new."

Meanwhile, *ravitoto* might appear as a refined plate of tender pork belly and cassava leaves, plated with modern techniques but steeped in ancestral flavors. Lalaina believes it's about bringing tradition into a new era, not leaving it behind.

For Lalaina, creativity arises from everyday life—from walking through the streets and discovering a local snack to being inspired by moods, music, or art. He stresses that having solid fundamentals in cooking techniques (like classic French mother sauces) is crucial to bring any new idea to life. Feedback from customers and colleagues helps refine each dish. Ultimately, he wants to remain true to his style and the restaurant's concept rather than try to please everyone's tastes (e.g., he chooses not to serve fries or strictly traditional Malagasy dishes).

One of Lalaina's greatest passions is marrying Malagasy flavors with Rova Caviar. As we talked, I asked how he manages to balance something as opulent as caviar with the often rustic profile of local cooking.

"Balance is key," he said. "Caviar can have a bold, salty character, so I usually pair it with gentler flavors—like sweet potato, cream, or coconut. They help keep the focus where it belongs."

"And how do you keep caviar as the main focus in your recipes?" I asked.

"It's about highlighting, not hiding," he replied. "Caviar's luxury demands simplicity. It's about letting its natural qualities shine through."

He added that caviar should never be cooked or paired with overly acidic or spicy flavors. Instead, he chooses minimal, complementary elements like brioche pan-fried in butter or a creamy asparagus carpaccio to showcase caviar's natural glow.

Two examples of recipes created by Lalaina based on traditional Malagasy products were a sweet potato *cromesquis* (a crispy sweet potato ball with a tender center, breaded and fried) served with a coconut *espuma* (foam), and a crispy mango and pineapple in a caviar crust.

"A beautiful quenelle of caviar, placed next to the prepared product, highlights its color and shine," he explained. "It's about letting caviar speak for itself."

I thumbed through the Marais menu and noticed a particular starter: Grilled Octopus with Rova Caviar. Curious, I asked what sparked that pairing.

"It's a tribute to Madagascar's exotic flavors," he replied. "When grilled, octopus has a smoky aftertaste that reminds me of the environment where the sturgeons are farmed at the Acipenser farm. The caviar's saline note highlights the octopus's oceanic essence."

Among his extensive repertoire of caviar dishes, two stood out to me:

- *Œuf dans l'Œuf* (Egg within an Egg): an egg emulsion with Baéri caviar, condiments, and apple.
- Glass Eel Nest with a Rova caviar heart, served alongside a light vanilla bisque. The glass eels are sourced from the east coast of Madagascar.

"Caviar is best enjoyed in simplicity," Lalaina said. "You don't want to bury its flavor. Everything else should enhance, never overshadow. It's not just about creating dishes; it's about respecting the caviar's flavor. That means minimal, well-chosen accompaniments. Starchy vegetables, cream, fish—these are ideal. They support, not dominate, the caviar's profile." He suggested that when tasting caviar, people should take the time to roll the eggs under the palate to better appreciate its texture.

He also mentioned pairing caviar with roasted bone marrow in the dish called Bone Marrow au Gratin with Fleur de Sel and Crispy Garlic. "Rich and buttery, the marrow balances caviar's brininess. People don't expect it, but it works beautifully." And yes, he has even tested it in desserts with chocolate and exotic fruit chips—an idea that, in his words, "springs straight from the natural abundance of the Red Island."

Before concluding our conversation, we touched on Lalaina's commitment to supporting underprivileged youth.

"I grew up modestly," he said, "and I want to show young people that discipline and persistence can open doors in the culinary world."

He often works with local associations, creating memorable experiences, such as a massive Christmas log project—to bring joy to children across Madagascar. In the future, he hopes to launch new dining concepts, develop a line of local spices, and open a culinary academy to train aspiring chefs.

I left Marais with a deeper understanding of not just the culinary art of caviar, but also the philosophy and passion that drives Chef Lalaina. His respect for ingredients and commitment to purity and simplicity is not just a cooking style, but a way of life.

I returned to Marais during each of my visits to Madagascar, and every time, the experience deepened. The food was consistently remarkable—thoughtful, elegant, and surprising—but it was Chef Lalaina's warm, unhurried presence that lingered. In his gorgeous restaurant, conversation flows easily, courses stretch gracefully, and time seems to slow. I never want to leave.

On my most recent visit, Lalaina surprised me with his signature creation, La Bible du Chef: thin layers of scallop with citrus caramel (Feuille en Feuille de Noix de Saint-Jacques au Caramel d'Agrumes), paired with a velvety leek-vanilla cream (Crémeux de Poireau à la Vanille), finished with a dramatic wisp of bitter cacao smoke. It was served in oversized oyster shells and presented inside an enormous book—as monumental in presence as it was in taste.

Voatsiperifery Pepper Mascarpone Mousse and Cucumber Combava Gelée with "Chaud-Froid" Perfect Egg and Rova Caviar

Recipe by Chef Lalaina Ravelomanana (Marais Restaurant in Antananarivo, Madagascar)

Serves 4 people

INGREDIENTS

Voatsiperifery Pepper Mascarpone Mousse

⅓ cup (80 g) mascarpone cheese
1 tbsp. heavy cream
Salt, to taste
2 pinches ground *voatsiperifery* pepper (wild pepper from Madagascar)

Cucumber Combava Gelée

1 firm cucumber
4 sheets gelatin, softened in cold water (or substitute 2 ½ tsp. powdered gelatin)
Juice and zest of 1 *combava* (Makrut lime)

"Chaud-Froid" Perfect Egg

4 large eggs, in shell
2 tbsp. (25 g) unsalted butter
2 tbsp. (25 g) all-purpose flour
1 cup (250 ml.) chicken stock
2 tbsp. (30 g) heavy cream
1 tsp cornstarch, pre-mixed with a little water
1 sheet gelatin, softened (or substitute ¾ tsp. powdered gelatin)
Pink peppercorn powder (to decorate the "chaud-froid")

TO ASSEMBLE AND SERVE

1. 2 jars (30 g each) Rova Caviar Madagascar (or premium caviar of choice)
2. A few sprouts and edible flowers

PREPARATION

For the Voatsiperifery Pepper Mascarpone Mousse

1. Whisk mascarpone until smooth.
2. Add heavy cream, a pinch of salt, and voatsiperifery pepper. Mix well until fully incorporated.
3. Transfer to a piping bag with a plain tip. Refrigerate until ready to serve.

For the Cucumber Combava Gelée

1. Roughly chop cucumber and juice it, using a juicer or blender and fine strainer to extract about 1 cup of juice.
2. Gently heat half of the juice in a saucepan.
3. Squeeze excess water from gelatin and dissolve it into the warm juice.
4. Combine with remaining cold juice and stir in lime juice.
5. Season to taste with salt. Chill until slightly thickened but still pourable.
6. Cook eggs at 149°F (65°C) using an immersion heater or in a bain-marie for 1 hour and 5 minutes.
7. Decant. Chill for about 3 hours. Peel and recover the yolk carefully to keep the spherical shape.

For the Chaud-Froid

1. In a saucepan, melt butter, then stir in flour to create a blond roux.
2. Gradually add chicken stock, whisking until smooth and thickened.
3. Stir in cream, followed by the cornstarch slurry. Cook gently until glossy.
4. Off the heat, add softened gelatin until fully melted.
5. Let cool slightly, then coat the egg yolks completely with the warm mixture.
6. Refrigerate until set with a gentle "glaze." Dust with pink peppercorn skin powder if available.

PLATING

1. Pour the cucumber jelly onto a shallow dish. Let the jelly set in the very cold temperature of the plate.
2. Arrange the mascarpone mousse with voatsiperifery pepper in a circle and place around 15 g of Rova Caviar in the middle.
3. Then place the "chaud-froid" perfect egg.
4. Decorate with a few sprouts and edible flowers. Sprinkle with lime zest.
5. Serve chilled.

Beverage Innovation: Mixologist K-Mëc

Randrianarisoa Mahery Tiana, known as K-Mëc, was born and raised in Antananarivo (Tana). Later, he moved to Mauritius for his studies, but he still reminisces about the food and aromas of his childhood—particularly fresh herbs such as coriander, mint, and basil, which his mother used in their family cooking.

"My first food memory is soup—*lasopy*," he recalled. "It's a famous Malagasy vegetable soup made with turnips, green beans, tomatoes, carrots, green onions, potatoes, and leeks."

After moving to Mauritius, he studied hospitality management and began his career in a small restaurant. One day, under somber circumstances—the sudden passing of a bartender—his manager asked if he could help out behind the bar. Though the situation was unexpected and heavy, stepping into that role marked a turning point for him. What followed was, in his words, a *coup de cœur*—an instant and profound connection with the craft of bartending. He threw himself into learning bar techniques, entered competitions like Jack Daniel's Barman Competition and World Class Mauritius, and came to see mixology as a true art form.

"Bartending is an art," he told me. "You don't just sell alcohol; you create experiences, you tell stories through cocktails."

When designing a new drink, K-Mëc meticulously plans every element. He writes recipes on paper, noting precise measurements, and sketches the desired appearance, envisioning how colors—like rum's amber hue combined with pink or red liqueur—will interact. Beyond taste, he emphasizes presentation, sometimes using family heirloom glassware or traditional Malagasy containers to underscore a cultural narrative. His conceptual approach often draws inspiration from specific ingredients or desserts, as with his Banana Split Cocktail.

He especially loves working with local Malagasy ingredients. "Madagascar has incredible local products: vanilla, *tsiperifery* pepper, *combava*, ginger, and *tsilandimilahy* chili—which means 'five men can't finish it.' It's also nicknamed 'seven pots' because a single chili can spice up seven pots of food."

Ginger is particularly popular in Madagascar, so he frequently incorporates fresh ginger into punches, cocktails, or infusions. One of his signature drinks, On the Way to Dago, highlights the island's bounty by combining aged Malagasy rum, a house-made *tsiperifery* pepper syrup, grapefruit juice spiced with cinnamon, local honey, lychee, ginger, and a dash of bitters. He serves it in an old-fashioned glass wrapped in woven *raffia* (symbolic of Madagascar's southeast region), garnished with wild pepper, orchid flowers, dehydrated grapefruit, and stirred with a zebu horn stirrer—each element paying homage to Malagasy heritage.

According to K-Mëc, Madagascar's cocktail scene is still in its infancy. Tourism and hospitality training remain limited, and many aspiring bartenders only learn the basics at culinary schools. Locally, bartending is often undervalued, seen merely as selling alcohol.

"Here, many people think a bartender is just someone who sells sodas, but we want to show it's a real craft."

To change these perceptions, K-Mëc has been training young bartenders, creating cocktail menus for various establishments, and demonstrating the art of mixology through workshops and private events. "The biggest challenge is we don't have access to many international spirits—they're too expensive due to heavy import taxes."

K-Mëc's place of work, La Teinturerie, is more than a bar; it's an artists' collective and cultural space that hosts musicians, painters, photographers, stylists, and artisans. Formerly a workshop and garage, the venue now houses a gallery, a concept store, a recording studio, and a restaurant-bar. Live music, art exhibitions, quizzes, and community initiatives—like painting rural schools and fundraising for social causes—are regular events. The bar, the "Comptoir des Artistes," blends seamlessly with this creative atmosphere, offering tiki-inspired cocktails and homemade infusions.

Renowned for its lengthy list of signature cocktails and mocktails, La Teinturerie strives to tell the story of Madagascar through flavor. Using local spices, fruits, and cultural references, each cocktail has its own narrative or regional inspiration, giving patrons a unique way to discover Malagasy tastes.

"I love to burn vetiver root inside a glass, so the smoke infuses the cocktail with a unique aroma," said K-Mëc.

Curious, I asked, "Can you give me other examples of signature cocktails from La Teinturerie?"

He nodded. "Let me give you four: Tso-drivotra, AK, Lychee Sour, and The *Combava* Fizz." He then described each one.

- **Tso-drivotra:** Inspired by the winds that sweep across Madagascar from the Indian Ocean to the Mozambique Channel. It features spiced rum, homemade Falernum (infused with *combava* peel, clove, star anise, cinnamon, and cardamom), and lime juice—evoking a fresh ocean breeze.
- **AK:** "AK isn't about the AK-47," K-Mëc said. "It's named after a young Franco-Vietnamese student, Ann Kim, who asked me for a cocktail that reflected her personality—small, with rosy cheeks. So it's very fruity and gentle." The drink is made with rum, blackberry liqueur, homemade blackberry syrup, and lemon juice.
- **Lychee Sour:** Showcasing Madagascar's bountiful lychee season, it uses rum infused with lychee, local lychee liqueur, sugar syrup, and fresh lime, all highlighting the fruit's delicate sweetness.
- **The *Combava* Fizz:** Another inventive creation, featuring local *combava*-flavored rum, blood orange liqueur, lemon, and yuzu, topped with a sparkling element. The result is reminiscent of a refreshing homemade lemonade, elevated by *combava* and the citrusy zing of Japanese yuzu.

Looking to the future, K-Mëc dreams of competing in international contests like World Class, which typically require sponsorships from global brands and easier access to imported spirits. Despite the logistical hurdles and cost challenges in Madagascar, he remains committed to advancing the local bar scene by experimenting with native ingredients, creating his own bitters, training emerging bartenders, and building connections with international spirits professionals. Ultimately, he envisions Madagascar as a recognized hub of inventive mixology.

Since the country's first craft cocktail competition in 2022, cocktail culture has undeniably grown. Bartenders around the city and beyond are upping their game, introducing signature drinks and experimenting with local ingredients. Meeting the American chefs and a visiting mixologist spurred a lively exchange of ideas and techniques, boosting general awareness and standards in the Malagasy bar scene.

The same competition propelled K-Mëc to broader acclaim. He began traveling around Madagascar to train bartenders and introduce new cocktails. In Fort-Dauphin, he developed signature drinks with local ingredients; in Nosy Be—famed for its ylang-ylang and rum distilleries—he focused on showcasing the island's aroma.

"In Nosy Be, I didn't mix the ylang-ylang flower into the drink. Instead, I used its scent on the rim of the glass, so it smelled like the island itself."

In Tamatave, he concentrated on honing bartending fundamentals and reorganizing bar layouts, setting the stage for future signature recipes. Drawing from Madagascar's remarkable biodiversity, K-Mëc introduced cocktails featuring *tsiperifery* and the fiery *tsilandimilahy* chili, pairing them with tequila or mezcal. These drinks balance salty, spicy, and citrusy flavors while spotlighting lesser-known local spices and peppers—an ongoing tribute to Madagascar's uniqueness.

Going forward, KMëc and his collaborators plan to make the annual craft cocktail competition a nationwide affair. Early rounds in coastal regions like Nosy Be and Tamatave will lead up to a final showdown in Antananarivo. The goal is to celebrate the island's bounty—its fruits, spices,

and rums—and to nourish the expanding talent and creativity of Madagascar's bartending community.

During my most recent visit in May 2025, K-Mëc invited me to his home and personal bar—the walls of the space were full of art pieces from Malagasy artists. Over the course of our conversation about the next edition of the competition, he poured a flight of new creations using rum from this year's sponsoring distillery. Among them was the APANGO cocktail, inspired by *ranon'apango*, the traditional Malagasy drink made by adding hot water to toasted rice remnants. He also revisited one of his earliest successes: the Lychee Sour, still a top seller at La Teinturerie, made with white rum, lychee liqueur, lemon juice, and sugarcane syrup.

"One day, I hope Madagascar will be recognized for its talented bartenders," K-Mëc said, his face lighting up with optimism. "We just need more support and the chance to show what we can do."

Tiomena

Recipes by Mixologist K-Mëc (La Teinturerie in Antananarivo, Madagascar)

INGREDIENTS

Infused Gin

3 cups gin (70 cl.)
2 tbsp. pink peppercorn

Red Cactus Puree

1⅓ cups cactus (or prickly pear as substitute) (31.5 cl.)
10.1 oz. water (30 cl.)
2.7 oz. honey (8 cl.)

Basil Syrup

17 fl. oz. water (50 cl.)
2¼ cups brown sugar (500 g)
12–15 basil leaves

TO ASSEMBLE AND SERVE

Makes 1 cocktail

1. 1⅔ oz. gin infused with pink peppercorn (5 cl. → 1 ⅔ oz. → 1 jigger + ⅔ jigger)
2. ⅔ oz. red cactus puree from southern Madagascar (substitute with prickly pear puree) (2 cl. → ⅔ oz. → 1 pony jigger)
3. ⅓ oz. lemon juice (1 cl. → ⅓ oz. → ⅓ pony jigger)
4. ½ oz. homemade basil syrup (1.5 cl. → ½ oz. → ½ pony jigger)

PREPARATION

For the Infused Gin

Combine gin with pink peppercorn and let sit for 2 weeks.

For the Red Cactus Puree

Place cactus (or prickly pear) and water in a blender, then add honey and reduce everything over low heat.

For the Basil Syrup

Boil water and brown sugar over a low heat for 15 to 20 minutes to obtain a sugar syrup. Allow the mixture to cool, then add basil leaves, which you will place in a blender, filtering out any leaf debris with a fine sieve. Pour the syrup into an airtight container and store in the fridge.

TO ASSEMBLE AND SERVE

1. Put all the ingredients in a shaker with ice and shake well.
2. Serve in a Mason jar.
3. Garnish with cactus slice and pink berry in the middle with a basil flower, optionally.

Mody Masoandro

Yields 1 cocktail

INGREDIENTS

For the Masoandro juice

1 pineapple
3 cucumbers
8 mint leaves
2 teaspoons freshly grated ginger

For the Carotanas juice

1 pineapple
1 pound carrots
2 ounces (¼ cup) fresh lime juice

TO ASSEMBLE AND SERVE

2¾ ounces (about ⅓ cup) Masoandro juice
1⅓ ounces (a little over 2½ tablespoons) "Carotanas" juice
⅔ ounce (about 4 teaspoons) basil syrup
¼ teaspoon freshly grated ginger

PREPARATION

1. For the Masoandro juice (in advance): Using a juicer, juice the pineapple and cucumbers. Add in the mint leaves and grated ginger. Stir.
2. For the Carotanas juice (in advance): Using a juicer, juice the pineapple and carrots. Add fresh lime juice. Stir.
3. Add Masoandro juice, Carotanas juice, basil syrup, and freshly grated ginger to a shaker with ice.
4. Shake vigorously until well chilled. Strain into a chilled cocktail glass.

A bridge between yesterday and tomorrow. The new generation of Malagasy chefs bridges the gap between traditional heritage and modern culinary techniques, ensuring that tradition flows seamlessly into the future.

From Mariette Andrianjaka's unwavering devotion to elevating local ingredients with modern culinary techniques, to Chef Henintsoa Moretti's regional explorations that spotlight the country's regional recipes, each culinary voice has demonstrated the power of tradition as a foundation for innovation. With Chef Farah Rabekijana's adventurous approach in discovering how people eat around the island, Chef Gilbert Kakulé's bold forays into fusion, and Chef Lalaina's avant-garde take on modern gastronomy on local produce, we see a collective push to redefine Madagascar's and Africa's dining culture in ways that honor its past while embracing global influences. Meanwhile, mixologist K-Mëc breaks ground in the beverage space, harnessing local flavors to create experiences that reflect both heritage and contemporary flair.

Together, these artisans embody a broader movement seen in regions around the world whose cuisines have long stood in the shadows of so-called "culinary capitals." We witness a parallel in countries where indigenous ingredients and cooking methods were dismissed by mainstream culinary elites—only to be rediscovered and celebrated for their depth, complexity, and cultural significance. The chefs and mixologists of Madagascar deserve to be included in this global culinary revival.

As they continue to blend traditional know-how with new techniques, their work signals an exciting era for Madagascar's dining scene—one in which the richness of the past coexists harmoniously with the promise of innovation. Madagascar's table is set for a bright, boundary-pushing future.

However, as Madagascar's gastronomic landscape evolves, a key challenge remains: ensuring this transformation benefits not only a select few, but also the broader community. While global recognition can elevate the country's culinary identity, it risks creating a divide where only those with access to resources, training, and international networks thrive. At the same time, there's the delicate balance of fostering growth without losing the soul of what makes it unique, avoiding the dilution that often comes with global commercial attention. How can Madagascar's food culture grow organically, stay true to its roots, and remain "cool" without becoming overly mainstream?

Some chefs are already finding ways to bridge this gap—like Chef Lalaina, who brought his team to the International Catering Cup, giving them valuable exposure on the world stage. Efforts like these suggest that Madagascar's culinary revival isn't just about redefining fine dining but also about creating pathways for a new generation of talent across the island.

Now is the time for curious travelers to come to the island and immerse themselves in the remarkable flavors and innovations these culinary leaders have to offer, forging a deeper connection to Madagascar's gastronomic heritage.

CHAPTER 11

Deforestation

The Hidden Cost of Culinary Bounty

Ny te-hihinam-boankazo tsy manapaka hazo.

Who wants figs does not cut down the tree.

—TRADITIONAL MALAGASY SAYING

"We're lost again," I sighed, feeling the familiar frustration rise.

Nirina chuckled, clearly amused by my nervousness. "Don't worry," he said, completely relaxed. "This is part of the adventure." His nonchalance was infectious, a testament to his intimate connection with his country and its mysteries.

◀ *Endemic, endangered, and emblematic—the black-and-white ruffed lemur's survival depends on the forest we choose to protect.*

Nirina had organized a surprise stop along our itinerary. After bidding farewell to Olivier Ramaherison amidst the wild *voatsiperifery* pepper–laden hills, we resumed our journey along the RN2. As the day waned, Nirina assured me that we would reach our mysterious destination by nightfall. We made a quick stop at a gas station to gather provisions. Curious about our destination, I asked Nirina for more details. With a hint of mystery in his voice, he said he wanted me to witness firsthand the valiant efforts of those combating deforestation.

We left the gas station, provisions in hand, and continued our journey. As the sun dipped below the horizon, I couldn't help but think about the stark realities I witnessed on this island. In some parts of the countryside, the acrid scent of burning wood hung heavy in the air, a constant reminder of the relentless human hand reshaping the landscape. Each plume of smoke rising from the ground seemed to carry away with it the soul of the forest—ghostly fingers against the sky. Driving along dusty roads, I saw countless bags of charcoal. "*Charbon de bois*," a common commodity in these rural stretches, stacked like sentinels of destruction. The sight filled me with a deep sense of sorrow. I also witnessed a macabre ballet of large boats on the picturesque and serene Pangalanes Canal, near Tamatave. Their decks, weighed down with the same charcoal bags, moved with a haunting rhythm. This mournful procession painted a heartbreaking picture of the island's tragic dependence on a vanishing resource.

In other areas, bare, eroded hillsides were stripped of their rich vegetation to make way for crops or to feed the ever-hungry fires of fuelwood production. Villages and roadside clearings were cluttered with piles of cut timber, the remnants of recent logging operations. The once-dense forests now displayed noticeable gaps, where patches of cleared land interrupted the verdant continuity. The edges of the forests seemed to retreat further each day, making way for expanding agricultural plots. In stark contrast to this destruction, groves of eucalyptus trees were emerging—offering a swift yet imperfect solution to reforestation. These rapidly growing trees consumed vast amounts of water and did little to nourish the soil, failing to restore the rich biodiversity that Madagascar's native forests once boasted.

Nirina's phone rang, breaking my thoughts. "Are we close?" I asked, trying to mask my frustration with curiosity.

"Patience," he replied with a grin. "We'll find them." His confidence was compelling.

Nirina continued to call our mysterious host, searching for clues in the pitch-black landscape. The voice on the phone instructed us to look for a simple wooden gate, but every dirt road we followed seemed to lead to identical gates.

"Another gate, Nirina. Are we circling?" I joked, attempting to lighten the mood.

"Maybe," he laughed. "Or maybe the gates are circling us."

Eventually, our host had to come find us. The beam of Nirina's car headlights revealed the writing on their van: "Ecovision Village." Relief washed over me as they guided us to our destination.

As we followed the van through the darkness, navigating the rugged terrain with its steep hills and rocky paths, Nirina started sharing stories about Ecovision Village. "This place," he said, "is more than just a project. It's a lifeline for both nature and the local community." He explained that Ecovision Village is a conservation initiative focused on protecting and reforesting a crucial forest corridor. This effort is essential for reconnecting fragmented habitats, allowing wildlife, especially the critically endangered Indri-Indri lemur, to move freely.

Nirina's tone was a mix of pride and concern as he described the project's goals. "We're not just planting trees. We're rebuilding an ecosystem. The village represents a significant effort to balance conservation with community development," he said, pausing to let the words sink in. "It's about ensuring the protection of Madagascar's unique biodiversity while supporting local livelihoods."

I could hear the passion in his voice as he spoke about his involvement. "The people here are deeply invested in the success of Ecovision Village. They know that their future is intertwined with the health of the forest. By participating in reforestation efforts and sustainable practices, they are securing a better future for themselves and their children. I am personally invested in the project."

As the van's taillights flickered in the distance, their red glow was like the eyes of a phantom guiding us through the black abyss. Nirina continued, "This isn't just about saving a species. It's about creating a sustainable model that can be replicated elsewhere. The forest corridor we're working on is crucial, not just for the lemurs, but for the entire ecosystem. Every plant, every insect, every bird plays a role."

We parked the car in front of the Base Vie or Life Base, the heart of Ecovision Village. The original metallic container, worn but proud, stood as a testament to the project's humble beginnings. Now repurposed into a storage area, it seamlessly integrated into a larger structure featuring a wooden deck, open kitchen, and communal table where we would gather for meals. The fire pit on the deck was the brightest light, casting a warm glow into the night, aside from a few scattered bulbs hanging around.

We gathered for dinner, a meal created from the provisions bought at the gas station. Chef Farah worked her magic, transforming simple noodle soup and omelet into a delightful feast. As we ate, I turned to Nirina and asked, "What keeps you going, even when the odds are against you?"

He gazed into the dark forest, the firelight reflecting in his eyes. "It's the future," he said quietly. "My children's future, our community's future. Every tree we plant is a step towards a sustainable life for them."

We ended our meal with vanilla cookies, a sweet finish to the evening. My accommodation was the first prototype of a luxury villa for project investors. Nirina, always the gracious host, offered me the villa. Located outside the main perimeter, it provided a touch of seclusion. A guard from Ecovision Village escorted me with a flashlight to my temporary home.

Morning arrived, replacing the previous night's darkness with a breathtaking panorama. Stepping onto the deck, I was greeted by a mist clinging to the rolling hills, creating a soft, ethereal blanket over the forest. Above, the

sky was a pristine blue, promising a clear day. The dense forest stretched out before me in a tapestry of green hues, with darker patches where the sun had yet to penetrate.

Making my way back to the Life Base, I followed the narrow dirt path that meandered, overlooking the valley, now fully visible in the daylight. Tall grasses and small shrubs flanked the path, leading to a rustic structure nestled harmoniously into the verdant hillside. Constructed with natural materials, it featured a thatched roof and woven bamboo walls. Wooden double doors at the front added to its earthy aesthetic, and the structure stood on stilts, slightly elevated above the ground.

Inside the Life Base, the atmosphere was warm and inviting, blending rustic charm with functional design. The main area featured an open-plan layout with a high thatched roof supported by sturdy wooden beams, creating a spacious and airy feel. A cozy seating area with a comfortable wicker chair dominated one corner. Adjacent was a large dining table covered with a vibrant, leaf-patterned tablecloth, set for meals and communal gatherings. The open kitchen was both practical and charming, equipped with essential appliances. Above the kitchen area, a sign read "*Atelier des Rêves,*" or "Workshop of Dreams," adding a whimsical touch. A deck extended outward, offering additional seating with wicker chairs around low tables, inviting guests to enjoy the surrounding nature. The entire structure exuded harmony with its environment, fostering a connection with the natural world.

As I sat comfortably, I gazed out at the panoramic view now completely clear of mist and saw the villa I stayed in blending harmoniously with the landscape. Below, the valley was a medley of verdant landscapes interspersed with small patches of farmland and groups of bee hives. The tall, wild grass near the edge of the deck swayed gently in the breeze. Chef Farah and Nirina joined me in front of the already-lit fire pit.

Breakfast was a feast of fresh fruits and scrambled eggs, complemented by Nirina's favorite, *sosoa*. Our hosts, Ntsoa Ramaro and Prisca, joined us, outlining the day's agenda: a long hike across the hills to witness firsthand the deforestation and Ecovision Village's efforts to combat it.

"The project covers the reforestation of seventy-four acres of abandoned pasture land with native tree species, creating a three-hundred-and-seventy-one-acre forest corridor." Our host spoke with steady passion, "This corridor will link the Andasibe-Mantadia National Park and the Analamazotra Special Reserve, crucial habitats for many endangered species, including twelve lemur species." When I inquired about community involvement, he nodded and smiled. "Beyond environmental benefits, Ecovision Village is deeply committed to community development. We're building a primary school and providing free lunches to ensure regular attendance. We also engage local community members in reforestation efforts, providing jobs and promoting sustainable practices."

"How did Ecovision start?" I inquired.

"Ecovision is situated in the rural commune of Andasibe, approximately one hundred and fifty kilometers, or ninety-five miles, from the capital, Antananarivo, along RN2," he explained. "We are an association under Malagasy law, established in 2020 to conserve Madagascar's biodiversity. The project operates on private property owned by Mr. Kazim, the association's president. We manage two thousand five hundred acres, including eight hundred sixty acres of biodiverse primary forest and sixteen hundred acres dedicated to income-generating activities like agribusiness."

"One of our main activities," he continued, "is ecological restoration. We aim to restore the original forest environment.

"To give you a firsthand experience of our efforts, let's go!" he said and explained that we were going to meet three forest guards involved in the project who would be our guide during the hike.

We drove for a while on a red dirt road unlike the bumpy and uncertain ride the night before. Three men were standing on the side of the road. The first man, barefoot, leaned on a machete. He greeted us with a warm smile, his light blue shirt and gray vest contrasting with the earthy tones of the road. His beanie sat snugly on his head, and his demeanor exuded a sense of ease and friendliness. Beside him, another man stood, dressed in a red jacket over a t-shirt and shorts. His baseball cap shaded his face as he rested his hands on his hips. The third man also held a machete, his stance calm but purposeful. Clad in a gray hoodie, red shorts, and sandals, he looked prepared for the day's work. These men were more than just forest guards; they were the heartbeat of the Ecovision Village project. We followed them along a path marked by a sign reading *"Le Rocher du Roi Lion"*—"The Lion King's Rock." Amused, I thought, "So this is where Simba's adventures really took place!"

As we walked, Ntsoa explained that one of Ecovision's crucial goals was to restore the ancient forest through ecological restoration.

"Geographically, Ecovision is positioned between three major protected areas in Andasibe," he said. "The Mantadia National Park to the north,

the Analamazaotra Special Reserve to the south, and the Vohimana Integral Natural Reserve to the east. Our location allows us to connect these three protected areas, ensuring the movement of genes and individuals between them, which is essential to prevent population fragmentation and maintain species fitness."

"Is one of these three zones more endangered because it is along a national road?" I asked. "If these movements cease, it is destined to disappear, correct?"

Confirming my understanding, he continued, "We're talking about the Analamazaotra Special Reserve, which is close to RN2. It's a small area of two thousand acres. Due to its isolation, species within it are forced to inbreed, showing signs of consanguinity and reduced reproductive success, leading to local extinction over time."

Our hike took us along a winding path through dense forest vegetation. As we descended the narrow trail, the trees enveloped us, their tall forms creating a natural embrace. Chef Farah led the way, her colorful shawl standing out vividly against the verdant backdrop. I followed, feeling the cool, damp air on my skin, with Nirina bringing up the rear. The trail, steep and uneven in places, was lined with wooden railings for support. The forest's symphony surrounded us—birds calling, leaves rustling, and the distant hum of unseen insects. Though the path was sometimes treacherous, with loose soil underfoot, the surrounding beauty made every step worthwhile. Tall, broad-leaved plants reached toward the sky, their green fronds contrasting with the rocky outcrops. Chef Farah, Nirina, and I paused occasionally, taking in the lush scenery, the sights and sounds of the forest etching themselves into our memories.

At one point, we ducked under a massive rock overhang, its surface worn smooth by time and elements. As we walked under the rock, the sheer size and natural architecture left us marveling at nature's grandeur. The path then twisted and turned, gradually ascending through lush, verdant surroundings. Each step brought us closer to the summit, the anticipation building with every breath. Finally, we emerged atop the rock, greeted by panoramic views that stretched as far as the eye could see. Standing on The Lion King's Rock, we felt a profound connection to the land, as if we were on the edge of the world, overlooking an endless horizon of wild splendor.

Chef Farah stepped to the edge of the rock, her outfit a bold mix of red, orange, and yellow, reflecting the vibrant culture of Madagascar. She sat with ease, looking out over the rolling green hills below. "Take a picture," she said, wanting to capture a moment where place, purpose, and identity came together. There's no photo on this page, but let these words frame the image: a woman shaped by heritage and ambition, staring into the horizon with quiet determination. Nirina, ever the tech enthusiast, was already preparing his drone for flight. The stunning backdrop of rolling hills and lush greenery spread out before us, a sight that Nirina was eager to capture from above. Throughout our trip, he made it a mission to use his drone to document the unique vibes and breathtaking landscapes of Madagascar. Each flight offered a new perspective, showcasing the island's raw elegance from the skies. His dedication to capturing these moments added a dynamic layer to our adventure, allowing us to relive the mesmerizing scenery long after we had descended from the heights of The Lion King's Rock.

Taking a break from our hike atop the rock, I continued conversing with Ntsoa and Prisca, eager to uncover the complex layers behind deforestation in this unique and fragile ecosystem. The lush surroundings masked a harsh reality—the relentless disappearance of forests that once thrived across the island.

“Deforestation,” Ntsoa began, “is simply the act of removing forest cover to use the land afterward.” This process, straightforward as it might sound, has deep and devastating roots in Madagascar.” He then pointed toward patches on the hills opposite us that were bare from trees and vegetation. “In the past twenty years,” he added, “twenty-nine percent of Madagascar’s forests have disappeared. Researchers predict that thirty-eight to ninety-three percent of the forest present in 2000 could disappear by 2050.”

Curious about the underlying causes, I asked, “Why does it happen here in Madagascar? What is the main reason for the problem of deforestation?”

“The main reason,” he explained, “is the lack of income and the need for daily subsistence, because there are no resources in the secondary and tertiary sectors. Agriculture dominates here. The traditional technique, known as slash-and-burn agriculture, is the foundation of deforestation in Madagascar. People clear, burn, and then plant. Even though the slash-and-burn method has been illegal since 1987, it continues to be practiced because almost nobody is prosecuted for forest clearance.”

As he spoke, the cycle became clearer. “And the next year, they go a bit further and do the same thing. Is that what you mean?” I asked.

“Exactly,” he replied. “Once the land is burned, it becomes unusable. That’s why they have to look for another piece of land to burn. This cycle has turned Madagascar from a green island into a Red Island year after year,” he said, his tone filled with a mix of frustration and resignation.

The harsh reality hit hard. Deforestation was not just about losing trees; it was about survival for many. “Ultimately, what is the main use for deforestation here in Madagascar? What do people turn the wood into?”

“Mainly charcoal, because it is the primary source of energy for now in Madagascar,” he replied. The wood is transformed into charcoal, which is essential for heating and cooking. This relentless demand drives deforestation across the island, from north to south, east to west. Each region, he explained, has its unique vegetation—from cacti and thorny trees in the south to evergreen trees in the east.

I wanted the conversation to shift toward hope—the ecological restoration process. “Can you elaborate on the ecological restoration process, particularly with endemic species across different altitudes?”

He responded, "Ecological restoration aims to emulate nature's processes by selecting species based on soil topology, properties, and altitude. We harness local expertise and traditional knowledge to plant species in valleys, mid-slopes, and high altitudes, ensuring a natural restoration process," he said, his passion evident. This method sought to heal the scars of deforestation, gradually restoring life to the devastated landscape.

But the scars run deep. "It also impacts what we call the primary forest, right?" I asked.

"Yes. Because it's the primary forest they destroy, since it has been there for years. After destroying the primary forest, which regenerates into what is called secondary forest, it will no longer be full of the species it once had. Even this secondary forest gets cut down again when the trees mature. After this second cut, the land is really left fallow and can't be used anymore due to a total lack of seeds and nutrients in the soil."

The primary forest, once teeming with life, faces a grim future. "Returning to the primary forest, can you give some examples of tree varieties?"

He listed them with familiarity, "The variety I know best are those the lemurs feed on. In Malagasy, for example, there's the *voapaka or Tapia* (. There's also *Chrysophyllum, Dalbergia (Uapaca bojeri),* and *Symphonia*. *Symphonia*, for example, is the basic food for the red-bellied lemur. These trees are found at altitude, and once cut, the brown lemur is lost."

The intricate connection between the forest and wildlife became undeniable. "So, the impact is not just on the forest, but also on the wildlife in Madagascar."

He nodded. "Most endemic species in Madagascar are dependent on the forest. If there's a forest, they are there. If there's no forest, they are gone."

The fate of these species was bleak. "What happens to these species? Do they leave or die?"

"They either leave, causing a local extinction, or die. This is scientifically known as extirpation, meaning the species removes itself from a certain locality and is no longer seen there," he concluded, the weight of his words hanging in the air.

This conversation painted a vivid picture of the challenges faced by Madagascar's forests and their inhabitants. The relentless cycle of

slash-and-burn agriculture, driven by necessity, continued to erode the island's green legacy, leaving behind a red, barren land.

As we hiked, Ntsoa delved into the historical roots of deforestation in Madagascar. He explained it accelerated during the French colonial period, from 1896 to 1960. The colonial administration's policies prioritized the economic exploitation of natural resources, leading to the clearing of large forest tracts for cash crops like coffee, significantly impacting the island's forests. The introduction of European agricultural practices, including extensive logging and land appropriation for plantations, further exacerbated forest loss.

Upon gaining independence from France in 1960, Madagascar faced profound political and economic instability. This tumultuous period saw many rural Malagasy communities retreat to forested areas for survival, resorting to shifting cultivation, or *tavy*. This agricultural practice, born of necessity, exacerbated deforestation. The nascent government, grappling with instability and limited resources, struggled to implement effective conservation policies, further accelerating the loss of precious forest cover.

Historically," he added, "during the colonial era, the locals primarily worked as railway laborers and charcoal makers. After independence, without the colonists and accustomed to farming, they had no sustainable income source and continued deforestation for charcoal and wood. The region between these three parks was greatly deforested in the sixties. And recently, the situation worsened with the COVID pandemic, which halted ecotourism, the main income source. Desperation drove more people to charcoal making, particularly in Ecovision's area, perceived as private and unprotected land."

We returned to the cars, but Ntsoa and Prisca had one final destination in mind before we parted ways. After bidding farewell to the forest guards, we drove to another part of Ecovision Village, known as "Le Bassin Bleu" or "The Blue Pool." The path led us along a serene stream, its clear waters mirroring the dense greenery overhead. We stopped near a wooden deck extending over a tranquil pond, aptly named "The Blue Pool." This peaceful spot offered a perfect moment to pause and soak in the natural beauty surrounding us. As I was admiring the tranquility of the surroundings, I didn't notice Nirina already in a swimsuit, ready to dive into the translucent waters. He called to me from the middle of the pool, sitting on a large rock, inviting me to join him.

I laughed and waved off Nirina's invitation and I turned back to Ntsoa, more interested in diving into our conversation than the water. Nirina shouted a few playful jabs in my direction, but I knew he understood. The discussion was too important to pause. We moved from casual observations to deeper truths—about deforestation's sweeping environmental effects and the harsh realities it imposes on local communities.

"We've talked about the consequences on nature, but does deforestation also have consequences for people?" I asked, anxious to understand the broader implications.

"Yes, especially in terms of the environment, like air quality," he began, his expression somber. "Deforestation releases carbon into the atmosphere, causing climate disruption. This leads to changes in the water cycle, because once the forest cover is gone, there's no water retention. For example, when it rains heavily, instead of water circulating over a week, it runs off to the sea or rivers in a day without the forest to retain it."

The image of rainwater, no longer held by the earth, rushing away to the sea, painted a vivid picture of the immediate impacts of deforestation. I pressed further, "Another consequence?"

"Deforestation," he continued, "especially in Madagascar, is not a sustainable technique. It takes fifty to one hundred years for natural regeneration. This increases the daily subsistence difficulties because once people cut a certain area, they have to look further for firewood and construction wood, leading to conflicts over land use."

The search for essential resources becomes increasingly difficult, creating tension and competition among communities. The narrative he wove revealed a cascade of consequences that extended far beyond the immediate environment.

The severe and multifaceted consequences of deforestation in Madagascar were clear:

- **Biodiversity Loss:** The island's unique flora and fauna are critically endangered. Many species have lost their habitats, leading to a decline in biodiversity. The forest, once a sanctuary for countless endemic species, now stands barren, its former inhabitants either displaced or perished.
- **Climate Change:** Deforestation contributes to global climate change by increasing greenhouse gas emissions. The loss of forest cover also affects local climate and weather patterns, disrupting the delicate balance that once sustained the island's ecosystems.
- **Soil Erosion:** Without tree roots to anchor the soil, deforestation leads to severe soil erosion. This not only reduces land fertility but also exacerbates agricultural challenges, making it harder for the land to support the people who depend on it.
- **Economic Impact:** The degradation of natural resources undermines the livelihoods of many Malagasy people who depend on forests for food, fuel, and income. The forest, once a source of sustenance and economic stability, now lies depleted, pushing communities into deeper poverty.

As our discussion deepened, the far-reaching consequences of deforestation became starkly clear. It was not just the forests that suffered; the effects rippled through every facet of life in Madagascar. The air grew more polluted, water sources dwindled, and the soil lost its vitality, all contributing to a cascade of challenges for the local communities. This complex web of environmental and social issues underscored the urgent need for a holistic approach to conservation—one that harmonizes human welfare with the health of the natural world.

The area was surrounded by tall trees and verdant undergrowth, creating a secluded haven where the sounds of the forest—rustling leaves and distant bird calls—enhanced the sense of calm and immersion in the wilderness. Chef Farah decided to stay on dry land like me, opting to sit on the wooden deck while our driver joined Nirina in the waters.

I delved into the story behind the conservation efforts that were transforming both the landscape and the lives of its inhabitants. Through my conversation with a key member of the Ecovision team, I discovered the intricate balance between conservation and community engagement.

"Ecovision's primary funding comes from self-financing and private companies in Antananarivo," my guide began, explaining how they offered companies a hectare to finance as part of their corporate social responsibility. "This is what Nirina did. It helps pay local workers, forest guards, nursery workers, and laborers," he continued, highlighting the project's multifaceted approach to sustainability.

The concept was both straightforward and powerful, leveraging corporate social responsibility to fund critical conservation efforts. However, the path to acceptance and cooperation within the local community had been fraught with challenges and required persistent effort.

"How did the locals initially react to Ecovision's arrival?" I inquired, eager to understand the community's first impressions of this ambitious project.

"Initially, it was a struggle," he admitted. "The land was used for charcoal making. It took time to convince locals of the benefits of conservation and provide alternative livelihoods. We showed them that four days of charcoal production equaled one day's work at Ecovision, without polluting or destroying the forest. This approach slowly won them over."

The challenge of shifting perceptions and livelihoods was palpable. I pressed for more detail. "Can you share an example of this difficult situation and how you managed to convince the locals to join your efforts?"

"Before Ecovision," he began, "a community association attempted reforestation projects for carbon credit subsidies. However, when the World Bank withheld approval due to land titling issues, the community felt betrayed, making it difficult to gain their trust initially. We demonstrated the economic benefits by comparing their losses from charcoal production to the steady income from working with us, which helped them see the advantages of conservation."

That early skepticism ran deep. But Ntsoa recalled a turning point that helped shift momentum: "One of our earliest supporters—one of the three forest guards you met today—joined us even against his family's wishes. He believed in our vision, and today, he's a key member of our team."

This personal commitment underscored the deep-rooted connection between the community and Ecovision's mission. "How has the situation evolved?" I asked, eager to hear about the current state of their efforts.

"Gradually, as people saw Ecovision's work and its benefits, they became more supportive. Now, many want to work with us, and our initial skeptics have become our strongest advocates," he said, a smile of satisfaction spreading across his face.

The transformation was evident. What began as a struggle against skepticism and tradition had blossomed into a collaborative effort to preserve and restore Madagascar's unique environment. The community, once wary, now stood united with Ecovision, forging a path toward a sustainable and prosperous future.

After Nirina and our driver had dried off, we returned to the Life Base to pack our belongings. I seized this moment to delve deeper into a conversation with our hosts, aiming to understand the intricate strategies they employed to balance environmental conservation with community needs. Their insights illuminated the delicate equilibrium they sought to maintain, blending immediate practical solutions with long-term sustainability. Ntsoa shared radical solutions and partnerships that were underpinning their efforts.

"Changing mindsets is difficult, especially when people have relied on charcoal for years," I began, referencing a point made by Nirina about the necessity of providing immediate support rather than distant promises. "Can you give examples of immediate solutions?"

"Our vision relies on continuous capacity building," my guide explained. "We train former charcoal makers in patrolling, biodiversity monitoring, nursery management, and other skills. Additionally, we introduce alternative income projects like vegetable gardening, composting, and fish farming. For example, we demonstrate how composting and permaculture can regenerate soil for sustainable agriculture, reducing the need to clear new land."

Among these alternative projects, one crop in particular caught my attention: coffee.

"Near the Vohimana Integral Natural Reserve, there's a community association that has been experimenting with growing Robusta coffee at altitudes around three thousand feet, or nine hundred meters. This initiative has shown significant potential for agribusiness," my guide explained.

"It suggests that coffee cultivation could be a viable and sustainable income source for local farmers." Reflecting on these innovative efforts, I couldn't help but feel inspired by the ingenuity and resilience of the communities we visited. The potential of coffee cultivation as an alternative income stream was promising.

This hands-on approach to training and alternative livelihoods was crucial in reducing reliance on destructive practices. Intrigued by the personal impacts, I asked, "Has this improved the situation for your colleague, the forest guard, regarding his relationship with his family? Did they manage to understand?"

"Unfortunately, they haven't made the connection between Ecovision and the broader projects like UNICEF. There's still a lot of skepticism and even jealousy towards Ecovision. However, we've made efforts to show our commitment, like using our vehicle for community emergencies, which helps build trust. For example, we've responded to medical emergencies, taking people to the hospital in the middle of the night."

The blend of practical support and emergency aid showcased Ecovision's dedication to the community's well-being.

Further exploring their collaborative efforts, my guide shared more about the ambitious plans that were beginning to take root. The Ecovision's latest collaboration with the Dr. Abigail Ross Foundation for Applied Conservation (TDARFAC) embarked on a pioneering initiative aimed at transforming the economic landscape of the region. The project was designed with a singular vision: to offer alternative incomes to the villages nestled within the forested corridors, all while ensuring that no village was left behind. At the heart of this initiative was a carefully orchestrated rotation planting system, a method that promised both sustainability and inclusivity. Every five days, a new wave of activity would sweep across the landscape as 1,500 saplings were carefully planted in the rich, dark soil. The process was meticulously planned to ensure that each village had its turn, rotating groups every two weeks to spread the benefits of the project evenly across the region.

He continued to explain that they plant around 1,500 saplings every five days, rotating groups every two weeks to rehabilitate 150 hectares over several years.

Intrigued by the logistics, I inquired about how the rotation system worked. Ntsoa said they bring in ten people from a village who plant for one or two weeks, depending on their speed, then they switch with another village. This approach ensures broad participation in conservation efforts. This rotational planting system not only fostered community involvement but also ensured sustainable land management. My guide explained the involvement of TDARFAC: providing direct training to our forest guards and increasing their knowledge and skills, which could transform individuals into local or national guides in the future.

The connection with international experts was pivotal in enhancing local capabilities. "Oh, one more thing," he added. "We've been working with the scientific community on agricultural potential here at Ecovision. For instance, we learned soil sampling techniques from a US student, helping us understand our soil's microbiome and texture. This is part of our plan to turn Ecovision's private property into a protected area under Malagasy law. We found that ginger is a significant crop here, often causing deforestation. By managing it better, we can reduce its impact."

The mention of ginger cultivation caught my interest. "Traditional ginger planting involves deforestation. How do you address this?"

"We use composting and permaculture. Unlike the traditional method of clearing new land each time, permaculture allows successive crops to use the same land without needing to clear more forest. This method isn't widely adopted yet but could significantly help manage land sustainably."

As our conversation ended, the narrative of Ecovision Village emerged as a complex fabric of immediate action, innovative practices, and collaborative efforts. Each strategy and partnership highlighted the ongoing journey toward sustainable development, demonstrating how local and global efforts can converge to create a brighter future for Madagascar's environment and its people. This story of resilience and hope stood in stark contrast to the growing threats to Madagascar's unique heritage.

As the fight against deforestation in Madagascar continues, various organizations and companies have stepped up to contribute to the cause in unique and impactful ways.

Back in Tana, I scheduled a lunch with Laurence Briand at the restaurant La Plantation. Laurence is my colleague at Symrise who heads up the organization in Madagascar. I wanted to hear from her what Symrise does against deforestation.

Laurence arrived as the waiter was bringing me a glass of soursop, my favorite fresh fruit juice. The menu featured Zebu Sirloin Steak with Spices from Madagascar. Tempting, but we both ordered the Duck Breast with Orange and *mokarana* Honey—the *mokarana* is a melliferous tropical tree native to the Anosy region of southern Madagascar.

After Laurence inquired about my journey across the northern part of the island, I asked her about Symrise's efforts against deforestation. She said the company implemented a comprehensive strategy designed to reduce the pressures on the island's parks and forests by introducing sustainable practices and alternatives that benefit both the environment and local communities. They focused on improving rice permaculture practices, aiming to increase productivity without relying on chemical inputs or slash-and-burn methods. By promoting these sustainable farming techniques, Symrise helps local vanilla farmers achieve better yields while preserving the land for future generations.

In addition to enhancing agricultural practices, Laurence added Symrise was supporting the cultivation of fast-growing tree species specifically for use in charcoal production, firewood, and energy for distilleries. By financing nurseries and providing technical support, they ensure that these resources are available without further depleting Madagascar's precious natural forests. Understanding the need to reduce the demand for wood, Symrise has also helped the production of improved stoves, reducing wood consumption for cooking by up to 50 percent, significantly lowering the environmental impact and reducing the strain on local forests.

She continued saying that beyond traditional reforestation efforts, Symrise has been active in developing bamboo cultivation as an alternative to wood for construction. Bamboo offers a fast-growing, sustainable option that can replace wood in many applications, helping to preserve existing forests. And they promoted agroforestry practices by integrating crops like vanilla, mandarin, and patchouli into the farming systems. These high-value crops provided farmers with additional income, reducing the need to clear more land for agriculture.

Symrise's commitment to sustainability is further demonstrated by its pledge to purchase only 100 percent certified products. By adhering to the strict standards of UEBT (Union for Ethical BioTrade) and Rainforest Alliance for spice and herb cultivation, Symrise ensures that all its suppliers comply with anti-deforestation practices, effectively excluding any producer involved in deforestation.

Finally, in a direct effort to restore Madagascar's degraded landscapes, Symrise supports the planting of endemic tree species and the restoration of these crucial ecosystems. Their reforestation initiatives not only replenish the forests but also contribute to the overall health of the environment, ensuring that these areas can thrive once again.

Witnessing these initiatives firsthand made me proud of my company's commitment. Symrise is not simply ticking boxes—it's contributing meaningfully to the fight against deforestation. Through sustainable practices and close collaboration with local communities, it's helping to build a more secure future for Madagascar's forests and the people who call them home.

Back in the United States, my reflections on these experiences lingered. I found myself wanting to understand more—particularly about the grassroots efforts that complement corporate sustainability work. Ntsoa's description of the role of TDARFAC in the Anjozorobe Angavo Forest Corridor had especially stayed with me. It was my curiosity that led me to Dr. Abigail Ross herself, intrigued by the possibility of learning more about the intersection of conservation and community involvement in this remote corner of the world.

My Zoom conversation with Dr. Ross did not disappoint. She welcomed me warmly, and her passion for Madagascar was immediately evident. Dr. Ross shared her connection with the country began over a decade ago during her PhD research on lemur ecology in the Ankarafantsika National Park (in the northwest part of the country). After finishing her PhD, Dr. Ross knew she wanted to return to Madagascar, though she wasn't sure how. It wasn't until the pandemic that the opportunity presented itself—an opportunity that led to the creation of TDARFAC.

Dr. Ross detailed how TDARFAC was born out of a collaboration between several professors and Malagasy colleagues who recognized the dire need for funding local students' research projects. The foundation's mission is simple yet profound: to empower Malagasy students to conduct their own research, independently of international funding constraints.

The pinnacle of this effort is their collaboration with Ecovision Village, where they are working to restore a vital ecological corridor between two protected areas. This reforestation project, spanning 370 acres (150 hectares), is crucial for maintaining biodiversity and supporting local communities.

Of course, such an ambitious project is not without its challenges. Dr. Ross spoke candidly about the difficulties they've encountered, including the spread of invasive plant species like *Desmodium*, which threatens both the newly planted trees and local wildlife. Additionally, logistical challenges such as coordinating the rotation of planters from different villages and managing relationships with existing tree nurseries have required creative solutions. Dr. Ross remains optimistic, driven by the progress they've already made and the potential for even greater impact.

During our conversation, Dr. Ross's deep connection to Madagascar became obvious. She described how the country has a way of capturing the hearts of those who visit, not just through its unique wildlife but through the warmth and resilience of its people. For Dr. Ross, the most rewarding aspect of her work has been mentoring Malagasy students, helping them develop their own research and careers. For Dr. Ross, Madagascar is more than a place of work—it's a place of personal connection and lifelong commitment.

As we wrapped up our discussion, Dr. Ross reflected on the broader implications of her work. She hopes that the reforestation corridor project will serve as a model for future conservation efforts across Madagascar, demonstrating the power of local leadership and the importance of long-term commitment. She also emphasized the importance of continued support, both for the foundation and for Madagascar's environmental future.

Our conversation, though held remotely, left a lasting impression. It deepened my understanding of how intertwined Madagascar's ecological future is with the daily lives and tradition of its people and gave me a deeper appreciation for the work being done on the island.

Madagascar, as I explained in previous chapters, is not just biologically diverse but culinarily rich as well. From the baobab fruit, often turned into a tangy drink or sweet candy, to the myriads of endemic spices that pepper Malagasy dishes, the island's forests serve as nature's pantry. Yet deforestation, often driven by slash-and-burn agriculture, threatens this diversity. The devastating impact of deforestation not only eradicates ancient trees but also distorts the very flowers that once gave birth to pure honey. Wild peppers, once a culinary staple, now face extinction. The island's unique biodiversity, which once thrived under the forest canopy, is fading—leaving both the nature and culinary traditions diminished. Ecovision, active in Andasibe, rehabilitates forests, engages communities, and collaborates with scientists. Beyond environmental conservation, Ecovision has offered tangible help to the local populations. The vanishing aromas of herbs and the echo of wildlife tell a tale of loss. As deforestation endangers Madagascar's culinary roots, what culinary wonders might we lose, and how can they be safeguarded?

CHAPTER 12

Departure and Transformation

Reflections on Madagascar

Ataovy dian-tana: jerena ny aloha, todihana ny afara.

Behave like the chameleon: look forward and observe behind.

—TRADITIONAL MALAGASY SAYING

The scent of vanilla still clung to my fingertips. Even days later, it lingered—earthy, floral, almost smoky—reminding me that the journey through Madagascar wasn't something I could easily leave behind.

As the trip came to a close, I find myself reflecting on the hidden gems of Madagascar that so often go unnoticed. The Red Island, with its untold stories and rich landscapes, is a treasure trove of ingredients, each one more unique and captivating than the last. But these are not just flavors; they embody the spirit of bold entrepreneurs, resilient communities, and the land itself—each connected through a shared narrative of strength and perseverance. It is in this intricate web of people, products, and places that true inspiration for this book was born.

◄ *Crossing the suspended bridge in Tsingy de Bemaraha National Park.*

For the chefs who traveled with me, that same shift took root. Watching them laugh with the farmers and taste familiar ingredients in unfamiliar ways, I recognized the same realizations taking shape. We all came away with a deeper respect for the ingredients we've known for years, now enriched by a fuller appreciation of their stories and origins.

Seeing the chefs rediscover familiar ingredients through the lens of Madagascar's landscapes mirrored my own personal shift. After engaging in meaningful conversations with the farmers, vanilla, once a simple flavor on the palate, now carried the weight of centuries of care, culture, and tradition—a lesson we all took back with us. Vanilla, a staple in their kitchens, now came layered with memory—with names, places, and centuries of care.

They were equally fascinated by other crops like vetiver, patchouli, and ylang-ylang, primarily known for their role in fragrances but also offering new avenues for flavor. Recalling the mixologists who used vetiver in cocktails, the chefs saw a deeper connection between aroma and taste. This experience, especially when considering the unique terroir of Madagascar, with its pink peppercorns and lesser-known ingredients, broadened their perspective on the region's potential. The diversity of flavors they encountered became one of their most lasting impressions.

What struck the chefs most was the blend of pride and determination in Madagascar's younger population. The topic of improving their country was a common theme during the evening of the cocktail competition. Many of the younger generation spoke about their desire to challenge the country's lingering conservative colonial mindset and push for more equality and progress. They were passionate about introducing new businesses. It was clear to the chefs that these aspirations were not just fleeting ideas but deeply held beliefs at the forefront of many minds. As we listened to their voices, you could not help but wonder if their desire to challenge the country's lingering conservative colonial mindset was part of a broader movement. Was this a sign of real, lasting change—a generational shift that could reshape Madagascar's future? With the effect of the pyramid of ages, the older system, steeped in tradition, would inevitably fade out, making way for new ideas and leadership. But was this truly the beginning of a broader movement? Or was it merely a spark, a momentary glimpse of hope that could fade with time, soon to be overshadowed by the weight of history? Only the future will tell whether these dreams will take root or be lost to the complexities of the country's long-standing traditions. I remember one comment from Nirina, who pointed out a shift had been quietly taking place in Madagascar. There was now a noticeable pattern of Malagasy who, after years abroad for education or work, were choosing to return home. This recent phenomenon stood in absolute contrast to the earlier decades, when those who left often did so with no intention of coming back. But now, there was a different energy—one marked by a sense of purpose. Those returning brought with them new ideas and a desire to contribute to the future of the country, a change that had slowly begun to reshape the landscape of opportunity and ambition.

The Malagasy youth expressed immense pride in their culture, heritage, and country, yet they were equally motivated to showcase Madagascar's potential and drive meaningful change. Their commitment to improving their homeland, while embracing their roots, was truly inspiring to the chefs and me. Every bartender during the night of the competition incorporated local ingredients like vanilla, pink peppercorn, or the endemic wild pepper, proudly declaring them as flavors of Madagascar. The chefs predicted that if they would return in five years, these ingredients would become staples on cocktail menus. Often mixology and pastry are at the forefront of flavor innovation. While savory cuisine has traditionally been slower to adopt these bold, local flavors, it is the cocktails and desserts that pave the way for new taste trends. Eventually, these innovations find their way into savory dishes, but it's always the sweet and the spirited that lead the charge.

The passion for innovation and tradition that the chefs witnessed in the cocktail competition mirrors what I encountered across Madagascar. The island's ingredients and flavors, while unique, were legacies of people determined to preserve their heritage. As I traveled through the island, I witnessed firsthand the courageous individuals and visionary companies who refuse to exploit the island's resources or its people. Instead, they have made it their mission to protect the land and its bounty, reinvesting in the communities that nurture these ingredients. These farmers and entrepreneurs are more than just producers—they are stewards of the future. They ensure the stories of these ingredients endure, not through mass production, but through sustainable practices, respect for the land, and a commitment to supporting the hands that cultivate them. In their fight to preserve these traditions, they offer something even more valuable than the flavors themselves—a future for the people and the land.

I realize that the most significant moments of my journey on the island were not just about what I saw (the magnificent sunset on either the Indian Ocean or the night in the lodge at the Ambohimanitra Domaine) or tasted (fresh *corossol* juice or zebu carpaccio). They were about the ways in which the island slowly unraveled parts of myself I had not yet understood. In each step I took, from crossing bridges to tasting local dishes, I was not just moving through a foreign land. I was moving through my own inner terrain, discovering new corners of myself.

Madagascar's landscapes, its people, and its food didn't just enrich my travels; they transformed me. As I recount these experiences, I see how each one pushed me closer to understanding not only this place but left a permanent imprint.

The transformative experience for me was the pivotal moment when I pollinated the vanilla orchid flower with my hand in the middle of these hills in the Ankara River. The tactile memory still lingers with me. I cannot see a vanilla bean the same way ever since. That moment reshaped my view of how ingredients and traditions are passed down, hand to hand, across generations. It's a lesson in the value of tradition and the importance of embracing a new culture fully.

My journey through Madagascar was a mix of unforgettable experiences—each piece shaped by adventure, culinary discovery, and cultural connection. These are the moments that left the greatest impression on me.

Adventure: Pushing Boundaries and Embracing the Unknown

From the moment I set foot on Madagascar's soil, I felt the pull of the island's wild, untamed spirit. A few moments I encountered along the way became more than just physical endeavors; they were metaphors for the personal challenges I was learning to overcome.

I realized that crossing the suspension bridge in Tsingy de Bemaraha National Park was a metaphor for facing fears and confronting the uncertainties that had lingered in my mind. This experience and the entire four-hour hike and *via ferrata* (or "iron path"—refers to metal rungs, ladders or permanently fixed safety wire as a means of crossing otherwise tricky and steep rocky terrain) symbolized a significant moment of inner strength.

Then there was the solitary walk down the Baobab Alley near Morondava. The towering trees stood as silent witnesses to my introspection. Alone with my thoughts, I considered how far I have come between the childhood stamps of baobab trees in my collection and the reality of standing among these ancient giants. Their centuries-long endurance felt like a harsh reminder of the temporary nature of my own time in the world. There, in the shadow of the ancient baobabs, I felt more connected to my inner self than I had in years.

But adventure was not without its risks. The nine-hour one-way dirt road trip (and back) to Tsingy, complete with the stress of having armed military in the car, was a harsh reminder that not all journeys are idyllic. The looming threat of the Dahalo, Madagascar's zebu rustlers, pushed me to confront the harsh realities of travel. It was a moment where I had to trust not only the process but the people around me. It reminded me that each challenge adds to the richness of the overall experience.

And then there was the drive from Tuléar to Fort-Dauphin: 387 miles that took thirty hours. We powered through twelve straight hours of nighttime driving, no sleep, and a lot of bouncing. A full rotation of the Earth, plus some bonus potholes. Between the craters, ridges, and surprise riverbeds, I think I realigned my spine...in several directions. Sometimes it's just not giving up, even when the road disappears.

Culinary Discovery: A Taste of Madagascar's Soul

Madagascar isn't just scenic landscapes—it's a feast for the senses.

One of the first aromas to captivate me was the subtle but intoxicating scent of ylang-ylang as I walked through the plantation in Nosy Be. Toward the end of the day, the air was thick with fragrance, and this represented a sensory awakening and an immediate connection to the earth—a fierce awareness of nature's beauty and how such experiences can ground you in the present.

The meal with Olivier Ramaherison in the *voatsiperifery* hills was a revelation. Surrounded by the very spices that seasoned the dish, I ate with the people whose connection to the land ran deep. It was a humble meal, but its simplicity spoke volumes. It reminded me of the mushroom foraging trips I took with my father as a child in France and the simple family dinners we shared afterwards. The flavor of the endemic Madagascar wild pepper wasn't just in the food; it lingered in the air and in the smiles of my companions. It was there, in this grounded experience, that I tasted the soul of Madagascar for the first time.

But perhaps the most striking culinary discovery came when I experienced Rova Caviar, the first Indian Ocean caviar from Madagascar. It was a moment of surprise and delight, a reminder that even in the most remote corners of the world, culinary treasures await discovery. This experience spoke to Madagascar's potential for innovation in the global culinary scene.

And then, there was the joy of prepping with the three American chefs at Ocean Momo hotel in Antalaha. Being in a remote part of the island, working in the kitchen with these renowned chefs, highlighted how food transcends borders and brings people together. It was a reminder of how the kitchen becomes a universal language, where passion and craftsmanship speak louder than words.

A defining moment in my culinary exploration was the meal with Chef Henintsoa Moretti at Haka Fy in Antananarivo, where her *manaramolotra*—a slow-cooked confit of zebu tail, tongue, tripe, and ribeye—captured the essence of Madagascar's regions in both flavor and philosophy.

Cultural Connections: People, Places, and Personal Growth

Although the landscapes and flavors of Madagascar made a profound impact on me, it was the people I met and the cultural exchanges I experienced that transformed me the most.

The most meaningful connection I made was developing a friendship with Nirina Ramanandraibe. What began as a casual interaction quickly grew into a friendship that deepened my understanding of the island. Through Nirina, I saw Madagascar not as a tourist but as a participant in its daily rhythms. We shared stories, meals, and laughter. I am forever grateful to Nirina, who not only introduced me to many people on the island but also for opening my eyes to a deeper cultural understanding.

Tasting the food from Chef Lalaina at the Marais restaurant in Tana was not just a meal but an extension of my experience in Madagascar, offering a lesson in blending local flavors with refined culinary techniques, showing how food can both honor tradition and embrace modernity. What stood out even more was his incredible support team. Chef Lalaina's kitchen was almost entirely made up of women, and the brigade worked with remarkable efficiency—something the three American chefs hadn't seen in a long time. The moment a task was assigned, each woman immediately jumped in, grabbed something, and got to work. The chefs noted that this level of eagerness and willingness to learn is becoming increasingly rare in kitchens today.

Another meaningful encounter during my time in Madagascar was with K-Mëc, the mixologist at La Teinturerie. This encounter reminded me that the most transformative moments often come from collaborations that transcend professional boundaries and delve into the shared values of curiosity, respect, and reinvention.

I have no doubt that the next time I see any of these three individuals, we'll effortlessly pick up our conversation right where we left off.

The moments of connection extended beyond humans to the wildlife as well. Experiencing lemurs jumping on my shoulders on the tiny island of Lake Mantasoa was a playful and unexpected reminder of Madagascar's unique ecosystem. This fleeting encounter embodied spontaneity and the joy of living in the moment.

Then there were the quieter moments, like crossing the Mania River on a local boat platform. The slow journey across the water, while seemingly simple, was a humbling experience that connected me to the rhythms of daily life in Madagascar. It was a simple yet symbolic crossing that paralleled the flow of my trip itself—sometimes smooth, sometimes uncertain, but always moving forward.

Among the many unforgettable moments etched into my memory during this journey, my encounter with the chief of the Bara tribe stands apart as something almost surreal.

Beyond the adventure, culinary discovery, and cultural connection, there was another layer to my time in Madagascar—one that spoke to the island's history and the shadows it still casts. The weight of Madagascar's colonial past was not just written into its history but felt in every conversation I had. As a visitor, I began to understand how the legacy of that past is still very much alive, shaping both the landscape and the lives of the people I met. I found myself in conversations with people who either lived through the transition or had inherited the stories from their parents. As someone born in France, I expected the scars of colonialism to have faded with time. What I encountered, however, was a lingering presence—a complex and deeply rooted impact that still shapes the lives and landscapes of the island.

The reflections I heard were nuanced and multifaceted. To my surprise, some people spoke nostalgically of the so-called "stability" of the colonial period, where infrastructure was established, and certain systems—like education and transportation—functioned with a degree of order. Yet this nostalgia was often tempered by an underlying criticism: the lack of preparation for independence and the absence of a clear plan for self-governance. I share this not to make a judgment, but to reflect voices that were generously and candidly shared with me.

This tension was reflected most clearly in the environment. Colonial land management practices, driven by the exploitation of natural resources, laid the foundation for a deforestation crisis that still grips Madagascar. The forests, once seen by the French as raw materials to be harvested, were never managed sustainably, leaving the Malagasy people to contend with the ecological fallout decades later. Colonialism's legacy is not just written into the history books but carved into the earth itself.

From conversations with those who remembered the end of colonialism, I realized that the process of decolonization is not just political; it is cultural, social, and environmental. The aftershocks of colonial rule continue to ripple through the Malagasy consciousness, in ways both visible and invisible.

Colonialism has left an indelible mark, woven into the very fabric of daily life in Madagascar. It isn't an abstract concept here—it's a memory embedded in landscapes, families, and institutions. As a Frenchman, I found myself quietly wrestling with that legacy—not just as history, but as something alive in the stories people shared and the places I visited. I don't presume to judge the past from the comfort of the present. I can't say how I might have acted had I lived through those times, nor do I claim to fully understand what that experience meant. Still, I felt a responsibility—not to speak for this history, but to listen more closely because of where I come from. Yet, despite everything I've learned about the island's history and its people, my understanding remains limited. I do not claim to know Madagascar, nor do I position myself as an expert on its complexities. My experiences, while rich and deeply meaningful, are those of a traveler—one who, thanks to my connection with Nirina, was granted a deeper insight than most tourists might ever encounter. Even so, I have only looked through a window into an unfamiliar world, not fully stepped inside. I have not lived the daily life of the Malagasy people; I have only glimpsed their reality through brief but profound encounters.

What I offer is a perspective shaped by curiosity, a passion for discovery, and a deep appreciation for the stories told through food. My explorations of Madagascar have been guided by the senses—the taste of its produce, the aromas of its markets, and the textures of its recipes. These sensory experiences have painted a picture for me, but I recognize that it is incomplete, seen through the prism of my own perspective as a visitor.

I do not pretend to know what truly takes place in Madagascar. Instead, I offer these reflections as a humble acknowledgment of my own position. I have walked its soil, tasted its flavors, and met its people, but my understanding remains partial. I hope through these pages, you too have caught a glimpse of this beautiful and complex land, and that it inspires you to explore, question, and appreciate the richness of cultures that may be unfamiliar to you.

But beyond the beauty of exploration and the pleasure of discovery, there are the quieter stories—those tied to the land and the people who nurture it. Madagascar's landscapes, intricately woven with both resilience and fragility, face real challenges like deforestation—challenges that ripple through communities whose lives depend on crops such as vanilla and honey. In sharing these stories, I aim to capture not only the work of those who farm and create but also the legacies they safeguard for future generations.

As I reflect on this journey, I find myself considering the choices I make more carefully. Perhaps, like me, you feel a connection to these stories, an echo that calls for deeper engagement. As you turn the pages, you'll find links to initiatives that seek to protect these traditions and landscapes, offering a chance to connect more deeply with these communities and become part of their story in your own way. If you're drawn to any of them, I encourage you to take a moment to explore further. It's a small step, yet one that can contribute to a larger movement to preserve these unique landscapes and traditions. It's a way to participate in something meaningful—something that helps ensure these stories are not lost to time.

Bibliography

Below is a list of major sources that I relied on for facts and information, or that influenced my thinking process.

2424.mg News & Reports. 2023. "Nécrologie – Cheffe Mariette Andrianjaka depose définitivement son tablier." *2424mg*. November 28. https://2424.mg/necrologie-cheffe-mariette-andrianjaka-depose-definitivement-son-tablier/#:~:text=Antananarivo%2C%2028%20Novembre%2C%207h10%20%E2%80%93,malgache%2C%20n'est%20plus.

Attoumani, Nassur. 2019. *Instinct de survie à Madagascar: de lîle au lagoon à la Grande île*. Orphie.

Boissard, Pierre. 1983. *Cuisine malgache, créole*. Librairie de Madagascar.

Cailler, Laurence, and François Pralu. 2008. *Cacao Vanilla: L'or Noir de Madagascar.* Agnès Viénot Éditions.

Dubois, Robert. 2003. *L'identité malgache – la tradition des ancêtres*. KARTHALA.

Lery François. 2002. *Madagascar: Les Sortilèges de l'ile rouge*. Editions L'Harmattan.

Marca, Claire and Reno Marca. 2011. *Madagascar: 3 mois de voyage sur l'île rouge.* MARTINIERE BL.

Mauro, Didier and Emeline Raholiarisoa. 1999. *Madagascar: L'ile mère.* Anako Editions.

Mauro, Didier. 2000. *Madagascar: L'île essentielle étude d'anthropologie culturelle (Grands témoins).* Anako Editions.

Rakotoson, Michèle. 2007. *Juliet au pays: Chroniques d'un retour à Madagascar. Elytis.*

Randrianja, Solofo and Stephen Ellis. 2009. *Madagascar: A Short History*. University of Chicago Press.

Ravelomanana, Lalaina. 2012. *Lartistika: Parfums de Madagascar & Saveurs des iles.* Carambole Éditions.

Serrière, Chantal. 2011. *Pangalanes: Retour à Madagascar.* Editions L'Harmattan.

Serva, Maurizo. 2012. "The Settlement of Madagascar: What Dialects and Languages Can Tell Us." *PLOS ONE* 7 (2): e30666. https://doi.org/10.1371/journal.pone.0030666

The African Gourmet. 2023. "Indonesia and Madagascar's Connection." *The African Gourmet*, December 3. https://www.theafricangourmet.com/2023/12/indonesia-and-madagascars-connection.htmlconnection.html.

The Editors of Encyclopædia Britannica. 2025. "Gondwana." *Encyclopædia Britannica*, June 25. https://www.britannica.com/place/Gondwana-supercontinent.

Trillard, Marc and Philippe Giraud. 2001. *Madagascar: L'île derrière l'île.* Vilo.

Vitale, Tom, Director. 2015. *Anthony Bourdain: Parts Unknown.* Season 5, episode 4, "Madagascar." Anthony Bourdain, Darren Aronofsky. Aired May 17, 2015, on CNN.

Wildmadagascar.org 2024-2025. https://www.wildmadagascar.org/

Featured Companies

Mikea Discovery

Mikea Discovery is a travel agency and tour operator committed to sustainable and responsible tourism in Madagascar.

Their mission is to support the island's economic and environmental development while offering unique experiences to travelers in search of adventure and cultural discovery.

They are convinced that tourism can be a positive force, combining solidarity and respect for the environment. It is with passion and pride that they create authentic and customized tours, designed to highlight Madagascar's breathtaking landscapes, exceptional biodiversity, and cultural heritage.

Jump into the heart of local life, discover Madagascar's traditions, and savor unforgettable moments as you explore places off the beaten track. Between heavenly beaches, idyllic islands, and exceptional cocoa farms, Mikea Discovery invites you to enjoy an enriching and instructive experience in northern Madagascar, for memories that will last a lifetime.

Find out more on their website.

Symrise symrise

Symrise is a global leader in flavor and fragrance production, with a rich history dating back to 1874, when its founders first synthesized vanillin. Over the years, the company has evolved, emphasizing sustainability and innovation in its operations.

Madagascar, particularly the SAVA region, is central to Symrise's vanilla sourcing. Recognizing the importance of sustainable practices, Symrise collaborates directly with more than seven thousand small-scale farmers across ninety-nine villages in Madagascar. This direct partnership ensures that the vanilla is of premium quality, traceable, and sustainably cultivated.

Beyond sourcing, Symrise is deeply invested in the well-being of the Malagasy communities. The company has implemented various initiatives:

- *Environmental Conservation:* Symrise restores and manages natural resources and works with the national parks that manage the reforestation efforts to preserve Madagascar's unique biodiversity.
- *Economic Diversification:* Farmers are encouraged to cultivate additional crops like cocoa and cloves, providing alternative income sources and reducing reliance on vanilla alone.
- *Health Insurance:* Symrise implemented a system that allowed farmers to afford medical care for their families without falling into debt, helping to break the cycle of financial insecurity.

Symrise's holistic approach not only ensures a stable supply of high-quality vanilla but also fosters resilient, sustainable communities in Madagascar.

Find out more on their website.

Domaine d'Ambohimanitra

If the name of this plantation literally translates as "the fragrant hill," it could just as easily have been translated as the hill of a thousand flavors. Flavors of hope, of doubt, of questioning, of rebound, of achievement, the flavors of a lifetime of travel.

Since its creation, the Domaine d'Ambohimanitra has been built on shared projects and inherited life lessons. The initial project was born of Ramanandraibe Exportation's desire to create a basis for the vertical integration of an industry to which it has been fully committed since 1973: vanilla! The cultivation of this exceptional spice has in turn rooted the company in the values of respect, acceptance, and recognition: respect for nature and the acceptance of harvesting the pods of success, as well as those of failure.

Each fragrance released by a Domaine d'Ambohimanitra spice is an ode to the courage of men and women who have tasted the flesh of the earth, measured the fragility of natural balance, and cultivated in their hearts the taste for perseverance.

Find out more on their website.

Chocolaterie Robert

For almost eighty-five years, Chocolaterie Robert has worked exclusively with cocoa beans from Madagascar, and has set itself on the mission of bringing out the delicacy and aromatic diversity of these beans, through chocolates of excellence.

This effort has been rewarded over the last ten years, with some thirty awards given by juries of internationally renowned competitions. The most gratifying ones are the Golden Bean 2017 and 2020, awarded by the Academy of Chocolate (London) to the two bars of 100 percent dark chocolate made by Chocolaterie Robert.

Backed by a 4,200-acre plantation in the Sambirano region, Chocolaterie Robert has successfully integrated vertically, enabling it to control quality at every stage, from the varietal choice of cocoa seed to the chocolate bar. In parallel with its own plantation, Chocolaterie Robert continues to ensure a stable and constant outlet for the fine cocoa produced by its longstanding partners, the farmer-producers, to promote their incomes.

Constantly striving for excellence, Chocolaterie Robert has been exploring Madagascar's terroirs for several years now. The aim is to establish a range of "rare terroir chocolates" to showcase the work of farmers in the island's other fine cocoa-producing regions.

Find out more on their website.

Beyond Good

Beyond Good makes chocolate and vanilla at the source in Madagascar. Their mission is to change the way the world experiences chocolate and vanilla.

It's a world with too many middlemen who walk away with too much of the profit. A world where beans are stripped of their natural taste and texture, and farmers are treated like photo-ops. A world where people have been blinded to the beauty of what real chocolate and vanilla can be.

Beyond Good is bringing that world to an end. By sourcing the best quality vanilla and cocoa in the world, directly from the farmers who grow it. By making chocolate at the source in Africa.

By pioneering a business model that has the power to change the food industry, forever.

And by inviting you to enjoy something that doesn't just taste better, it feels better.

This is chocolate and vanilla. Made right.

Click below to order online.

La Teinturerie

La Teinturerie is an artists' association founded in 2014 and dedicated to promoting art in all its forms. Over the years, La Teinturerie has established itself as a major cultural player in Antananarivo and Madagascar. Their many projects include monthly exhibitions, weekly concerts, the Art and Biodiversity project, creative workshops, and the production of one-off artistic events.

In particular, La Teinturerie has organized eight editions of the Festival d'Art Urbain in various cities of Madagascar, including Antananarivo, Antsiranana, Antsirabe and Mahajanga.

La Teinturerie is a must for art and culture lovers visiting Antananarivo. It's a place to relax and enjoy the bar's signature cocktails and mocktails. There are also items by local designers for those looking for authentic souvenirs.

Find out more on their website.

The Anja Reserve Lodge

The Anja Reserve Lodge is nestled in the spectacular landscape of southern Madagascar, close to the famous Catta lemur sanctuary. More than just a lodge, it's a purpose-driven initiative, born to support the Anja Community Reserve, managed with passion by the villagers themselves. Here, responsible tourism takes on its full meaning: each stay contributes directly to the protection of the forest, the lemurs, and the development of the village.

The elegant, comfortable suites have been designed to offer an upscale experience with total respect for the environment. Local woods, integrated architecture, sustainable management: every detail is carefully considered. The hospitality is heartfelt, and the dialogue is real. You leave the lodge with memories, but also with a deeper understanding of a unique place where nature, comfort, and community live in harmony. A hidden gem in Madagascar that preserves the heart of it all.

Find out more on their website.

La Compagnie du Miel

The Compagnie du Miel adventure began in 2017, with the founders' desire to promote and protect Madagascar's extraordinary biodiversity and produce honeys with exotic flavors that are still not widely available.

Their production model is centered on passing on beekeeping know-how and increasing beekeepers' purchasing power: with twenty hives, a beekeeper lives above the poverty line; with fifty hives, he or she enters the middle class.

- As their standard of living rises, they will move away from charcoal production, the main cause of deforestation in Madagascar.
- Bee pollination also helps to renew forests more rapidly.

- La Compagnie du Miel's honeys are traceable from the apiary to the jar, thanks to their mastery of the entire chain.
- Cold-extracted, they are 100 percent natural and can be enjoyed on toast or in the kitchen.
- Their uniqueness and creamy texture have convinced numerous customers in Europe, Japan, and the Middle East.

Click below to order online.

The Lemur Conservation Network

The Lemur Conservation Network believes that lemurs can be saved from extinction if we all work together. The Lemur Conservation Network unites more than fifty conservation organizations working across Madagascar and connects them with people around the world. They support this network through communications, education, and providing financial support and resources for Malagasy-led conservation programs.

The Lemur Conservation Network:

- Provides financial support through small grants and matched donations.
- Creates and shares educational materials with organizations, schools, and communities.
- Promotes the annual World Lemur Festival to engage communities in lemur conservation.
- Supports teachers and schools across the island through partnership with Teach for Madagascar.
- Shares the work of scientists and conservation organizations to increase their impact.

A full 98 percent of lemur species are at risk of extinction, and 31 percent are critically endangered. But you can help.

Find out more on their website.

The Dr. Abigail Ross Foundation for Applied Conservation (TDARFAC)

The Dr. Abigail Ross Foundation for Applied Conservation is a nonprofit organization dedicated to addressing critical conservation challenges by fostering innovative, community-led solutions. Founded in 2023, TDARFAC bridges the gap between academic research and practical conservation efforts, focusing on biodiversity hotspots like Madagascar. The foundation supports field-based research, reforestation projects, and capacity-building initiatives, particularly empowering early-career scientists and underrepresented communities. Through grants, mentorship, and collaborative partnerships, TDARFAC aims to implement actionable interventions that protect endangered species and their habitats, ensuring sustainable environmental stewardship for future generations.

Find out more on our website.

My Malagasy Soundtrack

Press Play to Travel Further

Curiosity is one of my defining traits—and a thread that runs through this entire journey.

I believe that discovering a place means engaging all the senses, and music is one of the most immediate ways to feel a culture's pulse.

Music was everywhere during my trips: echoing through markets, buzzing in the streets, pulsing from the car stereo during hours of bumpy driving, and spilling out of nightclubs late into the night. I tried keeping up with Nirina's energy—no easy feat.

Even if you don't speak Malagasy, the music still speaks. It tells stories—of celebration, resilience, longing, and love.

So, I've created a playlist for you. It gathers the songs that became the soundtrack to my travels. Local hits, unexpected influences, and rhythms that rooted themselves in my memory.

Scan the QR code below to listen as you read. Let the music transport you, set the mood, and draw you closer to the spirit of the island.

Press play, and let the music carry you to Madagascar.

Acknowledgments

My first thank you goes to the Malagasy people. Throughout my journeys across their extraordinary island, they welcomed me with open arms and open hearts. This book is a tribute to their resilience, generosity, and unwavering passion for preserving Madagascar's vibrant cultural and culinary heritage.

This project would never have taken shape without the time and knowledge of Nirina Ramanandraibe. His connections and deep understanding of Madagascar's food culture opened doors to stories and voices essential to this journey. His guidance and insider perspective have infused this journey with a richness and authenticity that would not have been possible otherwise. Nirina, thank you for being the compass that guided me through the island.

My deepest gratitude to Lantosoa Rakotomalala, Ambassador Extraordinary and Plenipotentiary of Madagascar to the United States of America—her generous spirit and profound connection to Madagascar bring an extraordinary depth to this book's foreword. It is a true honor to have your words open this book and bridge readers to the soul of Madagascar. Her dedication to representing homeland and its rich heritage is an inspiration, and I am profoundly grateful for her support.

To the brilliant minds and passionate souls who offered their time, stories, and expertise: Riaz Badouraly, Laurence Briand, Clément Cabrol, Delphyne Dabezies, Christiano Grosset, Gael Hankenne, Chef Gilbert Kakulé, K-Mëc, Tim McCollum, Chef Henintsoa Moretti, Dominique Ragon, Chef Farah Rabekijana, Olivier Ramaherison, Dina Rasanjison, Chef Lalaina Ravelomanana, Abby Ross, Gabriel Styvio, and Symrise's Perfumers: David Apel, Christelle Laprade, and Maurice Roucel. Thank you for opening your doors and sharing your lives and knowledge with me. Through your generosity, I was able to understand not only your ingredients, your work, and traditions but the deeper ties between land, culture, and identity. You've left a mark on every page.

To everyone who helped me along the way—offering directions, translating menus, introducing me to hidden gems, or simply sharing a meal—this book carries your fingerprints too.

To the chefs who offered their recipes: Shannon Tebay, Michael Gulotta, Elizabeth Falkner, Christophe Chiavola, Lalaina Ravelomanana, Guy Krenzer, K-Mëc, Henintsoa Moretti, Farah Rabekijana, and Gilbert Kakulé—thank you for adding your flavor, literally and metaphorically. You've seasoned these pages with your creativity and trust, and for that, I am truly grateful.

All pictures courtesy of me, Emmanuel Laroche, except the picture in Chapter 4, courtesy of Rova Caviar. Several of the recipe photographs in this book were generously shared by the talented chefs and mixologists featured in these pages.

Special thanks to Mimie Ravaroson, Sustainable Development Manager at Symrise, for introducing me to Chef Lalaina and mixologist K-Mec, and for setting in motion the journey that became this book.

A special thank you to Symrise—not only for supporting this project but for being an integral part of my professional journey over the past thirty years. The experiences, collaborations, and opportunities I've had through Symrise have shaped a career I truly love, and for that, I am deeply grateful.

A huge thanks to Florin Safner, illustrator, graphic designer, and cartography specialist based in Venezuela, for crafting the hand-drawn maps of Madagascar featured in this book. Not only did he make the island look stunning on paper, but he also somehow managed not to lose his sanity while navigating my endless notes, arrows, and "just one more revision" emails.

I tip my hat (and pen) to Laura Laroche, Dominique Laroche, and Dan Vollmer—my first readers and toughest critics. Your hours of thoughtful reading, questioning, encouraging (and sometimes lovingly challenging) made this book infinitely stronger.

To Paul Delfino, Yannick Leen, and Evan Unger: thank you for your insights, perspective, and good-humored honesty. Your contributions helped shape key chapters.

To my agent, Janice Shay: you didn't just shepherd this book into the world, you made sure it found the right home. Your belief and steely resolve kept me focused. Thank you for seeing the potential in both the book and its slightly obsessive author.

To Debby Englander and the entire team at Post Hill Press—thank you for believing in this project and helping bring it to life with care and intention. You made it feel real. I am truly grateful for the chance to bring this book to life with you.

And finally, a nod to ChatGPT, my ever-patient and delightfully tireless virtual assistant. You deserve a pat on the back—if only you had one!

I hope this book inspires you to journey to the Red Island, to immerse yourself in its breathtaking landscapes, and to experience the warmth and generosity of its people. More than that, I hope it changes the way you see vanilla—not just as an ingredient, but as a story of resilience, tradition, and craftsmanship.

And beyond vanilla, may it encourage you to think about the many extraordinary ingredients that come from different corners of the world, each carrying its own rich history and the dedication of those who cultivate or raise it. These ingredients, and the people who sustain their traditions, deserve our appreciation and respect.

About the Author

Born in Versailles, France in 1963, close to the famous chateau of King Louis XIV, Emmanuel Laroche grew up savoring the best food and drink that France offers, eventually earning him the American nickname "Champagne Charlie." His mother taught him to cook when he was six, starting with a simple yogurt cake, and moving on to Lorraine quiche, from the region where his mother grew up.

In 2002 he moved to the US for his role as VP of Marketing with Symrise North America—a global manufacturer of flavors and natural ingredients for the food and beverage industry. He now has more than thirty years of experience in the food and beverage industry, both in Europe and in the US.

Through his job, Emmanuel has access to a variety of acclaimed people in the food industry. In 2015, he developed an exclusive partnership with StarChefs, a trusted resource for the food and beverage industry, and began moderating panel discussions with successful culinary professionals.

He launched the popular podcast *Flavors Unknown* in 2018, which features conversations with acclaimed, award-winning cooks, chefs, and mixologists.

In 2022, Emmanuel published his first book, *Conversations Behind the Kitchen Door: 50 American Chefs Chart Today's Food Culture.*

His connection to Madagascar is linked to his role as VP of Marketing at Symrise. Several years back, he spearheaded a nationwide contest in the US in partnership with StarChefs, challenging chefs, pastry chefs, and mixologists to craft innovative creations using Symrise's premium vanilla extract and grade-A vanilla beans. In 2022, the winners traveled with him to Madagascar, immersing themselves in the origins of this extraordinary ingredient. This journey marked the beginning of his ongoing exploration of Madagascar's rich culinary and cultural heritage, which he revisited in June 2023 and deepened further during his visit in May 2025.

Emmanuel currently resides in New Jersey, which acts as a home base for his travels around the country, conducting tastings, lectures, and presentations on food and consumer trends.

Find him at:

Instagram

Facebook

LinkedIn